PANIC

Psychological Perspectives

PANIC

Psychological Perspectives

Edited by

S. Rachman
University of British Columbia

Jack D. Maser
National Institute of Mental Health

Routledge
Taylor & Francis Group
NEW YORK AND LONDON

First published 1988 by
Lawrence Erlbaum Associates, Inc., Publishers

This edition published 2014 by Routledge

Routledge
Taylor & Francis Group
711 Third Avenue
New York, NY 10017, USA

Routledge
Taylor & Francis Group
2 Park Square Milton Park,
Abingdon Oxfordshire OX14 4RN

First issued in paperback 2016

Routledge is an imprint of the Taylor & Francis Group, an informa business

Library of Congress Cataloging-in-Publication Data

Panic: psychological perspectives.

Includes bibliographies and index.
1. Panic disorders. 2. Panic attacks. I. Rachman, Stanley. II. Maser, Jack D. [DNLM: 1. Fear. 2. Phobic Disorders—psychology. WM 178 P192]
RC535.P36 1988 616.85'225 87-15741
ISBN 0-8058-0091-3

ISBN 13: 978-1-138-97788-4 (pbk)
ISBN 13: 978-0-8058-0091-3 (hbk)

Contents

Contributors

David H. Barlow, Ph.D. Department of Psychology, State University of New York at Albany, 1400 Washington Ave., Albany, NY 12222

Aaron T. Beck, M.D. Department of Psychiatry, School of Medicine, University of Pennsylvania, 133 South 36th St., Room 602, Philadelphia, PA 19104

Deborah C. Beidel, Ph.D. Western Psychiatric Institute and Clinic, University of Pittsburgh, 3811 O'Hara St., Pittsburgh, PA 15213

Dianne Chambless, Ph.D. Department of Psychology, American University, 321 Asbury Building, Washington, D.C. 20016

David M. Clark, Ph.D. University Department of Psychiatry, Warneford Hospital, Oxford, England 0X3 7JX

Michelle Craske, Ph.D. Department of Psychology, State University of New York at Albany, 1400 Washington Ave., Albany, NY 12222

Rolf G. Jacob, M.D. Western Psychiatric Institute and Clinic, University of Pittsburgh, 3811 O'Hara St., Pittsburgh, PA 15213

Peter J. Lang, Ph.D. Department of Clinical Psychology, JHMHC, Box J165, University of Florida, Gainesville, FL 32610

William Marshall, Ph.D. Department of Psychology, Queens University, Kingston, Ontario, Canada K7L 5C4

Jack D. Maser, Ph.D. Affective and Anxiety Disorders Research Branch, Division of Clinical Research, National Institute of Mental Health, Room 10C24, 5600 Fishers Lane, Rockville, MD 20857

Larry Michelson, Ph.D. Western Psychiatric Institute and Clinic, 3811 O'Hara St., University of Pittsburgh, Pittsburgh, PA 15213

S. Rachman, Ph.D. Department of Psychology, University of British Columbia, 2075 Wesbrook Mall, Vancouver, B.C., Canada V6T 1W5

Paul Salkovskis, Ph.D. University Department of Psychiatry, Warneford Hospital, Oxford, England 0X3 7JX

Martin E. P. Seligman, Ph.D. Department of Psychology, University of Pennsylvania, 3813 Walnut St., Philadelphia, PA 19104

M. Katherine Shear, M.D. Department of Psychiatry, New York Hospital-Payne Whitney Clinic, 525 East 68th St., New York, NY 10021

John Teasdale, Ph.D. Applied Psychology Unit, Medical Research Council, 15 Chaucer Rd., Cambridge, England CB2 2EF

Michael J. Telch, Ph.D. Department of Psychology, Mezes Hall, 330, University of Texas at Austin, Austin, TX 78712

Samuel Turner, Ph.D. Western Psychiatric Institute and Clinic, 3811 O'Hara St., University of Pittsburgh, Pittsburgh, PA 15213

Marcel van den Hout, Ph.D. Capaciteitsgroep Medische Psychologie, Rijksuniversiteit Limburg, Postbus 616, 6200 MD, Maastricht, Netherlands

Preface

Research groups at the National Institute of Mental Health (NIMH) and at medical schools in many countries have been actively pursuing the biological underpinnings of panic attacks. New and apparently effective drug treatments and the discovery of chemical methods that appeared to provoke states of panic in vulnerable individuals fueled the excitement of clinical investigators. A fillip was provided by a major pharmaceutical firm initiating an unprecedented world-wide study of the treatment of panic attacks. In a given year, more money was spent on panic research by this private sponsor than the NIMH extramural programs were spending on all anxiety disorders.

Independently, in 1983 the NIMH began work on a conference to bring together nearly 50 basic and clinical researchers to assess the state of the anxiety disorders field (see Tuma & Maser, 1985). Although that Conference enabled psychological and cognitive investigators to present their points of view in many areas of anxiety research, the topic of panic was still dominated by biological studies.

In our view, psychological research on panic should not be neglected, and therefore, we decided in 1985 that a workshop on psychological aspects of panic was necessary. The purpose of the planned meeting was to give those researchers with a psychobiological orientation an opportunity to present and discuss in depth their data and theories. The following year this plan came to fruition, papers were written, and after extensive revision, are being published in this volume. The contributors do not dispute the validity of biological findings, but rather argue that the biological data can be encompassed in psychological theory.

With the publication of this book, we believe that the original goal of the workshop—to present the psychological point of view on panic—has been met.

The writers of these timely chapters are enthusiastic and make a strong case for their position. The Editors are delighted with the result and take this opportunity to thank the contributors for the high quality of their efforts and their patience at our requests for changes and clarifications.

The Editors express their appreciation to Dr. Darrel Regier, Director of the Division of Clinical Research and Dr. Robert Hirschfeld, Chief, Affective and Anxiety Disorders Research Branch for their support of this work. We are indebted to Lawrence Erlbaum and his staff, especially Lori Baronian, for their cooperation in the production of the book. I would also like to thank Irma Maser for her help with proofreading significant portions of the text.

JDM and SR

1

Panic:
Psychological Contributions

S. Rachman
University of British Columbia

Jack D. Maser
Affective and Anxiety Disorders Research Branch, NIMH

INTRODUCTION

Our aim in compiling this volume is to inform students of psychopathology about recent findings on the subject of panic, and to promote attention to the extremely stimulating psychological perspectives on panic. This collection of chapters by psychologists and psychiatrists should prove to be a convenient medium for readers who wish to become familiar with contemporary thinking on this subject.[1]

The importance attached to the concept of panic is largely a result of the research carried out by Dr. Donald Klein and his colleagues over the past 20 years. It is not surprising, therefore, that his conception of the nature of panic as essentially a biological disorder, categorically distinguishable from other forms of mental disorder, was taken as authoritative. The reader is referred to Tuma and Maser (1985) for extensive considerations of this approach. *Panic: Psychological Perspectives* presents alternatives to a purely biological explanation of panic. The involvement of biological events and processes is accepted, but the contributors' ideas go beyond this acceptance and their data defy a purely biological explanation.

Definitions

According to the revised third edition of the *Diagnostic and Statistical Manual* (DSM–III–R; American Psychiatric Association, 1987) the essential features of

[1]The opinions expressed in this chapter are those of the authors and are not necessarily those of the National Institute of Mental Health.

a panic attack are discrete periods of intense fear or discomfort, and at least four of the following symptoms which appear during each attack: dyspnea (shortness of breath) or smothering sensations; choking; palpitations or accelerated heart rate (tachycardia); chest pain or discomfort; sweating; dizziness, unsteady feelings or, faintness; nausea or abdominal distress; depersonalization or derealization; numbness or paresthesias (tingling sensations); flushes (hot flashes) or chills; trembling or shaking; fear of dying; and fear of going crazy, or doing something uncontrolled.

During some of the attacks at least four of these symptoms develop suddenly and increase in intensity within 10 minutes of the first noticed symptom. Episodes involving fewer than four symptoms are called "limited symptom attacks." As the course of the disorder proceeds particular settings (e.g., in a car, in the market, on an elevator) may become associated with having a panic attack. The individual may fear having a panic attack in this setting, but is uncertain as to its timing or whether or not it will occur at all.

The Manual specifies that an organic etiology is excluded as a cause of these manifestations, and the disturbance must persist for at least 1 month beyond the cessation of any precipitating organic factor. DSM–III–R also states that the attack must be (a) unexpected, that is, not occur immediately before or on exposure to a situation that almost always caused anxiety, and (b) not triggered by situations in which the individual was the focus of others' attention.

In order to reach a diagnosis of panic disorder there is an additional criterion. Four attacks must occur within a 4-week period, or one or more attacks must be followed by a period of at least a month of persistent fear of having another attack.

There are two subtypes of panic disorder: panic disorder with agoraphobia and agoraphobia without history of panic disorder. Many believe that the etiology of agoraphobia results from the occurrence of panic attacks and that the patients with the former subtype far outnumber patients who have agoraphobia without panic. This issue will be discussed later in our chapter, but figures on the incidence of each subtype must await population-based epidemiology studies.

The DSM–III–R conception of panic disorder is strongly influenced by Klein's approach, which has been to categorize symptoms into syndromes. Some of the authors in this volume do not agree with the position of a separate category for panics, and they question the justification for viewing panic as other than an intense fear with rapid onset.

Background

Episodes of panic have been known under different names for many years (see Gelder, 1986), and numerous biological explanations have been proposed, including those based on hypoglycemia (see Gorman, Martinez, Liebowitz, Fyer, & Klein, 1984), mitral valve prolapse (Pariser, Pinta, & Jones, 1978), vestibular dysfunction (Jacob, Moller, Turner, & Wall, 1985), and thyroid disease (Hall,

1983; Lindemann, Zitrin, & Klein, 1984). None of these explanations has been confirmed (Fishman, Sheehan, & Carr, 1985; Gorman et al., 1984; Gorman et al., in preparation; Uhde, Vittone, & Post, 1984); psychodynamic theory also has its explanations, but these are essentially untestable.

Studies of the effects of antidepressant drugs on panic (Klein, 1964) first suggested that panic can be dissociated from generalized anxiety and agoraphobia. Then sodium lactate infusion (Pitts & McClure, 1967) was revived as a means of inducing panic (Klein, 1981; Liebowitz et al., 1984), and other compounds were also discovered to be capable of inducing panics (e.g., yohimbine; see Charney, Heninger, & Breier, 1984; caffeine, see Uhde, Roy–Byrne, Vittone, Boulenger, & Post, 1985). These two sets of findings (antidepressant effects and drug-induced panics) formed the foundation for the biological explanation of panic. However, there is no unifying, satisfying explanation of the original or subsequent findings, and the possible role of psychological factors was ignored (Margraf, Ehlers, & Roth, 1986a).

Interest in the psychological aspects of panic emerged rather late. Interviews with persons suffering from panic attacks suggested that cognitive events are related to the onset, timing, course, and consequences of their panics (e.g., Beck, Laude, & Bohnert, 1974). Patients worry and express alarm over the significance of their distressing symptoms; attribute their distress to a variety of causes; think they are going crazy; believe themselves to be in danger of dying or passing out; and often report that during a panic they have a confusing rush of thoughts or "stop" thinking. Convincing evidence of the role of psychological factors in laboratory inductions of panic strengthened the claim that such factors cannot be ignored.

The chapters in this book present information on the cognitions that people report having experienced during a panic, and how these cognitions are related to psychophysiological events. An important contribution of the psychological approach is that it promises to encompass and unify many of the diverse biological findings in a plausible manner.

The Chapters

During the past 3 years, David Barlow and his coworkers have paid particular attention to the relationship between Panic Disorders and other types of anxiety disorders, and this interest is clearly evident in his chapter on phenomenology. Barlow and Craske have organized the material according to a three-system analysis (Lang, 1968; Rachman, 1978). In addition to providing a general review, they consider some important but neglected aspects of panic, notably the occurrence of nocturnal panics, their possible significance for theory, and the importance of the initial panic. They consider the justification for regarding panics as being discontinuous from high levels of fear, and whether or not the term "spontaneous" is an accurate description of certain panic.

In answer to the first question, they cautiously accept the discontinuity hypothesis. Some of the other contributors (e.g., Chambless, Michelson, Turner, and Salkovskis) favor the continuity view, arguing that the evidence points more strongly to a continuum in which panics feature as extreme examples at one end of the continuum. The various contributors to this volume take their turn arguing for and against the proposition that panic is discontinuous from other forms of anxiety.

Turner, Beidel, and Jacob, for example, point out that panic occurs with some regularity in all of the anxiety categories (up to 83% in some of the nonpanic disorders), and that panics also occur in nonclinical samples. Turner et al. challenge the notion that panic disorders are qualitatively distinct, and prefer to construe panics dimensionally, in which panics are placed at the extreme end of a severity scale. The resolution of this issue is more likely to come out of the preponderance of evidence than from a definitive study.

The occurrence of nocturnal panics appears to present a major obstacle to cognitive theories of panic. The argument goes as follows: If panics are induced cognitively, why then do so many patients report that they were awakened by their panic? If these nocturnal panic awakenings occur in the absence of any associated or preceding cognitions, then cognitive theory is incomplete, at least. There are several contrary arguments, however. One is that when a person is awakened at night, for whatever reason, but presumably because of some discomfort, the occurrence or nonoccurrence of a panic depends on how the person interprets his or her perceived discomfort. Another is that dreaming is usually conceived of as a cognitive event, and the individual's panic might have been triggered by the perceived discomfort induced in the dream. In this context, we might also ask whether there is any relationship between night terrors and nocturnal panic attacks.

Dianne Chambless approaches panic cognitions from the vantage of her excellent work on the cognitive aspects of agoraphobia. As she points out, information about the content and the variations of the cognitions associated with panic is insufficient, but what is known is consistent with the notion that cognitions do play a part in the etiology of panic.

On the basis of her research experience with agoraphobia, she cites pitfalls to be avoided (or at least recognized), and provides suggestions for the collection and interpretation of dependable information on panic cognitions. Dr. Chambless postulates that patients with panic disorder believe that harm is more likely to befall them than other people, and they think more frequently about the possibility of harm, especially somatic harm. They are highly tuned to cues that might signal harm. The question of whether or not these differences are "due to current mood or to enduring characteristics" remains to be dealt with.

Rachman observes in his chapter that while most panics are distressing, the consequences of panic can be disabling. He focuses attention on three types of consequences: behavioral, psychophysiological, and cognitive. Along with Marshall (this volume) and others, Rachman believes that extensive avoidance behavior often is a consequence of panic, but avoidance may also have other origins. Many patients report the development of avoidance in the absence of panics, and as Barlow and Craske point out, panics are reported by patients with psychological problems that do not fit into the diagnosis of panic disorder or of agoraphobia. Patients who are seen in hospital clinics are more likely to report a sequence of panic followed by avoidance.

Presumably, those patients who experience panic which is not followed by disabling avoidance are less likely to seek help at a hospital clinic. For this reason they are likely to be underrepresented in hospital-based prevalence studies. Drawing conclusions solely from clinic samples can be misleading. In order to answer the question of what symptoms follow from other symptoms in the course of an illness, while avoiding Berkson's Paradox (1946), data from population samples are required.

Data from the population-based NIMH–Epidemiologic Catchment Area studies, particularly those reported by Boyd et al. (1984), are relevant. Table 4 in that report indicates that a person with agoraphobia is 18 times more likely to have panic disorder than someone without agoraphobia. For purposes of comparison, approximately the same odds ratio[2] (18.8) hold for having panic disorder if one is diagnosed as having an episode of major depression.

---

[2]An odds ratio is a statistic used in epidemiology. "Odds" is the ratio of the probability of the occurrence of an event to that of nonoccurrence (Last, 1983). An odds ratio or 2 by 2 cross-product ratio (AD/BC) for risk is the odds in favor of getting a disorder, if the proper conditions are present, to the odds in favor of getting this disorder, if these conditions are not present. The general 2 × 2 contingency table would be:

	Proper Conditions Present	Proper Conditions Absent
Disorder	A	B
No Disorder	C	D

In the case of panic and agoraphobia the contingency table would be:

	Agoraphobia Present	Agoraphobia Absent
Panic		
No Panic		

Although the odds are high (Boyd, personal communication), one needs to know the number of people occupying the cell defined by persons with agoraphobia and not panic. (This would be cell C in Footnote 2.) In 1986, Weissman, Leaf, Blazer, Boyd, and Florio reported that the lifetime rate of agoraphobia without panic disorder or panic symptoms ranged from 1.4 to 6.6 per 100 in the population. The lifetime rate of agoraphobia with panic disorder symptoms ranged from 1.7 to 2.6 per 100. On the basis of population studies there are many people for whom panic does not precede agoraphobia. Apparently, people with more than one disorder (agoraphobia plus panic) tend to seek help in clinics located in research centers, while those with only one disorder (agoraphobia) are less likely to come to such clinics. Data collected at research clinics, by virtue of an overrepresentation of patients with two diagnoses can give rise to a spurious correlation, even when the two diagnoses have independent probabilities of occurrence (Berkson, 1946).

Using a nonchemical method for inducing panic under controlled environmental conditions, Rachman found that panics tended to be followed by increases in *expected* fear, but not in *reported* fear. Unexpected panics contributed most to these changes in prediction, and expected panics had little effect on prediction or on reports of fear. Disconfirmed expectations of panic were followed by reductions in self-reported fear. Panics were followed by increases in the predictions of future panics. Although subjects correctly predicted roughly one in three of the induced panics, they showed a high rate of overprediction.

The possibility that some panics are caused by hyperventilation has been considered from time to time. Salkovskis concludes from his research that while hyperventilation often plays an important role, it is not a necessary condition for the development of a panic. His analysis of the influence of hyperventilation leads naturally to a consideration of other physiological information about panic, and he finds that the data are most consistent with the cognitive model. While acknowledging the strong association between panics and global avoidance behavior, Salkovskis notes that the behavioral components have been construed too narrowly. He also draws attention to the useful point that, contrary to what has been believed for some time, patients with generalized anxiety also show extensive avoidance behavior.

Van den Hout discusses the psychophysiological approach to panic, and attempts an ambitious integration of the psychological and physiological data on the experimental induction of panic. The data are often confusing and sometimes in apparent conflict, but his reconciliation is plausible and the explanation for the conflicting findings is promising and testable. Van den Hout also introduces an interoceptive model of fear that bears a resemblance to Seligman's outline of a conditioning theory of panic. Despite many attractive features, the concept of interoceptive conditioning does not easily lend itself to investigations of the genesis of panic, and it will need to be defined operationally before progress can be expected. The CR is easily defined, but the identity of the CS, UCS, and UCR is much less clear.

Much of the contemporary work on applying cognitive concepts to anxiety can be traced to the pioneering work carried out in 1976 by Beck. The implications of his work for anxiety were neglected because of the great interest that was then shown in forging cognitive theories of depression. It is only within the last 3 years that his attention, and that of others, has turned to the cognitions that precede, accompany, and follow episodes of panic (Beck & Emery, 1985).

Clark's theory that panics are induced by catastrophic misinterpretations of bodily sensations is the fullest and most advanced of the products of Beck's original claim that ideas and images play a vital role in determining anxiety states. It is not surprising to find connections between his writings and those of Beck. Both agree in general terms about the critical importance of ideation, but they differ in detail.

Beck recently added a new proposition to his original work: during panics the person experiences a significant loss of reasoning ability. Confirmation of this claim, or at least a more specifically formulated version of it, would bring to the fore the problem of how to prepare people for experiences in which their cognitive range is suddenly constricted. If it is correct that panics are caused by misinterpretations of bodily sensations, presumably we should try to establish the correct interpretation prior to panic episodes, during which time the person's ability to reason is reduced. It remains to be seen whether or not this tactic will be complicated by state-dependent problems of transfer of learning.

Clark's theory of catastrophic misinterpretations is concisely and clearly described. The theory is developed with considerable skill and is then used to incorporate a surprisingly wide range of information. The theory is consistent with the content of the cognitions reported by panic patients, with the sequence of events, the effects of panics induced in the laboratory, and with the occurrence of spontaneous panics. Moreover, a number of predictions are derived and his chapter describes the early results of experiments designed to test these predictions.

This deceptively simple model is, in fact, a highly ambitious attempt to provide a comprehensive account of panic. While it incorporates much of the biological data, it is not as precise operationally as one might wish. There is a great deal of research and clinical investigation to be carried out before the theory can be appraised fully, but Clark and Salkovskis have made an energetic start.

The extraordinarily promising early results of their newly developed treatment technique deserve full and extensive replication. Encouragement can be drawn from the fact that Beck has recently completed an uncontrolled clinical trial, using his own, but comparable, methods. The early responses to his treatment methods have been excellent. Other contributors to this volume, Michelson and Barlow, are separately engaged in treatment research of this nature. The completion of conventional controlled clinical trials of these cognitive/behavioral methods is awaited with impatience.

Peter Lang's chapter presents the most precise formulation of the psychological position. He points out problems with the attribution approach, introduces the computer program as a metaphor for mentation, and defines cognition as computation. The stage is thereby set to viewing behavior as the production of an information-processing system. In order to understand how the system works, research must elucidate the mechanisms of memory and its organization, how the brain processes images, and how efferent programs of action result. The theory is not easy to grasp on one reading, but its specificity is remarkable in a field long dominated and retarded by vague terminology.

After acknowledging the potential importance of the new research and theorizing on cognitive approaches to panic, Seligman introduces a constructively critical set of arguments. He draws attention to the need for more closely defined terms, and argues that "catastrophic misinterpretation" is too loose a construct, and bears little relationship to conventional cognitive psychology. He argues that the cognitive models of Clark and Beck are not sufficiently different from other, noncognitive, explanations. In the absence of differences, no differential predictions follow from these theories.

Seligman believes that much of the currently available information can be explained by conditioning theory. The explanatory value of conditioning theory is bound to attract increasing attention, especially if the dimensional view of panic comes to predominate. If the categorical classification of panic is verified, then separate explanations will be needed for panic and for other types of fear. A new (or greatly modified) conditioning theory will be required. On the other hand, if panic is better construed as an extreme point on a continuum of fear, then the existing conditioning theory of fear will need little revision. Panic can be encompassed simply by an extension of the theory.

In order to sharpen the definitions contained in cognitive theories and to test whether the theories have special value, Seligman proposes a number of differential predictions. The outcome of testing these predictions will no doubt help to elucidate and invigorate research on cognitive approaches to panic attacks.

Seligman also considers a number of unsolved problems. Distinguishing between the rational and irrational, the conscious and the unconscious, he argues that there are almost certainly two distinguishable cognitive processes, obeying different laws, which are blurred by both (cognitive and conditioning) theories. He reminds us of the persistently troublesome problem of the "neurotic paradox" and forcibly raises the question of why it is that certain kinds of fear appear to defy disconfirmation. Why does a person who has experienced hundreds of panic attacks fail to learn that his heart is not failing him? Why does he continue to believe that he is about to have a heart attack? Under all laws of disconfirmation of which I am aware, he received ample evidence that what he believed was false, and he should have abandoned it. Questions of this kind are critical and lie at the center of many of the remaining problems of neurotic behavior.

Teasdale's evaluation of cognitive theory poses three questions. He asks whether the cognitive theory presented is novel; is it superior to alternative accounts; and is the evidence for the clinical effectiveness of cognitive treatments satisfactory? He deals with these well-chosen questions in a balanced and searching manner, and his general answer is that cognitive theory is extremely promising, but by no means conclusive. Teasdale draws attention to the gaps in evidence, the overlap with alternative explanations, and the insufficiency of the evidence of therapeutic effectiveness.

In company with other contributors, Teasdale raises the intriguing question of why panic and other anxiety disorders are relatively easy to modify by exposure, but are slow to respond to purely cognitive changes. Observing that exposure procedures may be necessary, he considers whether purely verbal interventions may be of limited effectiveness unless backed up by experiential evidence. That is, cognitive changes need to be backed up by direct experience. His thoughtful consideration of this subject touches on Seligman's discussion of the resistance of panic cognitions to disconfirmatory experiences.

Starting from the basis of his clinical and research experience with cognitive treatments for depression, Teasdale proposes that it may prove necessary to combine two elements of therapy in order to change panic symptoms. First, patients have to be provided with credible explanations for their panics, and then provided with validating experiences in which they learn that symptoms can be controlled. Teasdale makes explicit the connection between the cognitive theory of panic and the better established and more fully investigated cognitive approach to the understanding and treatment of depression. In the case of Beck's work, of course, the connection is direct and personal, as he formulated the cognitive theory of depression that shows continuity with recent views of panic.

Clark has been an active contributor to research on depression and this influence on his thinking about panic is evident. The emerging links between the explanations for depression and anxiety, evident in parts of this volume, are parallel to new findings on the comorbidity between anxiety and depressive disorders.

Marshall reminds us of the predominant role of exposure in virtually all of the fear-reducing procedures, and warns against losing sight of this important fact. Although he favors the behavioral approach, Marshall is not unsympathetic to other views. He expresses a critical and slightly skeptical viewpoint, and uses the opportunity to draw attention to the ambiguous meanings attached to the term "avoidance behavior." In agreement with Salkovskis, he urges that greater specificity is required.

As far as the practical implications of the research and thinking described in this volume are concerned, the early results are a most encouraging first step. They have to be considered against a background of reasonable success reported by therapists who use pharmacological treatments for panic. Michael Telch concludes his review of the evidence on psychological and pharmacological treatments with the claim that, in combination, they can produce a superior result to either method used independently. However, the efficacy of the treatments has not been proven beyond doubt and Telch discusses the conflicting results. Unfortunately, the controlled treatment trials that are required are time consuming and expensive. Moreover, many methodological problems persist (e.g., how does one cope with the use, nonuse, or intermittent use, of the same or different drugs during the follow-up period?). Telch also directs attention to the lack of understanding of the mechanisms by which drugs act. Most of these drugs affect multiple neurotransmitter systems, and considerable experimental dissection will be required before final conclusions can be reached.

Using her familiarity with the biological and psychological approaches to panic, Shear proposes an integration. She argues that panic can be a manifestation of either biological or psychological disturbances, or a combination of the two. The type and strength of the coping mechanism influences the occurrence, type, and pervasiveness of pathological panic.

Shear also reports encouraging results from an exploratory study on the effects of cognitive behavioral therapy that are compatible with the findings already reported by Clark and by Beck. Conclusions on the effectiveness of psychological treatments for panic would be premature, but it is unwise to ignore the early signs. These early therapeutic results alone fully justify an energetic interest in the new developments.

The claim that psychological factors play a major role in the etiology and persistence of panics has received support. The importance of biological data is not disputed, but the interpretation of these findings as the sole cause of panic is questioned. The demonstration of significant psychological contributions to panic and the emergence of cognitive theory are useful advances, but the acid test of usefulness will come when investigators begin to make differential predictions between cognitive theory, a revived and refined conditioning theory, and purely biological explanations. After years of neglect there is a sudden, welcome profusion of ideas on the subject.

2

The Phenomenology of Panic

David H. Barlow and Michelle G. Craske
Center for Stress and Anxiety Disorders, State University of New York

INTRODUCTION

Subjectively, the feeling of panic is described as a rush of "apprehension, fear, or terror . . . or feelings of impending doom" that is distinguished from a high level of general anxiety by its sudden onset, usually within 10 minutes. The intense fright which often accompanies the first experience of panic is evident from the recollections of patients assessed at our Phobia and Anxiety Disorders Clinic; 81% of a group of 99 patients recalled that they left the situation or activity in which they were engaged, and approximately 25% attended an emergency medical facility or contacted a doctor or nurse, in response to their first panic attack. The extent to which avoidance patterns develop alongside panic attacks varies considerably both across individuals, and within individuals across time. Agoraphobia with panic (panic disorder with agoraphobia, DSM–III–R) is assigned as a diagnosis when anticipatory anxiety concerning the attacks results in reluctance to leave the house or to enter places in which panic is expected to occur. Anticipatory anxiety is commonly present in panic disorder, but is not associated with marked avoidance of specific situations.

PANIC TOPOGRAPHY

The following parametric data were obtained at the Phobia and Anxiety Disorders Clinic from the behavioral diaries of a group of 16 patients with a primary diagnosis of panic disorder who had been trained to record panic and therefore were sensitive to low intensity panics (i.e., attacks, episodes, etc.) as well as the more intense variety. At pretreatment assessment, these patients reported a mean frequency of 1.31 panics per week. The mean intensity of their panics was rated as 3.33, on a scale of 0 to 8, where 0 referred to no anxiety or discomfort and 8 referred to as much anxiety or discomfort as was imaginable. Their panics and the resulting residual anxiety lasted, on the average, 140.36 minutes. That is, their panic attack may have lasted 20 to 30 minutes but residual anxiety, as a consequence of the often unexpected attack, at an intensity of 4 or above, extended the episode to 140 minutes on the average. According to their data, these patients were experiencing a phenomenon relatively frequently and of sufficient duration and intensity to warrant the high level of general distress that typically accompanies this disorder.

In order to meet the criteria for definition as a panic attack, the sudden rush of fear or impending doom must be accompanied by at least four of the following list of symptoms, most of which are physical or somatic expressions of panic: dyspnea, palpitations, chest pain or discomfort, choking or smothering sensations, dizziness or unsteadiness, feelings of unreality, paresthesias, hot and cold flashes, sweating, faintness, trembling or shaking, fear of dying, and fear of going crazy or doing something uncontrolled during an attack. The prominence of particular symptoms varies across individuals and, like the avoidance component, sometimes varies within individuals across time.

TABLE 2.1
Number and Percentage of 41 Agoraphobics with Panic Reporting Each of the DSM–III Symptoms

	Agoraphobia with Panic N = 41	
Symptom	*Number*	*Percentage*
Dyspnea	37	(90)
Palpitations	40	(98)
Chest pain	31	(76)
Choking	30	(73)
Dizziness	39	(95)
Unreality	28	(68)
Paresthesias	26	(63)
Hot or cold flushes	35	(85)
Sweating	35	(93)
Faintness	31	(76)
Shaking	36	(88)
Fear of going crazy or losing control	37	(90)

Note. From *Panic, Anxiety and the Anxiety Disorders,* by D. H. Barlow, in press. New York: Guilford Press. Reprinted by permission.

TABLE 2.2
Rank Orders of the Intensity of Symptoms Experienced by Agoraphobes During Panic Attacks

Symptoms	*Ley's Rank*	*Barlow's Rank*	*Composite Rank*
Fear of dying, etc.	1	2	1
Palpitations	3	1	2
Trembling	2	4	3
Dyspnea	4	5.5	4
Dizziness	7	3	5
Hot or cold flashes	6	5.5	6
Faintness	8.5	7	7
Unreality	5	11	8
Sweating	8.5	8	9
Chest pain	10	10	10.5
Choking	11	9	10.5
Parasthesias	12	12	12

Note. From *Panic, anxiety and the anxiety disorders,* by D. H. Barlow (in press). New York: Guilford Press.

Typically, patients who experience panic report far more than the specified minimum number of four symptoms. The frequency with which each symptom was reported by a group of 41 agoraphobics who were assessed at the Phobia and Anxiety Disorders Clinic is listed in Table 2.1. Percentages are included in parentheses. The most frequently reported symptoms were palpitations and dizziness. In addition, dyspnea, sweating, and a fear of going crazy or losing control were reported by at least 90% of the sample. Since these descriptions were taken mostly from their "typical" panics, the specific number of symptoms associated with any one discrete panic may be somewhat less. The relative intensity of each symptom as reported by the same group of agoraphobics is shown in Table 2.2, from which it is seen that palpitations, fear of dying, and dizziness are rated as the strongest symptoms. Symptom intensity rankings parallel very closely those reported by Ley (in press), whose rankings are shown also in Table 2.2.

A certain percentage of people who experience repeated, full-blown panic attacks, also report the experience of limited symptom attacks. The latter refers to the discrete episodes of panic which are accompanied by fewer than four symptoms. Taylor et al. (1986) noted that approximately 25% of their group of panic disorder patients reported panic attacks that would be classified as minor or limited symptom on the basis of a three-symptom criterion for major attacks. The minor attacks were rated by patients as less intense than full-blown attacks (2.5 compared with 3.9, on a 0–10 scale), and were associated with average heartrate increases of 17.3 beats per minute (b.p.m.), compared with 49.2 b.p.m. for major attacks. However, in our clinical experience, this type of attack is relatively rare in the absence of full-blown panic attacks. In the series of 41 agoraphobics mentioned previously, only one reported the experience of limited symptom attacks without full-blown attacks.

TRIPARTITE DESCRIPTION OF PANIC

The supremely subjective phenomenon of panic can be operationalized to some extent by examination of each of the three major response systems that comprise anxiety reactions: physiological, subjective-cognitive, and behavioral. A brief description of each system follows.

Physiological Component. As early as 1970, Lader and Mathews captured the physiological concomitants of panic attacks in a laboratory setting. Physiological recording of unexpected panic has been reported by Cohen, Barlow, and Blanchard (1985). They recorded the responses of two subjects who panicked during the relaxation phase of a standard physiological assessment. The physiological profiles were very similar, as evident from Figs. 2.1 and 2.2. Initial decreases in heart rate and EMG indicated that the subjects relaxed well. These decreases were followed by abrupt increases during a panic, reaching a level of tachycardia within 1 minute for one subject and within 2 minutes for the other. EMG measures also increased during the panic episodes for both patients. Hand surface temperature change was consistent across both subjects, showing a decline during relaxation followed by an abrupt increase during panic, a pattern that differs from the usual finding of a decrease in peripheral temperature during stress.

Physiological patterns recorded from laboratory conditions that are designed to elicit panic (e.g., CO_2 inhalation, hyperventilation, lactate infusion) seem to match those recorded from unexpected panic. Liebowitz et al. (1985), for example, found that panic attacks which were induced in panic disorder patients through lactate infusions were characterized by abrupt heart rate increases (on average, 42 b.p.m.) and hyperventilation.

A third means of measuring the physiological component of panic is to record change during naturally occurring panic. This is made possible by advances in technology that allow relatively unobtrusive monitoring on a 24-hour basis. Freedman, Ianni, Ettedgui, and Puthezhath (1985) monitored patients with panic

---

FIG. 2.1. Heart rate, average integrated elecyromyograph (EMG), and hand-surface temperature for Subject 1. Note. From "Psychophysiology of relaxation-associated panic attacks," by A. Cohen et al., (1985), *Journal of Abnormal Psychology, 94,* p. 98. Copyright 1985 by American Psychological Association. Reprints by permission.

SUBJECT 1

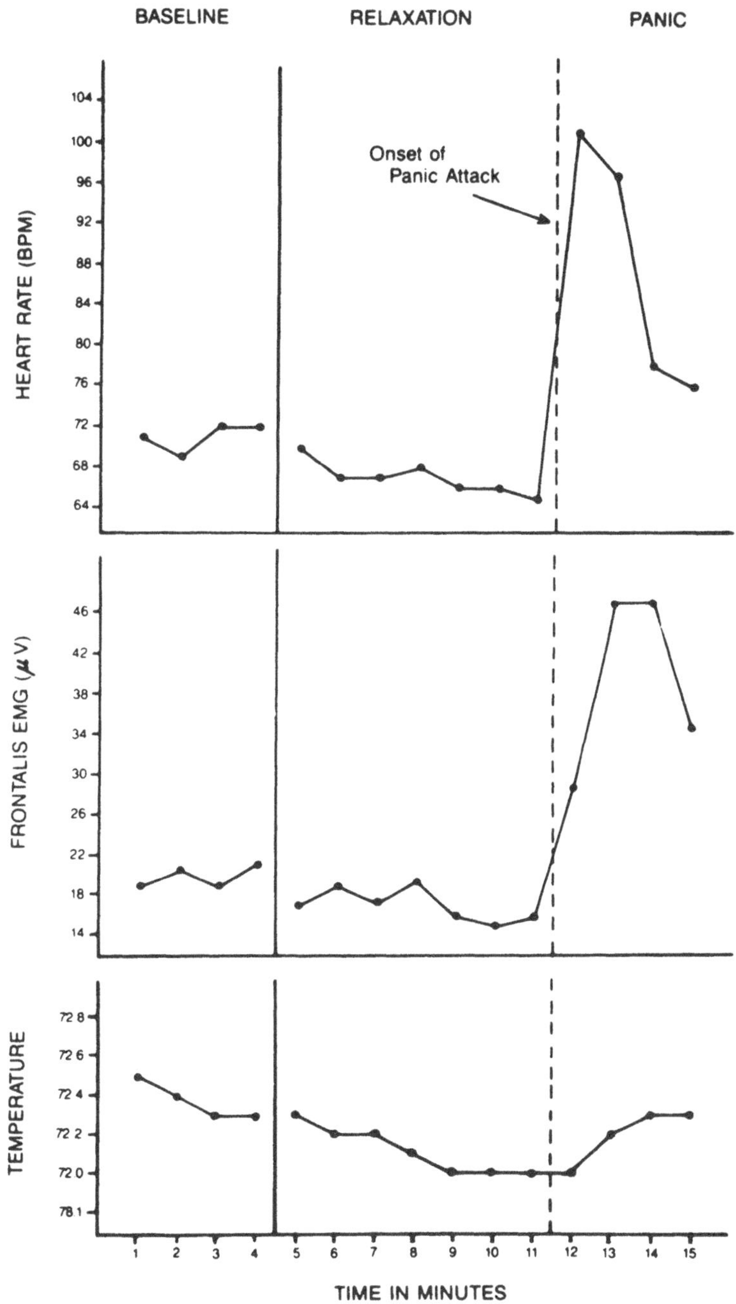

BASELINE
RELAXATION
PANIC
HEART RATE (BPM)
104
100
96
92
88
84
80
76
72
68
64
Onset of
Panic Attack
FRONTALIS EMG (μV)
46
42
38
34
30
26
22
18
14
TEMPERATURE
72.8
72.6
72.4
72.2
72.0
78.1
1
2
3
4
5
6
7
8
9
10
11
12
13
14
15
TIME IN MINUTES

SUBJECT 2

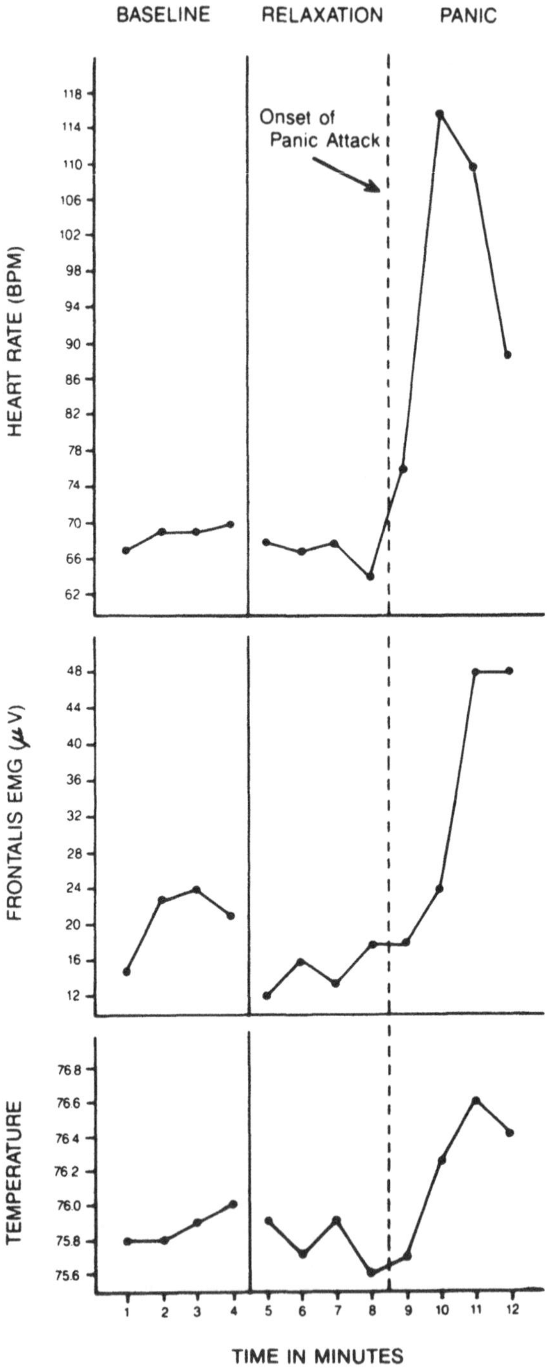
BASELINE
RELAXATION
PANIC
Onset of Panic Attack
HEART RATE (BPM)
118
114
110
106
102
98
94
90
86
82
78
74
70
66
62
FRONTALIS EMG (μV)
48
44
40
36
32
28
24
20
16
12
TEMPERATURE
76.8
76.6
76.4
76.2
76.0
75.8
75.6
1
2
3
4
5
6
7
8
9
10
11
12
TIME IN MINUTES

disorder over a period of 2 days, in which time they were able to record five panic attacks. During those episodes, substantial increases in heart rate and changes in other physiological indicators were recorded. Taylor and his colleagues have examined naturally occurring panic attacks in detail by removing statistically the amount of heart rate elevation due to physical activity per se from the level of heart rate elevation recorded during episodes of panic. Taylor et al. (1986) monitored 12 patients with panic disorder for 6 days, 24 hours a day. They were able to show that naturally occurring panic attacks could be identified by abrupt elevations of heart rate that could not be attributed to physical activity alone. Moreover, the physiological patterns they obtained were very similar to those that have characterized laboratory panics. The average heart rate increase of 38.6 b.p.m. generally peaked after 4 minutes. Mean panic duration of 20.2 minutes (using a heart rate criterion) was slightly longer than the typical 5-minute episode recorded in the laboratory setting. It is possible that the safety values of laboratory settings diminish the duration of panics. Surprisingly, Taylor et al. found that panic attacks occurred most often in the early hours of the morning when patients were sleeping.

Their results were of particular interest because they demonstrated occasional discordance between physiological and subjective measures of panic. Approximately 40% of the full-blown, self-reported, panic attacks were not accompanied by heart rate levels above those expected from normal activity, despite the report of panic symptoms. However, panic attacks that were accompanied by heart rate elevations were rated as more intense than those not accompanied by heart rate increases, as evident from the respective severity ratings of 4.7 versus 3.3, on a 0–7 scale. Moreover, Taylor et al. recorded heart rate elevations (not due to normal activity) that were comparable with those characteristic of panic attacks, but which were not labeled by the subject as panic. Their data suggest that heart rate elevation alone is insufficient as a marker of panic. In contrast, Liebowitz et al. (1985), on the basis of observed heart rate increases during lactate-induced panic, suggested that heart rate may be used as a marker for panic.

Discordance between physiological symptoms and the subjective element of panic was demonstrated also by Rapee (1986), who recorded physiological changes from 20 panickers under conditions of hyperventilation. At least 70% of his subjects reported the experience of dizziness, dry mouth, breathlessness, unsteadiness, flushed feelings, heart palpitations, faintness, trembling, difficulty in thinking clearly, and paresthesias when hyperventilating. These symptoms

FIG. 2.2. Heart rate, average integrated electromyograph (EMG), and hand-surface for Subject 2. *Note.* From "Psychophysiology of relaxation-associated panic attacks," by A. Cohen et al., 1985, *Journal of Abnormal Psychology, 94,* p. 98. Copyright 1985 by American Psychological Association. Reprints by permission.

were accompanied by an average heart rate increase of 15 b.p.m. Despite the presence of sympathetic arousal and the report of symptoms that were considered most often to be very similar to symptoms experienced during naturally occurring panics, no member of the group reported actual panic. "A number of subjects reported that although physical symptoms were the same, they did not panic because they knew what was causing the symptoms and they felt they were in a safe environment" (Rapee, 1986, p. 26). This has been a common observation in laboratory provocation studies for years (e.g., Bonn, Harrison, & Rees, 1971; Breggan, 1964). In agreement with Gorman, Askanazi et al. (1984), Rapee concluded that simply overbreathing is not sufficient to produce a panic attack. He suggested that misinterpretation of sensations may mediate the occurrence of panic.

The overriding influence of expectations and beliefs has been demonstrated by van den Hout and Griez (1982; this volume). They showed that states of relaxation or mild aversion resulting from carbon dioxide inhalation were determined largely by prior expectancy that was induced by experimental instruction. Similarly, Rapee, Mattick, and Murrell (1986) found that different experimental instructions regarding expected effects from carbon dioxide inhalation elicited different rates of panic. Customary instructions of panic induction experiments produced panic as frequently as is usually observed under such conditions. However, patients given detailed instructions concerning expected symptoms did not panic. Together, the data point to a primary role for cognitions in terms of (a) interpretations of physiological cues per se, and (b) interpretations of the context in which those cues occur. A complex interaction between physical sensations, subjective experience, and the surrounding environment is likely.

Further evidence pertinent to the concordance/discordance between subjective and physiological components derives from a recent follow-up examination of treated agoraphobics (Craske, Sanderson, & Barlow, 1987). It was found, paradoxically, that patients who experienced the highest heart rate during follow-up assessment behavioral testing were also those who responded most favorably to treatment. Panic was not measured directly, but the data showed that high heart rate can persist without forming part of a panic syndrome.

Cognitive Component. The cognitive component of panic is characterized frequently by a fear of dying, losing control, or going crazy. This aspect of panic attacks deserves further attention. Beck & Emery (1985; this volume) claim that panic is precipitated by danger signals which are based on the interpretation of internal sensations as indicative of heart attack and dying. Similarly, Clark and Salkovskis (1986a; this volume) propose that panic results from the catastrophic interpretations of certain bodily sensations; for example, perceiving palpitations as evidence of impending heart attack or racing thoughts as evidence of going crazy. Rapee (1986) noted that panic disorder patients tend to engage in "more cognitions associated with serious physical and mental illness than do subjects with generalized anxiety disorder'' (p. 26). In a survey study conducted by Craske, Rachman, and Tallman (1986), it was found that subjects who reported panicking in the previous week differed from those who did not panic in terms of cognitions. Responses to the Cognitions Questionnaire (Chambless, Caputo, Bright, & Gallagher, 1984) showed that panic subjects thought more frequently about passing out, heart attack, acting foolish, losing control, going crazy, screaming, babbling, and being paralyzed by fear when intensely anxious than subjects who had not reported panic in the preceding week. Unfortunately, panic was poorly specified on the questionnaire and the data pertained to a limited time period. However, despite those weaknesses, the differences obtained are more likely to be an underestimation than an overestimation of differences that would emerge under controlled comparison conditions.

Behavioral Component. The usual behavior avoidance component that reliably forms part of phobic disorders is much more variable in the case of panic disorders, ranging from extensive avoidance (which would characterize agoraphobia) to limited or no avoidance. Panickers continue to enter situations often despite the experience of panic and, as such, demonstrate courageous behavior (Rachman, 1978). Some panic patients report that they do not exhibit wide-ranging avoidance because the occurrence of panic is often unexpected, and therefore unreliably connected with specific situations. Conversely, others attribute their extensive avoidance pattern to the seemingly unpredictable experience of panic in any situation. Individual differences which could account for situational endurance versus avoidance is of great interest and worthy of the attention it has attracted recently, especially in terms of the relationship between avoidance and the expected–unexpected dimension of panic. It is sometimes observed that panickers avoid strenuous exercise, caffeine consumption, and other activities that elicit symptoms associated with the feeling of panic. Some patients have even reported deliberate attempts to breathe shallowly in order to minimize awareness of respiratory and cardiovascular symptoms. The degree to which avoidance of internal sensations accompanies avoidance of external situations is in need of assessment.

Panic Pervasiveness

The occurrence of panic is quite common in the normal population. In a survey conducted by Craske et al. (1986), it was found that 24% of a group of 173 students reported the experience of panic in the preceding week. Similarly, 21% of a group of 73 relatives of the student sample and 5% of a group of 58 senior citizens reported the experience of panic in the same time frame. These estimates are likely to be inflated given that panic criteria were specified by Chambless, Caputo, Jasin, Gracely, and Williams (1985) on their Mobility Inventory as follows: a high level of anxiety accompanied by strong body reactions (heart palpitations, sweating, muscle tremors, dizziness, nausea), temporary loss of the ability to plan, think, or reason and the intense desire to escape or flee the situation. This set of criteria is not as stringent as those specified by DSM–III (American Psychiatric Association, 1980), but, nevertheless, the substantial number of people reporting, or labeling an experience as panic is surprising. Nevertheless, Norton and his colleagues (Norton, Dorward, & Cox, 1986) have also found that up to 35% of a nonclinical population reported at least one panic in the last year. The latter study (Norton et al., 1986) employed well-defined and validated DSM–III criteria. Similar results have also been reported from England (G. Klerman, personal communication, 1986).

Panic disorder and agoraphobia with panic attacks together have a prevalence rate of approximately 4–7%, and are more frequently diagnosed in women, particularly in the case of agoraphobia (Myers et al., 1984). From a group of 99 panickers assessed at the Phobia and Anxiety Disorders Clinic, who presented with a range from mild to extensive avoidance, 78% were female and 22% were male. Uhlenhuth et al. (1983) also estimated the female to male ratio in agoraphobics with panic attacks as 3.5 to 1. The group of 99 panickers reportedly experienced their first panic at the average age of 28.5 years. Crowe, Noyes, Pauls, and Slyman (1983) reported a similar average age of onset of 26.3 years.

To determine the prevalence and phenomenology of DSM–III specified panic across various diagnostic categories, Barlow et al. (1985) completed a preliminary analysis with 108 patients, who were evaluated at the Phobia and Anxiety Disorders Clinic, using a structured interview schedule, the ADIS. All patients were interviewed on two separate occasions by two professionals. Reliability of differential diagnosis using the ADIS has been reported previously (DiNardo, O'Brien, Barlow, Waddell, & Blanchard, 1983). Each patient was questioned about the occurrence of panic attacks and their onset and frequency. Specifically, they were asked "Have you had times when you felt a sudden rush of intense fear or anxiety or feelings of impending doom?" An affirmative response was followed by ratings of the intensity of each DSM–III symptom of panic, using their typical or most recent attack as a point of reference. Each symptom was rated on a 5-point scale of severity, 0–4. Table 2.3 lists the frequency with which each primary diagnosis is represented, as are the mean age and sex distributions for each diagnostic category. The table also includes percentages of patients in each category who reported panic and the percentage who met the DSM–III criteria for panic disorder: the presence of at least 4 of the 12 symptoms at least three times in a 3-week period.

It is obvious from Table 2.3 that panic is an ubiquitous problem among patients with anxiety disorders, with at least 83% of patients in any diagnostic category reporting at least one panic attack. Almost all patients who reported the experience of panic satisfied the four symptom criteria. Differences emerge among the diagnostic categories when frequency of panic is considered. The percentage of patients in the social phobia, simple phobia, and generalized

TABLE 2.3
Sample Descriptors and Incidence of Panic Across Diagnostic Categories

	Agoraphobia with Panic	*Social Phobia*	*Simple Phobia*	*Panic Disorder*	*GAD*	*Obsessive Compulsive*	*Major Depressive Episode*	*Statistical Comparison*
Males (n)	2	10	2	6	8	2	1	
Females (n)	39	9	5	11	4	4	5	
Mean age (years)	36.2^{AB}	28.8^{A}	44.6^{BC}	34.8^{A}	36.1^{AB}	28.5^{A}	46.3^{C}	$F(6,101) = 4.64$, $p < .001$
Reports of panic (%)	98	89	100	100	83	83	83	$X^2(6) = 7.27$, NS
Diagnosis is met except for Panic Frequency (%)	98	84	85	100	75	83	83	$X^2(6) = 9.50$, NS
Diagnosis on DSM–III Panic Criteria (%)	74	50	33	82	29	*	*	$X^2(6) = 14.67$, $p < .03$

Categories sharing superscripts are not significantly different by Duncan's Multiple Range Test.

n's were too low to analyze, due to missing data on panic frequency. However, for the three obsessive compulsives and three depressed patients for whom we had complete data, 100% met the criteria.

Note. From "The phenomenon of panic," by D. H. Barlow et al., (1985), *Journal of Abnormal Psychology, 94,* p. 322. Copyright 1985 by American Psychological Association. Reprinted by permission.

TABLE 2.4
Average Severity Ratings of Specific Panic Symptoms Across Diagnostic Categories

Symptom	*Agoraphobia with Panic*	*Social Phobia*	*Simple Phobia*	*Panic Disorder*	*GAD*	*Obsessive Compulsive*	*Major Depressive Episode*	*Statistical Comparison*
Dyspnea (0–4)	1.71	1.33	1.33	1.29	1.67	1.80	1.10	$F(6,90) = .661$, NS
Palpitations (0–4)	2.35	2.03	1.67	2.21	1.67	2.10	.96	$F(6,91) = 2.05$, NS
Chest pain (0–4)	1.31^{B}	$.31^{A}$	$.92^{AB}$	1.29^{B}	1.00^{AB}	1.00^{B}	$.90^{AB}$	$F(6,91) = 2.39$, $p < .05$
Choking (0–4)	1.35	.90	1.17	1.06	.83	1.50	.70	$F(6,91) = .737$, NS
Dizziness (0–4)	2.04^{B}	$.91^{A}$	$.58^{A}$	1.76^{B}	1.39^{AB}	1.70^{AB}	$.70^{A}$	$F(6,91) = 5.04$, $p < .001$
Unreality (0–4)	1.28	.88	.83	1.83	.78	1.80	.90	$F(6,91) = 1.86$, NS
Paresthesias (0–4)	.76	.22	.92	1.00	.78	1.10	.80	$F(6,91) = 1.72$, NS
Hot or cold flushes (0–4)	1.71	.94	1.50	1.41	1.11	2.10	1.70	$F(6,91) = 2.12$, NS
Sweating (0–4)	1.51	1.38	1.33	1.44	.78	1.60	1.60	$F(6,91) = .76$, NS
Faintness (0–4)	1.61^{B}	$.66^{A}$	$.67^{AB}$	1.15^{AB}	$.94^{AB}$	1.10^{AB}	.10	$F(6,91) = .3.02$, $p < .01$
Shaking (0–4)	1.74	1.19	1.42	1.71	1.11	2.00	1.10	$F(6,91) = 1.33$, NS
Fear of going crazy, losing control (0–4)	2.11^{BC}	$.97^{A}$	1.58^{ABC}	2.50^{C}	$.89^{A}$	1.50^{ABC}	1.10^{AB}	$F(6,90) = 5.53$, $p < .001$
Average percentage of symptoms endorsed	85.6^{B}	61.3^{A}	68.0^{AB}	83.3^{B}	58.3^{A}	90.2^{B}	61.6^{A}	$F(6,91) = 6.21$, $p < .001$

Categories sharing superscripts are not significantly different by Duncan's Multiple Range Test

Severity ratings

0 = None 3 = Severe
1 = Mild 4 = Very Severe
2 = Moderate

Note. From "The Phenomenon of Panic" by D. H. Barlow et al., 1985, *Journal of Abnormal Psychology, 94,* p. 323.

anxiety disorder categories who met the frequency criterion is markedly lower than for the panic disorder category.

The severity with which each symptom was rated was also compared across diagnostic groups. Significant differences were found for two symptoms: dizziness and fear of going crazy or losing control. Patients with panic disorder and agoraphobia with panic reported more severe dizziness than patients with social phobia, simple phobia or major depressive episodes. These data are presented in Table 2.4. Panic disorder patients have the highest average severity rating for the symptom of fear of going crazy or losing control. It should be noted that the average severity ratings are lowered by the inclusion of zero scores for subjects who did not endorse a particular symptom. The percentage of symptoms endorsed by patients in each category are also presented. Agoraphobics with panic, panic disorder patients, and obsessive-compulsive patients all reported a high percentage of the 12 symptoms: 85.6%, 83.3%, 90.2%, respectively.

In general, few differences in panic phenonomenology emerge among diagnostic groups. Differences exist on only the severity of 2 of the 12 symptoms and in terms of the average percentage of symptoms endorsed.

The relationship between panic and major depression is currently a focus of research (see Beck, this volume). In an important series of studies, Leckman and his colleagues (Leckman, Weissman, Merikangas, Pauls, & Prusoff, 1983) reexamined 133 patients with a diagnosis of major depression to find that nearly 25% met very strict criteria for panic disorder or agoraphobia with panic. Their estimate may be low given that their criteria specified six panics in 6 weeks. Generally, the percentage of patients with major depression who experience panic attacks is estimated at 30% to 50% (Vermilyea, 1987).

PANIC UNIQUENESS

Given that the experience of panic is a relatively common phenomenon and occurs across a wide range of diagnostic groups, its uniqueness as an anxiety disorder becomes an issue. Justification for the differential status of panic from intense, generalized anxiety has been achieved by three methods of analysis, all of which fall short in some respects, but together converge to suggest that panic is an unique event. The first of these methods involves the observation of differential response to drug treatment. This was first noted by Donald Klein and his colleagues as early as 1959 (Klein, 1981). In this early work designed to test the effectiveness of a drug called imipramine, Klein observed that this drug seemed to reduce or eliminate panic attacks but had little effect on chronic levels of anticipatory anxiety. On that basis, he assumed that panic attacks were not simply severe states of general agitation. Klein thus "dissected" panic attacks from generalized, chronic, or anticipatory anxiety, as a qualitatively different state (Klein, 1964; Klein & Fink, 1962). Unfortunately, his reasoning was based on the logical fallacy of inferring pretreatment differences from treatment effects. Also, it now seems that any number of different pharmacological agents may be effective for panic (Liebowitz, 1985b). However, Klein's work suggests directions for future research.

The second method may be termed "psychological dissection"; it was employed by Waddell and colleagues (1984) in a study of the differential treatment effects of a combined treatment program on chronic background anxiety and panic attacks. In their multiple baseline across subjects design, three subjects were treated sequentially with relaxation training and cognitive restructuring. The patients self-monitored both number and duration of episodes of intense anxiety and panic, rated as 4 or higher on a scale of 0 to 8 points. In addition, they recorded level of general anxiety four times each day. These preliminary results indicated that all three patients demonstrated marked decreases in the number of episodes of intense anxiety/panic, an improvement that was maintained at a 3-month follow-up. Their response patterns are represented in Figs. 2.3 and 2.4. However, two patients exhibited a clear increase in background anxiety at the same time that episodes of intense anxiety were lessened. The third patient demonstrated synchronous reductions in background anxiety and episodes of panic.

It is tempting to conclude from these results that there are two different types of anxiety that respond differentially to the same treatment procedures. However, in so doing, the same logical error for which Klein and his coworkers were criticized is committed. In addition, the data are limited to three patients in whom a consistent pattern of differentiation between panic and chronic anxiety was not present. These data do not exclude the possibility that panic and chronic anxiety differ quantitatively but not qualitatively, and that the impact of psychological and pharmacological treatment is noticeable in the case of only intense levels of anxiety. Moreover, from a set of data collected recently from a group of 16 panickers who underwent a combined treatment of relaxation and cognitive restructuring at the Phobia and Anxiety Disorders Clinic, both number of panics and general anxiety ratings decreased from pre- to postassessment: number of panics per week decreased from 1.31 to 0.10; and mean anxiety ratings decreased from 2.31 to 1.37. However, group averages mask individual patterns of response, and it is likely that some patients within that group did not experience parallel changes in panic and generalized anxiety.

The third method by which the uniqueness of panic has been investigated is by direct comparison through physiological measures and psychometric scales. Taylor et al. (1986), as mentioned previously, were able to obtain physiological data in reference to episodes of panic and generalized anxiety during day-to-day activities. Heart rate remained relatively stable during periods of intense anticipatory anxiety, at a much lower level than during panic episodes, despite the fact that the episodes of anticipatory and panic anxiety were rated subjectively at similar levels of intensity. Heart rate averaged 89.2 b.p.m. during anticipatory

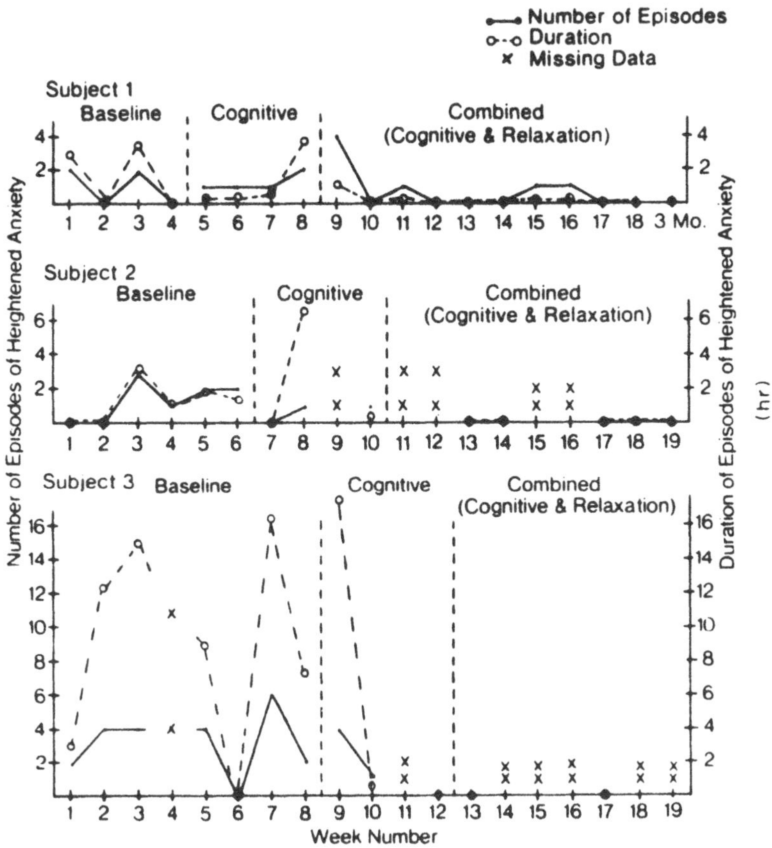

FIG. 2.3. Total number of episodes of heightened anxiety per week and duration of episodes. From "A Preliminary Investigation of Cognitive and Relaxation Treatment of Panic Disorder: Effects on Intense Anxiety vs "Background" Anxiety," by M. Waddell et al., 1984, *Behaviour Research & Therapy, 22,* p. 396. Copyright 1984 by Pergamon Press. Reprints by permission.

anxiety, compared with 108.2 b.p.m. during panic. A similar pattern of results was observed by Freedman et al. (1985), who compared heart rate recorded during panic attacks and during states of anxiety that were matched in terms of intensity but were not labeled as panic. The latter, which presumably represented periods of anticipatory or generalized anxiety, were not characterized by heart rate elevation.

However, physiological comparisons between panic episodes and anxiety states do not adequately rule out the possibility that panic is simply a severe level of generalized anxiety. It is conceivable that panic and generalized anxiety differ

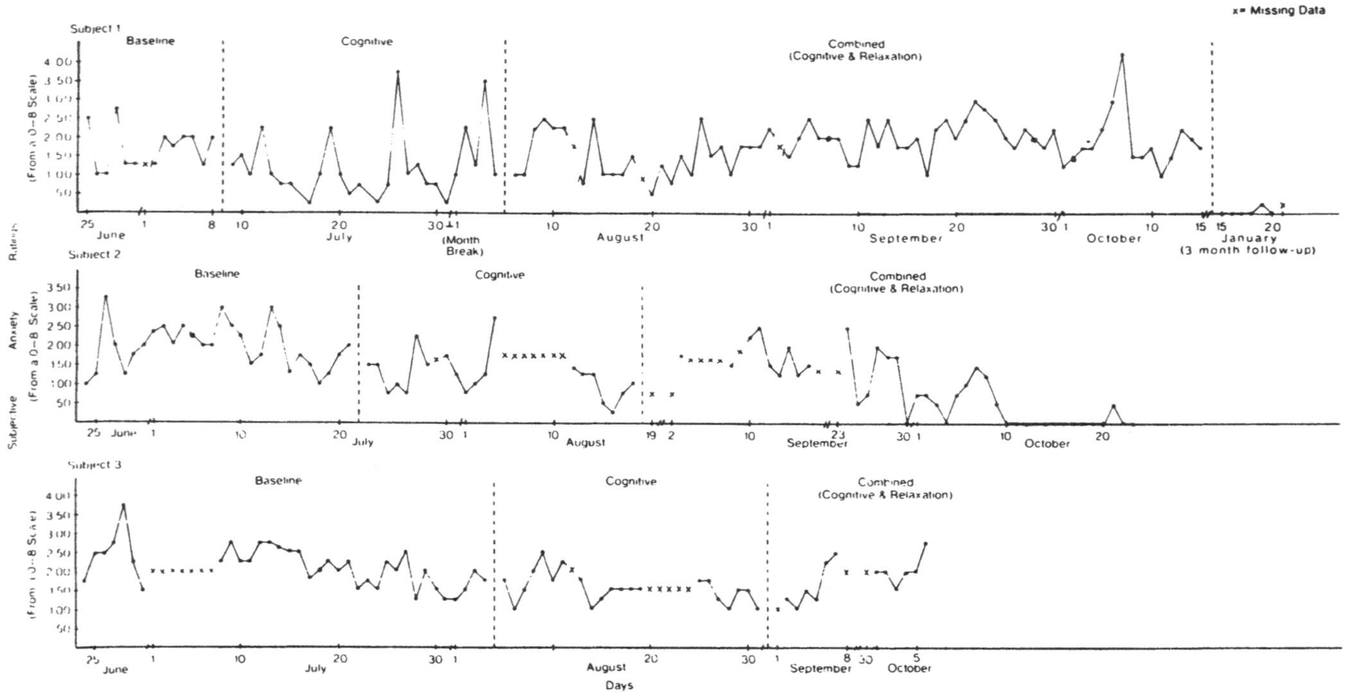

FIG. 2.4. Average of daily time-sampled ratings of anxiety. Based on a 0–8 anxiety scale. Ratings were recorded four times daily. X = missing data. From "A Preliminary Investigation of Cognitive and Relaxation Treatment of Panic Disorder: Effects on Intense Anxiety vs "Background" Anxiety," by M. Waddell et al., 1984, *Behaviour Research & Therapy, 22,* p. 398. Copyright 1984 by Pergamon Press. Reprints by permission.

only in terms of the degree of concordance between subjective fear and autonomic arousal in the expression of the same emotion. At the same intensity of subjective discomfort, physiological arousal may be present to a greater or lesser extent. Panic may characterize the state in which arousal is intense. This conceptualization, however, does not fit with the report of panic in the absence of elevated arousal, as was recorded by Taylor et al. (1986).

More compelling evidence for a qualitative difference between generalized anxiety and panic derives from studies that compare tonic arousal levels. Rapee (1985) recorded differences in baseline measures from 20 subjects with panic disorder (PD) and 13 subjects with generalized anxiety disorder (GAD). At rest, PD subjects showed a greater tendency to overbreathe than those with GAD. Rapee suggested that "such individuals may be predisposed to experiencing acute exacerbations of symptoms inasmuch as their body may no longer have the ability to buffer minor changes in pCO_2" (1986, p. 27). His data are consistent with evidence reported by Lum (1976) and Liebowitz, Gorman et al. (1985), who reported the chronic presence of lower bicarbonate and pCO_2 levels in patients with PD than in normal persons. Rapee found also that panic patients displayed higher resting heart rates than generalized anxiety patients: 92.4 compared with 76.4 b.p.m., respectively. Liebowitz et al. (1985) noted similar heart rate differences during baseline measurement; however, patient control differences were less marked the day before panic induction. They therefore attribute much of the chronic arousal to "nonspecific apprehension."

Recently, we have demonstrated that patients with panic disorder evidence a stronger somatic component to their anxiety than do patients with generalized anxiety disorder on questionnaire measures of anxiety (Barlow, Cohen et al. 1984). Subjects with panic disorder scored significantly higher on the somatic scale of the Cognitive Somatic Anxiety Questionnaire (Schwartz, Davidson, & Coleman, 1978); the means were 23.9 and 15.5. The groups did not differ significantly with respect to cognitive scores, although GAD patients tended to score higher. Hoehn–Saric (1982) compared the scores of 15 patients with GAD with the scores of 36 mixed anxiety disorder patients who were suffering panic attacks. The groups differed with respect to only the Somatic Symptom Scale, where the panic patients' high scores reflected more intensive and more somatic signs of anxiety, such as muscle tension and respiratory symptoms. The prevalence of the somatic component for panic patients has been reported by other researchers, including Anderson, Noyes, and Crowe (1984).

Of interest is the fact that these groups do not differ with respect to measures of general anxiety such as the State-Trait Anxiety Inventory. Scores from a group of 82 panickers and from 11 generalized anxiety disorder patients, assessed at our clinic, did not differ substantially on measures of general anxiety and depression using the Hamilton Anxiety Depression Scale; anxiety ratings were 18.4 and 19.8, respectively; and depression ratings were 12.9 and 14.4, respectively, Given the large somatic component found in panic disorder patients, one might expect them to report more physical complications of their disorder than generalized anxiety disorder patients. However, our preliminary findings suggest that panic disorder and generalized anxiety disorder patients are equally likely to report the presence of at least one physical complication, such as migraine headaches or irritable bowels (42% and 46% of the samples, respectively). Indeed, generalized anxiety disorder patients tended to report, on the average, more somatic complications (mean = 0.82) than panic patients (mean = 0.46). However, that evidence is subject to further investigation.

In general, the data converge to suggest that panic can be identified separately from intense generalized anxiety on measures of phasic response, tonic response, and questionnaire measures.

INITIAL PANIC

In an attempt to examine directly the characteristics of the first experience of panic, a group of 52 panic disorder patients and 47 agoraphobics with panic attacks were interviewed in detail concerning their first panic attack and surrounding circumstances, using the Anxiety Disorders Interview Schedule. Seventy-two percent of the sample reported stress at the time of initial panic, with a mean number of 1.71 stressors. The major stressors identified were: interpersonal conflict (23.3% of the sample), major life changes (22.2%), work/school stress (16.2%), death or loss of a significant other (12%), and birth or pregnancy (9.1%). When asked to describe the way in which their initial panic attack began, 56.5% of the clients reported panic symptomatology and 30.3% reported specific situations that may have triggered the panic episode, such as job interviews or plane travel. Only 6.1% referred to cognitions which may have precipitated the panic, such as worrying. Four percent referred to nocturnal panics and 3% to possible drug induction of their first panic episode.

This set of data provided some interesting information regarding the situation in which the first panic occurred and how that might relate to a differential diagnosis of panic disorder or agoraphobia with panic. Thirty-three percent of the panic disorder sample reported that their first panic occurred at home, compared with 13% of agoraphobics with panic. Thirty-six percent of agoraphobics with panic reported their first panic while driving or as a passenger in a car, compared with 12% of panickers. The groups reported comparable frequencies of panic in public places (approximately 30%). Also, 49% of agoraphobics with panic reported that their first panic occurred while alone, compared with 27% of panic disorder patients. The reliability of these data is questionable, given the problems of restrospective recall, but it is suggestive of the way in which the setting of initial panic may relate to subsequent avoidance behavior. The safety value of being accompanied and of the home environment in agoraphobics is understandable in light of these data.

NOCTURNAL PANIC

Worthy of mention is the phenomenon of nocturnal panic, the characteristics of which were assessed in a group of 41 individuals who presented for treatment at the Phobia and Anxiety Disorders Clinic. These people answered affirmatively to the question "Are there times when you awake from sleep in a panic?" They were then questioned specifically about the duration, amount of sleep before onset of panic, symptom intensity, and differences between nocturnal and daytime panics. The majority of nocturnal panics occurred within 1 to 4 hours of sleep onset (especially between the second and third hours), the time during which slow-wave sleep is most prevalent. Similarly, Taylor et al. (1986) noted that the panics they recorded on a 24-hour basis occurred most frequently between the hours of 1:30 A.M. and 3 A.M. Slow-wave sleep tends to be associated with reduced eye movements, lowered blood pressure and reduced heart rate, and respiration. These are also the common characteristics of wakeful relaxation. It is therefore tempting to make a connection between nocturnal panic and relaxation-induced panic (Cohen, Barlow, & Blanchard, 1985).

Relaxation is known to be associated with cognitive, physiological, or sensory side-effects which may be perceived as unpleasant (Heide & Borkovec, 1984). For example, a patient may become alarmed by a decreasing heart rate that occurs during relaxation, a cue to which the panic-prone patient is very sensitive and which may therefore trigger a panic attack. Similarly, a sleeping individual may be oblivious to his or her environment but remain attuned to personally significant stimuli. For example, a mother could be undisturbed by the noise of a loud truck driving past her house but may awaken to the sound of her baby crying. Hauri, Friedman, Ravaris, and Fisher (1985) were able to record five night panics in their sleep laboratory from a group of agoraphobics with panic attacks. They noted that the panics tended to occur in non-REM (rapid eye movement) sleep although occasionally an attack would occur during REM sleep. Non-REM sleep is associated with occasional violent muscular twitches. The agoraphobics were found to spend a greater number of minutes in delta or slow-wave sleep and to exhibit more large movements during sleep in comparison with a normal group and a group of psychophysiological insomniacs. It is possible that muscular movements served as cues that precipitated the elevation in physiological activation, which preceded awakening in this group of patients.

Approximately 25% of all panickers and agoraphobics with panic attacks who presented at the Phobia and Anxiety Disorders Clinic reported the experience of at least one nocturnal panic attack. Of those, 43% reported that their first symptom upon awakening was cognitive, such as fear of losing control, dying, or going crazy, whereas 57% reported that their first symptom upon awakening was somatic, such as a racing heart. Fifty-four percent reported that their nocturnal panics were more severe than their daytime panics, 25% said they were less severe, and 21% said they were of equal severity. In terms of symptom frequency, 46% reported that they experienced more symptoms during nocturnal panic, 21% reported fewer symptoms at night and 33% said there was an equal number. Nocturnal panic lasted, on the average, 24.6 minutes, with a range of 1 to 180 minutes.

Eighteen of the 41 subjects were questioned in detail concerning the occurrence and severity of each DSM–III panic symptom during their most recent nocturnal panic. The frequency with which each symptom was cited by the sample is shown in Table 2.5 (percentages are shown in parentheses). The symptoms which were reported with the greatest frequency were strong, rapid, or irregular heartbeat; shortness of breath; hot and cold flashes; choking or smothering sensations; trembling; and fear of dying. Also listed in Table 2.5 are mean severity ratings from which it can be seen that difficulty breathing, fear of dying, heart palpitations, and nausea are the most intensely experienced symptoms. Of interest is the finding that shortness of breath is also one of the most frequently and intensely experienced symptoms during that sample's daytime panics, a pattern which differentiates them somewhat from a representative sample of typical panickers who do not report the experience of nocturnal panic. In general, fewer symptoms are reported during nocturnal panics, but overall severity of symptoms is comparable across daytime and nocturnal panics (see Table 2.5).

Nocturnal panic attacks could possibly result from sleep apnea. Sleep apnea refers to a pause or complete cessation of breathing: "People with such apneas typically go through a repeating cycle of sleep apnea, arousal, resumption of breathing, and sleep once again" (Van Oot, Lane, & Borkovec, 1984, p. 711). The contributory role of sleep apnea is particularly likely, given the prominence of the reported shortness-of-breath symptom. However, two factors suggest otherwise. First, there was no evidence of obesity in our sample of nocturnal panickers (a characteristic associated very frequently with sleep apnea). Second, the concentration of nocturnal panic during the first 4 hours of the sleep cycle is not consistent with the repeating pattern of sleep apnea. Of interest will be the determination of the number of persons with sleep apnea who experience panic attacks.

Several changes in internal state that occur during different phases of the sleep cycle could serve as triggers for a panic-prone person: reduced heart rate and respiration during slow-wave and deep sleep, as would occur in the case of deep relaxation; erratic breathing patterns that occur during REM sleep; and major muscular twitches that occur during delta or slow-wave sleep. Nocturnal panic attacks could be considered the purest example of spontaneous panic, but even here, it seems possible to identify cues for the panic.

EXPECTED VERSUS UNEXPECTED PANIC

The expected/unexpected dimension of panic is of significance in terms of its relationship to diagnostic categories and to avoidance and fear responses. Panic

TABLE 2.5

Frequency (Percentage) and Average Severity for Those Subjects Reporting Each Symptom

	Nocturnal Panickers (n = 18)						*Panickers Without Nocturnal Panic (n = 46)*		
	Nocturnal			*Day*					
	#	%	*Mean Severity*	#	%	*Mean Severity*	#	%	*Mean Severity*
Dyspnea	12	(67)	2.42	13	(72)	2.15	23	(50)	2.09
Palpitations	17	(94)	2.29	13	(72)	2.06	37	(80)	2.54
Chest pain	6	(33)	1.33	9	(50)	1.56	15	(33)	1.73
Choking/smothering	11	(61)	1.90	11	(61)	2.00	15	(33)	1.73
Nausea	3	(17)	2.33	10	(56)	2.00	20	(43)	2.10
Dizziness	6	(33)	1.67	13	(72)	2.15	35	(76)	2.20
Feeling of unreality	10	(56)	1.33	11	(61)	1.73	30	(65)	2.20
Paresthesias	5	(28)	1.60	10	(56)	2.00	21	(46)	1.91
Hot/cold flashes	12	(67)	1.67	14	(78)	1.64	35	(76)	2.09
Sweating	10	(56)	2.00	13	(72)	1.62	26	(57)	2.08
Faintness	4	(22)	2.00	11	(61)	1.55	24	(52)	2.13
Trembling	11	(61)	1.73	14	(78)	1.93	29	(63)	2.28
Fear of dying	11	(61)	2.45	11	(61)	2.09	21	(46)	2.48
Fear of going crazy or losing control	7	(39)	1.98	12	(67)	2.17	23	(50)	2.52

disorder and agoraphobia with panic both assume at least some spontaneous or uncued panic attacks. Conversely, panic experienced by social phobics, obsessive-compulsive patients and simple phobics is assumed to be directly related to a phobic object; that is, clear cues for the panic exist.

Zitrin, Klein, and Woerner (1980) compared agoraphobics with panic attacks and mixed phobics (or, phobics with "spontaneous" panic who lacked a broad pattern of avoidance) with simple phobics. They found that agoraphobics and mixed phobics responded more favorably to exposure-based procedures if they additionally received imipramine as compared with placebo. The facilitatory effect of imipramine was not apparent for simple phobics. Cued and unexpected panics seemed, therefore, to differ in terms of their response to treatment. However, detailed examination of those results indicated that there was no substantial difference among patients identified as predominently cued versus uncued panickers. Sheehan, Ballenger, and Jacobsen (1980) reported similar differences in drug effects between agoraphobics and simple phobics. However, they did not measure panic directly and it is therefore difficult to draw conclusions. Overall, the results provide only modest support for a differential drug response between cued and unexpected panic. Moreover, these kinds of studies commit two basic errors: first, to assume that treatment effects reflect pathology; second, to assume that social phobics, simple phobics, and obsessive-compulsive patients never experience panic in the absence of their feared cues.

A less confounded analysis was performed by comparing the following groups of patients who were treated at our clinic (Barlow et al., 1985): patients who reported never experiencing a spontaneous panic; simple and social phobics and generalized anxiety disorder patients who reported at least one spontaneous panic in their lifetime; agoraphobics with panic; and panic disorder patients. The data presented in Table 2.6 lists the severity ratings of the 12 DSM–III panic symptoms for individuals who admitted having had a panic attack. Agoraphobics with panic and panic disorder patients endorsed significantly more of the symptoms than the other groups. They also reported significantly higher severity ratings on most of the symptoms, especially dizziness, fear of going crazy and losing control. However, when average severity is based only on those who reported having such a symptom, no differences emerge among the groups. Hence, patients with unexpected panic were more aware of the somatic symptoms associated with panic; that is, they endorsed more somatic symptoms than did patients with cued panic.

Some researchers suggest that the qualitative differences between cued and spontaneous panic arise from different biological processes (Klein, 1981). However, at this stage, it is equally likely that different cues are responsible for different panic manifestations. It is possible that the cues associated with the so-called "spontaneous" panics are either less discernible or inadequately measured or both. It has been a common procedure to record panic retrospectively, asking patients to recall their panic sensations and antecedents. However, the accuracy of such recall, especially in reference to subtle cues, is questionable,

TABLE 2.6
Average Severity Ratings for Only Those Patients Reporting Each Symptom in Four Groups Reporting Predictable or Unpredictable Panic
(The *N* reporting each symptom in each group accompanies the severity rating)

Symptom	Cued Panic $n = 27$		Mixed $n = 11$		Agoraphobia with Panic $n = 41$		Panic Disorder $n = 17$		Statistical Comparison
		N		*N*		*N*		*N*	
Dyspnea	1.65	17	2.19	8	1.85	37	1.57	14	Not significant
Palpitations	1.88	21	2.44	8	2.35	40	2.50	15	Not significant
Chest pain	1.11	9	1.58	6	1.69	31	1.83	12	Not significant
Choking	1.67	12	1.50	7	1.80	30	1.80	10	Not significant
Dizziness	1.63	12	1.57	7	2.09	39	1.77	17	Not significant
Unreality	1.46	12	1.7	5	1.82	28	1.94	16	Not significant
Paresthesias	1.33	6	1.6	5	1.17	26	1.42	12	Not significant
Hot or cold flushes	1.27^{A}	15	1.67^{AB}	9	1.96^{B}	35	1.71^{AB}	14	3.429 (3,69) $p < .02$
Sweating	1.66	16	1.75	9	1.73	35	1.75	14	Not significant
Faintness	1.36^{A}	11	1.14^{A}	7	2.07^{B}	31	1.77^{AB}	11	3.42 (3,56) $p < .02$
Shaking	1.67	15	1.56	8	1.93	36	1.81	16	Not significant
Fear of going crazy, losing control	1.83^{AB}	9	1.55^{A}	10	2.28^{B}	37	2.50^{B}	17	3.16 (3,69) $p < .03$

Note. "The Phenomenon of Panic," by D. H. Barlow et al., 1985, *Journal of Abnormal Psychology, 94,* p. 324. Copyright 1985 by American Psychological Association. Reprinted by permission.

and therefore, a panic is likely to be pronounced as "out of the blue" when not given due consideration. A more satisfactory procedure involves prospective self-monitoring of panic so that antecedents or cues can be recorded at the time of occurrence. There is increasing evidence that cues for spontaneous panic in agoraphobics with panic and in panic disorder patients are associated often with mild exercise, sexual relations, sudden temperature changes, stress, or other cues which alter physiological status in some discernible way, albeit out of the patient's immediate awareness. As with nocturnal panics, such physiological changes may signal anxiety much as a phobic object or situation signals anxiety in "situational" panics. Beck (this volume) for example, reported the experience of panic after the following kinds of events: fast consumption of a heavy meal, running up stairs, standing suddenly from a seated position, lifting a heavy object, relaxing, dozing, moving quickly from a hot to a cold area, and so on. The early notion of "effort syndrome," which referred to changes in physical well-being arising from exercise that triggered symptoms which would be now considered panic, is therefore being re-examined. It is also conceivable that the strong loss-of-control element in unexpected panic derives from the inability to explain the panic episode readily. That is, in the absence of cognizance of panic antecedents, an obvious attribution is the loss of control over one's bodily function, as opposed to an anxiety reaction to a specific situation.

Rachman and Levitt (1985) examined a different aspect of expected and unexpected panics. From 238 trials of enclosure in a small, dark room, 67 episodes of panic were experienced by 13 claustrophobics. Of those, 50 were correctly predicted and 17 were unexpected. Expected panics were those in which the subject rated the probability of panic at greater than 50% and unexpected panics were those rated with a probability of less than 50%. The experience of panic resulted in a significant increase in the expectation of subsequent fear, but did not influence the level of reported fear in the subsequent trial. Similarly, subjects overpredicted the loss of safety after a panic. Predictions of fear and safety, however, were affected differentially by whether the panic was predicted or unexpected. Predicted panics were not followed by changes in safety or fear predictions, whereas unexpected panics were followed by reductions in safety predictions and increases in fear predictions. Rachman and Levitt conclude that the experience of panic, particularly unexpected panic, has its main effect on anticipatory anxiety concerning the occurrence of subsequent panic rather than on actual fear itself. They were unable to find sufficient evidence for a relationship between unexpected panic and avoidance, but suggest that this is a fruitful area for future research.

SUMMARY

In summary, the sensations reported most frequently during panic attacks are dyspnea, sweating, and fear of going crazy and losing control. The most intensely experienced sensations are palpitations, dizziness, and fear of dying. In most cases, the reported sensations are accompanied by elevated physiological arousal, with an average heart rate increase of 40 b.p.m. However, discordance between arousal and the subjective report of panic does occasionally occur. Perceived safety and predictability seem to alleviate distress in response to sensations that accompany panic attacks. Avoidance of external situations and activities due to the fear of panic varies widely across individuals.

Panic is ubiquitous, as seen from its presence across many anxiety disorders. In fact, the quality of panic attacks seems to differ very little between panic disorder and the other anxiety disorders, with the exception of the frequency of occurrence. However, evidence from various sources converges to suggest that panic is not simply enhanced generalized anxiety.

Evidence concerning initial panic attacks suggests that location may relate to subsequent avoidance styles. Nocturnal panic attacks were reviewed in light of their apparent similarity to relaxation-induced panic. The expected or unexpected nature of panic attacks seems to be an important dimension in terms of the qualitative experience of panic and in terms of subsequent anticipation and, possibly, avoidance behavior.

CONCLUSIONS

Several aspects of the presentation of panic have been reviewed. As is often the case, many questions are unanswered. For example, while suggesting that panic is a unique event, we have not begun to address issues surrounding the basic nature of panic or its origins. While there are many recommendations emanating from the data that we have reported, one important area concerns measurement. We believe that the dimensions of expected–unexpected and cued–uncued are important modifiers of panic and should be routinely monitored. Furthermore, these dimensions seem orthogonal. Rachman and Levitt (1985) demonstrated that cued panic can be unexpected and that this is important to know in terms of predicting future anxiety. Similarly, uncued panic can be expected, as is evident in the common case of the patient who awakens knowing that he or she is going to have a "bad day," reacting most likely to uncued perturbations experienced upon awakening. "Cued" seems a better description than situational since there may be clearly discernible cognitions or somatic antecedents that the patient can identify, such as an obsessive thought. Of course, the cued–uncued distinction, while important in terms of treatment and of the prediction of future behavior, is most likely only in the mind of the patient since every panic probably has a "cue."

3

Assessment of Panic

Samuel M. Turner
Deborah C. Beidel
Rolf G. Jacob
Western Psychiatric Institute and Clinic,
University of Pittsburgh School of Medicine

INTRODUCTION

Since the introduction of the Diagnostic and Statistical Manual of Mental Disorders (DSM–III, 3d ed., APA, 1980), the phenomenon of panic has taken on major importance in the study of anxiety. In particular, panic episodes reported by those with Panic Disorder with or without agoraphobia, have been the object of intense investigation. The creation of a diagnostic category of panic disorder in DSM–III elevated the phenomenon of panic to the position of a discrete, qualitative entity, whereas in the past it had been viewed from a quantitative perspective. Since measurement strategies typically reflect the conceptualization of a construct, it follows that the manner in which a disorder is conceived will influence the development of assessment strategies. The purpose of this chapter is to discuss the current conceptualization of panic, review current methods of assessment, propose some alternative views of the phenomenon, and suggest additional approaches to its assessment.

Pharmacological Dissection as an Assessment Tool

The primary impetus for the separation of panic from other forms of anxiety stems from the work of Klein and his associates (e.g., Klein, 1964; Klein & Fink, 1962). It was observed that in phobic inpatients, ''episodic anxiety'' or ''panic attacks'' decreased following treatment with imipramine whereas anticipatory anxiety and avoidance remained unaffected. Among these drug-responsive phobic patients, two subgroups were identified (Klein, 1964). One subgroup consisted of patients who had suffered from chronic separation anxiety in childhood and whose panic attacks began during bereavement or separation. The other subgroup had unremarkable childhood histories. However, the onset of their disorder was associated with premenstrual states, parturition or posthysterectomy, all conditions indicative of altered endocrine functioning. The use of drug response as a pharmacological dissection tool, "allowing the discovery of specific developmental, physiological and social similarities within psychiatric subpopulations" was highlighted. However, the two groups identified by Klein and Fink were two panic groups. In these early papers, a distinction between panic disorder and generalized anxiety disorder as separate disorders was not made explicit.

By what appears to have been a semantic drift, "anticipatory anxiety," as discussed by Klein, became the equivalent of "general anxiety" or "chronic anxiety," while panic or endogenous anxiety retained a unique status (Liebowitz, 1985). It is unclear how the "pharmacological dissection" just described contributed to separating the categories of generalized anxiety and panic. Of course, as Klein (1964) pointed out, pharmacological dissection, although useful as a generator of hypotheses, cannot be considered as a diagnostic criterion by itself. Drug response cannot be the sole determinant of diagnostic classification because the effects of drugs are not discrete or unitary, and the mechanisms of action of most psychotropic drugs are not fully understood. For example, Detre (1985) noted that although Dilantin, an anticonvulsant, has proven effective in treating ventricular ectopic rhythms, few would call for the reclassification of cardiac arrhythmias or consider arrhythmia as an epilepsy equivalent. Similar restraint in interpreting various biological tests has been urged by Ross (1986).

Despite the fact that the original Klein studies did not directly compare treatments for panic versus anticipatory anxiety, these studies gave rise to the notion that panic is distinct from generalized anxiety and that panic anxiety should respond to antidepressants but not to minor tranquilizers, while general anxiety should respond to minor tranquilizers but not to antidepressants. A study by McNair and Kahn (1981) seemed to confirm the superiority of imipramine in the treatment of panic, but other pharmacological studies do not support this distinction. Imipramine was found to be effective for "high-anxiety subjects" (Kahn et al., 1981), while several minor tranquilizers, including diazepam, clonazepam, and alprazolam have been found to be effective for panic (Chouinard, Annable, Fontaine, & Solyom, 1982; Noyes, et al., 1984; Rickels & Schweizer, 1986; Sheehan, 1985; Spier, Tesar, Rosenbaum, & Woods, 1986). As a result of recent pharmacological studies, the biological boundaries between the two types of anxiety, upon which the original distinction has been based, have become blurred.

Spontaneous vs. Cued Panic

A second major factor in the evolution of panic disorder is the often noted occurrence of panic attacks "out of the blue." The seeming unpredictability of some panic attacks, independent of situational cues, served as an impetus for setting panic apart from usual anxiety or fear. Such attacks, it was reasoned, must result from some type of disordered biological process. However, the literature indicates that a number of factors (external and internal) may be serving as cues for what could be mistaken as "spontaneous" panic attacks. First, anxiety need not be conditioned to one specific stimulus, but is often conditioned to an entire class of stimuli (Hare & Levis, 1981). Thus, failure to be in the presence of a specific stimulus previously associated with a panic attack does not rule out the possibility that the cue has generalized to a variety of apparently innocuous stimuli. Second, cognitive factors in the form of intense worrying, apprehension, or negative expectation could serve as eliciting cues. Third, internal sensations might well serve as cues for the onset of what appears to be spontaneous panic attacks. Sensitivity to internal sensations could be the result of interoceptive conditioning, a form of classical conditioning in which the unconditioned and/or conditioned stimulus result from proprioceptive or visceral sensations (Razran, 1961). In the case of panic, internal sensations may serve as a stimulus for triggering a panic attack. Interoceptive conditioning could explain why patients are sometimes at a loss to associate any external stimulus with their panic. The ramification of interoceptive conditioning for panic has been discussed by a number of authors (e.g., Ackerman & Sachar, 1974; Evans, 1972; van den Hout & Griez, 1983; van den Hout, van der Molen, Griez, & Lousberg, 1987b). We will return to a discussion of interoceptive conditioning when we consider the various medical conditions related to panic.

There are two issues concerning cued or noncued panic attacks. The first relates to the occurrence of individual panic attacks and was discussed previously. The second pertains to the actual onset of panic disorder. Recent as well as older empirical studies suggest that the onset of the first panic attack is associated with a number of different precipitating stimuli, including biological, psychological, or environmental events. For example, Klein (1964) postulated that the onset of panic disorder is often associated with endocrine fluctuation, suggesting that some panic patients may be in a state of physiological disequilibrium at the onset of the first attack. Often, stressful life events, such as parturition or bereavement, are associated with the onset of panic attacks (Klein, 1964; Liebowitz & Klein, 1979). In a study of life events, Faravelli (1985) examined panic and nonpanic controls over 12 months prior to the onset of panic. Panic patients showed a significant number of stressful life events 2 months preceding the onset of panic attacks when compared with controls, indicating that panic patients experienced significant environmental stress prior to the onset of panic. There were no differences between patients and controls at other points during the study. Hoehn–Saric (1983) noted that in his sample, most panic patients had been chronically anxious prior to their first attack, with the actual attack triggered by some "minor incident." Furthermore, patients whose attacks are in remission report that panic returns with the onset of new psychosocial stressors, thereby suggesting that psychological parameters may serve as a triggering mechanism. Interestingly, autonomic parameters in laboratory studies of panic reveal that panic patients have higher heart rates during baseline than controls (see section on laboratory-induced panic, this chapter). This suggests that patients who experience panic may be in a chronic state of high arousal. Therefore, it appears that panic does not occur totally "out of the blue" (even though a particular episode might appear to), but rather in some meaningful psychological, biological, and/or environmental context.

Another issue enmeshed in the concept of cued and noncued panic concerns whether the diagnostic category of panic disorder is a valid one. A number of recent studies have questioned whether agoraphobics with panic and panic disorder patients can be empirically differentiated (Garvey & Tuason, 1984; Thyer, Himle, Curtis, Cameron, & Nesse, 1985; Turner, Williams, Beidel, & Mezzich, 1986). In one of these studies, Turner, Williams et al. (1987) found a high correlation between severity of panic attacks and degree of fear of certain situations. Individuals who endorsed mild to moderate panic symptoms also reported mild to moderate fear of "typical" agoraphobic situations which were listed on a fear survey schedule. Those endorsing severe panic symptoms also reported higher levels of fear in certain situations. Furthermore, agoraphobic and panic disorder patients did not differ in their ratings of fearfulness of agoraphobic situations.

Assessment of Panic Behavior

In the original paper by Klein and Fink (1962), the patients who responded to imipramine were described as having "sudden onset of inexplicable 'panic' attacks, accompanied by rapid breathing, palpitations, weakness, and a feeling of impending death" (p. 435). Earlier, Walker (1959) attributed special significance to a type of anxiety characterized as coming "as a complete surprise to the patient," with "sudden onset" but more gradual offset, and with the patient feeling "relatively normal although irritable and morose" between attacks. From these clinical descriptions, we can extract four characteristics of panic: (a) onset that is unexpected, noncued, unpredictable, "spontaneous"; (b) onset that is sudden, rapid, and instantaneous; (c) presence of somatic sensations (e.g., rapid breathing, palpitations, weakness); and (d) fear of embarrassment, fainting, heart attack or impending death. Studies attempting to measure the phenomenology of panic have primarily focused on the symptom characteristics, while the onset characteristics have received relatively little attention.

Even with respect to the symptom characteristics, assessment strategies have not been elegant. For example, in some studies in which lactate was used as a panic inducer, measures of panic were obtained solely by self-report. A more sophisticated approach was used by Liebowitz et al. (1984) who employed patient and independent assessor ratings of extreme anxiety and the subject's report of the presence of 4 of the 12 DSM–III symptoms to define panic. Both subjective apprehension and autonomic response had to be present for a judgment of panic to be made. Although this strategy had the advantage of requiring dual affirmation, only the patient was blind to what substance was being infused. Therefore, it is possible that the clinician's judgment was influenced by expectation effects. The occurrence and severity of panic symptoms have also been rated by using a checklist such as the Acute Panic Inventory (Liebowitz et al., 1984). This inventory consists of items assessing 17 panic symptoms and has been used in lactate studies to document the existence of specific physiological correlates of panic. However, as far as we know, no reliability or validity data for this inventory have been published. Validity is an important issue here because Rachman (this volume) found that symptoms included in the Acute Panic Inventory can be present in the absence of a panic attack.

Two promising instruments to measure both somatic symptoms and cognitions associated with panic are the Chambless Body Sensations (BSQ) and Agoraphobic Cognitions Questionnaires (ACQ; Chambless, Caputo, Bright, & Gallagher, 1984). The ACQ is a 14-item questionnaire with an internal consistency coefficient of .80 and a test-retest reliability coefficient of .79. The BSQ consists of 17 items which are internally consistent (alpha = .87) and has a test-retest reliability coefficient of .67. Although these instruments have not been used extensively, they have the capability of assessing cognition as well as somatic sensations, and it is likely they will be used more in future research.

To date, measurement of panic has focused primarily on somatic symptoms. The "sudden onset" criterion has not received much attention. The lack of an operational definition of this characteristic is a particular problem for lactate infusion studies (Margraf, Ehlers, & Roth, 1986b). However, physiological measures of naturally occurring panic attacks hold the promise of helping to solve this problem. The first physiologically recorded panic attack was reported as an incidental finding by Lader and Mathews (1970). During testing designed to assess physiological responses to auditory stimuli, three patients unexpectedly reported panic attacks. These attacks were accompanied by sudden heart rate increases of 35–40 b.p.m. and an abrupt rise in skin conductance. More recently, panic attacks have been reported during the course of relaxation training in two cases (Cohen, Barlow, & Blanchard, 1985). In both cases, tachycardia and synchronous electromyographic increases were noted. Surprisingly, hand surface temperature increased, contrary to what is typically found during anxiety. The data from both of these reports have been useful in confirming the rapid onset of autonomic hyperactivity during panic.

Although the results of both of these studies more closely reflect the characteristics of "natural" panic than studies which infuse foreign substances into the body, the circumstances under which panic occurred were not typical for the patient's normal activities. Data from ambulatory monitoring have provided a more naturalistic assessment of psychophysiology during panic (Freedman, Ianni, Ettedgui, & Puthezhath, 1985; Taylor et al., 1986; Taylor, Telch, & Hawick, 1983). In the Taylor et al. (1986) study, heart rate increased during panic by approximately 30 b.p.m. over a 4-minute period. Conversely, during anticipatory anxiety, the increase was approximately 15 b.p.m. Interestingly, in none of these studies did all patients show increases in heart rate in conjunction with self-report of panic. Taylor et al. (1983) found that only three out of eight (37%) self-reported panic attacks were accompanied by distinct cardiac changes. Similarly, Taylor et al. (1986) noted that 58% of reported panic attacks were accompanied by high heart rates. Only 4 of 14 heart rate episodes identified by the monitor as signifying panic actually were accompanied by subjective panic, resulting in a specificity of only 29%. However, Freedman et al. (1985) reported that seven out of eight patients experienced increased heart rate during panic episodes. Michelson (this volume) found that heart rates during a standardized behavioral task, as measured by an ambulatory monitor, were lower for patients who had the highest distress ratings, a surprising and somewhat perplexing finding.

The results of these investigations are limited by the presence of a number of methodological problems. First, understanding of all of the psychophysiological characteristics of panic is difficult because physiological measures were limited mostly to heart rate. Second, episodes of panic were based entirely upon self-report, and it is not clear to what degree these self-reports were influenced by factors other than panic experiences or how reactive these reports were to the measurement situation itself. The correlation of self-reported panic with other objective indexes of panic is in and of itself an important assessment issue. At the present time, we are unable to determine with certainty what psychophysiological parameters are characteristic of panic.

Laboratory-induced Panic

Under circumstances where the phenomenon of interest is difficult to capture in the natural environment, laboratory analogues can be helpful in understanding its nature. With the emergence of the biological view of panic, interest in the phenomenon of lactate-induced panic (Pitts & McClure, 1967) was revived. In order to evaluate whether the findings from studies on lactate-induced panic are generalizable to naturally occurring panic, at least two questions need to be answered. First, how similar is lactate-induced panic to naturally occurring panic; and second, how valid are the data from existing studies? With respect to the first question, Margraf et al. (1986), in their comprehensive review, concluded that the question of similarity is still open. For example, assessment of symptoms in lactate-induced panic have focused primarily on somatic anxiety symptoms per se, while more general indexes of discomfort or fear have been virtually omitted. In a study by Ehlers, Margraf, Roth, Taylor et al. (1986), seven patients rated lactate-induced symptoms as similar to their natural panic while three rated them as dissimilar. However, it has been observed that some patients identify the somatic symptoms of anxiety without the accompanying mental fear (Kelly, Mitchell–Heggs, & Sherman, 1971). In a study by Liebowitz et al. (1984), lactate-induced panic episodes, compared with naturally occurring panic episodes, were found to be associated with less fear of dying, confusion, unreality, difficulty with concentration, and with more urinary urgency and muscle twitching. A reasonable conclusion is that although the somatic symptoms of lactate-induced panic may resemble those found in naturally occurring panic, they do not appear to be identical and there appears to a particular difference in the cognitive domain.

Another avenue of assessing similarity of lactate-induced panic and natural panic is to compare psychophysiological changes. Most lactate studies report increases in heart rate, skin conductance, and muscle tension during panic (Margraf et al., 1986b). Interestingly, the cardiac changes were not inhibited by pharmacological blockade of the beta-adrenergic receptors which mediate the effect of the sympathetic nervous system on the heart. This finding might implicate reductions of parasympathetic output as a possible mediating mechanism for the heart rate increase. Nor do the beta-blocking agents seem helpful in reducing most naturally occurring panic attacks (Noyes et al., 1984). However, since it is unclear what actually occurs during naturally occurring panic, there is some limitation as to what can be learned from comparing changes between laboratory-induced panic and natural panic.

With respect to the issue of sudden onset, in most studies the panickers showed signs of elevated arousal before the infusion when compared with controls (e.g., Ehlers, Margraf, Roth, Taylor et al., 1986; Liebowitz et al., 1984). In the Ehlers Margraf, Roth, Taylor et al. (1986) study, anxiety ratings and heart rate showed parallel changes in panic patients and controls, suggesting that panic may constitute a threshold phenomenon. Furthermore, anxiety ratings and heart rate in this study increased steadily over the entire 5-minute period, questioning the "suddenness" of onset.

The validity of panic data obtained in lactate studies are open to question. As pointed out by Margraf et al. (1986b), most lactate studies had inadequate criteria for defining panic attacks, relied on self-report data, and employed single-blind procedures. Furthermore, patient expectation from the procedures employed may have contributed to the report of panic, inasmuch as patients often knew that the study was one involving panic induction. Indeed, Gorman et al. (1983) actually informed patients to expect an episode of panic. Informing patients to expect a panic attack may explain why baseline anxiety in these patients was elevated, and why a small percentage of patients panicked upon infusion with saline. Patients who panicked may have been "primed" to do so, and lactate might simply be one of many possible triggers for panic in highly anxious patients. That no satisfactory biochemical explanation for the effects of lactate has been forthcoming further supports this explanation.

The notion that lactate is one of many possible triggers for panic appears to be confirmed by the findings reviewed by van den Hout et al. (this volume). A number of different substances, including carbon dioxide, isoproternol, caffeine, and yohimbine induce panic in patients with a history of panic attacks. Furthermore, the apparent treatability of panic with conditioning treatments points toward the need for an increased psychological understanding of the lactate panic phenomenon.

It should be noted that biological methods are not the only means by which panic can be induced in the laboratory. Rachman (this volume) reported that placing claustrophobics in enclosed spaces can serve as a behavioral inducer of panic. This method appears to be a promising addition to the assessment arsenal for panic and further data are needed to determine if panic induced in this fashion is equivalent to naturally occurring panic. In particular, panic induced by this maneuver would appear to fall under the "predictable" category which might differ with respect to symptomatology from "unpredictable" panic attacks (Barlow et al., 1985).

The Role of Cognitive Processes in Panic

Although the role of cognitive activity was alluded to in the preceding discussions, at this point more specific comments will be made. Cognitive variables might be operative on at least three different, and not necessarily mutually exclusive levels. First, there are cognitions that might be considered secondary to, or the result of physiological phenonema. Examples of such cognitions would be attributions concerning one's somatic state, or preoccupation with physical well-being. Little attention has been devoted to assessing this class of thoughts. One unanswerered question is how important are such cognitions in cueing the first or future panic episodes. Second, panic attacks are often associated with temporary changes in cognitive functioning. An example of this impaired cognitive functioning can be found as part of Chambless et al.'s (1984) definition of panic attack, that is, "the temporary loss of the ability to plan, think or reason, and the intense desire to escape or flee the situation." What is the role of these temporary decrements of cognitive functioning in the actual experience of panic, how are they related to maintaining panic, and how are they related to thoughts associated with somatic sensations, fear of going crazy, or other stimuli associated with the onset of panic?

Worry is another category of cognitive phenomena. With the exception of Borkovec (1985) and a few others, the role of worry in the anxiety disorders has been neglected. However, among clinicians, the importance of worry is freely acknowledged. Worry could well be a common psychological pathway for the triggering of panic by stimuli from multiple sources. For example, chronic worry could create a state of heightened arousal such that the organism is more likely to be distressed by stimuli from a variety of sources. Worry could instigate somatic cues that trigger apparently spontaneous panic. In the case of overtly cued panic, worry about contact with the specific stimulus could play a similar role. Chronic worry might also make the individual more susceptible to the conditioning of fear, or the mere presence of worry could fuel avoidance behavior because of the concern about negative consequences (e.g., possible onset of another panic attack). The presence of rigid avoidance might then preclude natural recovery through extinction or modification of expectation. The fact that worry plays such an important role in the phenomenology of all of the anxiety disorders is sufficient to warrant efforts designed to assess and clarify its possible role in panic.

Panic as a Discrete vs. Dimensional Construct

Up to this point, panic has been discussed mainly as a phenomenon rather than as a variable for diagnostic classification. In this section, the focus will be on data bearing directly on the issue of classification. There are two questions of relevance here: Is cued or noncued panic unique to certain diagnostic categories, and, is panic uniquely different from other anxiety? Among the anxiety disorders, panic episodes occur at a fairly high frequency in all of the diagnostic categories. For example, Barlow et al. (1985, see also this volume) reported that panic attacks occurred in all of the anxiety disorders, ranging from 100% in simple phobia and panic disorder, to 83% in generalized anxiety disorder and obsessive-compulsive disorder. Almost all of these panic attacks were associated with 4 of the 12 DSM–III panic criteria. Unpredictable as well as predictable panic attacks occurred in all diagnostic groups. However, panic disorder and agoraphobic patients reported a larger percentage of panic symptoms. Unpredictable panic was associated with more symptoms, particularly dizziness and fear of losing control, than was predictable panic. The finding that panic, both predictable and unpredictable, occurs frequently among all of the anxiety disorders raises questions about the nature of panic. An important question that has received little attention is whether panic should be viewed as a discrete or a dimensional construct.

In addition to panic not being limited to panic disorder or agoraphobia, panic is not even specific for the anxiety disorders. For example, Breier, Charney, and Heninger (1985) reported that panic attacks occurred in 37% of patients with a diagnosis of major depression. Even more important, Norton, Harrison, Hauch, and Rhodes (1985) reported that 34% of a sample of apparently normal college students reported one or more panic attacks within the past year. Although this figure is substantially higher than the figure reported in the NIMH Epidemiologic

Catchment Area Survey (Myers et al., 1984), it seems clear that the experience of panic, cued and noncued, is highly prevalent in the general population.

As is evident in DSM–III and DSM–III–R, and as seems to be accepted by authors in this volume, panic is a unique emotion, similar phenomenologically, but qualitatively distinct from "typical" anxiety, However, this position has not been unequivocally demonstrated. The question that needs to be answered is whether or not there is a panic factor among the various anxiety symptoms that is independent of severity. Until this issue is addressed, one cannot logically conclude that panic is a unique emotion. Other authors have suggested that the current DSM view of panic does not conform to clinical reality (Tyrer, 1984). These issues, together with the data discussed previously, and the Robins, Helzer, Croughan, and Ratcliff (1981) finding of low diagnostic reliability for panic disorder using the Diagnostic Interview Schedule raise questions about the validity of panic disorder as a unique diagnostic entity. On the other hand, DiNardo et al. (1983) reported acceptable interrater reliability for panic disorder, using the Anxiety Disorders Interview Schedule.

Multiple Medical Conditions and Panic

Cognitive appraisal of internal stimuli as signifying immediate danger may be an intermediary link in the sequence of sensation to panic (e.g., Butler & Mathews, 1983; Hibbert, 1984b). Furthermore, unexplained bodily sensations produce a bias toward negatively toned emotions (Marshall & Zimbardo, 1979). In a study of the link between bodily symptoms and emotions, Pennebaker (1982) found that the presence of any bodily sensation tended to be associated with negative or unpleasant emotions, while positive emotions were characterized by the absence of bodily sensations. For example, Pennebaker (1982) studied the correlations between ratings of current symptoms and current emotions by having 177 students complete a checklist consisting of 14 symptom items (e.g., racing heart) and seven emotions (e.g., tense, angry, happy). He found that the correlations between negative emotions (tense, angry, jealous, sad, guilty, unhealthy) and physical symptoms were positive, whereas the correlation between physical symptoms and the positive emotion of happiness was negative. Thus, the occurrence of happiness was associated with a relative absence of bodily sensations. In a supplementary study, 9 subjects filled out a symptom-emotion checklist repeated once per hour and the symptom–emotion correlations were calculated separately for each subject across the hourly ratings. This study revealed that while the difference in correlations between individuals was substantial, there was still a tendency for the emotions of "happiness" and "health" to be negatively associated with symptoms, while the unpleasant emotions showed positive correlations. The differences between individuals occurred primarily in what particular symptom was associated with a particular emotion.

Bodily sensations may lead to increased self-focused attention. This self-focused attention in turn could further augment negative affect in certain individuals (cf. Gibbons et al., 1985). Self-focus or self-preoccupation is also a common effect of stress (Sarason, 1979). Thus, stress might predispose an individual to panic attacks via increased self-monitoring of bodily symptoms. As pointed out by Clark (this volume), similar mechanisms have been postulated for hypochondriasis.

Since the introduction of DSM–III, much attention has been given to the somatic symptoms of panic. In fact, the somatic emphasis is so great that a specific number of somatic symptoms (4) is required in order to warrant a diagnosis of panic. It is unclear how the developers of DSM–III arrived at this figure, nor has it been empirically demonstrated that panic consisting of 3 symptoms is qualitatively different from panic with 4 or more. It is also unclear whether certain symptoms should be more heavily weighted than others. With 12 symptoms from which to choose, it is possible for as many as three individuals to manifest completely different clinical pictures and yet receive the same diagnosis. In a study summarizing data gathered in the NIMH Epidemiologic Catchment Area Survey, Von Korff, Eaton, and Key (1985) presented data illustrating that patients experiencing "simple attacks," "severe and recurrent attacks," and those meeting criteria for panic disorder showed the same symptom patterns. There was no unambiguous demarcation between panic disorder and severe and recurrent panic attacks in terms of autonomic symptom expression, age at onset distribution or distribution by demographic factors (p. 979). It is apparent, then, that studies assessing the importance of these phenomenological parameters are needed.

The notion that the symptom profile of panickers may differ may be a constructive one, serving to highlight medical conditions which have been associated with panic. As one example, the role of mitral valve prolapse has been discussed as a possible etiological factor in panic, and although the most current data do not indicate an increased incidence of mitral valve prolapse in panic patients, other medical findings continue to fuel the speculation. Studies have suggested neurological abnormalities, including two recent PET scan studies that revealed unilateral hippocampal lesions in lactate-sensitive panic patients but not in lactate-nonsensitive patients (Reiman, Raichle, Butler, Herscovitch, & Robins, 1984; Reiman et al., 1986). Further research is needed to explicate the significance of these findings. For example, the patients with hippocampal lesions tended to show abnormalities of blood gases indicating respiratory alkalosis; it is well known that hyperventilation has profound effects on cerebral perfusion (Jacob & Rapport, 1984). Could it be that the blood flow abnormalities identified by Reiman and his colleagues are related to behavioral changes in respiration?

Although the relationship of these various abnormalities to anxiety has been thought to be medical in nature, it might be that somatic symptoms serve to trigger panic through the mechanism of interoceptive conditioning. Once triggered, various associated stimuli might serve to elicit future panic episodes, especially if there is a tendency to worry or engage in catastrophic prediction. An example of how such a process might work can be generated from observations regarding patients with vestibular abnormalities (Jacob, Moller, Turner, & Wall, 1985). These patients frequently reported experiencing episodes of dizziness or imbalance prior to the onset of panic, sensations for which they had no explanation. Their concern increased when their physicians also were unable to offer an explanation after extensive examinations. Frightening, unexplainable symptoms such as these could serve to provoke a panic episode, particularly in the presence of other predisposing factors (see Multiple Determinants of Panic, below). Many of these patients were considerably relieved when they were provided with some explanatory information about their balance disturbance. However, this explanation did not prevent future panic attacks from occurring. It would appear that once panic occurs, it is phenomenologically the same, regardless of factors associated with its etiology.

MULTIPLE DETERMINANTS OF PANIC

Based on these considerations, there appear to be many variables that might predispose a person to develope panic, such as certain psychiatric disorders, environmental stress, and internal stimuli perhaps triggered by medical or hormonal aberrations. They may also include variables that can be subsumed under the label of anxiety-proneness, such as a tendency for overappraisal of immediate danger, greater physiological reactivity, and a family history of panic. Thus, although none of these factors in isolation may be sufficient to induce panic, a combination of such factors may predispose a person to develop panic disorder. The role of all of these factors in the genesis of anxiety disorders has already been the subject of some theorizing and investigation (e.g., Beck & Emery, 1985; Mineka, Davidson, Cook, & Keir, 1984; Torgersen, 1983).

Prospective studies that include measures of anxiety-proneness are needed to document empirically the degree of importance of each of these factors. Several assessment instruments are suitable for measuring this construct. For example, Reiss, Peterson, Gursky, and McNally (1986) reported that the Anxiety Sensitivity Inventory is a useful measure of anxiety proneness independent of state anxiety. Another instrument suitable for measuring the tendency to respond in an anxious fashion is the Spielberger Trait Anxiety Inventory (Spielberger, Gorsuch, & Lushene, 1970). The child's version of this instrument (Spielberger, 1973) was successfully employed in a study of the offspring of anxiety disorders patients by Turner, Beidel, & Costello (1987). Finally, the introversion factor of the Eysenck Personality Inventory (Eysenck & Eysenck, 1968) might be a useful measure of anxiety-proneness.

A group that can be considered at risk for developing panic are the relatives of panic disorder patients. For example, Crowe (1985) noted that 17.3% of relatives of panic patients met criteria for panic disorder, and an additional 7.4% reported infrequent attacks. Turner, Beidel, & Costello (1987) found significant differences on measures of fear and anxiety between the offspring of anxiety patients and the offspring of normal parents. Forty-four percent of the anxiety offspring met criteria for a DSM–III anxiety disorder, whereas only 9% of the offspring of normal parents had a diagnosable disorder. The offspring of patients with an anxiety disorder constitute an easily identifiable group at high risk for experiencing panic and may provide important information about etiological variables.

Identification of biological precipitants or determinants is also needed. Since not all individuals with, for example, mitral valve prolapse or vestibular dysfunction develop panic disorder, such precipitants may be more important for individuals who are already anxiety-prone. In a prospective study, somatic symptoms could be monitored in a high-risk population so that their role in precipitating panic can be studied. In addition, somatic sensations could be elicited experimentally in anxiety-prone samples to examine the role of internal sensations as conditioned stimuli for panic. Conversely, the mediating role of anxiety-proneness could be studied in medical disorders characterized by a high incidence of panic-like symptoms, such as cardiac patients or patients with vestibular disorders.

SUMMARY

This discussion of the assessment of panic has highlighted the state of the art, as well as some of the deficiencies in our current efforts. A number of specific assessment strategies that should be considered for future empirical endeavors have also been delineated. Within the context of this discussion of assessment, data bearing on how the phenomenon of panic is currently conceptualized were reviewed. At this time, it must be concluded that the evidence for a qualitatively distinct panic disorder is relatively weak. Moreover, the issue of whether or not panic is a unique type of anxiety has not been resolved.

The focus on panic as a discrete diagnostic entity, and more or less as a purely biological phenomenon, has resulted in somatic symptoms receiving the greatest amount of attention. Yet, anxiety has always been viewed as a multidimensional construct with the accompanying necessity of attending to all of its various parameters. Because of the preoccupation with somatic sensations, insufficient attention has been given to the role of cognitive activity. In particular, the role of chronic worrying, a phenomenon known to be an important part of the clinical picture for panic as well as other anxiety states, has been virtually ignored. Greater attention should be devoted to studying those person variables that could play a role in both the vulnerability to, and in the maintenance of, the panic phenomenon. Finally, it was suggested that medical conditions associated with panic might exert their influence through psychological mechanisms. Specifically, medical conditions that might play a role in panic by creating somatic symptoms that provoke panic were discussed. Subsequent panic episodes could then be provoked as a result of interoceptively conditioned cues.

Future assessment studies of panic will need to address a number of areas that have received little or no attention to date. First, the role of anxiety-sensitivity or proneness is seen as important for a complete understanding of panic, and those who develop frequent panic attacks. Second, the relationship of worry to anxiety-sensitivity or proneness, and to current environmental as well as somatic symptoms, is judged to be a critical area in need of study. Third, family studies focusing on possible psychological mechanisms of transmission of fearful behavior, extreme emotionality, and overconcern with bodily symptoms and health could yield useful data with respect to basic psychopathology as well as for treatment. Fourth, there is a need for studies designed to elucidate the psychophysiological characteristics of naturally occurring panic attacks. This is essential information to have before the results of analogue studies can be properly interpreted. Fifth, as was discussed, studies examining the role of interoceptive conditioning have the potential to make a critical contribution to understanding spontaneous panic. Sixth, there is a need to expand the range of subjects who are the focus of study. For example, populations at risk, particularly prior to some significant life event, such as the loss of a loved one or childbirth, are prime candidates. Studies of normal subjects are critical to a full understanding of panic, with respect to its nature as well as how it should be conceptualized. Seventh, objective means for determining the onset and end of panic episodes are needed. Finally, studies addressing the role of thought processes that might be related to initial onset, but also resulting from panic and perhaps increasing the probability of future panic, should be studied.

4

Cognitive and Biological Models of Panic:
Toward an Integration

M. Katherine Shear, M.D.
New York Hospital-Payne Whitney Clinic

INTRODUCTION

The delineation of panic disorder as a specific diagnostic category is one of the innovations in DSM–III, the current psychiatric diagnostic system (American Psychiatric Association, 1980). Patients who are diagnosed as having this disorder have recurrent unexpected episodes of panic, defined as sudden onset of intense fear associated with somatic symptoms such as chest pain, heart palpitations, shortness of breath, dizziness, tingling sensations, hot or cold flashes or faintness. Panic episodes are accompanied by varying degrees of nonpanic anxiety and phobic avoidance. The clinical psychopathology of panic disorder is determined by both panic and its consequences. Neurobiological studies (Brier, Charney, & Heninger, 1985; Rainey & Nesse, 1985) family studies (Harris, Noyes, Crowe, Chaudhry, 1983; Surman, Sheehan, Fuller, Gallo, 1983; Torgersen, 1983) and treatment studies (Barlow, Cohen, Waddell, Vermilyea, Klosko, Blanchard, DiNardo, 1984; Klein, 1964, 1982; Rohs & Noyes, 1978; Sheehan, Ballenger, & Jacobsen, 1980; Zitrin, Klein, & Woerner, 1980) support the diagnostic validity of the panic disorder category.

Work is currently under way to elucidate the pathophysiological and psychopathological underpinnings of panic as a symptom and syndrome. Most investigators use either a biological approach, aimed at understanding the neurophysiological basis of panic, or a cognitive-behavioral approach, aimed at understanding psychological mechanisms of panic and its consequences. The model of panic disorder proposed in this chapter is an integrated one, drawn from the paradigm used by investigators in the field of psychosomatic medicine. This approach uses a biological conception of panic, as a disturbance of brain function. The principles of psychosomatic medicine are based on a view of health and disease which includes the effects of psychophysiological reactivity on organic function. Psychological factors are seen as important mediators of physiological changes and vice versa. Social relationships and environmental events are taken into account since such events influence mental and bodily function. Psychosocial input probably acts via neurohormonal mechanisms regulated by the central nervous system, and has both immediate and long-term effects on the central nervous system. In the psychosomatic paradigm, symptomatic illness represents a final common pathway of a variable series of interacting psychological and biological disturbances.

An integrated paradigm allows the construction of a heuristic model that takes into consideration interindividual variabilty. Clinically, such a model encourages an open-minded search for the relevant pathogenic factors operating in any given patient. The premise of this chapter is that research and treatment of panic disorder patients benefit by the use of a psychosomatic paradigm. This chapter will include a discussion of the panic disorder syndrome from biological and cognitive-behavioral perspectives and from a third perspective, which is based on current notions of psychosomatic illness. The material is organized in three parts: (1) Definition and descriptive characteristics of panic, (2) Clinical psychopathology of panic disorder, and (3) Pathogenic mechanisms: cognitive, biological, and psychobiological views.

Definition and Descriptive Characteristics of Panic

Panic is well described in both the lay and scientific literature. The dictionary (Webster, 1969) definition, "sudden overpowering fright" or "sudden unreasoning terror often associated with mass flight" captures the core descriptive characteristics: (a) intense fear, (b) sudden onset, (c) a sense of being overpowered or out of control, (d) loss of reasoning capacity and (e) a strong urge to flee.

Panic can be conceptualized as an emergency biobehavioral response to situations of catastrophic and immediate threat. As such, panic includes a cognitive appraisal of danger accompanied by physiological and behavioral activation. Panic is also an affective state related to anxiety and possibly depression. Physical sensations are prominent and include heart palpitations, shortness of breath, sweating, trembling, weakness, dizziness, and nausea, or diarrhea. Physiological changes, such as heart rate acceleration (Freedman, Ianni, Ettedgui, Puthezhath, 1985; Liebowitz, Gorman et al., 1985; Shear et al., 1987; Taylor et al., 1986), blood pressure increase (Liebowitz, Gorman et al., 1985; Shear et al., unpublished manuscript), and alterations in blood chemistries (Liebowitz, Gorman et al., 1985) and hormones (Ko et al., 1983; Liebowitz, Gorman et al., 1985) have been documented. Although no specific pattern of physiological accompaniments of panic has been identified, these findings point to a role for neurobiological mechanisms in panic. It is likely that there is an area in the brain center which directs the panic response.

The capacity for panic appears to be widely distributed among humans as well as other animals. Experiences of panic occur in normal individuals (Norton, Harrison, Hauch, & Rhodes, 1985). Panic is a normal response to conditions where personal coping capacities are totally overwhelmed, in the face of immediate danger. The panicking person utilizes last-ditch, emergency coping behaviors which are primitive, automatic, simple, and rigid. These behaviors consist of efforts to flee to safety and/or recruit immediate help. If escape is blocked, freezing or aggressive behavior may occur. The experience of panic is highly aversive and thus stimulates conditioned avoidance of associated situations. In short, panic can be conceptualized as an organism's total, single-minded commitment to immediate removal from, and inclination toward future avoidance of, a situation perceived as highly threatening situation. It is possible to imagine a scenario where such a response would be adaptive: If primitive man or woman chanced upon a watering hole frequented by a group of panthers, a single, close encounter with one of the beasts could lead to a panic episode facilitating quick escape and future avoidance of the watering hole.

On the other hand, panic inhibits the ability to consider alternative actions and will be adaptive only when assessment of catastrophic danger is accurate, and when primitive behaviors, such as flight or freezing, are the best choices. Panic becomes pathological when it occurs maladaptively, in the absence of real threat. The causes of pathological panic have not yet been fully elucidated. Biological and cognitive researchers have different working models for explaining pathological panic. It is likely that neither model alone is fully explanatory, and that each reflects a different perspective on the problem. An integrated psychobiological perspective incorporates notions from each of the other models.

The Biological Perspective

Donald Klein (1964) can be credited with the identification of panic as a discrete psychopathological symptom. Studies by Klein and his colleagues (Klein, 1964; Klein, Zitrin, Woerner, Ross, 1983; Liebowitz & Klein, 1982; Zitrin et al., 1980; Zitrin 1983) revealed that panic symptoms were alleviated by tricyclic antidepressant medication, a responsiveness that differentiated panic from anticipatory and phobic anxiety. Descriptive studies (DiNardo, O'Brien, Barlow, Waddell, & Blanchard, 1983; Hoenn-Saric, 1982; Raskin, Peeke, Dickman, & Pinsker, 1982; Sheehan & Sheehan, 1984) have further delineated phenomenological differences between panic, depression, and other types of anxiety.

Full-blown panic attacks are distinguished from limited symptom episodes by intensity and number of symptoms. In many studies, and in the revision of DSM–III, full-blown panic is defined as consisting or four or more symptoms from the DSM–III list, while partial panic (also called near-panic, limited symptom attacks, or subpanic) has fewer than four. Full-blown panic is usually longer in duration and/or higher in intensity than partial panic. Sudden onset and rapid peak differentiates panic from generalized anxiety, and lack of triggers differentiates panic from phobic anxiety. In the biological model, panic is conceptualized as resulting from excessive firing of the central nervous system, which regulates the biobehavioral expression of fear and its associated somatic symptoms. Panic attacks are viewed as analogous to a seizure disorder in which the threshold for neuronal firing is abnormally lowered. Research efforts are directed at trying to identify which areas of the brain are involved and which neurotransmitter functions are abnormal. Current hypotheses focus on the locus coeruleus (Charney, Heninger, & Brier, 1984; Levin, Liebowitz, Fyer, Gorman, & Klein, 1984; Uhde, Boulenger, & Vittone, & Post, 1984; Redmond, 1979) parahippocampal area (Reiman, Raiche, Butler, Herscovitch, & Robbins, 1984) and/or the medullary chemoreceptor (Carr & Sheehan, 1984b) as anatomical sites responsible for regulation of panic. Cortical projections from these centers may also have a role (Boulenger, Marangos, Patel, Uhde, & Post, 1984). Noradrenergic, adrenergic, benzodiazepine, serotonin, and adenosine receptors have been postulated to have a role in panicogenesis. Neurotransmitter abnormalities may reflect defects in synthesis, release, degradation, or receptor function. These abnormalities may be due to changes in intracellular processes, membrane physiology, or extracellular microenvironment (e.g., ionic gradient, hormonal constitution, metabolical state). Studies are in progress to try to tease apart these various alternatives.

The Cognitive-Behavioral Perspective

The cognitive-behavioral model is different from the biological model in that panic is seen as a manifestation of sudden, intense anxiety and/or fear. Panic attacks are always cued by a frightening situation, though the content of the fear may be out of awareness. Panic occurs in all anxiety disorders (see Barlow, this volume) and may or may not warrant a separate diagnostic category.

The states of fear, anxiety, and panic are triggered in reaction to appraisal of danger. Appraisal of danger is a subjective matter which involves simultaneous processing of threat and safety information. In other words an identified danger situation can be conceptualized as the net result of appriasal of degree of external threat, and effectiveness of protective mechanisms (sense of safety). In normal individuals, the presence of a severe external threat in an unsafe setting can trigger panic. A fire (serious threat) in a crowded theater (an unsafe setting) is an example. Intriguing recent research (Norton et al. 1985; Kennedy & Shear, unpublished data) suggests that normal individuals may also experience occasional panic attacks in the absence of external threat.

Panic disorder patients regularly have panic attacks in the absence of external threat. The cognitive model holds that these patients have abnormal cognitive processes which lead them to perceive threats in the absence of an actually threatening situation. Research efforts are directed at trying to identify which cognitive processes are involved. There is some evidence that panic patients feel themselves to be unsafe in ordinary situations. Panic patients may be preoccupied with ideas of catastrophic personal or social harm, from which they feel helpless to protect themselves (see Beck, this volume). In this setting, they are likely to misconstrue small changes in bodily sensations as indicative of life-threatening illness, loss of consciousness, or going crazy (see Clark, Salkovskis this volume). Once a panic episode has occurred, further panics may be triggered in response to associated cues by a mechanism of classical conditioning. Operant conditioning may also increase panic susceptibility after successful reduction of panic sensations through escape.

An Integrated Psychobiological Perspective

Panic can be conceptualized from a psychobiological perspective as involving interacting factors: specific physiological and biochemical as well as specific psychological mechanisms determine vulnerability to a panic episode and to panic disorder. The psychobiological model has been used fruitfully in studies of physical illness (Weiner, 1977a). The model theory predicts that there will be etiological heterogeneity within each illness category, and consequent difficulty in clearly identifying a single pathogenical mechanism. One patient may have prominent psychological abnormalities while another may have more pronounced physiological disturbance. Yet another may have a combination of subthreshold disturbance in each area. There are also likely to be variable and interacting factors leading to illness onset, according to this model. In general, a stressful situation will increase the likelihood of symptom formation. Stress may be nonspecific or specific, psychological or biological, or some combination of these.

Pathological panic can be conceptualized as a psychosomatic disorder in which psychological and biological factors interact to determine panic vulnerability, onset, and consequences. Panic can occur either as a manifestation of sudden, extreme anxiety and/or fear, or as a manifestation of a disturbance in brain function unrelated to a psychological state of anxiety or fear. The model suggests a research approach which includes identification of both psychological and biological features, and consideration of their interaction. The model predicts that stressful environmental events, maladaptive cognitive processing style, abnormal behavioral reactivity and/or defective physiological processes interact to produce symptoms. Different patients may have different patterns of abnormalities. The same patient may experience exacerbation or remission of symptoms as a result of different mechanisms at different times.

Clinical Psychopathology of Panic Disorder

The pathological syndrome of panic disorder includes vulnerability to recurrent panic episodes and/or maladaptive consequences of panic. The typical course includes a prodromal period (often associated with major life stresses), an initial panic episode, recurrent panic and associated anticipatory anxiety and phobic avoidance. Treatment can be accomplished by using antidepressant medication and/or cognitive-behavioral interventions.

Panic Vulnerability and the Prodromal State

The clinical syndrome begins with an initial panic episode. This initial attack is usually experienced as "coming out of the blue" and is extremely frightening. Barlow (this volume) found that 81% of his patients discontinued their activities and 25% contacted a medical facility at the time of the first panic. In panic disorder patients, the first panic is followed by recurrent panic episodes. Interestingly, it is now clear that a large number of people (perhaps as high as 20%) have occasional panic episodes without developing further complications (see Barlow, this volume).

The prodromal state has not been well studied. There are indications that life stresses play a role in contributing to panic onset. Panic disorder patients are likely to report one or more stressors at the time of the initial panic. Klein (1981) Last, Barlow, and O'Brien (1984) found that prior to the onset of panic a significant loss was particularly common in women and the onset of physical illness in men. In some patients, panic disorder begins with a drug-related panic episode. The mechanisms mediating the development of panic disorder in response to life stresses have not been elucidated. It is possible that one of several pathways may be involved. Speculations about these mechanisms will be elaborated.

Family and twin studies (Harris et al., 1983; Surman et al., 1983; Torgersen, 1983) suggest a genetic basis for panic vulnerability. Again, the mechanism which explains this vulnerability is not known. There is some evidence for a biological vulnerability to panic. Studies of agoraphobics and anxiety neurotics show slow habituation of skin conductance response to repeated auditory tone (Lader, 1980), although these studies have not been done in panic disorder patients. Heightened responsiveness to sodium lactate, yohimbine, caffeine, and CO_2 may reflect biological differences in panic patients. Psychological traits or personality types may also predispose to panic. A significant number of patients report a history of school phobia as a child (Gittelman & Klein, 1985). We found a high prevalence of personality disorder diagnoses in panic patients (Friedman, Shear, & Frances, 1987).

Panic Consequences: The Panic Disorder Syndrome

The initial panic is followed by development of a panic-prone state. There are recurrent panic attacks and mild or aborted forms of panic called limited symptom attacks, near-panic, or partial panic. Patients begin to fear having another attack. Much of the morbidity of the panic disorder syndrome is determined by panic consequences. Patients develop fear and begin avoiding of situations where panic has occurred or where they would not be able to leave or get help if panic did occur. The experience of recurrent panics leads to anxiety and self-criticism. Demoralization and depression are common (Breier, Charney, & Heninger, 1985).

Nonpanic anxiety may be related to fear of having a panic episode, fear of entering a phobic situation or general worries and insecurities, which are typical of generalized anxiety states. Nonpanic anxiety accounts for much of panic disorder morbidity. In a 24-hour monitoring study of 23 panic disorder patients (Shear et al., 1987) we found all patients had symptoms of anxiety and/or panic on the day of the recording. 70% had nonpanic anxiety, 65% had partial panic, and 21% had panic attacks.

Recurrent panics might occur unexpectedly or expected, in a cued or noncued setting (see Rachman; and Barlow, this volume). Rachman's data (this volume) suggest that there is a tendency toward overprediction of panic in claustrophobics exposed to their phobic situation. When predicted panic does not occur, extinction of the associated fear is a slow process. It would be interesting to know if this result is also true of patients with panic disorder. The use of overprediction could increase the sense of safety and decrease panics. However, this mechanism would also be likely to enhance escape or avoidance behavior.

Phobic avoidance is typical in panic disorder patients. It is not yet clear what factors contribute to the development of phobias in some patients but not others. Barlow's data (this volume) suggest that agoraphobics have different patterns of panic occurence than nonagoraphobics. Specifically, panic patients were more likely than agoraphobics to have experienced panic at home and less likely to have had a panic episode in a car or to have been alone at the time of the first panic. Barlow suggests that this pattern may indicate a role for safety searching in the avoidance behavior. Deltito et al. (1986) found a stronger history of school phobia in the agoraphobic, compared with panic patients. There may be a difference in personality traits between panic patients with limited, compared with extensive, phobic avoidance. In a pilot study, we found extensive phobic avoidance was associated with dependent personality traits, while panic disorder subjects with compulsive traits had limited avoidance (Friedman et al., in press).

Treatment Responsiveness

Recent advances in psychopharmacology include the discovery that tricyclic antidepressant medication (imipramine in particular) is highly effective in treating panic symptoms (Charney & Heninger, 1985a, b; Chouinard, Annabel, Fontaine, & Solym, 1982; Davis, Nasar, Spira, & Vogel, 1981; Gloger, Gruenhaus, Birmacher, & Troudart, 1981; Klein, 1982). These studies suggest that antipanic efficacy is usually achieved at dosages similar to those required for antidepressant effects. Although some workers continue to question the mechanism of action of imipramine in agoraphobics, the cited clinical trials and studies with pharmacological provocative agents (Kelly, Mitchell–Heggs, & Sherman, 1971; Ortiz, Rainey, Frohman, 1985; Rifkin, Klein, Dillon, & Levitt, 1981) support the proposed antipanic effects of these antidepressant drugs. In addition to imipramine, Monoamine oxidase inhibitors and a new triazolo-benzodiazepine (alprazolam) are also of proven efficacy as antipanic agents. Behavioral treatment studies also show efficacy in treating patients with agoraphobia (see Michelson this volume). However, outcome measures focus on phobic avoidance, fearfulness, and generalized anxiety, rather than panic. The careful studies reviewed by Michelson (this volume) reveal only moderate antipanic effects of standard behavioral treatment. More recently, several groups (Barlow, Cohen et al., 1984; Beck, this volume; Clark, 1986a; Gitlin et al., 1986) have developed cognitive-behavioral treatment approaches specifically targeted at panic and have achieved good results. Each group has a slightly different method, but the overall approach is similar. Patients are taught panic management skills, which include cognitive and/or physiological techniques. An exposure program is then developed to provide actual experience using the techniques. A more detailed description of our own treatment study provides an example of this approach.

Pilot Study of Cognitive Behavioral Treatment

We treated 15 patients who met DSM–III–R diagnoses of panic disorder. Patients were recruited from Payne Whitney Anxiety Disorders Clinic, for a study of the effects of behavioral therapy on sodium lactate vulnerability. All patients were free of significant illness, medical or psychiatric. Two of the 15 patients had uncomplicated panic disorder, 9 had limited phobic avoidance and 4 were agoraphobic. There were 6 males and 9 females. Mean age was 33 years and mean duration of illness was 5.7 years.

Patients were taught slow abdominal breathing and progressive muscle relaxation to decrease physiological arousal. Cognitive restructuring and behavioral techniques were used to modify catastrophic thinking and escape responses during panic. The therapist and patient then developed a program of daily exposure to a graded hierarchy of anxiety-provoking situations. Patients with no phobic avoidance were able to identify situations such as relaxation, emotional arousal, physical exercise, or specific interpersonal situations, which regularly provoked panic.

Two patients dropped out of treatment before 4 weeks. Of the 13 patients who remained in the study, all completed treatment to meet termination criteria. The mean length of treatment was 17 weeks. Twelve patients (92%) were free of spontaneous full-blown panic attacks by the time of termination. In all cases, there was also a decrease in situational panic, situational, and unexpected limited symptom episodes, and in generalized anxiety ratings. Nine patients (69%) were completely free of all clinically significant panic or panic-related symptoms.

Three subjects continued to have limited symptom episodes. In these three cases, overall panic frequency was significantly less than at treatment onset. There was also improvement in the patient's self-rated fears, although this was less dramatic than the improvement in panic symptoms, further suggesting that the effectiveness of this treatment was related to direct effects on panic.

Pathogenic Mechanisms in Panic Disorder

The panic disorder syndrome is a psychopathological state in which panic attacks are the central pathognomonic feature. As noted above, an initial panic episode is followed by vulnerability to recurrent panic and near-panic experiences and to secondary anxiety and phobic avoidance. In order to understand the pathogenesis of panic disorder, it is useful to ask a number of questions, such as: What is the mechanism of production of panic symptoms? What accounts for the onset of a panic episode and the particular quality of the symptoms? What terminates a panic episode? What are the mechanisms involved in vulnerability to panic, both before and after the initial panic episode? What processes are involved in the development of anxiety and avoidance responses? What mechanisms block panic? What processes enhance or mitigate panic frequency, anxiety, and phobic avoidance? While these questions have not yet been answered, some data are now available. The section that follows will review results of studies and proposed theoretical mechanisms from biological and psychological perspectives.

Biological Studies of Panic

There have been two main trends in biological studies of panic patients. The first grew out of Klein's observation that pharmacological treatment was effective in ameliorating panic symptoms. This line of research has focused on elucidating mechanisms of action of drug treatment. There has been an effort to identify neurotransmitter dysfunction which could be corrected pharmacologically by agents known to have antipanic efficacy. Much of the work in this area has utilized pharmacological provocative testing, which will be summarized herein.

The second trend in biological research is related to the prominence of physical symptoms in panic patients. This line of research has focused on elucidating underlying medical illness and/or autonomic dysfunction which might explain the somatic aspects of panic. We will also outline results of these studies. In summary, it has not yet been possible to implicate a specific neurotransmitter or neurophysiological abnormality which produces panic. Similarly, with the possible exception of mitral valve prolapse, no organic illness has been found to occur with a high prevalence in panic patients.

Biological Underpinnings of Panic Symptoms

1. Pathophysiological Implications of Pharmacological Treatment Studies. Pharmacological treatment studies reveal good antipanic efficacy of imipramine, desipramine, phenelzine, and alprazolam. Standard benzodiazepines are often helpful to panic patients, but do not appear to block panic with the same degree of efficacy as the newer triazolobenzodiazepines, tricyclic antidepressants, or monamine oxidase inhibitors. Beta adrenergic blocking agents have been used, but are not generally effective in treating panic (Noyes et al. 1984). The alpha-adrenergic agonist, clonidine (Hoehnn-Saric, Merchant, Keyser, & Smith, 1981) appears to be effective initially, but may lose antipanic efficacy with continued use.

The implications of these pharmacological results for understanding treatment mechanisms have been well reviewed by Klein, Rabkin, and Gorman (1985). These authors conclude that pharmacological studies to date have not elucidated pathophysiological mechanisms and they propose two main reasons to explain this failure. First, etiological heterogeneity may mean that large samples are needed to dissect subgroups with specific pharamacological responsiveness. Second, there is a need for a systems model of pathology to replace the rheostat model often used. This means that pathogenesis may relate to abnormal feedback circuits or changes in the character of neural responses, rather than to rheostatic changes in transmitter release or receptor sensitivity. It is also possible that the best model of panic requires consideration of multiple, interacting neurophysiological systems.

2. *Pharmacological Provocative Studies.* Pharmacological agents have been used in attempts to provoke anxiety for nearly 50 years (Gorman, 1984; Guttmacher, Murphy, & Insel, 1983). Most recently this work has been focused on panic provocative testing. One strategy used in pharmacological provocative studies of panic involves testing agents which cause panic in vulnerable individuals, but not normals. Sodium lactate infusion and carbon dioxide inhalation are used in this way. Pharmacological effects of these agents have not been fully elucidated, and several neurotransmitter systems may be involved. However lactate infusion, and possible carbon dioxide appears to be highly specific in provoking panic only in patients with clinically diagnosed panic or agoraphobia with panic attacks. This approach is used to study preinfusion differences between panickers and nonpanickers, and to document physiological changes which occur during panic attacks. Some preinfusion differences between panickers and nonpanickers have been identified. Reiman et al. (1984) used Positron Emission Tomography scans to compare regional cerebral blood flow distribution in normal controls and panic disorder patients during a panic-free period. Patients who showed subsequent sodium lactate vulnerability had significantly increased blood flow assymmetry in the region of the parahippocampal gyrus. Liebowitz et al. (1985b) reported that lactate infusion alone (without panic) produces significant physiological changes: increases in heart rate, systolic blood pressure, blood lactate, pyruvate, bicarbonate prolactin, and decreases in blood cortisol, pCO_2, calcium, and phosphorus. The onset of a panic attack is associ-

ated with significant and abrupt physiological changes, beyond the increases produced by lactate alone. There is a sudden, further increase in heart rate associated with a further decrease in pCO_2 and bicarbonate.

The mechanism of action of lactate panicogenesis remains unknown. A number of theories have been proposed. These include lowered ionized calcium, metabolical alkalosis, beta-adrenergic hypersensitivity, stimulation of central noradrenergic centers, excessive peripheral catecholamine release, alteration of acid/base-regulation chemoreceptor hypersensitivity and cognitive psychophysiological explanations. Studies to date have failed to provide consistent support for any of these theories. In general, the role of psychological factors has not been adequately explored. This omission may be responsible for some of the confusion about lactate mechanisms. There is further discussion of this issue in chapters by Clark, Salkovskis, and van den Hout in this volume.

A second strategy in pharmacological provocative testing is to use agents with known neurotransmitter specificity to study responsiveness of panic patients, compared with controls. Challenge tests using the alpha-adrenegic antagonist, yohimbine, and beta-adrenergic agonist, isoproterenol, are examples of this strategy.

One theory of the biological basis of panic is locus coeruleus activation. The locus coeruleus is the brain nucleus containing most of the noradrenergic neuron cell bodies. Noradrenergic transmission is regulated by a complex system of excitatory and inhibitory inputs to the locus coeruleus. The noradrenergic presynaptic membrane contains an alpha-adrenergic autoreceptor, an autoreceptor is a presynaptic receptor which helps regulate neurotransmitter relese. In this case, the alpha-2 autoreceptor is a noradrenergic receptor which inhibits release of noradrenalin from the nerve the alpha-2 receptor. Activation of this receptor leads to inhibition of locus coeruleus discharge. If noradrenergic activation is important in the etiology of panic disorder, panic vulnerability should be influenced by pharmacological agents which act on the locus coeruleus. Yohimbine is an alpha-2 adrenergic antagonist which interferes with presynaptic receptor mediated inhibition of noradrenergic transmission. Studies using oral yohimbine document robust increases in plasma-free 3 methoxy-4-hydroxyphenyglycol (MHPG) and mild increases in systolic blood pressure, anxiety, and autonomic symptoms in normals (Charney, Heninger, & Sternberg, 1982). Since plasma-free MHPG is thought to provide a reliable estimate of norepinephrine (NE) turnover in brain, yohimbine administration provides a method for assessing central NE function in panic patients.

Charney and colleagues have published several reports of studies using this approach (Charney & Heninger, 1985a, b; Charney, Heninger, & Brier, 1984). They found a significant yohimbine effect on plasma MHPG but no significant differences between patients and controls. However, patients experienced significantly more anxiety and somatic symptoms than controls and reported the anxiety to be similar to that experienced during panic. In low, but not high, frequency panickers, MHPG correlated with anxiety ratings. There was a significant patient-control difference in MHPG response when patients with frequent (> 2.5 attacks/week) panic were compared with controls. Greater response of MHPG, blood pressure, and somatic symptoms in high-frequency panickers support hypotheses of increased presynaptic norepinephrine (NE) activity. The fact that this finding was limited to high-frequency panickers may be related to the dosage level of yohimbine. At higher doses, more patients may show this response. In low-frequency panic patients MHPG increases were similar to normals, but, unlike normals, these elevations correlated with anxiety. This may be due to a functional abnormality in postsynaptic receptors or to the fact that anxiogenic responses in this group are due to a learned association with unpleasant bodily sensations.

Further work by this group has shown measurable changes in central NE activity with effective pharmacological treatment. Alprazolam (Charney & Heninger, 1985a) resulted in a small but significant decrement in baseline MHPG and blunting of the yohimbine-stimulated rise. Imipramine (Charney & Heninger, 1985b) induced a substantial and significant fall in baseline MHPG with no effect on yohimbine stimulation. The differing physiological responses to two effective antipanic drugs suggests that the pathophysiology of panic involves complex interacting mechanisms.

Hypersensitivity of peripheral beta-adrenergic receptors has also been considered as a possible etiological mechanism for panic disorder. Patients with beta-adrenergic hyperactivity have symptoms similar to panic patients (Easton & Sherman, 1976). These patients respond well to treatment with beta blockers and have heightened cardiovascular and behavioral reactivity to infusion of the beta-adrenergic agonist isoproterenol. Isoproterenol does not cross the blood-brain barrier well, so studies with this agent test peripheral responsiveness primarily. Isoproterenol has been reported to produce panic symptoms in panic disorder patients (Rainey, Pohl et al., 1984). Response to low-dose isproterenol is also different in panic patients compared with normals. Patients show higher resting heart rates, but significantly less heart rate increase per unit dose of isoproterenol than controls (Nesse, Cameron, Curtis, McCann, & Huber-Smith, 1984). This response fails to support theories of beta-adrenergic hypersensitivity in panic disorder. Instead, there is a suggestion of receptor desensitization. We have pilot data suggesting decreased isoproterenol-stimulated production of cyclic adenosine monophosphate lymphocytes from panic patients, compared with normals, which provide further support for this notion.

In summary, it appears that infusion of isoproterenol leads to panic symptoms in panic disorder patients, but not normal subjects. Panic induced by isoproternol could occur because of receptor hyperresponsiveness of panic patients, but the evidence does not support this possibility. Instead, it is likely that isoproterenol infusion produces unpleasant and frightening bodily sensations which trigger panic through a mechanism of differential reactivity to these sensations in panic patients.

Biological Explanations of Panic Vulnerability

1. Underlying Physical Illness. Panic attacks are usually accompanied by prominent somatic symptoms. The symptoms often begin abruptly, without obvious psychological triggers. These two characteristics have led to speculations about a primary physiological basis for panic episodes. One line of research in this area is to ask whether panic is really a manifestation of underlying physical illness. Possibilities which have been studied include neurogenic hypertension, idiopathic cardiac arrhythmias, mitral valve prolapse (Gorman, Fyer, Gliklich, King, & Klein, 1981; Grunhaus & Gloger, 1982; Kantor, Zitrin, & Zeldis, 1980; Pariser, Pinta, & Jones, 1978) hyperventilation (Garssen, van Veenendaal, & Bloemink, 1983; Hibbert, 1984a; Ley, 1985) hypoglycemia (Uhde, Vitton, & Post, 1984), pheochromocytoma (Starkman, Zelnik, Nesse, & Cameron, 1985) and vestibular dysfunction (Jacob, Moller, Turner, & Wall, 1985). Study results fail to show hypoglycemia as a cause of panic. Hyperventilation produces panic-like symptoms, but does not appear to be necessary or sufficient for panic pathogenesis. An interesting study by Jacob et al. (1985) of vestibular function in panic disorder patients revealed significant abnormalities. However, the identified vestibular deficits were nonspecific and not associated with any known disorder. It is possible that the findings are secondary to panic or anxiety rather than etiologically important. Prevalence of panic attacks was low in Starkman et al.'s study of pheochromocytoma.

A special comment is needed regarding a series of studies which addressed the possibility of a relationship between mitral valve prolapse (MVP) and panic disorder. While the majority of these studies report a high prevalence of MVP in panic disorder patients, the meaning of this relationship remains unclear. A number of studies are available which fail to support a strong relationship between the two disorders (Gorman, Shear, Devereux, King, & Klein, 1986; Mavissakalian, Salerni, Thompson, & Michelson, 1983; Shear, Devereux, Kramer–Fox, Frances, & Mann, 1984). We found a low prevalence of MVP in a group of agoraphobic subjects and hypothesized this difference was related to the use of stringent diagnostic criteria for MVP. This hypothesis was supported in the study by Gorman et al. (1986), which revealed striking differences in interpretation of echo-cardiograms by our cardiologist, compared with the reader at another institution. Ascertainment bias may also explain prevalence differences. Hartman et al. (Hartman, Kramer, Brown, & Devereux, 1982) reported a high prevalence of panic disorder in a group of probands (self-identified patients) with MVP. This relationship did not hold up in an unselected group of subjects with MVP, who had a rate of panic disorder no higher than a control group of normals. Importantly, family studies (Crowe, Pauls, Slyman, & Noyes, 1980) and treatment studies (Gorman, Fyer, & Gliklich, 1981) suggest that even when MVP and panic disorder are found in the same individual, there is no evidence that panic attacks are different from those that occur in patients without MVP. Together, these findings suggest that panic should not be conceptualized as a symptom of MVP, but rather that MVP may be overdiagnosed inpatients with frequent panic symptoms.

In summary, studies to date indicate a high prevalence of nonspecific physiological abnormalities in panic patients, but no evidence of a clear-cut role for medical illness in explaining the pathophysiology of panic. Nevertheless, clinical work reveals a number of medical problems which mimic panic. Examples include temporal lobe epilepsy, hyperthyroidism, and paroxysmal atrial tachycardia. Although further studies are certainly needed, current evidence warrants two conclusions: (1) underlying medical illness is not likely to be the most common explanation of panic symtoms, and (2) underlying medical illness may cause panic-like symptoms, and should be identified and treated if present.

2. *Resting Physiological Abnormalities and Spontaneous Physiological Fluctuations.* Another line of research has been conducted to address the possibility that panic vulnerability results from transient, nonspecific peripheral physiological changes which occur more frequently in panic patients. Such changes might include sudden heart rate changes, heart rhythm disturbances, blood pressure changes, blood pH change, or hormonal changes. They may occur against a backround of tonic hyperactivity, or in an otherwise normal individual.

Several groups, including our own, have studied cardiovascular functioning in panic patients during ambulatory monitoring. These studies reveal normal, 24-hour-average heart rate (Freedman et al. , 1985; Taylor et al., 1986) and blood pressure (Shear et al., unpublished) and elevations during both anxiety and panic episodes. Most but not all panic attacks are associated with a sudden, marked increase in heart rate. There is some evidence for differences in heart rate variability in panic patients, compared with normals. Overall, however, it seems unlikely that a primary disturbance in peripheral physiological activity is the basis for panic vulnerability.

Cognitive Studies

Research in cognitive aspects of panic has been conducted, using clinical and experimental paradigms. Clinical studies include clarification of clinical characteristics of panic. Clinical work has been done in the areas of descriptive phenomenology, treatment strategies, and treatment mechanisms. The successful development of cognitive-behavioral treatment of agoraphobia broadened to include techniques focused directly on alleviation of panic. Research is under way to clarify clinical characteristics of panic patients with and without agoraphobia (see Barlow, Turner, this volume) and to elucidate mechanism of action of treatments (see Michelson, Chambless, Beck, Clark, van den Hout, this volume). Experimental work includes fear-processing studies (Lang, this volume), mechanisms of production of panic consequences (Rachman, this volume) and the influence of appraisal, expectation, and attribution on clinical symtoms and pharmacological provocation of panic (Clark, Salkovskis, van den Hout, this volume). Since the rest of this volume is devoted to extensive discussion of these issues, they will be summarized briefly here.

Cognitive-behavioral Underpinnings of Panic Symptoms

1. Pathogenic Implications of Cognitive-Behavioral Treatment Studies. There are now a number of studies showing efficacy of nonpharmacological treatment in blocking panic. The approach used by each research group is similar, with some differences. Successful treatments differ with respect to specific techniques but appear to share a common strategy which includes: (a) modification of response elements (cognitive, behavioral and physiological), (b) stimulus–response dissociation and (c) an experiential (exposure) component. It is not yet clear which, if any, of these ingredients is essential to successful outcome. It is possible that different programs should be used for different individuals. Foa and Kozak (1985) have written a thought-provoking review regarding the implications of treatment for psychopathology of anxiety disorders. They point out that fear structures of phobics are noted for their persistence, coherence, and irrationality; there is erroneous evaluation of the probability and/or consequences of an event; there is a failure of normal mechanisms which usually promote spontaneous recovery from fears, through exposure. The authors suggest several possible ways this failure may occur: actual avoidance, use of cognitive distraction or distortion, excessive arousal with decreased habituation, misinterpretation of information acquired through exposure or impairments in rules of inference. Beck (this volume) suggests that impairment of realistic appraisal which occurs during panic is pathognomonic. This impairment blocks processing of repeated disconfirmations of catastrophic consequences. It is likely that there are several abnormalities which occur alone or in combination to provide access routes to the final common pathway of panic. These include altered quality and/or quantity of stimulus–response associations, excessive tendency to behavioral avoidance, or cognitive processing errors.

2. Experimental Studies of Panic

Experimental studies of fear and phobias have a long and rich history in behavioral psychology. These studies have elucidated patterns of cognitive, emotional and physiological responses to fear which will not be reviewed in detail here. Cognitive mechanisms related to attention, evaluation, appraisal, valence, and cue sensitivity have been studied in anxious subjects and agoraphobics (see Chambless, this volume). Such studies provide a basis for hypotheses about panic mechanisms, but studies with panic patients have not yet been done.

The evidence to date would suggest that panic patients attend selectively to fear-related cues, either in or out of awareness. Attention to fear-provoking cues may lead to heightened arousal and physiological activation, which, in turn, may predispose to panic through cognitive and/or physiological mechanisms. Attention to fear-relevant stimuli may also operate to distract the patient from task performance and lead to a sense of inadequacy or confusion. Such interference may generate anxiety or even trigger panic. Studies testing such hypotheses need to be done.

An interesting experimental study of panic is provided by Rachman's work (this volume). Attention to the role of predictions and consequences of panic is a novel approach which needs repetition in an agoraphobic or even nonphobic population of panickers.

3. Descriptive Studies

Descriptive studies of cognitive aspects of panic have been completed (Beck, Laude, & Bohnert, 1974; Chambless, Caputo, Bright, & Gallagher, 1984; Hibbert, 1984b; Rapee, 1985). These studies reveal a high prevalence of frightening thoughts and catastrophic images at the inception of panic episodes. Panic patients tend to misinterpret specific types of bodily sensations. Clark's study (this volume) showed increased likelihood of negative interpretations of bodily sensations but not of other ambiguous situations.

Cognitive-Behavioral Explanations of Vulnerability

1. Defects in Cognitive Processing. Cognitive features have been best characterized during and immediately preceding panic episodes. However, there is some evidence that cognitive disturbances may also lead to panic vulnerability. Such distrubances may include chronic preoccupation with bodily sensations, excessive attention to environmental threat cues, overexpectation of the probability or harmfulness of threats, recurrent intrusive fear images or thoughts, or appraisal of loss of safety (enhanced vulnerability). The occurence and origin of predisposing cognitive traits have not yet been clarified, but it is likely that cognitive patterns play a role in panic vulnerability, at least in some patients.

2. Panic as a Conditioned Emotional Response. Panic may also be explained as a conditioned emotional response which occurs in response to cues associated with an inital panic episode (see van den Hout & Seligman, this volume). The cues may be internal bodily sensations or external signals. The fact that some people have initial panic episodes without developing recurrent episodes or other symptoms of panic disorder suggests that this possibility is not fully explanatory. The heightened state of conditionability must still be explained. A stressful life circumstance which increases overall arousal is one possibility.

Panic as a Psychosomatic Illness

Researchers using a psychosomatic model focus on elucidating both psychological and biological factors and on their interactions. This approach can be applied to panic disorder in clinical and experimental studies. Treatment studies include both biological and psychological outcome measures and compare biological, psychological, and combination therapeutic strategies. Descriptive studies of panic symptomatology include both cognitive-behavioral characteristics and neurohormonal features. Experimental provocation of panic includes a comparison of pharmacological with nonpharmacological methods as well as manipulation of cognitive variables during pharmacological provocation. Cognitive, behavioral, and physiological responses are all measured. Psychobiological studies of panic vulnerability include a role for early experience and consideration of potential panicogenic effects of losses and other life stresses.

Psychobiological Underpinnings of Panic Symptoms

1. Pathogenic Implications of Treatment Studies. As noted, treatment studies have shown effectiveness of both pharmacological and cognitive-behavioral treatment of panic and of their combined effects (reviewed by Telch, this volume). Three studies with agoraphobics show better effectiveness of drug (Zitrin et al., 1983) or psychotherapy (Telch, Agras, Taylor, Roth, & Gallen, 1985) treatments or equivalence (Michelson, this volume). However, these studies have been done by clinic researchers with considerable expertise in one or the other but not both forms of treatment. Studies using the same referral source, random assignment to drug or psychotherapy treatments, therapists with monitored training in the respective treatment modes, and outcome measures, which include clinical, behavioral, cognitive and physiological response measures, are necessary. Such studies should help tease apart specificity and/or commonality of treatment effects.

2. Experimental Studies of Panic. Experimental studies of panic have centered primarily on pharmacological provocation. Physiological results are reviewed in previous sections and psychological aspects of pharmacologically provoked panic have been in other chapters of this volume and elsewhere. Rachman's work (this volume) suggests that panic can also be provoked using exposure to phobic stimuli. Cohen, Barlow, Blanchard, & 1986) have reported relaxation-induced panic. We have also been able to provoke panic attacks using imagined fear, exercise, and loud noise startle. Physiological, but not psychological aspects of panic have been measured during ambulatory monitoring studies. Such studies also have the potential of identifying patterns of thinking (see Michelson, this volume) and specific thoughts and/or situations related to panic episodes, and of correlating cognitive and affective changes with physiological measures before and during panic episodes.

Psychobiological Explanations of Panic Vulnerability

1. Effects of Early Experience. Psychobiological studies suggest that early experiences can affect later mental and bodily functioning. Several series of animal experiments demonstrate effects of deficient sensory stimulation on neuronal development and function. Early social experience and nutrition can modify brain chemistry. This modification may become apparent only when the adult animal is challenged by stress (Ackerman, Hofer, & Weiner, 1975; Henry, Meehan, & Stephens, 1967; Levine, 1968). Animal studies of young monkeys show persisting heart rate differences in novel situations between early separated and normal subjects (Reite, Short, Kaufman, Stynes, & Pauley, 1978). While these results are not directly generalizable to study of the panic disorder syndrome, they suggest that early experiences could increase vulnerability to panic by affecting neuroendocrine and/of behavioral reactivity to stress. Development of an animal model of panic (see Seligman, this volume) would allow testing of this hypothesis.

It is also likely that differences in fear modulation are present from birth in susceptible individuals but that these are only obvious at a later maturational stage (postpuberty) and under specific circumstances (initiating stress). Studies of infants of panic disorder patients could document differences in panic-prone, compared with normal, subjects. Studies might also be done comparing responsiveness with fear-provoking stimuli subjects in high-risk, compared with normal, subjects might also be done. High-risk populations might include recently bereaved subjects and/or family members of panic patients.

2. Effects of Recent Stressors. Stressful situations, and loss of important relationships in particular, have been known to cause profound physiological as well as psychological changes (Hofer, 1983). Studies by Last, Barlow, & O'Brien (1984) and others have shown a high prevalence of life stresses prior to panic onset. Separation has been postulated to play an important role in panic vulnerability (Klein, 1981). The mechanism of development of this vulnerability is not known. Studies of animals and humans have demonstrated that bereavement or maternal infant separation can lead to disturbance in autonomic regulatory systems. Autonomic regulatory disturbance may provide the substrate for development of an initial panic episode. Weiner (1977b) suggested several possible models for explaining environmental effects on bodily and mental functioning: environmental events produce physiological changes directly related to evoked affect: Stressful events lead to physiological changes via behavioral changes (e.g., dietary, medication, drinking, etc.), stressful events produce internal changes via the effects of a part of the experience, or there may be physiological changes which affect the CNS and lead to increasingly primitive ways of evaluating, thinking about, and coping with stress.

CONCLUSION

Biological psychiatrists and psychopharmacologists conducted pioneering studies in describing and treating the panic disorder syndrome. Researchers have identified specificity of pharmacological responsiveness to both treatment and provocative agents. The biological perspective is that panic is a manifestation of central or peripheral neurophysiological dysfunction. However, so far, biological studies have not fully elucidated the pathophysiology of panic, and physiological theories at the biomolecular level may not be fully explanatory. In general, biological models of a psychological syndrome are meaningful only if they incorporate bridging mechanisms to explain cognitive, behavioral, and affective manifestations.

In the context of our current, limited understanding of brain physiology, a second research strategy is to focus on the psychological mechanisms underlying symptom development and expression. Cognitive-behavioral psychologists have taken this approach. The other chapters in this book summarize major findings in cognitive-behavioral research in panic.

A third strategy in studying mechanisms of illness is an integrated psychobiological approach. Little has been done directly in the area of panic disorder using this model. However, the positive findings that have emerged from both biological and psychological studies suggest that each has a role. A psychosomatic hypothesis would state that panic attacks occur because of an interaction of a stressor(s) with underlying psychological and/or biological vulnerability (ies). Panic is a manifestation of either biological or psychological disturbance or a combination of the two. The type and strength of coping mechanisms influence the occurence, type, and pervasiveness of pathological panic consequences.

This model encourages the clinician to assess multiple aspects of the patient's functioning, and to tailor treatment to the specific disturbance(s) which are found. The psychosomatic approach encourages the researcher to consider study of biological and psychological factors in the same subjects and in the same settings. For example, drug treatment studies should include pre- and post treatment assessment of cognitive functioning and cognitive-behavioral studies should measure neurobiological outcome. This may allow subtyping of clinical populations according to the primary disturbance and the type of responsiveness to treatment. Hypotheses related to interaction effects should also be considered. The human body is a complex machine which has many built in compensatory systems when one system fails. Compensatory mechanisms in the brain are undoubtedly even more extensive. It is unlikely that a single factor will emerge which fully explains the pathogenic underpinnings of panic. A psychosomatic model takes this observation into consideration, and makes predictions which may better approximate the complexity of biological reality.

5

A Cognitive Model of Panic Attacks

David M. Clark
University of Oxford

INTRODUCTION

Ever since Freud's (1894/1940a) classic essay on anxiety neurosis, it has been accepted that panic attacks are a frequent accompaniment of certain types of anxiety state. However, it is only relatively recently that panic attacks have become a focus of research interest in their own right. This shift in emphasis is largely a result of the work of Donald Klein. In a series of studies which started in the 1960s, Klein and his colleagues (Klein, 1964; Zitrin, Klein, & Woerner, 1980; Zitrin, Klein, Woerner & Ross, 1983; Zitrin, Woerner & Klein, 1981) obtained results which they interpreted as indicating that anxiety disorders which are characterized by panic attacks respond to imipramine while anxiety disorders which are not characterized by panic attacks fail to respond to imipramine. This apparent "pharmacological dissociation" led Klein (1981) to propose that panic anxiety is *qualitatively* different from nonpanic anxiety. This view was endorsed by the writers of *the diagnostic and statistical manual,* 3rd Revision (DSM–III, American Psychiatric Association, 1980) when they created the two diagnostic categories of panic disorder and agoraphobia with panic, and used the presence or absence of panic attacks as a major criterion for distinguishing between different types of anxiety disorder.

Following publication of DSM–III, there was an enormous increase in research on panic attacks. Perhaps because drug studies were the major stimulus for the creation of the diagnostic category of panic disorder, most recent research has concentrated on biological approaches to the understanding of panic. However, Beck, Emery, and Greenberg, (1985) and Clark (1979, 1986a) have argued that panic attacks might be best understood from a cognitive perspective. In this chapter, a cognitive model of panic attacks is described, the extent to which the model is consistent with existing knowledge is discussed, and the initial findings from a series of experiments which are designed to test predictions derived from the model are reported.

Paradoxically, the cognitive model of panic attacks is perhaps most easily introduced by discussing neurochemical and pharmacological approaches to the understanding of panic. A large number of studies have shown that several biochemical and physiological manipulations frequently induce panic attacks in patients who suffer from attacks but rarely induce attacks in nonpanic patients or normal controls. These manipulations include infusions of sodium lactate (Appleby, Klein, Sachar, & Levitt, 1981; Liebowitz et al., 1984), yohimbine (Charney, Heninger, & Breier, 1984), and isoproterenol (Rainey, Pohl et al., 1984); oral administration of caffeine (Charney, Heninger, & Jatlow, 1985); intravenous administration of caffeine (Uhde, Roy–Byrne, Vittone et al., 1985) voluntary hyperventilation (Clark, Salkovskis, & Chalkley, 1985), and inhalation of carbon dioxide (van den Hout & Griez, 1984). The success of these chemical, physiological, and gaseous manipulations in inducing panic attacks in patients who suffer from attacks has been taken to indicate that certain biochemical changes have a direct panic-inducing effect, and also that panic is a biological disorder. These conclusions have provided a rationale for the further exploration of drug treatments for panic (Chouinard, Annabie, Fontaine, & Solyom, 1982; Zitrin, 1983), and also for studies which attempt to identify neurochemical abnormalities in panic patients (Charney et al., 1984; Nesse, Cameron, Curtis, McCann, & Huber–Smith, 1984).

However, studies of two of the induction techniques in normal subjects suggest an alternative, psychological explanation for the effectiveness of these diverse manipulations. The first study (Clark & Hemsley, 1982) investigated individual differences in affective response to hyperventilation. A group of normal subjects were asked to hyperventilate in a highly standardized fashion for 2 minutes. Although many subjects became somewhat anxious, considerable individual variation in affective response was observed, with some subjects experiencing hyperventilation as pleasurable. Furthermore, there was some indication that variability in affective response was partly determined by cognitive factors. In particular, subjects' recollection of the context in which they had previously experienced the induced sensations appeared to relate to whether they experienced hyperventilation as pleasant or unpleasant. Subjects who recollected having experienced the sensations during a drug-induced high or during sex experienced hyperventilation as pleasant. Subjects who recollected having experienced the sensations when about to faint or in other unpleasant contexts experienced hyperventilation as aversive.

The second study (van den Hout & Griez, 1982b) directly investigated the role of cognitive factors in determining response to the CO_2 inhalation technique by systematically manipulating subjects' expectancy of affective change following CO_2 inhalation. One group of subjects were given the expectation that CO_2 would produce a calm state of relaxation, while another group were told that CO_2 would produce a mildly aversive state. The results were broadly consistent with the experimenters' hypothesis. Subjects given the expectation that CO_2 would produce a pleasant state did indeed experience a pleasant state, while those who were given the opposite expectation tended (nonsignificantly) to experience an unpleasant state. Both of these studies raise the possibility that panic-induction techniques may not have a direct panic-producing effect but may only provoke panic if the bodily sensations which they induce are interpreted in a particular way. This is the central notion behind the cognitive model of panic.

A COGNITIVE MODEL OF PANIC ATTACKS

In the cognitive model it is proposed that panic attacks result from the catastrophic misinterpretation of certain bodily sensations. The sensations which are misinterpreted are mainly those which are involved in normal anxiety responses (e.g., palpitations, breathlessness and dizziness) but also include some other sensations. The catastrophic misinterpretation involves perceiving these sensations as much more dangerous than they really are, and in particular, interpreting the sensations as indicative of an *immediate,* impending disaster. Examples of catastrophic misinterpretations would be a healthy individual perceiving heart palpitations as evidence of an impending heart attack; perceiving a slight feeling of breathlessness as evidence of impending respiratory arrest and consequent death; or perceiving a shaky feeling as evidence of impending loss of control and insanity.[1]

Figure 5.1 illustrates the sequence of events that is suggested to occur in a panic attack. A wide range of stimuli appear to provoke attacks. These stimuli can be external (such as a supermarket for an agoraphobic who has previously had an attack in a supermarket) but more often are internal (body sensation, thought, or image). If these stimuli are perceived as a threat, a state of mild

---

[1]Although derived independently, the present model has similarities with the models of panic which have recently been proposed by Beck, Emery and Greenberg (1985), by Beck (this volume) and by Griez and van den Hout (1984).

The present model was developed from clinical experience with patients who complained of recurrent panic attacks, some of which appeared to come "out of the blue." Within DSM–III, such patients would mainly fall into the diagnostic categories of panic disorder or agoraphobia with panic. Barlow and Craske (this volume) report that panic attacks are also experienced, albeit less frequently, by other diagnostic groups such as social phobics and simple phobics. Further research is required to determine whether the cognitive model also applies to panic attacks experienced by these groups. Logically, the model only applies to panic attacks in which part of an individual's perception of threat is related to internal sensations. It seems likely that many of the panic attacks experienced by simple phobics will not fall into this category.

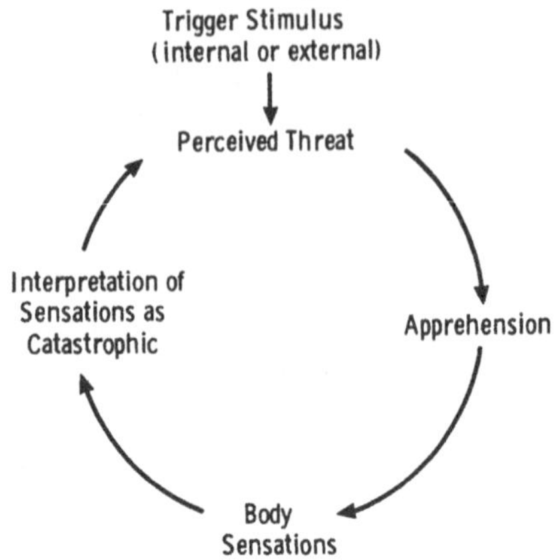

FIG. 5.1. A cognitive model of panic attacks. Reprinted with permission from *Behaviour Research and Therapy, 24,* p. 463, D. M. Clark, A Cognitive Approach to Panic, Copyright 1986a, Pergamon Journals Ltd.

apprehension results. This state is accompanied by a wide range of bodily sensations. If these anxiety-produced sensations are interpreted in a catastrophic fashion a further increase in apprehension occurs. This produces a further increase in body sensations and so on, round in a vicious circle, which culminates in a panic attack.

Types of Panic Attack

The model shown in Fig. 5.1 can account for both panic attacks which are preceded by a period of heightened anxiety and panic attacks which are not but instead appear to come "out of the blue."

In the case of attacks which are preceded by heightened anxiety, two distinct types of attack can be distinguished. In the first, the heightened anxiety is concerned with the anticipation of an attack. This is often the case when agoraphobics experience an attack in a situation (such as a supermarket) where they have previously panicked. On entering such a place they tend to become anxious in anticipation of a further attack, then selectively focus on their body, notice an unpleasant bodily sensation, interpret this as evidence of an impending attack, and consequently activate the vicious circle which produces an attack. In other cases the heightened anxiety which precedes an attack may be quite unconnected with anticipation of an attack. For example, an individual may become nervous as a consequence of discussing an emotional topic during a dispute with a spouse, notice his or her bodily reaction to the argument, interpret these sensations in a catastrophic fashion, and then panic.

In the case of panic attacks which are not preceded by a period of heightened anxiety, the trigger for an attack often seems to be the perception of a bodily sensation which itself is caused by a different emotional state (excitement, anger) or by some quite innocuous event such as suddenly getting up from the sitting position (dizziness, palpitations), exercise (breathlessness, palpitations) or drinking coffee (palpitations). Once perceived, the bodily sensation is interpreted in a catastrophic fashion and a panic attack results. In such attacks patients often fail to distinguish between the triggering bodily sensation and the subsequent panic attack and so perceive the attacks as having no cause and coming "out of the blue." This is understandable given the patients' general beliefs about the meaning of an attack. For example, if an individual believes that there is something wrong with his heart, he or she is unlikely to view the palpitation which triggers an attack as different from the attack itself. Instead he or she is likely to view both as aspects of the same thing—a heart attack or near-miss.

This type of explanation for the occurrence of spontaneous attacks can also be applied to nighttime attacks, in which the patient wakes up in a panic. Sleep studies (Oswald, 1966) have shown that we monitor the external world for personally significant sounds while asleep and tend to have our sleep disturbed or be woken up by such sounds. It seems reasonable to suppose that we also monitor our *internal* environment for significant events. If this is the case, then an individual who is concerned about his or her heart might have a panic attack triggered by a palpitation which was detected and misinterpreted during sleep. He or she would then wake up in a state of panic.

Which Sensations Are Misinterpreted?

In Fig. 5.1 it is hypothesized that the misinterpretation of bodily symptoms of anxiety is always involved in the vicious circle which culminates in a panic attack. However, other sensations can also play a role in panic, particularly as triggering stimuli. We have already mentioned sensations, such as breathlessness and palpitations, which sometimes are produced by anxiety but other times can initially be produced by innocuous events or positive emotions. In addition, occasionally panic attacks are triggered by sensations which are never part of an anxiety response. For example, floaters in the visual field are not symptoms of anxiety, but if an individual was concerned about the possibility of a deterioration in sight then perception of a floater could trigger a panic. The individual might interpret the floater as a sign of impending visual deterioration, and become anxious; blurred vision arising from this anxiety, would further reinforce the belief that something was seriously wrong with his or her vision, and so activate a circle of misinterpretation and increasing blurred vision which culminates in a panic attack.

So far our discussion has mainly concentrated on sensations which arise from the perception of internal physical processes (e.g., palpitations). These are the most common sensations involved in the production of panic attacks. However, sensations which arise from the perception of mental processes can also contribute to the vicious circle which culminates in a panic attack. For example, the belief of some patients that they are about to go mad is based partly on moments when their mind suddenly goes blank or they have a profound difficulty in thinking. These moments are interpreted as evidence of impending loss of control over thinking and consequent insanity.

A further aspect of the cognitive model which requires comment concerns the temporal stability of patients' catastrophic interpretations of bodily sensations. For some patients the panic-triggering sensations and their interpretations of those sensations remain fairly constant across time. In other patients both the sensations and interpretations change over time. For example, some patients appear to have a rather vague belief that they are going to suffer from some serious illness. This belief leads them to misinterpret a wide range of bodily sensations; their particular misinterpretations varying with which bodily sensations they notice, what illnesses they have information about, and what illnesses they have already been able to discount.

Are Catastrophic Misinterpretations Always Conscious?

In elaborating cognitive theories of emotional disorders, many workers have concentrated on conscious cognitive events. However, as cognitive psychologists are well aware, many cognitive processes are not conscious and it is likely that nonconscious processes play an important role in the production of panic attacks (see Lang, this volume). In patients who experience recurrent attacks, catastrophic misinterpretations may be so fast and automatic that patients may not always be aware of the interpretive process. This possibility is particularly likely early in therapy. Our clinical experience is that as cognitively orientated therapies progress, patients tend to become increasingly aware of the interpretative process.

The suggestion that catastrophic misinterpretations may on occasions be so fast and automatic that patients may not be aware of them raises potential problems for studies evaluating the cognitive model of panic. However, cognitive psychologists have developed a wide range of tasks for assessing this type of cognitive event and it should be possible to utilize some of these in panic research. One paradigm which may be of particular value is the contextual priming task described by Fischler and Bloom (1979). In this task subjects are shown a sentence which is complete except for the last word. Having read this sentence frame, they are then presented on some trials with a word, and on other trials with a nonword, and their task is to decide as quickly as possible whether the letter string which they see forms a word or a nonword. When the letter string forms a word, subjects typically make faster lexical decisions if the word is one which they would expect from the sentence frame than if it is a word which they would not expect, given the sentence frame. This speeding of lexical decision times by a match between a word and the meaning of the preceding sentence frame is called contextual priming. The phenomenon could be exploited to assess misinterpretation if sentence frames and target words were constructed so that the target word completes an interpretation of a bodily sensation. Two such sentences follow, with the target words underlined:

1. John had palpitations because he was *dying*.
2. John had palpitations because he was *excited*.

If panic patients are particularly likely to make catastrophic interpretations then, compared with control subjects, they should show more contextual priming for the word "dying" than for the word "excited."

Are Catastrophic Misinterpretations a State or Trait Characteristic?

I have earlier argued that the cognitive model can account for panic attacks that are not preceded by a period of heightened anxiety by proposing that these attacks are triggered by the catastrophic misinterpretation of a bodily sensation caused by an emotional state other than anxiety (e.g., excitement, anger, relaxation) or by some quite innocuous event, such as exercise. For this type of triggering to occur, it is necessary to postulate that panic patients have a tendency to misinterpret bodily sensations even when they are not anxious. This relatively enduring cognitive *trait* would then be amplified when a individual enters an anxious *state*.

The First Panic Attack and the Cognitive Model

Although this discussion suggests that individuals who have recurrent panic attacks have a tendency to misinterpret bodily sensations even when they are not anxious, it is not clear whether this "trait" antedates the first panic attack. It could be that in some individuals adverse life events (a relative dying suddenly and unexpectedly) may produce a tendency to misinterpret bodily sensations before the first attack occurs. However, the data on initial attack cognitions reported by Barlow and Craske (this volume), suggest that in most people this tendency develops after the first attack, as a consequence of the way they perceive the attack. For example, if during a first panic attack a relative or general practitioner gives the patient a clear, noncatastrophic explanation for the bodily sensations that are experienced, a negative interpretive style and further attacks are unlikely to develop. However, if such an explanation is not provided, the patient is likely to be left with the lingering doubt that there could be something seriously wrong with him or her and this could then lead him to misinterpret subsequent changes in bodily state and hence experience further attacks. Suitable noncatastrophic explanations for the surge of autonomic symptoms occurring during the first attack would include clear and unambiguous descriptions of how these symptoms could have been produced by stress-induced hyperventilation, hormonal changes, extreme emotional stress, diet, or drugs.

Fear of Fear and the Cognitive Model

It has often been suggested that panic attacks are the result of a fear of fear. The proposed cognitive model has similarities to the fear of fear hypothesis, but there are also important differences. First, the simple statement that panic results from a fear of fear would lead one to predict that panic patients would always panic when they notice themselves becoming anxious. This is clearly not the case. There are many occasions in which panic patients notice that they are fairly severely anxious but do not panic. For example, a patient who experiences panic attacks may notice that he or she is becoming anxious before an interview but not panic. Instead the patient may simply ascribe the bodily sensations being experienced to the understandable apprehension produced by a difficult situation. The cognitive model avoids the problem of overprediction by specifying that individuals only panic when they notice themselves becoming anxious if they interpret the bodily symptoms of anxiety as indicating an immediately impending disaster. In many situations, knowledge about the situation and other contextual factors will prevent individuals from making a catastrophic interpretation of their anxiety responses.

A second difference between the fear of fear hypothesis and the cognitive model concerns the triggering of panic. In the fear of fear hypothesis panic must always be triggered by an anxiety response. This is not necessary in the cognitive model. Instead it is supposed that sometimes the bodily sensations whose misinterpretation triggers a panic do not arise from anxiety, but as a result of seemingly innocuous events (such as exercise or caffeine) or as a result of other emotions, such as anger and excitement.

Hypochondriasis and the Cognitive Model

Relatively little is known about the psychological processes involved in hypochondriasis. However, it seems likely that hypochondriacal complaints are at least partly based on catastrophic misinterpretations of bodily sensations and signs. The question therefore arises, what is the difference between the psychological processes involved in panic and those involved in hypochondriasis without panic? One important difference may be the distinction between immediate and long-term threat. Interpretations of bodily sensations which lead patients to believe that they are in immediate danger of dying, going mad or losing control may be particularly characteristic of panic, while interpretations which imply more distant danger may be more characteristic of hypochondriasis.

A second possible difference between hypochondraisis and panic concerns the bodily stimuli which are misinterpreted. Clinically it would appear that a wider range of bodily stimuli are misinterpreted in hypochondriasis and many of these stimuli are not commonly occurring elements of the anxiety response (i.e., spots, aches, and pains). As such stimuli are not autonomic nervous system responses, there is no efficient mechanism for markedly increasing their intensity and so producing the surge response characteristic of panic.

A BRIEF REVIEW OF RESEARCH

Having presented a cognitive model of panic, I will now briefly review the literature on panic to determine the extent to which it is consistent with the proposed model.

1. Ideational Components of Panic. If the cognitive model is correct, one would expect that the thinking of panic patients would be characterized by thoughts which are concerned with the catastrophic misinterpretation of bodily sensations or at least which could be interpreted that way. Data from two recent interview studies provide support for this hypothesis. Hibbert (1984a) compared the ideation of nonphobic patients who experienced panic attacks (n = 17) with that of nonphobic patients who did not experience panic attacks (n = 8). The two groups did not differ in the frequency of thoughts concerned with general inability to cope or with social embarrassment, but they did differ in the frequency of thoughts concerned with the anticipation of death, illness or loss of control—all thoughts which could be based on a misinterpretation of a bodily sensation. Rapee (1985) obtained essentially similar results in a larger study that compared the ideation of panic disorder patients (n = 38) with that of generalized anxiety patients who had never experienced panic attacks (n = 48). Discriminant analysis indicated that panic patients were more likely to have thoughts concerned with the anticipation of having a heart attack, fainting, dying or going mad, while generalized anxiety patients were more likely to believe that they were unreasonably anxious.

2. Perceived Sequence of Events in a Panic Attack. As the cognitive model specifies that panic attacks result from the catastrophic misinterpretation of bodily sensations, one would expect that a bodily sensation would be one of the first things noticed during an attack. Two studies have asked patients about the perceived sequence of events in an attack and both have provided results consistent with this expectation. Hibbert (1984a) and Ley (1985) both found that panic patients frequently report that the first thing they notice during an episode of anxiety is a physical feeling. In addition, Hibbert (1984a) found that this sequence of events was reported significantly more often by patients with panic attacks than by patients without panic attacks (53% and 0%, respectively).

3. The Role of Hyperventilation in Panic Attacks. The bodily sensations which are produced by voluntary hyperventilation are very similar to those experienced in naturally occurring panic attacks. This observation has led a number of writers to suggest that hyperventilation may play an important role in the production of panic attacks (Clark, 1979; Clark & Hemsley, 1982; Gibson, 1978; Hibbert, 1984b; Kerr, Dalton, & Gliebe, 1937; Lewis, 1954; Lum, 1976; Wolpe, 1973). Consistent with this suggestion it has been shown that in some panic patients (a) voluntary hyperventilation produces a panic-like state (Clark et al., 1985), and (b) hyperventilation accompanies naturally occuring panic attacks (Hibbert, 1986; Salkovskis, Warwick, Clark, & Wessels, 1986), panic attacks produced by contrived psychological stress (Salkovskis, Clark, & Jones, 1986) and panic attacks induced by sodium lactate (Liebowitz, Gorman et al., 1985). These observations suggest that hyperventilation plays a role in some panic attacks.[2] However, it is clear that hyperventilation per se does not produce panic. As already mentioned, studies of the effects of hyperventilation in normals (Clark & Hemsley, 1982; Svebak & Grossman, 1985) have shown that individuals vary considerably in their affective response to hyperventilation, with some individuals actually finding the experience enjoyable. It is therefore suggested that hyperventilation only produces panic if the bodily sensations which it induces are perceived as unpleasant, and interpreted in a catastrophic fashion.

4. Lactate-induced Panic. Infusions of sodium lactate are the most frequently used technique for inducing panic attacks in the laboratory.[3] Between 60% to 90% of panic patients and 0% to 20% of normals and nonpanic anxious patients experience an attack when given an intravenous infusion of 0.5–1.0M racemic sodium lactate (Appleby et al., 1981; Liebowitz et al., 1984; Liebowitz, Fyer et al., 1985; Rainey, Pohl et al., 1984). Even when subjects do not panic, lactate infusions are accompanied by a wide range of physiological and biochemical changes. Liebowitz, Gorman et al. (1985) reported that lactate produces significant increases in heart rate, systolic blood pressure, pyruvate, prolactin and bicarbonate, and significant decreases in cortisol, partial pressure of carbon dioxide (pCO_2), phosphate, and ionized calcium. As some of these

[2]Gorman et al. (1984) reported a study in which 12 panic patients were asked to hyperventilate in room air, breath 5% CO_2 and participate in a sodium lactate infusion. Eight of the patients had a panic attack during sodium lactate, 7 during CO_2 inhalation, and 3 during hyperventilation. Gorman et al. interpreted these findings as indicating that hyperventilation does not play an important role in the production of panic attacks. However, in all subjects hyperventilation followed lactate infusion and CO_2 inhalation. It is therefore equally plausible to suggest that order effects explain why patients were less likely to panic during hyperventilation. Consistent with this suggestion, Bonn, Harrison, and Rees (1971) and Griez and van den Hout (1986) have reported data suggesting that repetition leads to a decrease in patients' affective response to panic induction procedures.

[3]Margraf, Ehlers, and Roth (1986b) provided a more detailed review and critique of lactate infusion studies.

changes in bodily function are likely to be perceived, the cognitive model could account for the panic-inducing effects of lactate by proposing that individuals who panic do so because they interpret the induced sensations in a catastrophic fashion. This explanation is consistent with Liebowitz, Gorman et al.'s (1985, p. 718) observation that individuals who panic during lactate infusion perceive bodily changes, such as tremor and paresthesias, well before the onset of panic. The fact that more patients than controls panic during lactate infusion would be explained mainly by supposing that patients have, as a relatively enduring characteristic, a particularly marked tendency to interpret certain bodily sensations in a catastrophic fashion. However, in some studies part of the difference in response between patients and controls may be due to differences in the instructions given to the two groups. For example, in their preinfusion instructions, Appleby et al. (1981) told patients that they "might experience a panic attack" (p. 413), but told controls that they "might experience an attack with symptoms analogous to those of 'public speaking' " (p. 413). As the controls presumably had never experienced a panic attack but probably had been slightly nervous during public speaking these instructions are likely to lead controls to expect a less frightening experience than patients. Such differences in expectation can have marked effects on the affect produced by biochemical interventions (van den Hout & Griez, 1982b).

5. *Effects of Psychological Treatment.* The proposal that panic attacks result from the catastrophic interpretation of certain bodily sensations suggests both a cognitive-behavioral and a behavioral approach to the treatment of panic attacks. The cognitive-behavioral approach would involve identifying patients' negative interpretations of the bodily sensations which they experience in panic attacks; suggesting alternative noncatastrophic interpretations of the sensations; and then helping the patient to test the validity of these alternative interpretations through discussion and behavioral experiments. The behavioral approach would capitalize on the observation that fear of specific stimuli can often be treated by repeated, controlled exposure to those stimuli and would consist of graded exposure to the bodily sensations which accompany panic. Recently both of these approaches have been tried and the initial results are highly encouraging.

Clark et al. (1985) adopted the cognitive-behavioral approach and concentrated on one particular alternative interpretation—the view that the bodily sensations which patients experience in a panic attack are the result of stress-induced hyperventilation rather than the more catastrophic things which they usually fear (impending heart attack, insanity, loss of control). Their treatment had several stages. In the first stage the cognitions and bodily sensations which are associated with panic are elicited. These vary considerably from patient to patient. Next the therapist tries to demonstrate that hyperventilation could have produced the symptoms of panic by asking the patient to overbreathe for about 2 minutes. Patients are *not* told that overbreathing may reproduce their attacks. Instead, hyperventilation is simply introduced as a diagnostic test. If the patient recognizes the bodily sensations induced by hyperventilation as similar to those experienced during naturally occurring attacks, this observation is used as the basis for a discussion in which the therapist tries to help the patient to reattribute the sensations away from catastrophic interpretations and toward the notion that he or she is suffering from stress-induced hyperventilation. This is an important step in the treatment and great care must be taken to ensure that any doubts which the patient has about the validity of the model are carefully discussed. For example, the patient may say, "Well, during overbreathing I experienced all the sensations I get during a panic attack and your explanation makes some sense, but you were talking about stress-induced hyperventilation, and I get attacks when I am trying to relax." In such an instance, the therapist would carefully review with the patient the sequence of events which occurred during the last "relaxation-induced" panic in order to determine whether such attacks could be encompassed within the model. A probable sequence of events to emerge from such a review would be that the patient started to relax, in so doing focused on his or her body, noticed an innocuous body sensation (e.g., palpitation) misinterpreted this sensation in a catastrophic fashion and then the attack was triggered. Following the reattribution discussion, the next step in the treatment involves training in a pattern of controlled respiration which is incompatible with hyperventilation. This is a slow, shallow pattern of breathing, which is intended to be used as a coping technique when a patient thinks a panic is about to start. As well as using controlled breathing as a coping technique, patients are encouraged to rehearse more appropriate cognitive responses to bodily symptoms and to use these when they notice a panic attack is about to start. Lastly, attempts are made to identify and modify panic triggers. Early in treatment, nonphobic patients may be unable to identify triggers for their panic attacks. However, by inspecting their daily panic diaries it is often possible to identify triggers (e.g., caffeine, exercise, effects of a hangover, postural hypotension, phase in the menstrual cycle, and bizzare fleeting images). This process of identification helps to make attacks seem more understandable, and hence, less frightening. It also often suggests ways of directly reducing the frequency of panic triggers.

To date, Clark and Salkovskis have conducted two evaluations of this cognitive-behavioral treatment. In the first evaluation (Clark et al., 1985) patients were selected who perceived a similarity between the effects of overbreathing and naturally occurring panic attacks. Substantial reductions in panic attack frequency were observed during the first few weeks of treatment. These initial gains, which occurred in the absence of exposure to feared external situations, were improved upon with further treatment (including exposure to feared situations if appropriate) and were maintained at 2-year follow-up.

In the second evaluation (Salkovskis, Jones, & Clark, 1986) an unselected group of panic patients were studied. Again a substantial reduction in attack frequency was observed. In addition, there was some evidence that outcome was positively correlated with the extent to which patients perceived a marked similarity between the effects of voluntary overbreathing and naturally occurring attacks. Neither study employed a wait-list control group. However, it is unlikely that the improvements observed in these studies were due to spontaneous remission as stable baselines were established before treatment and significant improvements from baseline occurred in a treatment period shorter than the baseline. It therefore appears that the cognitive-behavioral package is an effective treatment for panic, especially in patients who perceive a marked similarity between hyperventilation and naturally occurring panic. Patients who fail to perceive a marked similarity between the effects of hyperventilation and naturally occurring panic would probably benefit from the inclusion of additional discussions and behavioral experiments related to other, noncatastrophic explanations of bodily sensations (see Clark, 1986b, for an example).

Further evidence for the effectiveness of the cognitive-behavioral treatment comes from two recent studies which have independently replicated the results obtained by Clark et al. (1985) and by Salkovskis, Jones et al. (1986). In Hungary, Kopp, Mihaly, Tringer, and Vadasz (1986) found that a mixed group of panic disorder, and agoraphobia with panic patients, showed substantial reductions in panic frequency during a 6-week application of Clark et al.'s cognitive-behavioral treatment. In the United States, Beck and colleagues (Beck, this volume) incorporated this treatment within their cognitive therapy program. Panic disorder patients showed substantial reductions in panic frequency during the course of treatment, and these gains were maintained at 3-month follow-up.

Griez and van den Hout (1983, 1986) adopted the behavioral approach to treatment and used inhalations of 35% CO_2/65% O_2 as a way of repeatedly exposing patients to the bodily sensations which accompany panic attacks. Inhalation of 35% CO_2/65% O_2 is a highly effective technique for inducing the bodily sensations of panic (van den Hout & Griez, 1984). Its effects appear to result from the sudden drop in pCO_2 (hyperventilation) which follows exhalation of the gas rather than from the increase in pCO_2 (hypercapnia) which accompanies inhalation (van den Hout & Griez, 1985). When used as a treatment, inhalations are introduced in a graded fashion. Initially, subjects take small inhalations, as their anxiety to small inhalations drops they are encouraged to take a fuller depth inhalations and eventually take several fuller depth inhalations each session. Griez and van den Hout (1986) evaluated the short-term effectiveness of this treatment using a crossover design in which 2 weeks of CO_2 inhalation therapy was compared with 2 weeks of propranolol. Inhalation therapy was associated with significant reductions in panic frequency and fear of autonomic sensations. Propranolol failed to have significant effects on either of these measures. However, the difference in change scores between treatments only reached significance on the measure of fear of autonomic sensations. In view of the unusually brief duration of therapy, Griez and van den Hout's (1986) results may be an underestimate of the effectiveness of CO_2 inhalation therapy. Although the therapy was associated with substantial drops in panic frequency, most patients were not panic-free at the end of the 2 weeks. Further improvements might have been observed if the therapy had been extended.

At this stage, neither Clark et al.'s (1985) cognitive-behavioral treatment nor Griez and van den Hout's (1986) behavioral treatment have been compared against an alternative psychological treatment in order to control for nonspecific therapy ingredients. Until this is done it is not possible to say whether the apparent effectiveness of the treatments is due to their specific emphasis on fear of internal sensations. However, it is encouraging to note that both treatments appear to be effective with panic disorder patients as these patients form a group for whom there is no generally accepted psychological treatment. In Clark et al.'s (1985) study, these patients (termed "nonsituationals") did extremely well, all becoming panic-free by the end of treatment. Subsequently Beck and colleagues (Beck, this volume) have also reported finding that most panic disorder patients are free of panic after cognitive-behavioral treatment.

In contrast to panic disorder, there is a generally accepted psychological treatment for agoraphobia with panics. Numerous studies (see Mathews, Gelder, & Johnston, 1981) have shown that graded, in vivo exposure to feared external situations is an effective treatment for agoraphobic avoidance and situational fear. Early studies did not include direct measures of panic, but it was assumed that panic attacks would decline as situational fear declined and recent studies have confirmed this assumption (Marks et al., 1983; Michelson, Marchione & Mavissakalian, 1985; Mavissakalian & Michelson, 1986a). The question therefore arises whether the cognitive-behavioral and behavioral treatments described previously have anything to add to graded, in vivo exposure. Several authors (Freud, 1895/1940b; Goldstein & Chambless, 1978; Hallam, 1978; Klein, 1981; Westphal, 1872) have argued that in many cases agorpahobia is best viewed as a fear of panic rather than a fear of specific situations. This view suggests that treatments which tackle panic directly may produce more generalized change. In particular, they may be more effective than graded exposure alone in reducing the frequency of "spontaneous" panic attacks and panic attacks which occur in patient's homes. Certainly there is room for further improvement in these areas. In a recent study, Michelson, Marchione, and Mavissakalian (1985) found that 45% of patients given the DSM–III diagnosis of agoraphobia with panic were still experiencing panic attacks at home without obvious environmental provocation after 3 months of in vivo, therapist-assisted exposure to feared situations.

6. The Role of Biological Factors in Panic. By specifying that the catastrophic interpretation of certain bodily sensations is a necessary condition for the production of a panic attack, the cognitive model provides a different perspective to that offered by biological models of panic and also provides a rationale for psychological approaches to treatment. However, the cognitive model does *not* assume that biological factors have no role to play in panic attacks.

There are, *in principle,* at least three ways in which biological factors might increase an individual's vulnerability to the vicious circle shown in Fig. 5.1.

First, biological factors may contribute to the triggering of an attack. As already mentioned, panic attacks are often triggered by a perceived bodily sensation, such as breathlessness or palipitations, and such sensations appear to be reported more frequently by panic patients than by other patients or normals. Bodily sensations are particularly likely to be noticed when there is a change in bodily processes (Pennebaker, 1982). It is therefore possible that the increase in perceived sensations observed in panic patients occurs because such patients experience more, or more intense, benign fluctuations in bodily state than others.

Second, biological factors are likely to influence the extent to which a perceived threat produces an increase in bodily sensations as shown in Fig. 5.1. The reduced efficiency of central adrenergic $alpha_2$-autoreceptors, which Charney et al. (1984) suggested could be characteristic of panic patients, would be an example of such an effect. Noradrenergic neurons in the locus coeruleus and other brain stem areas play an important role in the central control of the autonomic nervous system. The $alpha_2$-adrenergic autoreceptor has an inhibitory influence on presynaptic noradrenergic neurons. A deficiency in this autoreceptor would mean that release of noradrenaline would not be damped down by presynaptic inhibition. Individuals with such a deficiency would experience larger than normal surges in noradrenaline and sympathetic nervous system activation in response to a perceived threat. A further example of a biological influence on the extent to which a perceived threat produces an increase in body sensations comes from the literature on hyperventilation. As already mentioned, in some patients the bodily sensations which occur in a panic attack are partly a result of hyperventilation and the effects of hyperventilation vary with resting levels of pCO_2, which in turn, vary with phase in the menstrual cycle (Damas–Mora, Davies, Taylor, & Jenner, 1980).

Third, the extent to which bodily sensations which accompany anxiety are interpreted in a catastrophic fashion will largely be determined by psychological factors. However, biological factors may also have a small role to play in this aspect of the vicious circle. For example, the hypothesized deficiency in central $alpha_2$-adrenergic autoreceptors would mean that individuals would be more likely to experience sudden surges in sympathetic activity, and surges in activity may be more likely to be interpreted in a catastrophic fashion than gradual buildups.

Having specified several ways in which biological factors can be accommodated within the cognitive model, it should also be pointed out that cognitive model has important implications for biological research. If, as the cognitive model states, the catastrophic misinterpretation of bodily sensations is a necessary condition for the producfion of panic, then biological researchers may find it useful to incorporate this knowledge in the design of experiments attempting to identify biological factors which make individuals vulnerable to panic. There may be a number of biological variations which are no more common in panic patients than in nonpanic patients but which nevertheless contribute to the development of panic attacks. These variations would only come into play in individuals who already have a tendency to misinterpret bodily sensations. This methological point is very similar to the arguments used in schizophrenia research. There it is suggested that in order to investigate the effects of social factors it is necessary to take into account individuals' genetic vulnerability. In the case of panic it is suggested that psychological vulnerability needs to be taken into account when assessing biological factors.

The cognitive model has a second implication for biological research. As pointed out, it has been argued that the increased vulnerability of panic patients to substances such as lactate indicates the presence of a biological disturbance. An alternative explanation is that panic patients have a psychological disturbance (misinterpretation of interoceptive sensations) which makes them react in a more negative fashion to such substances. Biological researchers wishing to avoid this interpretive ambiguity will need to use pharmacological agents which can test for biological disturbance without inducing the sort of sensations which are feared by panic patients. To date, I am aware of only one group of workers who have attempted to do this.

Charney has hypothesized that panic patients suffer from an abnormality in central $alpha_2$-adrenoceptor function. As a first test of this hypothesis, Charney et al. (1984) gave panic patients an $alpha_2$ antagonist (yohimbine). Panic patients showed a greater increase in plasma levels of 3-methoxy-4-hydroxyphenyglycol (MHPG, a breakdown product of central noradrenaline) and blood pressure than nonpanic patients or normal controls. This finding is consistent with an abnormality in $alpha_2$-adrenoceptor function, but as yohimbine induces a wide range of sensations which are feared by panic patients, it could also be argued that these patients' stronger MHPG response could be psychologically mediated. This objection does not apply to two more recent studies (Charney & Heninger, 1986; Nutt, 1986) in which panic patients were given an $alpha_2$-adrenergic receptor agonist (clonidine). This decreases blood pressure and MHPG and Charney and Heninger (1986) found that these decreases were *larger* in panic patients than normal controls. Essentially similar results were obtained by Nutt (1986). As panic patients in these studies are demonstrating a bigger *decrease* in anxiety-related variables it is unlikely that the results can be explained entirely psychologically. Instead, it seems reasonable to suppose that there may be an abnormality in the regulation of central noradrenergic function in panic disorders. Although as neither study included other anxious controls these studies should be replicated with such controls to ensure that the results are not a function of anxiety per se rather than panic vulnerability.

7. *Effects of Pharmacological Treatment.* Within the model shown in Fig. 5.1, there are several ways in which drugs could be effective in reducing the frequency of panic attacks. Blockade of, or exposure to the bodily sensations

which accompany anxiety, and a reduction in the frequency of bodily fluctuations which can trigger panic could all have short-term effects on panic. However, if a patient's tendency to interpret bodily sensations in a catastrophic fashion is not changed while a drug is being administered, discontinuation of drug treatment should be associated with a high rate of relapse.

So far, three drugs (propranolol, diazepam, and imipramine) have been investigated in controlled trials which include measures of panic. Propranolol appears to be ineffective, even when given in doses which are sufficient to effect beta-blockade (Griez & van den Hout, 1984; Noyes et al., 1984). This is perhaps because beta-blockade reduces the cardiovascular aspects of panic, but appears to leave some other bodily sensations unaffected (Gorman et al., 1983). Noyes et al. (1984) found that high doses of diazepam (up to 30 mg) were effective in reducing panic frequency over a period of 2 weeks, but the report did not provide data on the long-term effectiveness of diazepam. Other studies (e.g., Catalan & Gath, 1985) have raised serious doubts about the long-term effectiveness of diazepam as a treatment for anxiety.

In contrast to propranolol and diazepam, more positive results have been obtained with imipramine. Three controlled trials (McNair & Kahn, 1981; Zitrin et al., 1980, 1983) have found that imipramine is more effective than an inert placebo in reducing the frequency of panic attacks in agoraphobics with panic and a further trial (Telch et al., 1985) obtained a trend toward a significant difference between imipramine and placebo ($p < .1$). However, two further studies with agoraphobics failed to find differences between imipramine and placebo on measures of panic (Marks et al., 1983; Mavissakalian & Michelson, 1986a). Where imipramine has been more effective than placebo, it has always been combined with graded exposure to feared situations. This raises the possibility that imipramine may not have direct antipanic effects, but instead potentiates the effects of self-initiated and/or therapist-initiated graded exposure. Consistent with this suggestion, Telch et al. (1985) found that imipramine had no effect on panic when given in conjunction with counterexposure instructions. However, in the only study to investigate the effects of imipramine in panic disorder (as opposed to agoraphobia with panic), Garakani, Zitrin, and Klein (1984) found that imipramine without the addition of psychological treatment was associated with a marked reduction in panic attacks. This study was a case series and so did not include a placebo control group. Until a study is reported which includes such a group, it will remain unclear whether imipramine has a specific antipanic effect in panic disorder.

TESTING PREDICTIONS DERIVED FROM THE COGNITIVE MODEL

From this review it would appear that the proposed model is consistent with existing research on the nature of panic. This conclusion is encouraging. However, if a model is to be useful it must not only account for existing research but also generate predictions which can be tested by future research. There are three main predictions which can be derived from the cognitive model. These are:

1. Compared with other anxious patients and normal controls, patients who suffer from panic attacks will be more likely to interpret certain bodily sensations in a catastrophic fashion.
2. Pharmacological agents which provoke panic (such as sodium lactate) do so only when the somatic sensations produced by the agent are interpreted in a catastrophic fashion, and the panic-inducing effects of these agents can be blocked by instructional manipulations.
3. Treatments which fail to change a patient's tendency to interpret bodily sensations in a catastrophic fashion will have higher rates of relapse than treatments which succeed in changing those interpretations.

Recently, with the help of colleagues, I have started a program of research which will test these predictions. To date we have completed the two experiments and the results are as predicted. In the first experiment (Clark, Salkovskis, Koehler, & Gelder, 1987) we tested Prediction 1 by comparing panic patients, other anxious patients, and normal controls in terms of the extent to which they are likely to interpret ambiguous events in a negative fashion. Using a questionnaire four types of ambiguous event were presented. These were (a) descriptions of bodily sensations which the cognitive model predicts will be particularly likely to be misinterpreted by panic patients (e.g., "You notice your heart is beating quickly and pounding"); (b) ambiguous social events (e.g., "You have visitors over for a meal and they leave sooner than you expected"); (c) other ambiguous events (e.g., "A member of your family is late arriving home") and (d) descriptions of bodily symptoms which should not be markedly misinterpreted by panic patients (e.g., "You have developed a small spot on the back of your hand"). Consistent with prediction, panic patients were significantly more likely to interpret bodily sensations in a negative fashion than either other anxious patients ($p < .01$) or normal controls ($p < .01$). This result appears to reflect a highly specific cognitive disturbance as panic patients did not differ from other anxious patients in their interpretation of the three other ambiguous events.

This first experiment clearly demonstrates that panic patients are particularly prone to misinterpret certain bodily sensations catastrophically. However, it could be argued that this cognitive style does not play a causal role in the production of panic attacks but instead is epiphenomenal, perhaps arising as a consequence of an individual having experienced repeated attacks. More substantial support for the cognitive model would be provided by experiments in which the bodily sensations characteristic of panic are induced and then patients' interpretations of these sensations are systematically manipulated (Prediction 2).

Voluntary hyperventilation is known to induce panic attacks in some patients

(Clark et al., 1985). Our second experiment (Salkovskis & Clark, 1987) investigated whether manipulating individual's interpretation of hyperventilation-induced sensations would influence the extent to which overbreathing is perceived as pleasant or unpleasant. Once again the results of this experiment were as predicted. Nonpatient, student volunteers who were given a positive interpretation found overbreathing a pleasant experience, while those who were given a negative interpretation found overbreathing an unpleasant experience. The difference in affect experienced by the two groups was highly significant ($p < .001$). Furthermore, consistent with the cognitive hypothesis, correlational analyses indicated that within each instructional group individuals who experienced the strongest bodily sensations also experienced the strongest induced affect. Within the positive instruction group there was a significant correlation between induced bodily sensations and induced positive affect ($r = .6$, $p < .001$); within the negative instruction group there was a significant correlation between bodily sensations and induced negative affect ($r = .74$, $p < .001$). We now plan to follow up these results in a further experiment with panic patients. This experiment will investigate whether it is possible to block the panic-inducing effects of sodium lactate by providing patients with a noncatastrophic interpretation of the bodily sensations induced by lactate.[4] Additional experiments will test Prediction 3.

ACKNOWLEDGMENTS

The author is grateful to the Medical Research Council of the United Kingdom for its support. In addition, he would like to thank Aaron T. Beck, Michael Gelder, Ruth Greenberg, Eric Griez, Elizabeth Knox, Maryanne Martin, David Nutt, Jack Rachman, John Rush, Paul Salkovskis, Martin Seligman and Marcel van den Hout for helpful discussions.

[4]With reference to this experiment, it is encouraging to note that van den Hout (this volume) has already succeeded in demonstrating that cognitive factors can influence *normal* subjects' affective response to lactate. In his experiment, subjects' expectancies of mood change were manipulated prior to lactate infusion. Subjects given a positive expectancy showed a smaller increase in anxiety than subjects given a negative expectancy. This result clearly demonstrates the influence of *a* cognitive factor. However, as expectancies rather than interpretations were manipulated it is not a direct test of Prediction 2.

6

Cognitive Approaches to Panic Disorder: *Theory and Therapy*

Aaron T. Beck, M.D.
University of Pennsylvania

INTRODUCTION

Panic attacks are particularly intriguing for a variety of reasons. First, they illustrate the human tendency to focus attention on internal experiences as a source of information regarding the integrity of vital somatic and psychic functions. In studying conditions such as depression, cognitive investigators have concentrated on the way individuals selectively abstract and construe (or misconstrue) signals from the *environment*. The study of panic attacks (as well as of hypochondriasis and hysteria) has prompted examination of the way individuals process signals originating *within the body*.

In view of the fact that functions such as respiration, circulation, and consciousness are critical for immediate survival, it is not surprising that certain vulnerable individuals will be hypersensitive to any indications that their hearts will stop beating, that they will be unable to catch their breath, or that they will pass out. Further, some patients are particularly fearful of signs that indicate (to them) that they may be losing control over destructive impulses (directed toward themselves or others). Similarly, some patients are especially sensitive to signs of psychological or behavioral dyscontrol because of the projected consequences of being hospitalized for "crazy" behavior, or possibly humiliated for uncontrolled behavior. The patient's fear that a vital organ (e.g., heart, lungs, or brain) or behavioral system is about to cease functioning is an essential component of the cognitive structure of panic attacks. Because of these concerns, panic-prone patients tend to fix their attention on any bodily or mental experiences that are not explicable as normal.

A second feature of panic attacks that poses a challenge to the clinician and presents a gold mine for the cognitive therapist is the fixation of attention on the concept of an impending disaster. The disaster that they fear after the attack starts is not simply the progression of the panic attack, but the possibility of the much graver alternative explanation of their symptoms; namely, that *this time* it may not be the usual panic, but a rapidly fatal process or an acute disruption of mental or behavioral operations. In addition to the fixation on internal sensations, the concept of impending disaster occupies the center of the patient's thinking and is often so vivid that the patient believes that he or she is indeed dying, losing control, or going crazy.

Associated with the attention fixation is an inability (once the panic attack has reached its apogee) to apply reasoning and logic or to draw on past experience or previous knowledge to re-evaluate the symptoms or to examine the frightening concept objectively. This concept of sudden disaster has the properties of a closed or impermeable system that seems to have a life of its own; it becomes autonomous relative to other psychological processes. Having run its inexorable course, it gradually becomes inactive.

Among the questions that are raised by this phenomenon are: Does this fixation represent in a more acute form the kind of "tunnel vision" observed in depression and generalized anxiety disorder? Is the capacity for realistic thinking about the nature of the physical or mental problem lost during the attack? Is there an actual *inhibition* of realistic thinking about the explanation for the symptoms? One can also ponder the possible survival value of an event that is so disruptive and unpleasant.

Another by-product of the study of Panic Disorders is the opportunity to observe the interplay of cognitive and physiological factors. The following observations should promote reformulation of a more comprehensive psychobiological model than is currently available. First, panic attacks can be instigated in susceptible individuals by certain procedures designed to upset the biochemistry of the blood (for example, by hyperventilation, inhalation of carbon dioxide, and infusion with sodium lactate). But attacks can also be triggered by "non-biochemical" events such as imaging a frightening scene, deep relaxation, standing up suddenly (producing hypotension) or a sudden physical jolt (producing chest pain). Further, attacks may be aborted by restoring the biochemical imbalance (by breathing into a paper bag, for example), by an abrupt shift in attention to an external object, or by utilizing the cognitive technique of "rational reappraisal."

What do these facts reveal about the pathopsychophysiology of panic disorders? The most parsimonious explanation is that certain individuals are predisposed both neurophysiologically *and* cognitively to experience panic attacks under specifiable circumstances. The neurophysiological and the cognitive aspects may represent different sides of the same coin. The predisposition may take the form of a chronically increased physiological arousal (in some of the patients), an increased tendency to exaggerate or misconstrue the meaning of certain symptoms, and most likely, an inability to reappraise these misinterpretations realistically.

There appears to be a deficiency in information processing that may be conceptualized either in cognitive or neurochemical terms. The administration of a drug may have a direct effect on information processing in panic cases (in a way similar to that which I have postulated in depression, Beck, 1984) or it may act to damp down the peripheral stimuli that activate the panic mechanism. Interestingly, there is evidence that these drugs alone are not sufficient to reduce or eliminate panic attacks (Telch, this volume). Some input via the information-processing system (through exposure therapy, for example) seems necessary to enable relearning to take hold. The processing of information leading to the panic appears to be automatic.

On the basis of the patients' reports, it appears that much of the corrective processing (reality testing) is also automatic. The modification of a belief that a particular sensation is dangerous can be based on experience alone. Cognitive restructuring does not necessarily require conscious reflection and deliberate correction of erroneous ideas. The utilization of the "higher mental processes," however, is important to prepare the individual to respond to corrective learning experiences as well as to reinforce the modification of the erroneous beliefs.

THE COGNITIVE MODEL

The cognitive model of Panic Disorders is essentially a descriptive model. It is derived from clinical examinations such as that reported in the vignette which follows. In a previous description of panic attacks (Beck, 1976, p. 146), I pointed out the following characteristics of the patient's fear during the attacks.

"From the patient's standpoint, the danger is quite real and plausible. What do we learn if we ask the patient what he is afraid of? At first, he may be so concerned with his anxiety, his peculiar feeling states, and his preoccupations, he may find it difficult to focus on the question. With a minimum of introspection, however, it is possible for the patient to provide the pertinent information. Often, but not always, the acutely anxious patient is overwhelmed by thoughts that he is dying. The fear of dying may be triggered by some unexpected or severe physical sensation. The patient interprets the physical distress as a sign of physical disease, becomes anxious, and a chain reaction is set up."

The basic theses of the cognitive model of panic disorder are as follows:

1. Panic-prone individuals are particularly sensitive to internal sensations (somatic or mental) that do not seem normal.
2. They are particularly prone to be hypervigilant for the experience of these sensations and focus attention on them if they cannot find a nonpathological explanation for them *and* if they may be explainable as a manifesta-

tion of an impending biological (death), mental (insanity or loss of consciousness), or behavioral (loss of control) disaster.

3. The fixation of attention on the panicogenic sensations is involuntary and enhances the patient's concept of an imminent danger which leads to increased activation of the autonomic nervous system.
4. A vicious cycle is created by the interaction between the catastrophic interpretation of sensations and the consequent intensification of anxiety-related symptoms.
5. The next stage which is crucial to the experience of panic, as contrasted to simply severe anxiety, is the loss of the capacity to appraise the symptoms realistically, which is associated with the fixation on the symptoms. At this point, the patient is "scared out of his wits."

This progression of cognitive-affective events does not imply exclusive somatic or psychological causation. Irrespective of the investigator's perspective, the model can serve a variety of purposes: as an aid to diagnosis, as a backdrop for studying the psychological effects of neurochemical events or pharmacological interventions, or as a blueprint for making psychological interventions.

There is considerable controversy regarding the initial processes leading to the panic attack. Although some investigators regard the attacks as spontaneous, it appears that many patients do not report sensations leading to the attack unless they are specifically questioned about them. A number of studies, in fact, have suggested that anxious people may respond to anxiety-related stimuli without being conscious of them. Although the patient may not recognize them, these stimuli in themselves can interfere with carrying out goal-directed activities. Mathews and MacLeod (1986), for instance, have demonstrated how the input of anxiety-related words through the "unattended channel" can selectively intrude on the anxious patient's focus on another task. It is conceivable that in a similar way certain internal stimuli can draw away the panic patient's attention from other tasks—even prior to their consciously recognizing the stimulus—and somewhat disrupt their conscious cognitive processes. This automatic processing of information and consequent redeployment of attention could play a role in the loosening of voluntary control over cognitive processes. This is, the patients are simultaneously forced to process data that previously have been incorrectly categorized as connoting danger and then, as a result of the automatic fixation of attention on the specific internal sensations and the concept of danger, they are hampered from reflectively reappraising the pathogenic nature of the stimuli.

The concept of automatic, nonconscious processing of information has achieved prominence in recent years (Hasher & Zacks, 1979). It is possible that much of the apparent obliviousness of anxiety-prone patients to the activating stimuli may be attributed to the nonconscious nature of the incipient stages of the reactions. There is clinical evidence, for example, that agoraphobics do have specific fears of the "disastrous" consequences of traveling on buses, automobiles, and trains; of being in crowded places; of busy streets, heights, elevators, and escalators (Beck, 1976). On first inquiry, the patients may simply state that they are afraid of these places because they represent the type of situation in which they had experienced panic attacks. When trained to observe their sensations and interpretations, these patients frequently recognize that each situation represents a danger to their physical or mental functioning: closed situations threaten suffocation; buses, cars, trains, and city streets, the risk of being injured or killed; high places and bridges, the danger of falling. Interestingly, the specific fear may be expressed in the type of symptom experienced: fear of suffocating in tightness in the chest and gasping; fear of falling in a faint feeling; and fear of being injured in generalized tightening of the muscles.

It should also be noted that the patients will begin to focus their attention on their bodily sensations when they approach a situation in which they have previously had a panic attack. This *hypervigilance,* in itself, contributes to the vicious cycle in panic attacks: The more the patients focus their attention on these sensations, the stronger the sensations become. When the experience exceeds a certain threshold, the catastrophic misinterpretation occurs. Sometimes, the passing through such as, "Wouldn't it be awful if I had a panic attack here?," may be sufficient to channel the patient's attention to his or her bodily sensations and set the stage for an attack.

EMPIRICAL FINDINGS

The amount of research relevant to the cognitive model of panic is scanty, but the available reports are supportive of the cognitive model. The studies will be reported in terms of the major hypotheses of the model: the catastrophic misinterpretation hypothesis and the cognitive dysfunction hypothesis.

Hypothesis 1: Catastrophic Content of Ideation

In an attempt to pin down the cognitive themes in clinical anxiety and panic attacks, ideational material has been collected from patients with these disorders in a series of studies.

Beck (1970) reported that of 11 patients reported to have free-floating anxiety, all had automatic thoughts and images regarding danger. Beck, Laude, and Bohnert (1974) conducted a study of patients diagnosed as having an anxiety disorder. Themes of danger permeated the cognitions and imagery of all 32 patients. Twenty-eight patients were reported to have acute anxiety (panic) attacks. Since panic disorder was not a category of the DSM–III classification, it is not possible to state how many of the patients would have fulfilled the current criteria of this disorder. However, the cognitive components of the anxiety attacks were essentially the same as those described in panic disorder. Other characteristics, such as rapid onset, severe distress, total disability during the episode, and duration were essentially similar to signs and symptoms observed in panic attacks. In all patients, the images and automatic thoughts associated with the attack revolved around the same type of "catastrophe" reported herein. Eight of these patients, for example, had recurrent, anxiety-associated ideation about dying.

Themes similar to the above were reported by Hibbert (1984b) in his study of generalized anxiety disorder patients. Those patients who had clear-cut panic attacks reported fears centering on physical danger. Those patients without panic attacks primarily had fears of not coping with psychological problems.

In a study by Ottaviani and Beck (1987), the cognitions associated with panic were examined in 30 patients diagnosed as panic disorder according to the *Diagnostic and Statistical Manual of Mental Disorders* (3rd Edition). In all cases, arousal of panic was associated with thoughts and images related to physical and mental catastrophe. The imagery of physical catastrophe included fainting (8 patients), death (3), heart attack (6), loss of breath (2), and choking (1). The images of mental or behavioral catastrophe included loss of control (11) and going crazy (3).

The initial episode of panic was precipitated by either psychosocial stress (17 patients) or physical stress (10). In all of the patients, fixation on somatic or mental experiences triggered panic attacks, even though some attacks initially appeared to occur "out of the blue." These internal experiences were typically instigated by social situations, phobic situations, or being alone, but sometimes occurred as the result of physiological factors such as orthostatic hypotension, exercise, or hypoglycemia. The next step in the genesis of the panic attack was the catastrophic interpretation of these sensations.

In a recent outcome study, to be described subsequently (Sokol–Kessler & Beck, 1987), we found that a wide variety of somatic sensations or psychological states led to the typical catastrophic misinterpretations involved in the genesis of panic attacks. In a random sample of 13 patients who were questioned regarding the onset of their most recent panic attack, only 4 described internal sensations that could be attributed to anxiety. The sensations in the other 9 cases ranged from euphoric excitation, fullness in the abdomen, slowing of breathing, and acute anger, to sudden tearing of the eyes. There was a logical relationship between the precipitating event and the specific sensation. A female patient, for example, heard that her painting was going to be on exhibit in a prestigious gallery. She became extremely excited and was aware of "palpitations of the heart," which she interpreted as a sign of a heart attack. A male patient, upon hearing a relative had died, began to have tears and then had an image of himself crying uncontrollably. He then experienced the typical symptoms of a panic attack.

Many of these patients had believed that their panic attacks were brought on spontaneously. However, once they began to focus on the premonitory symptoms, they recognized some sensation that alarmed them just prior to the attack. Table 6.1 describes the onset of the panic attacks in these 13 patients.

Greenberg (1987) carried out a study to determine the nature of imagery and automatic thoughts when a panic attack was induced. Among the eight patients in which it was possible to induce a panic attack through hyperventilation, the patients had vivid imagery (during the panic attack) with automatic thoughts regarding the typical fears of a physical or mental disaster.

It seems clear from the studies by Beck et al. (1974), Hibbert (1984b), Ottaviani and Beck (1987), and Greenberg (1987) that when there is acute anxiety that is diagnosable as panic, the cognitive content centers on the fear of impending physical, mental, or behavioral disaster. When the patient experiences anxiety but not panic, then the main cognitive theme centers on less immediately threatening problems, such as social relations, performance, and achievement. Similarly, if the fear is of some condition that is not immediately threatening to survival, such as gastrointestinal, musculoskeletal, or kidney disease, panic is less likely to occur.

Another approach to testing the hypothesis regarding the content of the ideation is the administration of standard questionnaires following a panic attack. One study directly addressed the question of whether particular cognitions were associated with relevant sensations during the panic attack. In a study of panic disorder patients, Chambless (personal communication, 1985) extracted three factors with an orthogonal solution. She found, in line with my predictions, that the "frightening body sensations load on the same factors with their related cognitions: e.g., heart palpitations and fear of heart attack." These responses were drawn from two questionnaires that were administered separately: The Chambless Body Sensations Questionnaire and the Agoraphobic Cognitions Questionnaire. The construction and administration of the tests were not formulated so as to suggest to the patients that there might be any particular association of sensation and cognition.

The first factor had 12 items relevant to physical sensations and cognitions regarding a serious medical disorder. Among the sensations were "numb limbs, palpitations, short breath, numb or tingling fingers, dizzy, blurred vision." Among the fearful anticipations were "heart attack, stroke, pass out, tumor, choke to death." For each sensation item there was at least one cognition item in the factor that could be related to the sensation. The second factor had loadings of 10 sensations and cognitions relevant to mental, psychological, or behavioral collapse. Among the sensations were "disoriented," "disconnected," and "wobbly legs." Among the fears were "go crazy, lose control, paralyzed, babble, act foolish, scream, hurt someone." The third factor included sensations relevant to gastrointestinal stimulation, such as "butterflies, knot in the stomach, and nausea." The only cognition loading on this factor was "throw up."

TABLE 6.1
Precipitating External and Internal Events in Panic Attacks (N = 13)

	Precipitating "Events"		
Patient	*Typical External Event*	*"Internal Reaction"*	*Fear*
1	Receiving very good news	Excited; increased heart rate	Losing control; Having heart attack
2	Argument with husband or children	Acutely angry	Losing control; Will harm them
3	Looking down from top of escalator	Dizzy; faint	Losing consciousness
4	Driving	Strange feelings in limbs; mental clouding	Having an epileptic fit
5	Ate a heavy meal very fast	Fullness in abdomen	Having heart attack
6	Ran up flight of stairs	Rapid heartbeat	Having heart attack
7	Going into strange place	"Strange feelings of unreality"	Going crazy
8	Got up suddenly from chair	Feeling faint	Losing consciousness; Having heart attack
9	Lifting heavy object	Pain in chest	Having heart attack
10	Relaxing; dozing	Breathing slowed	Respiratory arrest
11	From hot to cold room	Difficulty breathing (Bronchospasm)	Suffocating
12	Eating food fast	Difficulty in swallowing	Choking to death
13	Hearing about sad event	Eyes begin to tear	Starting to cry uncontrollably and will be humiliated

The notion that it is always the symptoms of *anxiety* that are initially misinterpreted in panic attacks is contradicted by these observations in different patients with panic disorder. Seventeen other patients had symptoms referable to anxiety.

These studies support the hypothesis that panic attacks are characterized by catastrophic ideation associated with fixation on physical or psychological experiences. The studies have investigated this hypothesis through a variety of technical procedures: direct questioning, induction of imagery through forced fantasy technique, induction of imagery through hyperventilation, and use of standardized questionnaire. The convergence of findings point to the importance of the patient's imagery and misinterpretation in the genesis of the panic attack.

Hypothesis 2: Loss of Reappraisal Capability

In addition to regarding their fears as completely plausible, the panic patients in our study (Sokol–Kessler & Beck, 1987) seemed to be incapable of accessing relevant information that could be utilized to neutralize their catastrophic ideation, and thereby modify a panic attack. Panickers are somewhat more successful when the information regarding the nonpathological nature of their sensations is presented to them by another person. When they shift focus from their symptoms and refocus on statements from another person, the corrective information becomes more salient or perhaps, the "closed system" characteristic of panicky thinking becomes more permeable to external information.

In order to investigate this clinical observation, we developed a 16-item scale labeled the Cognitive Dysfunction Inventory (Beck & Sokol–Kessler, 1986). This instrument consisted of statements that patients were asked to rate according to how well each statement described them during the attack. Ratings were made on a 4-point Likert-type scale ranging from "Not At All" (0) to "Completely" (3). Typical items were: (1) "I have difficulty reasoning"; (7) "All I can think of is how I feel"; (13) "I am not able to think objectively about my symptoms." These items were counterbalanced by negatively keyed items such as: (2) "I remain cool-headed"; (6) "I remember others' advice and apply it"; (8) "I am able to focus on the facts." One item was included to test for acquiescence set; namely, "My mind goes blank" (a description that is not characteristic of the panic attack). This inventory was administered prior to treatment and at intervals during treatment to 28 panic disorder patients receiving cognitive therapy. Table 6.2 shows the items and reponse categories in the Cognitive Dysfunction Inventory.

The scores on the Cognitive Dysfunction Inventory (CDI) for the various diagnostic groups were as follows: pretreatment score 38.5; 6 weeks, 27.65; 12 weeks, 19.0. In the category of agoraphobia with panic attacks (n = 5), the scores were essentially similar: 36.4, 27.6, 19.8. For the combined group (N = 28), scores were 38.1, 27.6, and 19.1.

The mean score on "My mind went blank" item was close to zero (indicating the absence of a response set) and therefore should not be included in further calculations. The total mean score of 38.5 for the other 15 items at admission approached the maximum of 45. As the panic attacks diminished in intensity and

TABLE 6.2
Cognitive Dysfunction Inventory: Scoring Key

INSTRUCTIONS: Try to think back to your recent panic attacks and then determine how well each of the statements below seems to describe you at the time of the attack.

When I am having a panic attack . . .

	Not at All	*Slightly*	*Moderately*	*Completely*
1. I have difficulty reasoning.	0	1	2	3
2. I remain coolheaded.	3	2	1	0
3. My mind goes blank.	0	1	2	3
4. I can think clearly about what is happening to me.	3	2	1	0
5. I can examine my fears realistically.	3	2	1	0
6. I remember others' advice and apply it.	3	2	1	0
7. All I can think of is how I feel.	0	1	2	3
8. I am able to focus on the facts.	3	2	1	0
9. I think of a variety of solutions.	3	2	1	0
10. I imagine the worst.	0	1	2	3
11. I can distract myself.	3	2	1	0
12. My mind does not function normally.	0	1	2	3
13. I am not able to think objectively about my symptoms.	0	1	2	3
14. I picture frightening things that could happen to me.	0	1	2	3
15. I am able to apply logic to my problem.	3	2	1	0
16. I can't think straight.	0	1	2	3

frequency, these scores diminished. When the scores dropped below 19, the patients no longer regarded the episodes as full-blown panic attacks but looked at them either as "miniattacks" or aggravation of ordinary anxiety. At this point, the scores dropped to zero.

In order to determine whether the cognitive dysfunction was specifically characteristic of panic disorders or was typical of episodes of acute anxiety, a comparison of CDI scores was made between panic disorder patients and 10 patients with generalized anxiety disorder (GAD) with episodes of acute anxiety. We found that the 25 panic patients scored significantly higher (M = 38.2) than did the GAD patients (M = 28.2).

From the standpoint of the impact of our treatment program, scores on the CDI were consistent with the patients' personal records of a decrease in the frequency and intensity of the panic attacks. All of the patients showed substantial improvement by 12 weeks.

We may find for panic attacks, as in delusions, that there is a disruption or loss of reality testing of the *idée fixe*. When the channels for appraising reality are reopened (via administration of drugs or input of corrective information) the patient is enabled to learn at the most fundamental level that his or her catastrophic thinking is incorrect. For example, habituation due to repeated administration of agents (such as sodium lactate or carbon dioxide), or desensitization as a result of repeated exposure to threatening stimuli, may involve cognitive restructuring. The patient learns through repeated experiences of the sensations produced by exogenous agents that these bodily sensations are not signals of impending disaster. Durable effects from drugs, such as imipramine or alprazolam, cannot be expected in all cases, especially if the action of the drugs is only to reduce arousal. In any event, the utilization of drugs and/or psychological-behavioral interventions plus the assessment of cognitive and physiological changes can expand our understanding of how we interpret stimuli, form beliefs, utilize corrective information, and test reality. In this way the functioning of our complex mental apparatus can be revealed by studying its aberrations.

A feature of the mental functioning that appears to be delineated by panic is the dissociation between reflective, directed thinking and automatic "reflexive" processing (Hasher & Zacks, 1979). *Reflective* processing, which ordinarily can serve as a check on *reflexive* processing, is immobilized as it were. Only when attention is diverted from the concept of impending disaster (as a result of application of various distraction techniques) does the higher mental function become operative again. The learning or unlearning that occurs with desensitization seems to modify these automatic processes. Even the educative maneuvers (e.g., demonstrating to the patients that they can control the attack, that their somatic experiences are due to normal physiological changes, etc.) seem to work by preparing or priming automatic channels to respond to corrective experience. Without the actual exposure, all of the preliminary *briefing* about the actual mechanics of the attack, repeated *instigation* of the symptoms, and finally *debriefing* following exposure regarding the meaning of the attack, can serve to recalibrate the automatic mechanisms.

My focus on the cognitive processes leads to a tentative thesis: The necessary condition for a panic attack is the dissociation of the higher-level reflective processes from the automatic cognitive processing. The essential feature of the panic attack is not the physiobiological activation, since some patients have panic attacks when pulse and respiration are normal (Barlow, this volume).

The various therapeutic maneuvers which we will describe can be viewed as quasi-experiments to test the theory outlined previously. Although we do not have empirical data regarding the efficacy of each maneuver, we have clinical information suggesting that each contributes in some way.

The role of fearful appraisal of the symptoms can be gauged by the apparent benefit of re-education (for example, in demonstrating that the patient can instigate the attack by overbreathing, vigorous exercise, or imaging a catastrophe; that the induced symptoms are the same as or similar to those experienced during a spontaneous attack; and that the attack can be terminated). The patient changes his or her belief of the pathogenic nature of the symptoms. This change can be measured by various instruments (e.g., the Cognitive Dysfunction Inventory) used to assess cognitive appraisal of symptoms.

TREATMENT OF PANIC DISORDERS

Our standard treatment of panic attacks falls within the framework of the cognitive model. The main thrust is the demonstration to the patients, by using their own experiences, that the panicogenic sensations are not dangerous. We presume that part of the learning is automatic (as in exposure therapy) and part is conscious (as in re-education therapy). The formal treatment program consists of several steps:

The patient first receives a course of instruction regarding the nature of panic attacks and a specific reeducation regarding his or her own particular set of symptoms and his interpretations of them. In this way the patient is prepared to restructure cognitively the interpretation of the sensations preceding the attack. (It is important before proceeding with cognitive therapy to determine through appropriate medical procedures that the patient's symptoms are *not* indicative of some underlying physical pathology.)

Agoraphobic patients may wait until they have mastered the new information and the techniques before going into the agoraphobic situation. The patients with "spontaneous Panic Disorder" need to be prepared in advance for the unexpected occurrence of the episode. As they become more aware of the typical premonitory sensations that precede an attack (the prodromal symptoms), they can apply various techniques to head off the attack—provided that terminating the attack is the goal at this stage of the therapy.

Outline of Treatment Procedures

Patients who have received cognitive therapy for this disorder state that they are able to abort or "short out" the panic attack by applying certain techniques as soon as they recognize the warning signs. They report that they are able to "tell" themselves that the symptom (e.g., shortness of breath, fullness in abdomen, faintness) is not a sign of an impending disaster. Also, they find that they can successfully distract themselves, for example, by engaging actively in conversation. Applying relaxation or controlled breathing techniques further diminishes the sense of impending disaster. Most patients are able to employ all of these methods.

In the preparation period, the patients are provided with a more realistic interpretation of their frightening body sensations. They learn, for example, that sudden faintness (if that is their problem) may be due to a faulty adjustment of the blood pressure mechanism to a change in posture. Also, the therapist may explain that hyperventilation can be an innocuous reaction to stress, or demonstrate that chest pain is due to tension in the intercostal muscles.

The next phase is the patients' acquisition of various techniques for dealing with the panic disorder itself. The first therapeutic component is *exploration* with the patient of the specific frightening phenomena experienced during the incipient and full-blown attack. The patient's specific thoughts, meanings, interpretations, and images are elicited retrospectively (recollection of previous attacks) and prospectively. Fortified by the knowledge that their ideation about the pathological nature of their experience is erroneous, the patients can *reappraise* their specific interpretations and images. If the patient experiences tightness in the chest, for example, and ascribes this to a coronary attack or to imminent cessation of breathing, he can tell him/herself that it simply is a tightness of the muscles in the rib cage (if he can indeed demonstrate that this is the case) and not a sign of serious abnormality.

The application of *relaxation* techniques is generally useful only in the incipient stage of the panic attack. At this point, the relaxation itself may reduce the symptom, such as tightness of the chest or abdominal pain, and therefore assure the patient that it is not pathological. On the other hand, if the patient is experiencing faintness or is already totally preoccupied with the notion of sudden death, then the relaxation may undermine his or her ability to deal effectively with the problem. Some patients find that a panic attack can be precipitated by relaxation. One young man, for example, noted that his breathing and heart rate slowed down when he was about to fall asleep. He became fearful that his breathing would continue to slow down until it stopped completely. At this point he was likely to have a panic attack.

Another effective technique, particularly for those patients whose attacks seem to be brought on by hyperventilation, is training in *breathing techniques*. The patient may be given a breathing tape to listen to and then learn to time his or her breathing according to the instructions on the tape. This breathing exercise ostensibly works by reducing the blowing off of carbon dioxide. Related to the use of the breathing technique is the utilization of a method to restore the acid-base balance by rebreathing carbon dioxide. This restoration is accomplished by having the patient breathe into a paper bag.

Distraction techniques are a third method of treatment. Depending on the individual and the situation, a wide variety of techniques of varying usefulness are used. In a social situation, for example, the patient may benefit by becoming actively engaged in conversation with other people as he begins to experience the symptoms of panic. He or she attempts to break his fixation on his or her sensations by focusing attention on nearby objects. Above all, it is important that the patient become physically active. Some patients benefit from working on a puzzle; others do well by becoming actively engaged in a task, such as writing a description of the experience.

Induction of "Minipanic Attacks"

Reproduction of the symptoms of the panic attack in the therapist's office is a central component of our treatment, following Clark (this volume). This procedure enables the therapist to obtain a direct report of the patient's thinking processes as the attack develops and gives the patient first-hand instructions for dealing with the attack. It takes a combination of ingenuity and trial-and-error to instigate the symptoms of an attack in the office. Basically, it is important to reproduce the type of situation that can precipitate an attack. In about 60% of the patients, hyperventilation itself is sufficient to initiate a miniattack.

Once the attack has started, the patient is instructed in following a sequence consisting of breathing more regularly and more slowly, using the bag for rebreathing, distraction, and reappraising the significance of his or her symptoms. Patients learn that they can turn off as well as turn on an attack. The increased sense of control reduces their sense of vulnerability and consequently reduces susceptibility to full-blown attacks.

For patients who are alarmed by a rapid heart rate, a miniattack may be induced by jumping up and down for a few minutes or running up a flight of stairs. The patient is then (a) given a relaxation exercise, (b) shown how to distract him/herself, and (c) prompted to reinterpret the symptoms. Sometimes induced imagery can be utilized to induce a miniattack. The vivid visualization of a scene that is specifically frightening to a patient may be sufficient to produce frightening sensations that lead to the panic cycle. Since most patients do not experience a full-blown attack in the office, it is useful to enhance the experience of the symptoms by asking the patient to focus on bodily sensations (Clark, this volume).

In cases of agoraphobia, it is important to determine those external aspects of the agoraphobic situation that trigger unpleasant sensations initially: a sense of being crowded in a bus or subway; a feeling of strangeness in a large, open place, like an auditorium or a supermarket; some mental disorientation induced by the long, horizontal dimensions of the aisles, lanes, or corridors of public places. It is also important for the patient to undergo a series of practice sessions in the office to build him/herself up for going into the supermarket or other public place and staying there for a period of time.

Ultimately, it is crucial for the patients to learn not only to cut off the panic attacks, but to experience them. In this way, they can consolidate the new belief that the panic attack is not a serious threat to their physical or mental viability.

This consolidation can be accomplished through having the patients imagine—as vividly as possible while in the office—the experience of entering the frightening place (cognitive rehearsal).

Graded Exposure

It should be emphasized that after the preliminary ''training sessions'' in the office, it is essential to utilize the techniques and new information in situations that are likely to produce a panic attack. It is important to go through the entire experience of panic attacks. At this point, panickers should be discouraged from using techniques, such as distraction, to abort the attack. The therapist needs to explain that in order to learn fully that a panic attack is not dangerous, the patients have to undergo the complete experience. The therapist also explains that their panic attacks prior to treatment did not result in new learning because the patient did not have a solid framework to reinterpret the symptoms. With the new framework, however, the panic symptoms can be reconceptualized and a stable recovery from the disorder facilitated.

One of the major merits of the office induction of panic attacks is the opportunity it provides for therapist and patient to test many of the assumptions regarding the panic, such as its uncontrollability, inexorability, and catastrophic implications. The successful use of the rebreathing bag undermines the notion of uncontrollability; the inexorability construct is counteracted by successful application of relaxation techniques in the incipient or prodromal period; and the catastrophic construct is negated by the successful use of cognitive restructuring through the re-education period, rational responses, and exposure therapy.

The induced attack, in summary, is valuable from many standpoints. First, it enables the therapist to observe first-hand the actual behavior of the patients and to hear their description of the episode and their report of automatic thoughts and images. Second, it provides an opportunity for the therapist to coach the patient in various techniques developed to terminate an attack: distraction, relaxation, rebreathing, reevaluation of symptoms, reasoning with automatic thoughts. Finally, the induced attack enables the patient to practice these techniques in preparation for applying them to in vivo attacks. The patient, consequently, is primed to meet his panic attacks head on whether they occur spontaneously or in the context of particular situations.

The stages in treating panic disorders are outlined in Table 6.3.

The graded exposure for agoraphobics follows the same principles outlined by behavior therapists such as Barlow (this volume) and Chambless and Goldstein (1982). In addition, patients are expected to track their automatic thoughts and images and report them to the therapist, who generally accompanies the patient for the first few trials. The in vivo practice of the techniques is particularly useful when the therapist rides in the car with the patient who is afraid of having an attack when driving.

Antiavoidance Program: Patients who have panic attacks without agoraphobia are still prone to avoid situations that have precipitated panic attacks in the

TABLE 6.3
Steps in Treating Panic Disorders

1.	Explanation of the nonpathological nature of symptoms.
2.	Reappraisal of the panicogenic sensations and of the idiosyncratic meanings and interpretations.
3.	Eliciting automatic thoughts and images asssociated with attack.
4.	Enhancement and re-evaluation of symptoms and responding to automatic thoughts.
5.	Relaxation, breathing exercises.
6.	Induction of miniattacks in office by hyperventilation, exercise, imagery, etc.
7.	Distraction.
8.	Systematic exposure.
9.	Use of flash cards.

past—for example, confrontations with family members, strenuous exercises, sitting in the middle of a row in a theater, being alone overnight. The panicogenic situations are not as concrete as in the case of the agoraphobics, and panic attacks can occur in any geographical locale. The panicogenic situations are characterized by their ability to induce sensations that are interpreted as a sign of danger. Consequently, the therapist identifies the situations, and with the patient, sets up a schedule of "mastery experiences"—exposure to the situation plus utilization of the standard cognitive techniques.

Outcome Study

Becuase of the newness of the cognitive approach to panic disorders, outcome studies have been undertaken only recently. Clark (this volume) reported two studies of successful outcome using a specific focus on the catastrophic misinterpretations of bodily sensations.

Sokol–Kessler and Beck (1987) have reported the results of the cognitive program outlined in this chapter in two studies. In the first study, 25 patients with the primary diagnosis of panic disorder were divided into two groups: those without personality disorders ($n = 18$) and those with personality disorders ($n = 7$). The former group, who came to treatment primarily for panic disorder, had a range of 10 to 30 weeks of treatment with a mean of 17 weeks. Typically, the patients were seen weekly for about 12 weeks and were then seen several times at biweekly intervals. The patients with personality disorders requested treatment for their personality and situational problems, in addition to the panic-oriented treatment. Treatment for this group of patients ranged from 14 to 44 weeks with a mean of 30 weeks. For the entire sample, the mean was 32.

Combining the no-personality-disorder group with the personality-disorder

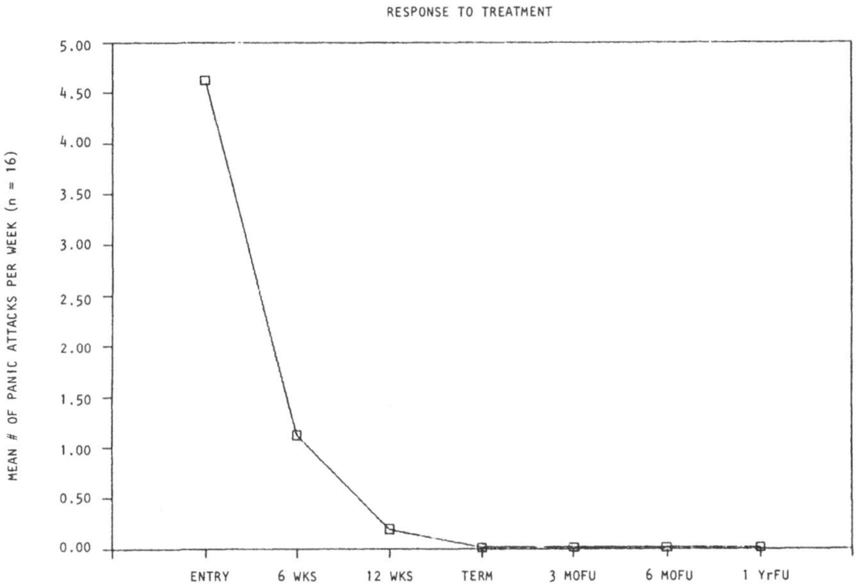

FIG. 6.1. Mean number of panic attacks per week.

group yields a total of 16 patients that have been followed for 1 year post treatment termination. The number of panic attacks per week reduced significantly from a mean of 4.62 panic attacks per week at intake, 1.12 at 6 weeks, and .19 at 12 weeks, and then to 0 upon termination. The complete remission continued at all follow-up points as shown in figure 6.1. There were no drop outs from treatment or follow-up.

A one-way repeated measures ANOVA showed the changes in panic frequency significantly changed over time with treatment (F (6,90) = 10.76, $p < .000$). These findings were supported by a Greenhouse-Geisser statistic (G-G (6, 90) = .1747, $p < .004$), which takes into account nonhomogeneity of variance. All univariate contrasts were also significant.

In the second study the effectiveness of cognitive therapy in the treatment of panic disorder was assessed in a *controlled* outcome study. Patients were randomly assigned to either (a) cognitive therapy, consisting of 12 weekly individual meetings with a trained cognitive therapist (n = 13) or (b) brief supportive therapy, consisting of 8 weeks of monitoring symptoms and brief weekly supportive therapy with a trained therapist (n = 16).

In the cognitive therapy group, the number of panic attacks per week was reduced significantly from a mean of 5.06 per week at intake, .71 at 4 weeks, .31 at 8 weeks, and 0 at 12 weeks (termination). At this time, 13 patients had completed 8 weeks of cognitive therapy and 7 had finished 12

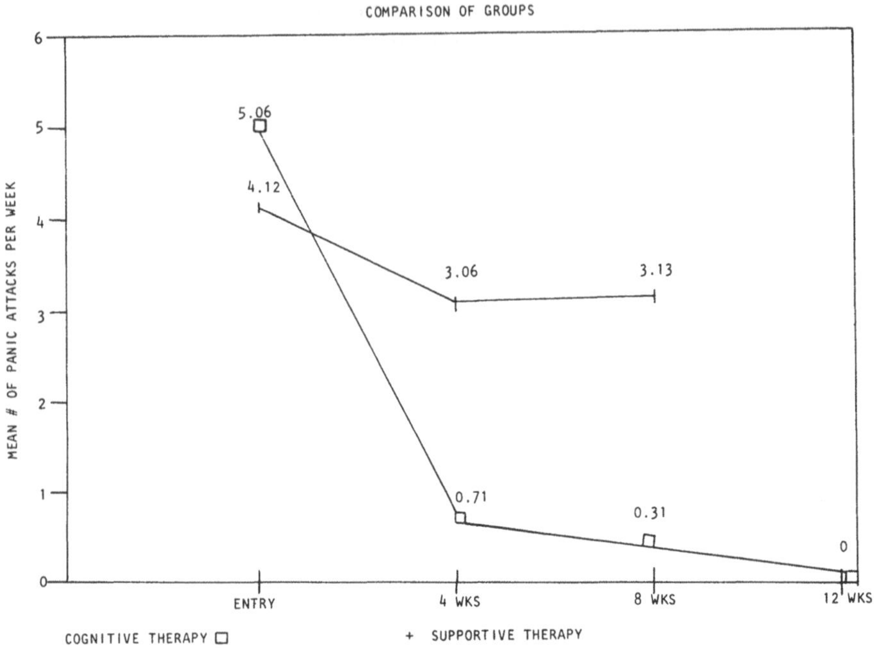

FIG. 6.2. Study 2: Response to treatment.

weeks. In the brief supportive therapy condition, the mean number of panic attacks per week were 4.12 at intake, 3.06 at 4 weeks, and 3.13 at 8 weeks. 16 patients had completed 8 weeks of brief supportive therapy (see Figure 6.2). There were no dropouts in either group.

A two-way repeated measure ANCOVA was performed in order to determine whether changes in panic frequency were significantly different for the two groups over the course of treatment. Covarying out pretest mean panic scores showed a significant superiority in reduction of panic attacks in the cognitive therapy group (F (1,26) = 12.26, $p < .001$).

In summary, in both an "open" and a controlled clinical trial, patients treated with cognitive therapy showed a complete remission of symptoms at the end of treatment and follow-up.

SUMMARY

A cognitive model of panic attacks is described. The model is based on the clinical observation that panic-prone patients are particularly sensitive to the experience of any physical sensation or mental state that they cannot dismiss as normal. Panickers are disposed to fix their attention and to apply a catastrophic interpretation to such sensations of states. When they begin to fear an impending disaster, they seem to lose the ability to apply reason or prior information to neutralize or correct misinterpretations of their sensations. Systematic study of automatic thoughts and images, as well as of descriptions of their cognitive dysfunctions, support this observation.

The treatment of panic disorder consists of several steps. The patients are initially briefed on the nature of the panic attacks, the specific quality of their bodily sensations or psychological state just prior to the attack, and their catastrophic interpretations and imagery regarding the meaning of these sensations. They learn to recognize and reality-test their automatic thoughts and images regarding these sensations. When possible, the symptoms of the panic attack are reproduced in the office so that the patient can learn how to restructure their significance. Relaxation techniques are also taught to forestall an attack and distraction techniques to terminate it. Finally, the patients are induced to expose themselves to a full-blown attack in vivo and apply their therapeutic technique to restructure the panic.

A preliminary study of 25 patients with panic disorder indicates that these methods have a robust effect on the frequency of panic attacks. All of the patients reported a total elimination of panic attacks by the end of treatment. This improvement persisted for 6 months posttreatment in those patients who had already completed treatment and entered the follow-up phase.

7

Phenomenology, Assessment, and the Cognitive Model of Panic

Paul M. Salkovskis
University of Oxford

Phenomenology and assessment are closely linked in function. Research into the comparative phenomenology of particular disorders may serve to generate working hypotheses about the nature of the conditions being investigated because general phenomena more characteristic of one disorder than another can be identified. Such work should lead to the formulation of hypotheses regarding the etiology and maintainance of the disorder, and hence to treatment strategies. On the other hand, the main function of assessment is to identify the presence and probable importance of variables which may be involved in the etiology or maintainance of a disorder (or both) for any particular patient. This allows the clinician to formulate individualized treatment goals and tactics. In this way, there is an intimate link between phenomenology, theoretical models, and the processes of assessment and treatment. Two other chapters in this volume have examined more general aspects of phenomenology and assessment of panic (Barlow & Craske, this volume; Turner, Beidel, & Jacob, this volume). This chapter will consider aspects of phenomenology and assessment of panic attacks and panic disorder which have implications for the cognitive model, described by Clark (1986a) and Salkovskis and Clark (1986a).

Understanding the phenomenology of a particular disorder involves the examination of descriptive and experimental studies. Similarly, cognitive-behavioral assessment commonly involves descriptive information provided by the patient, gathering observational data and carrying out systematic experimental manipulation of variables thought to be important in particular individuals. Functional analysis, in which the primary intention is assessment for treatment, may thus generate useful information relevant to a more general understanding of the disorder. Examples of this are to be found in our own work on panic, when assessments (carried out in the context of routine clinical treatment of panic patients) have helped illuminate specific facets of the cognitive model (Salkovskis, Clark, & Jones, 1986; Salkovskis, Warwick, Clark, & Wessels, 1986).

There are a number of general considerations which affect phenomenological studies of panic. Most research into panic is based on the analysis of different patient (diagnostic) groups. It has recently been shown that some patients in all of the anxiety categories in the third edition of the *Diagnostic and Statistical Manual* (DSM–III; American Psychiatric Association, 1980) suffer from panic attacks and generalized anxiety (Barlow, Blanchard, Vermilyea, Vermilyea, & DiNardo, 1986; Barlow et al. 1985). Comparison between Panic Disorder patients and other diagnostic categories can be misleading, because nonpanic groups may include patients who are having panic attacks. A solution is to use DSM–III criteria to define diagnostic groupings, but also to require the absence of panic for at least the previous 6 months in nonpanic control groups. Panic patients can also be subdivided on the basis of their recent frequency of panic. A completely different approach is to examine factors which influence panic within subject. This type of research has the additional virtue of producing information which can be particularly applicable to psychological assessment and treatment strategies in clinical practice (also dependent on within subject analyses). A good example of within subject investigation of panic in a normal population is provided by Rachman (this volume).

Investigation of the difference between panic, as opposed to other anxiety disorders, is crucial for both psychological and biological models. In particular, the biological model is based on the notion that panic is qualitatively different from other forms of anxiety. This chapter will examine the phenomenological evidence relevant to such an hypothesized distinction, and consider the likely nature of the complex interaction between cognitive and physiological factors in panic. In order to integrate phenomenology and assessment within the framework of a cognitive model of panic, the relevant studies and concepts are considered from a tripartite (cognitive/physiological/behavioral) view. In the conclusion, specific aspects of the cognitive model relevant to research and assessment are identified.

IS PANIC QUALITATIVELY DISTINCT?

The extent to which panic, as it is presently defined, can be regarded as a unique phenomenon or set of phenomena distinct from other forms of anxiety (e.g., anticipatory or phobic) has, rightly or wrongly, become central to the debate between advocates of biological and psychological approaches. Biological models of panic are firmly based on the closely related arguments that panic represents a discrete and therefore pathological endogenous process, and that panic is relatively impervious to environmental influence and requiring biochemical cor-

TABLE 7.1
Scores of Panic and Other Anxious Patients on Spielberger STAI (State)

Patient Group	*Anxious Controls*	*Panic (n)*
Butler	49 (19)	60 (21) $p < 0.05$
Present group	45.1 (20)	53.2 (20) $p < 0.05$
Student norms	40.01 (334)	

rection. Of course, a possible explanation of the apparent distinctness of panic found in some group studies would be that DSM–III operational definitions result in the selection of groups differing in the very characteristics specified by these definitions. Panic attacks are explicitly defined as sudden onset, discrete, and accompanied by at least four intense somatic sensations. When such diagnostic criteria are used, considerable care is needed to ensure that results do not reflect directly associated characteristics (criterion contamination). For example, panic patients selected on the basis of DSM–III criteria will show a more rapid increase of anxiety during periods of heightened anxiety than other anxious patients. Some, although not all, of the differences noted between groups may be due to selection criteria.

The simplest psychological hypothesis which could account for the phenomenon of panic attacks is that panic anxiety might simply represent particularly severe episodes of general anxiety. As we have described, the presence or absence of acute somatic sensations may be accounted for by DSM–III diagnostic criteria themselves, so that data relevant to this issue must not depend solely on the report of body sensations. We have noted a significant difference in self-reported anxiety (measured by the state version of the State-Trait Anxiety Inventory (STAI; Spielberger, Gorsuch, & Lushene, 1970) between panic disorder, compared with a control group of anxious patients (Table 7.1). In a study evaluating a treatment for general anxiety, (Butler, Cullington, Hibbert, Klimes, & Gelder, in press) data were collected on state and trait anxiety scores of PD and generalized anxiety disorder (GAD) patient groups. Once again PD patients scored significantly higher on state anxiety, despite the groups not being significantly different on trait anxiety scores.[1] These differences may occur because it is relatively more likely that PD patients will have experienced an episode of severe anxiety on the day of or days preceding testing. Margraf, Ehlers, and Roth (1986) review data showing that there are differences in resting anxiety and physiological arousal between panic patients and controls. The results of studies carried out on self-reported anxiety levels of PD, compared with other anxious patients do not exclude the possibility that panic simply represents a particularly

[1]I am most grateful to Gillian Butler for her kind permission to use this data.

severe form of general anxiety. Studies intended to investigate possible qualitative differences in panic must either employ strategies which allow the effects of general anxiety to be controlled, or they must demonstrate effects which run counter to such an influence.

Anderson, Noyes, and Crowe (1984) and Rapee (1985) reported that GAD has a significantly earlier age of onset than PD; Anderson et al. also report a more chronic course in GAD. Rapee reports a preponderance of sudden onset in PD and gradual onset in GAD. It is most unlikely that such results could be explained by PD patients being more anxious than GAD patients. These findings are most consistent with the suggestion of Barlow et al. (1986) that GAD might represent a problem characterized by chronic patterns of concern about life circumstances. Other data show that the cognitions typical of panic concern the possibility of immediate personal catastrophe, as opposed to cognitions in generalized anxiety which are more likely to involve unpleasant negative, but non-catastrophic, circumstances at some more distant point in the future. These differences, which do not reflect differences in state anxiety, are discussed further in the section on cognitions.

Relationship between Panic and Hyperventilation

One of the most frequently discussed observations with respect to the phenomenology of panic relates to the pattern of somatic symptoms reported by patients who experience panic attacks. In particular, a number of workers have noted similarities between patients who panic and patients who have repeated episodes of hyperventilation (defined as breathing in excess of metabolic requirements). Such observations raise the interesting possibility that panic may be distinct because it is specifically associated with hyperventilation. Similarities have been noted in terms of symptoms reported, physiological function at rest, sensitivity to respiratory changes, and respiratory changes under stress and when panicking (Clark, 1979; Kerr, Dalton, & Gliebe, 1937; Lum, 1976; Rapee, 1986; Salkovskis & Clark, 1986a). Furthermore, there is evidence (Clark et al., 1985; Kopp, Mihaly, Tringer, & Vadasz, 1986; Salkovskis, Jones, & Clark, 1986) that treatments which include components of breathing control are effective in the treatment of panic (although it has not been established that breathing control is the effective component). Rather than indicating a causal effect, these reports of low CO_2 may simply show that respiratory changes can arise from severe anxiety (Seuss, Alexander, Smith, Sweeney, & Marion, 1980). It is certainly true that hyperventilation is neither necessary nor sufficient for panic to occur; on the other hand, acute respiratory change of the magnitude measured in panic patients (Salkovskis & Clark, 1986a) is normally associated with the range of somatic sensations which accompany respiratory alkalosis.

If hyperventilation is involved in the origin or maintainance of panic in some patients as seems likely (Salkovskis & Clark, 1986a), is there any evidence of a qualitative difference in respiratory function (hyperventilation syndrome) in panic patients (e.g., Garssen, van Veenendaal, & Bloemink, 1983)? Alternatively, should respiratory changes be regarded as part of normal pychophysiological responding to stress (Seuss et al., 1980)? Put in another way, is the respiratory function of panic patients qualitatively different from persons who do not experience panic, or should respiration simply be regarded as a system which is particularly likely to have effects on other psychological and physiological responses? A cognitive-psychophysiological response model, in which changes in respiration as a response to physiological or psychological challenge lead to increases in perceived bodily sensations which, if interpreted in a catastrophic fashion, result in further bodily sensations and hyperventilation, and so on, round in a vicious circle culminating in a panic attack. This type of incrementation through the interaction of cognitive and physiological mechanisms is most consistent with the data on the association between hyperventilation and panic. Hyperventilation is neither necessary nor sufficient for the occurrence of panic, but appears to play an important role in a proportion of panic attacks. This is is considered in greater detail in the section describing physiological correlates of panic.

Differential Response to Treatment

Turner and his coworkers (this volume) point out that there is a logical fallacy inherent in the proposal that differential response to treatment *between* patient groups reflects fundamental differences in processes. However, if psychological treatments specifically intended to reduce anxiety differentially affect panic but not general anxiety *within subjects* then the argument that panic represents a more severe form of anxiety would be considerably weakened. Waddel, Barlow, and O'Brien (1984) presented data which they interpreted as showing a reduction in panic, independent of any reduction in general anxiety, indicating that specificity in response to treatment does occur. Our own data suggest that both panic attacks and general anxiety do respond to a cognitively based treatment (See Fig. 7.1). This finding has since been independently replicated (Kopp et al., 1986). The effects of treatment within subjects, therefore, are not inconsistent with the view that panic is a more severe form of anxiety.

A POSSIBLE DIMENSIONAL BASIS OF PANIC

As already described, biological models of panic as presently formulated are predicated on the view that panic *qualitatively* rather than quantitatively distinct from severe anxiety, and that such distinctness is an indication of "disordered physiologic mechanisms divorced from cognitions" (Lesser & Rubin, 1986). On the first of these points, data already reviewed do not rule out the possibility that

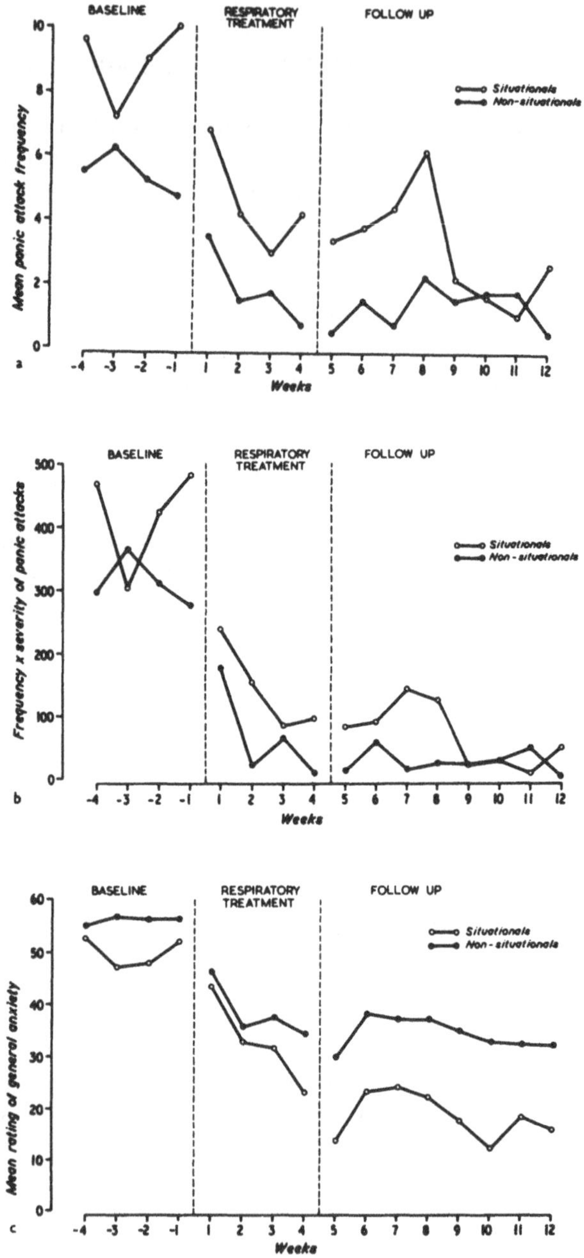

FIG. 7.1. Self-ratings (from patients' daily diary) of panic frequency, general anxiety, and panic severity × frequency for situational and nonsituational groups in the second treatment study. The period marked "respiratory control" is the period during which cognitive treatment in which reattribution of panic symptoms to respiratory factors was carried out. Counterexposure instructions were given during the respiratory control period; during follow-up, graded exposure was added where appropriate. (From Salkovskis, Jones, & Clark 1986 p. 529; reproduced with permission.)

panic simply represents a severe form of anxiety; indeed, there is some support for this view (Table 7.1). However, even if it is possible to identify unique phenomenological aspects of panic, the implied specific abnormality of panic is not consistent with two further observations: (1) Panic is prevalent in almost all anxiety disorders and in depression (Barlow et al., 1985); (2) Panic occurs frequently in nonclinic populations (Norton, Dorward, & Cox, 1986; Norton, Harrison, Hauch, & Rhodes, 1985; Wittchen, 1986). A broad view of all the evidence is consistent with the hypothesis that clinical panic represents the extreme of a normal distribution. The simplest dimension which could underly such a distribution would be: Calmness ⇒⇒ Anxiety ⇒⇒ Panic. The distribution of panic in normal and clinical populations would reflect the degree to which individuals reacted along such a dimension at any particular time.

However, this dimension cannot account for a number of important observations: for instance, panic occurring during relaxation, the ineffectiveness of most benzodiazepines in the treatment of panic and the effectiveness of biochemical methods of provoking panic. Furthermore, there are data concerning the cognitive correlates of panic which do suggest a qualitative distinction from general anxiety (Clark, this volume; see also the "cognitions" section). When PD and GAD patients are asked what goes through their mind when anxiety is at its most severe, panic patients are more likely to report having thoughts of serious physical or mental harm, while generally anxious patients are more likely to have thoughts concerning negative outcomes in terms of social behavior or general coping under pressure.

The cognitive model was devised to account for these and other observations (Clark, 1986a; this volume). It is based on the idea that panic results from the perception and catastrophic misinterpretation of bodily sensations which often, but not always, result from autonomic arousal. This misinterpretation in turn increases anxiety and results in further bodily sensations which are misinterpreted catastrophically, and so on, in a vicious circle. This model forms the basis for a more comprehensive dimensional view. Panic arises from a tendency to perceive and interpret bodily sensations in a catastrophic fashion. This tendency in turn might be influenced by previous experience of illness in self or others, beliefs and assumptions regarding the nature of bodily sensations, physical state, and mood. The cognitive dimension would therefore be:

Tends to interpret bodily sensations as benign	⇒	Slight Tendency to over interpret bodily sensations as catastrophic	⇒	Tends to interpret bodily sensations as catastrophic
⇓		⇓		⇓
No Panic	⇒ ⇒	Infrequent/ Mild Panic	⇒ ⇒	Frequent/ Severe Panic

Norton et al. (1986) evaluated the characteristics of panic experienced by normal subjects not seeking treatment, who the cognitive model predict should fall in the middle of such a dimension. They report that normal panickers differ from patients

> in the severity with which they experience fears of dying, going crazy, or doing something uncontrolled during a panic attack. Barlow et al.'s (1985) patients report the "fears" symptom as being second only to palpitations in severity. Our subjects rated the "fears" symptoms as sixth most severe. (Norton et al., 1986)

The cognitive model also needs to account for the tendency for increases in general anxiety to result in panic. The most consistent explanation would be that general anxiety or worry contributes to panic to the extent that the autonomic symptoms associated with this anxiety are interpreted catastrophically (as opposed to being understood by the patient as innocuous symptoms of anxiety). That is, individuals experiencing anxiety often experience a variety of somatic sensations. Usually, they are aware that these are part of the anxiety response and are able to interpret symptoms in these terms. However, increased anxiety predisposes to negative interpretations by altering the perception of threat (Butler & Mathews, 1983). This means that, when someone is generally anxious, a number of unpleasant bodily sensations will be experienced at a time when negative interpretations are at their most acessible, and panic is therefore more likely to result. In some instances this occurs despite initially accurate attribution of sensations to anxiety. For example, a typical thought in generally anxious patients who do develop panic is "I've been anxious for so long that the stress has damaged my heart, which is why it is pounding so much; it may fail completely."

According to the proposed cognitive model, the panic continuum may be identified as a vulnerability to forming ideas about the imminence of catastrophic circumstances which are based on the misinterpretation (misattribution) of bodily or mental sensations. These sometimes arise as a result of the experience of anxiety (Beck, this volume; Clark, 1986a; this volume), but may also come from other sources (e.g., exercise, caffeine). A further distinguishing feature of panic is that bodily sensations are not only misattributed to imminent catastrophic internal events (for instance, cardiac sensations interpreted as symptoms of an impending heart attack), but also that perceived changes in arousal resulting from such interpretations may function to reinforce the worry itself ("the sensations are getting more severe, and I'm becoming dizzy and breathless as well"). This important difference between the mechanisms involved in panic and general anxiety allows us to dispense with poorly specified incubation/incrementation models, and instead allows the simple proposition that the degree of anxiety experienced is proportional to the perceived probability and "awfulness" of anticipated danger. There is a quantitative difference in the amount of anxiety provoked by the perception that one will offend a friend as opposed to the idea that you are about to die *within the next few seconds.*[2] Moreover, the presence of perceptibly worsening bodily sensations consistent with the feared catastrophe is likely to confirm the apparent validity of the catastrophic interpretation.

Consistent with the hypothesis that panic attacks result from the catastrophic misinterpretation of bodily sensations, work carried out with David Clark and Michael Gelder has shown that panic patients interpret ambiguous situations involving bodily sensations more negatively than do anxious patients not experiencing panic; these results are not the result of higher levels of anxiety among panic patients, and are specific to bodily sensations (see Clark, this volume).

In summary, research does not fully support the view that panic represents a severe form of anxiety. It is certainly true that PD patients score higher than GAD patients on most self-report measures, and on some physiological measures. On the other hand, there is evidence that panic patients have shorter duration of disorder and more sudden onset. The other outstanding difference between panic patients and other anxious patients lies in the cognitions typical of episodes of severe anxiety, which are much more likely to concern catastrophic internal events (such as heart attacks or madness) in panic patients than in other anxious groups. This difference in cognitions provides the basis for a cognitive model in which bodily sensations are increased by the fear generated by catastrophic interpretations of those sensations. In this way, the cognitive hypothesis provides the basis for a panic dimension distinct from but related to more general anxiety. Panic does not simply represent a severe form of anxiety; rather it is an idiosyncratic anxiety response to the catastrophic misinterpretation of bodily sensations, thereby explaining phenomena such as panic in nonclinic subjects and relaxation-induced panic. Panic can therefore be seen as a specific form of severe anxiety, but not all severe anxiety will result in panic.

THREE-SYSTEM DESCRIPTION OF PANIC

A three-system analysis of the phenomena of panic is useful because it reflects the way in which both clinical research into the psychology of fear and the actual

[2]Note, however, that if DSM-III criteria are applied to severe situational anxiety and the associated autonomic symptoms, then "panic" would be identified without the catastrophic misinterpretation of bodily sensations. This reflects part of the mechanism postulated for panic, that is, that severe threat increases ANS arousal. The prediction from the cognitive model is specifically that attacks categorized as "spontaneous" or "unexpected" will necessarily involve the catastrophic misinterpretation of bodily sensations; situational panic may (and often does) involve sensations; such sensations may be subject to misinterpretation, but this is *not* necessary, as for instance, in anxiety experienced during parachute jumps.

practice of behavioral assessment are usually conceptualized and carried out. A three-system analysis, while not necessarily implying functional relationships between responses within any system, represents a convenient way of summarizing the available data. The introduction of DSM–III reflected the trend for psychiatric research to adopt more multifceted accounts of psychological disorders. The division into PD and agoraphobia with panic explicitly recognizes the importance of assessing behavior independently of reported symptomatology. Unfortunately, at least one clinical interview used to derive DSM–III diagnoses, the Scheduled Clinical Interview for DSM–III (SCID), sets criteria which may result in panic being identified as present in the absence of anxiety provided that "discrete preiods of anxiety" had occurred in the initial attacks on which the diagnosis is based. If DSM–III is applied rigidly, an episode of dizziness, flushing, sweating, and palpitations is regarded as a panic attack even if the patient reacted in the most stoical way possible. A three-system approach would resolve this anomaly. Further subdivision of panic symptom criteria into cognitive and physiological would be a useful progression. Furthermore, such an analysis should allow further integration of phenomenology, assessment, and treatment. In the discussion which follows, the highlighted phenomena are those which the evidence suggests are functionally related to panic, or which are considered important by advocates of cognitively based treatment (Beck, this volume; Chambless, this volume; Clark 1986a, this volume; Clark, Salkovskis, & Chalkley, 1985).

Cognition

Three major cognitive factors said to be important in the phenomenology of panic have been identified: thoughts of catastrophic harm, imagery, and loss of appraisal capacity. Of these, there is most evidence for the importance of catastrophic thoughts. A strong and apparently specific association between panic and cognitions relating to serious physical and mental harm has been reported by several authors (Chambless, Caputo, Gallagher, & Bright 1984; Hibbert, 1984b; Rapee, 1985). This finding is consistent with the cognitive model of panic (Clark, 1986a; this volume), in which the interpretation of bodily sensations as *catastrophic* is a key element. We have been able to demonstrate that patients who experience frequent panic attacks judge catastrophic explanations of ambiguous situations involving bodily sensations as significantly more probable than do socially and generally anxious patients who do not experience panic attacks. Furthermore, there is no difference between patients who panic and other anxious patients with respect to negative interpretations of other ambiguous situations, and the observed effects cannot be accounted for by severity of anxiety.

At present there is little information about how such interpretations may originate. Turner et al. (this volume) discuss the possible importance of cognitions in cueing the first panic attack. Certainly, there is evidence that many or even the majority of panic patients perceive their first attack as causally unrelated to anxiety, and are most likely to regard the sensations they experience as signs of a serious physical condition (Rapee, 1985); Katon (1985) not only noted a similar pattern among panic patients, but also noted that many such patients are wrongly diagnosed as suffering from an organic condition; this medical diagnosis often persists for months and occasionally for years, bolstered by findings such as depression of the S–T segment in electrocardiograms, apparent paroxysmal tachycardia, and so on. Turner et al. (this volume) also note the possibility that multiple medical conditions may trigger panic through interoceptive conditioning, combined with "a tendency to worry or engage in catastrophic prediction."

My experience in dealing with anxiety in general medical settings has tended to support the latter, cognitive factor rather than interoceptive conditioning. Where otherwise frightening and often life-threatening symptoms are readily explicable in medical terms (regardless of previous frequent pairings with potential conditioned stimuli), they are appropriately attributed and do not result in panic, although anxiety commensurate with actual threat is usually present. Panic is much more likely when symptoms are unusual, apparently inexplicable or interpreted in particularly frightening ways. Giving explanatory information may block such responses, but simple explanations and reassurance are not always effective (Salkovskis, Warwick et al., 1986), probably because of the way that explanatory information is provided and understood (Salkovskis & Warwick, 1986; Warwick & Salkovskis, 1986). Exploration of the difference between cognitions associated with panic and those associated with hypochondriasis suggests that there may be similarities between cognitive aspects of these conditions, with the one of the principal differences being the immediacy of the feared consequences (and hence the nature of the associated behavior). For example, the panic patient's belief that dizziness means they are having or about to have a stroke requiring immediate medical attention as opposed to the hypochondriacal patient's belief that they are in the early stages of development of a brain tumor requiring a series of diagnostic investigations.

The other principal difference may be that the bodily phenomena misinterpreted in panic are those liable to incrementation under conditions of autonomic arousal as opposed to those in hypochondriasis are more likely to likely to be bodily sensations not prone to autonomic incrementation (for instance, in response systems without autonomic inputs) and bodily signs or perceived changes. (In hypochondriasis, behavioral mechanisms, including voluntary covert behavior, such as active focusing of attention, may account for longer-term increases in anxiety, Warwick & Salkovskis, 1986).

The other cognitive phenomena which may make specific contributions to the psychopathology of panic are imagery and loss of or change in appraisal capacity.

Imagery

Imagery has been identified as a prominent cognitive phenomenon in anxiety (Beck, Emery, & Greenberg, 1985; Clark & Beck, 1986). That anxiety-related imagery is prevalent in both normal and clinical populations is well established (de Silva 1986; Dent & Salkovskis, 1987; Salkovskis & Dent, in preparation). It is possible that fleeting, unpleasant images of catastrophic personal consequences may play a role in the occurrence of panic, either because of the autonomic responses induced by such images or as readily acessible examples of elaborated catastrophic events. If the images are not directly attended to, they may have an effect on arousal or attributions without the patient having any clear awareness of their importance, thus making panic apparently inexplicable. Beck (this volume) describes a study by Greenberg, in which eight patients who were asked to monitor the occurrence of images did experience vivid imagery during panic induction. Assuming that imagery is found to provoke or maintain panic, then specific assessment of imagery is required especially if it is to be modified directly (Clark & Beck, 1986).

Cognitive Appraisal

Beck (this volume) suggests that, once a panic has started, patients lose their ability to utilize information which would otherwise modify the course of an attack. He presents evidence of this in panic patients but without controlling for anxiety; the inability to use information may not be unique to panic and may occur in all forms of anxiety. The occurrence of such decreased external and increased internal focusing is certainly consistent with clinical reports, and might represent an important element to take account of in assessment and treatment. My experience of using a hyperventilation provocation test clinically to induce physical sensations which frequently resemble the arousal experienced during panic suggests that the effect is unlikely to be due to arousal level and physiological changes associated with arousal (see also Rapee, 1986); patients who appeared to lose appraisal capacity were those who became intensely preoccupied with catastrophic thoughts concerning the sensations they were experiencing at that particular moment.

It seems most likely that the explanation for loss of appraisal is that anxious patients, under conditions of threat, actively deploy their attention toward the perceived source of threat. In panic patients this means that attention will be actively focused on internal sensations and their supposed catastrophic origins, and away from the external environment. (A similar phenomenon may be observed in phobic anxiety; for instance, in the height phobic traveling in an external, glass-fronted scenic lift. He or she is minutely aware of slight vibrations in the ascending lift while being almost totally unaware of the view unfolding before him or her.) Investigation of the nature of this apparent deficit in the processing of external information may be useful in attempts to change this type of response in individuals who are convinced of the imminence of catastrophe. We have found that more compelling strategies than distraction alone are required (Clark & Salkovskis, 1986b), and that a clear, convincing demonstration of the noncatastrophic nature of the bodily sensations the patient is experiencing is one of the principal components of the cognitive approach to panic. Generally, it seems likely that treatments involving active coping (cognitive or behavioral) need to allow increasing penetration of such coping material. The use of active and positive coping strategies counteracts the tendency to focus internally on sensations salient to catastrophic consequences and thereby prevents the partial exclusion of other material.

Physiology

Physiological responding in panic has received much attention, not least because of the popularity of various biological or endogenous models of panic. Specifically, physiological indexes are regarded as possible markers of biological processes. Although such a view has found some favor among the more psychologically oriented (Thyer, 1986) alternative views are now more popular; within a cognitive-behavioral framework physiological changes are regarded as an integrated part of the psychophysiological pattern involved in panic. In particular, the importance of *perceived* bodily sensations to the cognitive model lies primarily in their "signal" function, so that bodily sensations are stimuli which may result in panic if interpreted in a catastrophic fashion. It is important to realize that evidence of the importance of both biological and psychological factors in panic is not mutually contradictory. Few would reject the notion that physiological factors may serve to potentiate cognitive effects and vice versa (Schachter & Singer, 1962).

Differences found between panic patients and others in the experience of bodily symptoms mostly come from studies which use self-report measures of the perception of bodily sensations (as do the criteria employed in DSM–III and most routinely employed methods of behavioral assessment). Given that the perception of bodily sensations is most usual when physiological changes occur, (Pennebaker, 1982), bodily sensations may be perceived either because panic patients experience more physiological fluctuations than others or because they notice bodily sensations more than others. Evidence bearing on this point is not available, and will require data comparing the extent and perception of physiological changes in panic and nonpanic anxious patients at times when they are not severely anxious. Most group differences in psychophysiological measures between panic patients and others have been in resting levels rather than degree of change. As noted, panic patients score significantly higher on state anxiety than other anxious patients, which may account for group differences, both physiological and psychological. Margraf et al. (1986b) have presented data which they interpret as indicating that differential responses to pharmacological panic-inducing agents can be accounted for by differences in the resting levels of psychological and physiological measures. Unfortunately, they fail to take account of problems associated with interpreting responses occurring from markedly differing initial values. For instance, if anxiety, rated on a 100-point scale, increases 30 points from an initial level of 20 to 50, this cannot be assumed to be the same as a change from 60 to 90. Similarly, if heart rate increases by 40 b.p.m. from an initial value of 60, this may be substantially different from a similar increase where the resting level was 100 b.p.m.

A number of investigations have examined the physiological concomitants of naturally occurring panic and, more recently, psychological influences on panic-induction techniques have been experimentally manipulated. Using a cognitive model of panic, it is useful to divide peripheral physiological variables into two major categories to aid understanding of these results.

Perceived Bodily Sensations. Physiological responses may give rise to the perception of bodily sensations through the perception of change in the responding system (although it also seems likely that other processes play a role in such perception). Assessment of the magnitude and type of physiological response, as well as the way in which the patient interprets such changes, is important; treatment may involve specific education about or interventions with the particular system involved. In a recent experiment, we were able to demonstrate that providing positive or negative interpretations of the sensations induced by a brief period of hyperventilation produced substantial differences in whether bodily sensations were experienced as pleasant or unpleasant (Salkovskis & Clark, 1986b). Furthermore, the degree of bodily sensations experienced was significantly correlated only with the affect appropriate to the interpretation which had been provided. This experiment demonstrated that bodily sensations are not necessarily aversive, but can acquire hedonic tone consistent with the particular interpretation made by the person experiencing them. This experiment was even more convincing in this respect because the mean heart rate increase in both groups over the period of a minute was more than 40 b.p.m., with the magnitude and timing of this change being closely comparable with that experienced by patients experiencing panic in laboratory conditions (Cohen, Barlow, & Blanchard, 1985).

Rapee, Mattick, and Murrel (1986) demonstrated that panic patients' experience of the effects of carbon dioxide (CO_2) inhalation was strongly influenced by their interpretation and espectations of sensations. In this experiment, Rapee and his coworkers compared the provision of accurate information regarding the effects of the inhalation with minimal instructions. The information given had a significant effect on the frequency of catastrophic cognitions, amount of panic, and similarity to the experience of naturally occurring panic attacks. Furthermore, this result was specific to panic patients as opposed to social phobics, providing further support for the view that panic patients are more likely than other patients to misinterpret bodily sensations arising from physiological responses.

Physiological Responses Producing Bodily Sensations (Directly or Indirectly). Physiological mechanisms may be involved in the production of other responses and/or central nervous system changes without their mechanism necessarily involving direct perception. One important example of this is change in respiration.

Hyperventilation, defined as breathing in excess of metabolic requirements, has received considerable attention as a mechanism which may be involved in producing panic attacks. Breathing is unique as a physiological system because of a number of attributes: (a) Respiration is under partial voluntary control, and is subject to behavioral influences; (b) Hyperventilation is capable of producing a wide range of intense bodily sensations within a short time; (c) The sensations produced by hyperventilation closely resemble those characteristic of panic attacks; (d) There is evidence that hyperventilation can be both a cause and effect of increased anxiety; (e) Few patients are aware of the *effects* of changes in respiration (or may even think breathing more will reduce symptoms), although it is frequently a focus for nonspecific professional and lay coping strategies (e.g., "take deep breaths when you get anxious"); (f) Respiration itself is a readily perceived physiological process when attention is focused on it; (g) Prolonged increases in respiration can have the effect of altering both chronic resting levels and the regulatory system (by the same mechanism which operates in altitude adaptation), thus increasing sensitivity to physiological and psychological challenge.

The evidence for involvement of hyperventilation in some patients who panic is based on a number of observations. Particularly important are: the resemblance between the bodily sensations associated with panic and those observed in hyperventilation, so that patients identify the somatic sensations experienced as a result of hyperventilation as similar to those experienced during panic (Clark, 1979; Lum, 1976; Rapee, 1986); low resting partial pressure of carbon dioxide in blood (pCO_2) (Kopp et al., 1986; Salkovskis, Jones, & Clark, 1986; Rapee, 1986); pCO_2 is acutely lowered to levels normally associated with a range of intense bodily sensations during biologically induced panic (Gorman, Fyer, Ross, Cohen et al., 1985), during psychologically induced panic (Salkovskis, Clark, & Jones, 1986) and during naturally occurring panic (Hibbert, 1986; Salkovskis, Warwick et al., 1986); normalization of pCO_2 following successful treatment (Gorman, Fyer et al., 1985; Kopp et al., 1986; Salkovskis, Jones, & Clark, 1986). Other work suggests that hyperventilation cannot fully account for the psychological phenomena associated with panic, and may be serving as an important mechanism for the production of bodily sensations, the subsequent *reaction* to those sensations probably accounting for the affective disturbance.

This view is supported by studies such as those of Clark and Hemsley (1982), Svebak and Grossman (1985), Rapee (1986), Rapee et al. (1986), and our own work on the manipulation of interpretations described previously.

A further physiological factor arising from the consideration of hyperventilation as a source of somatic sensations suggests a possible basis for biological vulnerability to panic. Repeated episodes of prolonged hyperventilation are known to lead to renal excretion of bicarbonate in order to return pH to normal (Gledhill, Beirne, & Dempsey, 1975). That such a mechanism probably operates in panic patients is shown by the repeated findings of low resting pCO_2 (Gorman, Fyer et al., 1985; Salkovskis, Jones, & Clark, 1986). Renal excretion of bicarbonate results in a reduced buffering capacity and greater susceptibility to pH challenge (for instance, lactate infusion, hyperventilation). That is, a given amount of respiratory change, will result in more symptoms occurring with a shorter latency. This increased sensitivity is also associated with an enhanced exercise response, reduced breath-holding capacity, and is maintained at the cost of chronically elevated respiration and associated fatigue, chest pain and breathlessness (which appear inexplicable to the patient, further fueling their anxiety).

Physiological data from panic patients are most consistent with the cognitive model. A specific physiological process, hyperventilation, can interact with cognitive mechanisms in individuals prone to catastrophic interpretation of bodily sensations. Hyperventilation appears to have an effect on panic by (1) providing a potentially frightening pattern of bodily sensations; (2) because changes in resting pCO_2, produced by renal excretion of bicarbonate, increase patients' vulnerability to the development of such sensations. Fig. 7.2 illustrates the cognitive model as specifically applied to hyperventilation related sensations, together with the principal physiological and psychological factors which have been demonstrated to have an effect.

Behavioral Components

A major and pervasive diagnostic distinction is made on the basis of the behavioral correlates of panic. Patients who experience "anticipatory fear of helplessness or loss of control during a panic attack . . . when alone or in public places [and avoid] many situations of the kind" receive a diagnosis of panic with agoraphobia, while patients who do not are diagnosed as having panic disorder (American Psychiatric Association, 1980). This distinction is said to be based on the view that agoraphobic avoidance is simply secondary to panic (i.e., avoidance is maintained by anxiety) (Klein, 1981). This hypothesized link between panic and avoidance is in contrast to behavioral formulations in which avoidance is said to develop as a way of reducing anxiety; once avoidance has developed, it retards extinction of anxiety (i.e., anxiety can generate avoidance, which in turn maintains continued anxiety and hence avoidance, Gray, 1975). This difference with regard to the putative functional role of behavior is considered by some to

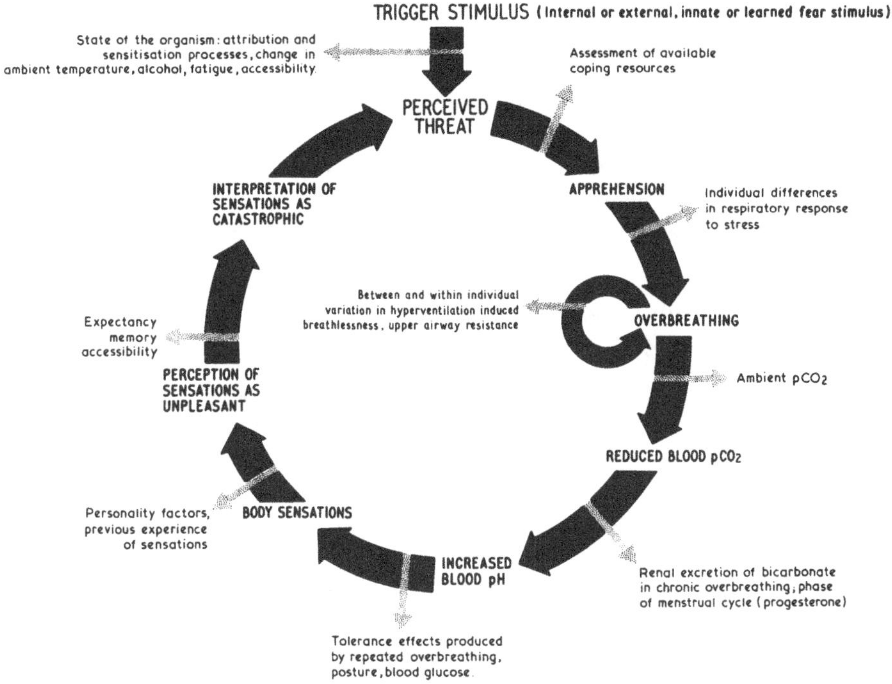

FIG. 7.2. The cognitive model of panic as applied to panic in which hyperventilation is involved in the production of sensations. Psychological and physiological factors for which there is evidence of a modulatory influence are given by each step. (From Salkovskis, Clark, & Jones, 1986 p. 241).

be a crucial aspect of the debate between biological and psychological models of panic.

However, it is difficult to see why evidence regarding the importance of anxiety in the generation of avoidance behavior should be seen as evidence of the endogeneity of panic and agoraphobia. It seems most likely that the hypothesized primacy of "endogenous panic" is based on an inadequate understanding of the role of anxiety in cognitive and behavioral models. The idea that panic is uniquely or causally related to avoidance is not well supported. Mavissakalian and Michelson (1986b) and Michelson (this volume) report data which indicate that the reduction of avoidance has substantial effects on anxiety and panic (see also Marks, Gray, Cohen et al., 1983). This evidence of the effectiveness of treatments directed at reducing avoidance is consistent with the weight of evidence from studies predating DSM–III, which convincingly demonstrate the effectiveness of behavioral treatments for agoraphobia (Marks, 1980; Mathews, Gelder, & Johnston, 1981; Munby & Johnston, 1980). If panic were indeed the primary phenomenon in agoraphobia, then the global therapeutic gains reported from behavioral treatments would not be predicted; nor would the longer-term follow-ups be as encouraging. Interestingly, Butler, (personal communication) reports that GAD patients show extensive avoidance. In order to examine the importance of the behavioral dimension of panic, I will consider the relationship between panic and agoraphobia, then examine more general behavioral correlates of panic relevant to cognitive and behavioral approaches.

The Relationship between Panic and Agoraphobic Behavior

In patients with a diagnosis of agoraphobia with panic, there is now increasing evidence that the characteristic global avoidance behavior is functionally associated with the occurrence of panic (Thyer, 1986; Thyer & Himle, 1985). Thyer, Himle, Curtis, Cameron, and Nesse (1985) compared PD patients and agoraphobics with panic, and found few differences. They conclude that spontaneous, biologically determined panic is the core condition, and that agoraphobia with panic represents a later stage of panic, with agoraphobic avoidance arising through negatively reinforced superstitious conditioning (Thyer, 1986). That negative reinforcement is a factor in agoraphobia seems likely; that it is the predominant mode of acquisition of avoidance behavior and that panic is biologically determined is considerably more dubious. A simple view in which avoidance is merely a passive consequence of panic is inconsistent with the fact that panic disorder patients show a nonsignificantly *longer* duration of disorder (Thyer et al., 1985), as opposed to a significantly shorter duration which would be predicted.

An alternative view is suggested by Noyes et al. (1986), who present clinical and familial data which they interpret as showing that agoraphobia is a more severe variant of panic disorder. The findings are consistent with two treatment studies (Clark, Salkovskis, & Chalkley, 1985; Salkovskis, Jones, & Clark, 1986), in which panic patients who avoided particular situations had significantly higher scores on measures of panic frequency, avoidance *and* anxiety than those who did not. In another study examining the effects of hyperventilation as a challenge, the same degree of hyperventilation (as indexed by $p_{mv}CO_2$) resulted in significantly higher ratings of bodily sensations and negative affect in 10 patients with agoraphobia with panic than in 10 patients with panic disorder (Salkovskis, in preparation).

In the second treatment study, Salkovskis Jones, and Clark (1986) measured nonpanic anxiety, and found that nonsituational panic patients were (nonsignificantly) higher in diary ratings of generalized anxiety (i.e., anxiety between panic attacks) only (See Fig. 7.1). This is interesting to consider in the light of Rachman's (1984a) formulation of agoraphobia from a safety signal perspective; if panic is tied to particular situations, then anxiety between panics should be lower for such patients, as not being in the phobic situation would act as a safety signal.

Turner et al. (this volume) reports that patients with agoraphobia with panic did not differ from Panic Disorder patients in their rating of fearfulness of agoraphobic situations on the Fear Survey Schedule. This report is surprising, since agoraphobic patients are clearly more fearful in behavioral terms. Failure to find differences in fearfulness could arise as a function of the patient's current level of actual avoidance (and hence recent experience of fear in agoraphobic sitations) which would be lower among the agoraphobic patients. The Fear Survey Schedule specifically asks for ratings of "how much you are disturbed by (the situation) nowadays." This means that similarities in fearfulness as opposed to avoidance may be a function of recent exposure to those situations. Generally, the failure to find differences between panic disorder and agoraphobia with panic, on these and other variables, is relatively weak evidence for the view that the two conditions are the same. This is particularly true when the apparently crucial component (i.e., behavior itself) has seldom been directly examined; self-reported fearfulness and behavior are often observed to be discordant. The evidence in this respect is consistent with the notion of an association between agoraphobia and severe anxiety; clearly, the development of avoidance could have been influenced by the severity of anxiety, *or* the severity of anxiety may be a result of the development of avoidance behavior. The key difference between the two groups lies in the behavior itself; this difference is vital to cognitive and behavioral approaches to treatment. The relationship between panic and agoraphobia does not appear to afford any crucial tests of either psychological or biological models of panic. As the next section will describe, it also appears that the way in which behavioral components of panic have been conceptualized may have been too narrow in any case.

Panic-related Behavior

Behavioral components of panic itself (as distinct from agoraphobic avoidance) have been neglected because of the commonly held belief that avoidance did not feature in panic disorder. For instance, Barlow, Cohen et al. (1984) comment that "exposure is of little or no use to those suffering from Generalized Anxiety Disorder (or panic disorder) since they avoid nothing to begin with." Although this view is now less prevalent, the focus has not substantially shifted from the relationship between panic and agoraphobic avoidance. Barlow and Craske (this volume) make the interesting observation that patients frequently avoid activities which may result in somatic sensations. In previous work (Clark & Salkovskis, 1986a,b), we have argued that such activities and stimuli serve as triggers for panic, so that the occurrence of bodily sensations is frequently misinterpreted in a catastrophic fashion. It is also apparent that patients will often avoid other stimuli which may trigger catastrophic thoughts (such as news reports involving details of illness) and frequently make determined attempts to block out unpleasant thoughts or images (covert avoidance). In the later stages of treatment, such triggering situations and thoughts are identified by examining the pattern of panic and avoidance; once this has been done, *the way in which the effects of such triggering stimuli are interpreted* is directly modified. This can involve deliberate exposure to the trigger, thus allowing confirmation of the innocuous origin of the sensations triggered and reappraisal of the nature of the "threat" posed (Clark & Salkovskis, 1986b).

When patients first develop panic attacks, their pattern of behavior is more consistent with the avoidance of *catastrophes* than with the avoidance of *panic*. For instance, we have described an extreme example of this phenomenon in a single case report (Salkovskis, Warwick, Clark, & Wessels, 1986). In this report, the avoidance itself was life threatening, and the relationship between avoidance and catastrophic cognitions was clear. The patient was undergoing regular dialysis sessions for chronic renal failure. During dialysis, he experienced bodily sensations (those normally arising as a consequence of the pH changes which occur during dialysis) which served to trigger panic. He believed that the dialysis itself was damaging him in a way likely to be fatal during the dialysis session. Because of this belief, he missed dialysis on a number of occasions (a course of action that he acknowledged to be risky) and was contemplating refusing it altogether—a course of action he knew was certain to be fatal, but not immediately. His avoidance behavior, which he knew to be dangerous in itself, was not intended to avoid panic, but to avoid being killed by the machine.

Most attention has focused on anticipatory avoidance behavior such as that described, because such behavior may serve to prevent exposure to fear cues (and hence retard extinction and reappraisal). Identification of the range and ramifications of such behavior is important, and allows definition of assessment strategies in people who panic. A great deal is already known about the phenomenology and assessment of such behavior from the literature on exposure treatments for agoraphobia (Mathews, Gelder, & Johnston, 1981). However, consideration of behavior reported by panic patients suggests that avoidance continues or even starts with the onset of panic. Patients sit down, hold onto walls, seek medical attention, take deep breaths and generally engage in behaviors which they believe may abort imminent disaster. This suggests a subdivision into: (a) behavior designed to prevent exposure to the possibility of catastrophic consequences (avoidance of exposure to fear cues), (b) behavior arising as a *consequence* of panic and intended to avert an imminent catastrophe (escape behaviors, seeking safety signals). This second category is likely to be important because in some circumstances it might, as Turner (this volume) points out, serve to "preclude natural recovery . . ." (which may otherwise occur) ". . .through extinction." Such behavior would seem to serve the same function as compulsive rituals (overt or covert) among obsessional-compulsive patients; that is, to terminate exposure or to prevent functional exposure. Panic-related and catastrophe-avoiding behavior may also have the effect of maintaining preoccupation. For as long as efforts are directed at the avoidance of feared disasters, then cognitive activity is likely to remain centered on the possible disasters, and may result in cognitive elaboration.

The range of behavior which may be observed in panic patients can be categorized into:

1. Doing nothing (no change in behavior).
2. Behaving as if the immediate problem is imminence of the feared catastrophe (e.g., dying, going mad), viz. (a) overt: taking safety measures, such as attempting to remove oneself from the "dangerous" situation; e.g., escaping from situation, sitting down, calling for help; (b) covert: seeking confirmation of catastrophic interpretation of the situation (increased scanning of body for sensations, taking pulse).
3. Behaving as if the immediate problem is having frightening thoughts. The panicker may (a) seek disconfirmation of catastrophic interpretations; (b) engage in active coping attempts (relaxation, talking to oneself, distraction).

If the relative salience of these reactions is considered, (2) would be expected to retard habituation and anxiety reduction and maintain preoccupation, while (1) and (3) should result in decreased anxiety and reappraisal of actual threat. It seems most plausible that panic will be characterized by (2), but studies of behavior immediately consequent on panic are required in order to investigate the possible importance of such factors, and evolve appropriate assessment strategies. There is some evidence of the importance of such factors in obsessions. Some preliminary evidence emerging from the cognitive behavioral treatment of hypochondriasis (Salkovskis & Warwick, 1986; Warwick & Salkovskis, 1985, 1986), suggests that such factors may be of great importance. Phenomenologically, hypochondriasis has much in common with panic. It is also notable that the treatment employed by our group (Clark & Salkovskis, 1986a,b) had, as a central feature, strategies directed at (or having the effect of) shifting patients' behavior during panic from (2) to (1) and (3).

CONCLUSIONS

The issues that I have discussed lead to a number of specific conclusions regarding the phenomenology of panic and issues important to research in this area.

Implications for Research into Panic

1. Care is needed in distinguishing between studies investigating the phenomenon of panic and those comparing people having a panic-related diagnosis and those without. Both types of study are important, and generate complementary information.

2. It is not sufficient to compare panic patients with normals, because the resulting differences may be due to patients' anxiety levels rather than panic per se. Even comparisons of panic patients with other anxiety patients should include measures of mood (particularly state anxiety) at the time of testing to ensure that differences observed do not simply reflect pre-existing differences in mood intensity (which frequently occur) rather than characteristics specific to panic.

3. The validity of considering severe anxiety as synonymous with panic is not established. Severe anxiety is not sufficient for the occurrence of panic, which probably represents a phenomenon related to but not identical with anxiety per se. The cognitive model provides a framework which distinguishes between panic and severe anxiety, with panic being specific to catastrophic as opposed to general threat. Further clarification of the relationship between general anxiety and panic is needed; preliminary data from cognitive studies support a distinction on the basis of catastrophic ideation in panic but not general anxiety.

4. Panic should be considered from a three-system perspective. The present influential status of DSM–III should not lead those concerned with psychological approaches to psychopathology to abandon the powerful descriptive approach afforded by a three-system model, which still appears to describe nature better than any categorical/lump system. Viewed from this perspective, there is a great deal of scope for further work within each system, and careful examination of the relationship between them should also prove rewarding. In the cognitive system, cognitions concerning feared catastrophes appear important, particularly those related to the perception of bodily sensations; the nature of interactions with behavior has been neglected. In the physiological system, respiration is an important and relatively neglected physiological response partly under voluntary control, known to produce acute attacks of bodily sensations, having marked effects on other physiological systems, consciousness, and anxiety; it is subject to changes liable to increase vulnerability to subsequent acute challenge through alterations in buffering capacity. Voluntary modification of respiration has been shown to be beneficial in the control of panic; it is unclear as to how much these effects have been mediated by cognitive, physiological, and/or behavioral mechanisms. In the behavioral system, behavior related to panic has been largely disregarded because of the (almost certainly erroneous) belief that panic disorder is not associated with specific avoidance, and that panic is not consistently associated with particular stimuli. The possible functional role of behavior needs direct evaluation.

5. Although hypochondriasis is in a different DSM–III group, there are sufficient similarities to warrant careful comparison with panic in terms of psychopathology and treatment.

6. Psychological and biological models of panic are not mutually incompatible. Examination of possible interactions is likely to be most illuminating (van den Hout, this volume; Lang, this volume).

Implications for the Assessment of Panic and panic related Behavior

Finally, I have identified those characteristics of panic patients and panic attacks important in the context of the cognitive model both in terms of assessment for treatment and evaluation of outcome. Specific assessment techniques are also listed where appropriate.

Areas Important from a Cognitive Perspective

(i) Identifying Catastrophic Interpretations. When the cognitive approach to treatment is used, it is crucial to identify catstrophic misinterpretation of bodily sensations because these misinterpreatations are subsequently the principal focus of intervention. These are identified in a variety of ways: asking the patient questions such as "When you are having a panic attack, what goes through your mind at that time?". If the patient cannot clearly identify thoughts in this way, asking "What, during panic, do you think is the worst thing that could happen?" may be helpful. Identifying negative automatic thoughts in this way is often sufficient, although it should be remembered that when the patient is being assessed in the office they have much better access to rational responses (e.g., "I know I'm not really going to have a heart attack.") in a way which they may not during panic. Other techniques which are useful in gaining access to the catastrophic interpretations made by panic patients include homework emphasizing thought monitoring and diaries for use at times when panic occurs, and questioning the patient during in vivo behavioral testing. Imagery and rehearsal of previous recent panic can be used in the same way. Our group has been using a questionnaire in which patients are asked to described their most likely thoughts in ambiguous situations involving the experience of bodily sensations (e.g., "You notice that your are feeling dizzy . . . why?").

(ii) Identifying Behavior and Symptom Patterns Characteristic of Hyperventilation. As described, hyperventilation can be involved in panic by producing bodily sensations which serve as triggering stimuli for inexplicable bodily sensations which are then catastrophically interpreted, and also be a mechanism by which sensations increment. The effects of hyperventilation can serve to promote further hyperventilation through anxiety related to catastrophic interpretations and hyperventilation-induced breathlessness, where overbreathing results in paradoxical attempts by patients to breathe more in an attempt to overcome breathlessness, thereby further increasing symptoms of hyperventilation. Hyperventilation can be detected through the measurement of resting breathing rate, by counting observed breaths, or by using a polygraph with appropriate transducers. It should be noted that awareness of breathing usually results in increased respiration. The presence of pCO_2 can be measured by a variety of means, and will

give indications of reduced resting or acute levels, depending on the method used and the circumstances in which measurements are taken. Rebreathing measurements of mixed venous pCO_2 have been used in our treatment studies and are relatively easy to use clinically as brief, spot checks, particularly of resting levels. End tidal pCO_2 is the easiest of the continuous measures, although it is subject to considerable artefact. Transcutaneous pCO_2 has particular advantages; it is possible to use with 24-hour ambulatory systems and it does not interfere with the airway. Transcutanous measures are, however, technically difficult and expensive and have poor response times.

Symptom checklists can be an easy to apply and useful alternative, although there are some doubts about their validity in the detection of hyperventilation per se. Checklists do correlate reasonably well with the reproduction of sensations by voluntary hyperventilation and hence may be a useful indication of whether or not hyperventilation will be useful in reattribution procedures, whether or not hyperventilation is indeed crucial to panic in any particular patient. From this viewpoint, evaluating the response to brief, forced ventilation (provocation test) is the most relevant assessment for the specific version of cognitive treatment which utilizes reattribution of the symptoms of panic on to stress-induced hyperventilation. The latency of symptoms produced by voluntary overbreathing tends to be reduced in patients who chronically overbreathe, so asking the patient to indicate the time of onset of symptoms during the provocation test is helpful initially in deciding on this point and in evaluating the patient's response during the course of treatment. When the provocation test is carried out, it is useful to evaluate the degree of breathlessness as a response; this may give some indication of the extent to which this may be inducing further hyperventilation in naturally occurring panic attacks. Breath-holding time is also reduced in patients with low resting CO_2, and can provide helpful indications of progress through treatment.

(iii) Avoidance Behavior. Identification of behaviors intended to prevent exposure (a) to panic and (b) to the possibility of feared catastrophes, can be done on the basis of interview data, avoidance questionnaires, behavioral diaries, behavior tests, and direct observation by therapist or others in the patient's environment.

(iv) Panic-related Behavior. Behaviors consequent upon catastrophic interpretations may serve to maintain, reinforce, or prevent inhibition of, the vicious circle. It is important to identify these behaviors because of their maintenance function and because they may disguise catastrophic interpretations. Assessment can be through behavior tests, diaries, behavioral experiments, and direct observation. The patient's belief about the function of such behaviors can be assessed by questions such as "Supposing you didn't hang on to the supermarket cart, what did you think might happen then?"

(v) Beliefs. The cognitive approach to panic predicts that identification and modification of beliefs/assumptions which result in a tendency for particular bodily sensations to be interpreted catastrophically is important for the prevention of relapse. Techniques which have been applied to cognitive treatment of other disorders (Beck, Emery, & Greenberg, 1985) are effective in this respect: for instance, a vertical arrow (in which particular thoughts are followed through to their conclusion [see Burns 1980]). It is also useful to identify patients' previous experiences of particular bodily sensations and their perceived relationship to severe illness; for instance, by asking if they ever knew anyone else who had similar symptoms, and what had happened to them.

(vi) Specific Physiological Mechanisms. Identification of physiological processes directly leading to bodily sensations; e.g.,

breathlessness ⇛ increased ventilation ⇛ symptoms (including further breathlessness)

Behavioral experiments, such as periods of overbreathing in situations like those in which the patient panics may be helpful, sometimes combined with psychophysiological monitoring (laboratory and ambulatory [see, for instance, Salkovskis, Warwick et al., 1986]). Another important example is asking patients who experience chest pain to breathe for 5 minutes at normal tidal volumes with lungs alternately full and empty (i.e., at top and bottom of their vital capacity).

(vii) Panic Triggers. In the later stages of treatment, identification of "triggers" producing somatic sensations, which are the subject of misinterpretation and lead into the panic feedback loop is important to the completion of treatment and to relapse prevention. The panic diaries are most helpful in this respect; patients record the occurrence of panic and relevant antecedent of concurrent events and symptoms each day. On the basis of these and/or discussion with the patient, assessment proceeds a stage further with behavioral experiments designed to test hypotheses about possible triggers. For example, it may emerge that panic frequently precedes mealtimes or follows coffee breaks; changing mealtimes and reducing (or increasing) caffeine intake allows direct assessment of these factors.

Consideration of the phenomenology of panic provides some support for a cognitive-behavioral model. However, many of the crucial questions remain to be investigated. Some of the data from biological studies of panic support the view that there might be biological predisposing factors to panic, although much of the data are biologically inconsistent and is best explained by a cognitive rather than a biological model (Clark, this volume). Direct investigation of the interaction between biological, behavioral, and cognitive aspects of panic are urgently needed, rather than the overenthusiastic embracing of the tabula rasa afforded by DSM–III at the expense of so much carefully conducted previous research into anxiety and agoraphobia (e.g., Klerman, 1986). While welcoming the adoption of the useful operational definitions embodied in DSM–III, those researching psychological factors should guard against uncritical adoption of the other assumptions implicit in a categorical diagnostic approach. Finally, the primary purpose of cognitive-behavioral assessment is still the establishment of functional relationships between the patient's complaint on the one hand and psychological and physiological processes on the other.

ACKNOWLEDGMENTS

The author is grateful to the Medical Research Council of the United Kingdom for its support. I would also like to thank Pavlos Anastasiades, Gillian Butler, David M. Clark, Lorna Hogg, and Hilary M. C. Warwick for comments on earlier versions of this manuscript.

8

Cognitive, Behavioral, and Psychophysiological Treatments and Correlates of Panic

Larry Michelson
University of Pittsburgh, School of Medicine
Western Psychiatric Institute and Clinic

Panic is receiving considerable research attention due to myriad factors which are converging in psychology and psychiatry. The convening of scientists in the anxiety field by the National Institute of Mental Health is one reflection of this trend. The present volume represents the state of the art in research and practice. Reviews of panic have been addressed in previous chapters with regard to epidemiology, etiology, assessment, taxonomy, and treatment. The aim here, therefore, is to examine two critical areas of panic empirically. First, what are the relative and combined effects of behavioral, cognitive, and pharmacological treatments on a short- and long-term basis? Second, are there differential patterns across the tripartite systems for subjects identified as in vivo panickers versus nonpanickers to address the controversial issue of whether panic is a distinct entity or merely one end of the anxiety continuum.

The objective of the first study was to ascertain the short- and long-term effectiveness of diverse psychosocial and pharmacological treatments for panic. In Study 1 an intracenter (University of Pittsburgh), multistudy comparison of four outcome investigations representing 11 treatment conditions and 174 subjects was performed. The relative efficacy of cognitive, behavioral, physiological, and pharmacological modalities in reducing agoraphobics' panic attacks was examined at mid- and posttreatment and during a follow-up period of 2 years. Both outcome and maintenance effects were examined within and across the four outcome studies. Meta-analyses, comparing groupings of psychosocial and pharmacological modalities, were also conducted.

In Study II, the cognitive, behavioral, and physiological correlates of in vivo panic were examined empirically. Differential patterns of cognitive, behavioral, and physiological functioning were identified across anxious, fearful, and panicked subjects. This tripartite micro/macroanalysis of in vivo panic offers a unique and important perspective on the relative contributions and possible mediating influences of each of the tridimensional systems.

STUDY 1

A total of 174 subjects, meeting DSM–III criteria (American Psychiatric Association, 1980) for agoraphobia with panic attacks participated in one of four separate comparative outcome studies, representing 11 treatment conditions. Additional criteria for inclusion consisted of age prior to 40 years for onset of the condition, duration of illness of at least 1 year, and age between 18 and 65. Social phobics and anxiety neurotics exhibiting the typical fears of leaving home, entering public places, or using public transportation were excluded. Also excluded were subjects in a major depressive episode or those with a history of affective disorder preceding the onset of agoraphobia or a diagnosis of organic brain syndrome, schizophrenia, obsessive-compulsive disorder, antisocial personality, Briquet's syndrome, substance abuse, or alcoholism.

Overall, the 174 subjects had an average duration of illness of 9.5 years, with a mean age of 37, with a mean age of onset of 27; 83% were female, and 76% were married. Pretreatment clinical ratings are presented in Table 8.1.

The assessment, diagnostic, and protocol evaluations were relatively consistent across investigations. A measure of panic was administered in all studies at each assessment, instructing subjects to rate the "frequency and intensity of panic attacks, palpitations, breathlessness, sweating or trembling which you have had for no obvious reason during the past 3 days." (The only exception to the "last 3 days" instructions occurred in the "Imipramine versus Imipramine plus Programmed Practice" study, where 15 subjects rated their panic for the previous 3 weeks.) On a 9-point scale, subjects endorsed their panic experiences with ratings from 0 (no panic), 2 (mild panic), 4 (moderate panic), 6 (severe

TABLE 8.1

Pretreatment Test Scores	*Mean*	*Range*
Global assessment of severity	4.49	Minimum = 1 Maximum = 5
Fear questionnaire agoraphobia subscale	30.2	Severe range
Fear questionnaire total	70.01	Severe range
Self-rating of severity	6.3	Minimum = 0 Maximum = 8
Phobic anxiety and avoidance	7.67	Minimum = 0 Maximum = 8

panic) to 8 (very severe panic). Examination of the panic values for this study reveals that they closely approximated the scores from the other investigations.

The four separate outcome studies were conducted at the University of Pittsburgh. A brief outline of each of the investigations, and their respective treatments is presented in Table 8.2. Subjects in all studies were randomly assigned to one of the treatments, representing either cognitive, behavioral, psychophysiologic, or pharmacological modalities. A brief overview of each study is presented followed by a series of meta-analyses examining the entire data set.

In 1986(a) Mavissakalian and Michelson reported an investigation examining the relative and combined effectiveness of therapist-assisted in vivo exposure and imipramine. Sixty-two DSM–III diagnosed agoraphobics with panic attacks were randomly assigned to one of four treatments using a 2 (exposure versus programmed practice) × 2 (imipramine versus placebo) factorial design, which included Imipramine plus Exposure, Imipramine, Exposure and Control (Programmed Practice) conditions.

Treatment consisted of 12 weekly visits that included individual 15-minute sessions with a psychiatrist for administration of drug treatment and 90-minute group sessions of either exposure or programmed practice discussion with a clinical psychologist.

All subjects were given the same behavioral rationale for their condition, with an emphasis on the role of habitual avoidance in maintaining their fears, and were instructed and encouraged to practice self-directed, prolonged, in vivo exposure between sessions. They were told that any additional treatments they received, such as the medication and the group treatments, were designed to facilitate their attempts at self-directed exposure. They were strongly urged to confront and remain in phobic situations until their anxiety discomfort decreased to fairly comfortable levels or until their urge to escape abated. They were also advised to proceed with their practice of self-directed exposure along the hierarchy from the least to the most phobic situations.

The drug conditions were double-blind, and treatment started with one 25 mg tablet of imipramine or one matched placebo tablet. The average stable dosage of imipramine during the last month of treatment was 130 mg/day. Exposure, conducted in groups of eight, typically involved accompanying the therapist and an assistant in the hospital van to the center of town or to large shopping malls. Once on site, subjects were encouraged to leave the group as soon as possible and to pursue prolonged exposure, on their own or with the help of a therapist by entering the stores or walking in congested areas. Subjects consistently were encouraged to apply the principle of prolonged exposure by remaining in these situations until they felt comfortable. After 90 minutes, the group reconvened and returned to the clinic. In the later phases of treatment, subjects took the bus, either alone or in small groups, to go downtown or return to the clinic, or both. Subjects assigned to the control group (programmed practice) also met in groups of eight with the same therapist to discuss their efforts and progress with self-directed exposure. Assessments were conducted at pretreatment and at weeks 4,

TABLE 8.2
Multistudy Description of Designs, Demographics and Clinical Measures of Severity

Study	*Year*	*Treatment Conditions*	*Sample Sizes*	*Assessment Phases*	*% Female /Male*	*Mean Age*
I. NIMH/2 × 2	(1986)	IE	*N* = 14	Pre, Mid, Post, 1 mo., 6 mo., 1 yr., 2 yr.	F 79 M 21	39.8
		I	*N* = 17		F 88 M 12	35.5
		E	*N* = 17		F 89 M 11	33.1
		C	*N* = 14		F 86 M 14	33.4
II. IMI	(1983)	I	*N* = 7	Pre, Mid, Post	F 100 M 00	33.6
		I + PP	*N* = 8		F 100 M 00	33.4
III. PI/SST	(1983)	PI	*N* = 12	Pre, Mid, Post, 1 mo., 6 mo.	F 92 M 8	42.8
		SST	*N* = 12		F 75 M 25	40.7
IV. CBM/NIMH	(1985)	PI	*N* = 26	Pre, Mid, Post, 3 mo., 6 mo., 1 yr., 2 yr.	F 73 M 27	36.7
		GE	*N* = 22		F 96 M 4	39.5
		RT	*N* = 25		F 68 M 32	34.9

Note. IE = Imipramine + Exposure; I = Imipramine; E = Exposure; C = Control (Programmed Practice); I + PP = Imipramine + Programmed Practice; PI = Paradoxical Intention; SST = Self-Statement Training; GE = Graduated Exposure; RT = Relaxation Training.

8, and 12 (posttreatment), and again at follow-ups of 1, 3, 6, 12, and 24 months. (The fourth- and eighth-week panic measures were averaged to yield a mean for the midassessment to permit cross-study comparisons.)

The results revealed statistically significant improvements in all conditions from pre- to posttreatment. Relatively few between-group differences emerged.

TABLE 8.2
(Continued)

Mean Duration of Illness	*% Marital Status*	*Global Assess. of Severity*	*Self-Rating of Severity*	*Phobic Anxiety and Avoidance*
11.9 yr.	Married = 79	4.79	6.31	7.77
10.3 yr.	Married = 88	4.63	6.31	7.81
8.1 yr.	Married = 61	4.61	6.50	7.91
7.3 yr.	Married = 64	4.71	6.64	7.49
4.7 yr.	Married = 75	4.13	5.86	7.60
10.2 yr.	Married = 43	4.57	6.33	7.91
10.4 yr.	Married = 75	3.91	4.70	6.98
9.7 yr.	Married = 83	3.45	4.90	6.93
9.1 yr.	Married = 77	4.50	6.42	7.55
10.5 yr.	Married = 82	4.82	6.32	7.91
9.9 yr.	Married = 88	4.56	6.16	7.95

Absence of interaction effects between exposure and imipramine were probably due to the fact that all subjects received intensive and systematic behavioral (programmed practice) instructions and were actively practicing self-directed in vivo exposure, rendering the exposure condition only a small portion of the subjects' total exposure experience. This protocol also rendered the imipramine condition a combined pharmacological-behavioral treatment. Approximately one-third of the control (i.e., programmed practice) subjects improved and were functional at posttreatment. Imipramine plus exposure. imipramine plus programmed practice and exposure alone exhibited twice the level of high Endstate functioning (an operationalized composite measure of absolute clinical functioning). No dose–response relationships were found between blood plasma levels and panic attacks. Posttreatment follow-up comparisons revealed a tendency for reversals among imipramine subjects. Conversely, behavioral treatments alone exhibited further improvement.

The objective of the second study (Mavissakalian, Michelson & Dealy, 1983) was to examine the relative contribution of behavioral instructions (programmed practice) to the effectiveness of imipramine on anxiety, panic, mood, and behavioral measures. Eighteen DSM–III-diagnosed agoraphobics with panic attacks were randomly assigned to either imipramine or imipramine plus programmed practice. Subjects were seen individually on a weekly basis for the first 6 weeks and at the 8th- and 12th-week treatment phases. In the imipramine condition, subjects received an average dosage of 125 mg/day. The sole rationale provided to these subjects emphasized the antipanic effect of imipramine and its utility in the treatment of agoraphobia. Mention of exposure to phobic stimuli was consistently and deliberately avoided, and questions concerning activities were met with a standard response such as "Well, you can be the best judge for that" or, "You will decide when the time comes and when you feel ready." The aim of this treatment was on improving mood and providing maximal antipanic benefit.

Subjects in the imipramine plus programmed practice condition received an average dosage of 125 mg/day. However, the rationale of treatment was entirely different. Subject met with a clinical psychologist for 1 hour at each session for detailed, systematic instructions and reinforcement for self-directed, in vivo practice. Subjects in this group were told that the reason why their fears had continued and even increased with time was due to their habitual avoidance behavior. In order to overcome their fears and anxieties they should stop avoiding and start entering their phobic situations. It was strongly suggested that once in a phobic situation, they should remain there and tolerate their anxiety until it decreased to fairly comfortable levels and/or until their urge to escape abated. It was emphasized that imipramime was an additional treatment designed to facilitate self-directed in vivo exposure.

The results of the study revealed consistent and substantial differences between the two groups, the imipramine plus programmed practice condition being significantly superior on major outcome measures. Although subjects in the imipramine condition showed some clinical improvement, substantially greater absolute and percentage of pre–post changes were observed in the imipramine plus programmed practice condition.

The objective of the third study (Michelson, Mavissakalian, Greenwald, Kornblith, & Greenwald, 1983) was to ascertain the relative effectiveness of two promising cognitive treatments for agoraphobia; Self-Statement Training (SST) and Paradoxical Intention (PI). The treatments utilized diametrically opposed instructional sets and content. The SST consisted of cognitive restructuring, designed to replace self-defeating cognitions with adaptive thoughts. Conversely, PI offered a counterintuitive, experiential approach to managing phobic anxiety, avoidance, and panic.

Treatment consisted of 12 weekly sessions of 90 minutes each. Subjects were seen in groups of 4 to 5. The first 2 sessions were identical across treatment conditions, providing subjects with the same rationale and information about the nature of agoraphobia, the role of habitual avoidance, and faulty cognitions in maintaining their fears. Subjects were told that a significant part of their anxiety was caused by the type of statements they were saying to themselves. Subjects were informed that treatment would focus on teaching them how to change these self-defeating statements in ways that would help them cope more effectively with their phobic anxiety, phobic avoidance, and panic attacks. The importance of in vivo exposure practice was explained. Subjects were informed that the cognitive coping strategies they were about to learn were intended to help them confront and/or remain in their phobic situations without undue anxiety. The emphasis of treatment was not just on increasing approach behavior, but also on the management of anticipatory and phobic anxiety experienced in vivo. The specific treatments were introduced at the third session and continued throughout the treatment phase.

The SST was similar to Meichenbaum's approach (1977) and consisted of training subjects to emit adaptive self-statements regarding: (a) preparaing for, (b) confronting, and (c) coping with anxiety and self-reinforcement. Self-statement training subjects were instructed on methods for identifying and replacing negative, maladaptive thoughts with positive, adaptive cognitions. They were also taught to apply SST prior to entering phobic situations, during in vivo outings, and after completing the outing, to reinforce themselves for their performance.

Paradoxical intention subjects were told that anticipatory anxiety brings about precisely what one fears, and excessive intention about one's performance interferes with functioning. Examples included the insomniac's excessive intention to fall asleep (to no avail), and the self-imposed pressures for sexual performance which usually lead to failure. A more relevant example was the subject's usual pattern of trying hard to control their anxiety, with its paradoxical effects. During every session, each subject was asked to describe an anxiety-provoking situation. Typically, difficulties in entering phobic situations during the previous week were made the focus of the in-session practice for each subject. Subjects imagined themselves in that situation and verbalized appropriate cognitive techniques. For example, subjects assigned to SST imagined they were entering a fearful situation and that they were learning to prepare, handle, cope, and reinforce themselves with appropriate self-statements drawn from the examples that we have given. Subjects in the PI condition imagined they were entering a fearful situation with the intention of becoming anxious, panicky and of sweating, blushing, and fainting at that moment. The therapist provided feedback and, when indicated, modeled alternative statements. The therapist also encouraged the introjection of humor, which was considered to be an important component of the treatment. The results indicated statistically significant improvement for both treatments, from pre- to posttreatment, with several between-group advantages observed for paradoxical intention. However, by the 6-month follow-up, SST subjects exhibited continued improvement, in effect "catching up" to the PI subjects.

The primary aim of the fourth investigation (Michelson, Mavissakalian, & Marchione, 1985) was to conduct a comparative outcome study of cognitive (Paradoxical Intention—PI), behavioral (Graduated Exposure—GE) and psychophysiological (Progressive Deep Muscle Relaxation Training—RT) treatments for agoraphobia. Tripartite monitoring was conducted at pre-, mid- and posttreatment and at 3-, 6-, 12-, and 24-month follow-up assessments. Seventy-three agoraphobics with panic attacks were randomly assigned to one of three treatment conditions. Treatment consisted of 12 weekly, 2-hour group sessions composed of 4 to 5 subjects each. The initial two sessions were identical across treatment conditions, providing subjects with a rationale of the program and information about the nature of agoraphobia and the role of exposure/habituation in treating phobias.

Treatment sessions across all modalities focused on teaching subjects how to modify their habitual phobic anxiety and avoidance patterns. The importance of self-directed, graduated, prolonged, in vivo, exposure practice was reviewed. Progress was reviewed weekly, reported gains and improvement reinforced, and progressively more difficult phobic tasks to be completed between sessions were assigned. The specific interventions were introduced at the third session and continued throughout the treatment phase.

Graduated Exposure. Only subjects assigned to GE received therapist-assisted, graduated, in vivo exposure, which typically involved accompanying the therapist and an assistant to the center of town, or to large shopping malls in the hospital van. Once there, subjects were encouraged to leave the group as soon as they were able to pursue graduated, prolonged exposure on their own or with the help of a therapist. At first they entered stores independently or walked alone on congested areas. Subjects were encouraged to apply the principle of graduated exposure consistently by remaining in situations until they felt comfortable. After 90 minutes, the exposure group reconvened and returned to the clinic. In the later phases of treatment, subjects were encouraged to take the bus, either individually or in groups of two or three, to go downtown and return to the clinic, a distance of 8 miles.

Paradixocal Intention. The therapeutic instructions given in the PI condition for this study are identical to those described in the previous Michelson et al. (1983) investigation.

Progressive Deep Muscle Relaxation Training. Subjects assigned to RT received intensive, systematic, and programmatic instruction in all phases of relaxation training. The RT included a series of graduated steps, each with coaching, modeling, practice, rehearsal, and instructions. Subjects were sequentially exposed to relaxation and learned how to differentiate tension from relaxation, utilize RT exercises, master differential relaxation training, develop cue-controlled relaxation skills, use facilitative (diaphragmatic-yogic) breathing techniques, and practice instantaneous "letting go" techniques and related RT coping skills. In addition, they were instructed to practice RT skills a minimum of 20 minutes per day and to utilize these coping skills when in phobic situations. The results indicated that all treatments yielded statistically significant improvements on major outcome measures, although exposure and relaxation training evoked more rapid, stable, and potent effects than paradoxical intention.

META-ANALYSES OF STUDIES 1–4

Prior to comparing the relative efficacy of the modalities in reducing panic, multivariate analyses of variance (MANOVAs) were performed on demographic and clinical measures. There were no significant pretreatment differences across either the four studies or 11 treatment conditions. A significant analysis of variance was performed between the individual treatment conditions on the pretreatment panic measure, although Neuman–Keuls post hoc analyses could not identify specific differences.

The four outcome studies, with their 11 respective treatments, are summarized in Table 8.2. As seen in the table, the 174 subjects were judged as clinically severe and had a chronic history of agoraphobia with panic attacks. Mean panic ratings across the 11 therapeutic conditions are presented in Table 8.3. Follow-up data are provided, where available. Clinical inspection of the panic ratings reveals marked decreases from pre- to posttreatment, with conditions exhibiting differential trajectories over the follow-up. To quantify both outcome and maintenance phenomena empirically across the 11 modalities, treatment effect size computations were performed within each intervention using the formula:

$$\frac{\text{mean}_x - \text{mean}_y}{\textit{pooled Standard Deviation}}$$

The individual treatment effect size deviations are presented in Table 8.4. Examining the within-group treatment effects from Study 1 [imipramine plus exposure (IE), imipramine (I), exposure (E), control (C)], the combined treatment (IE) yielded large effects both at posttreatment and at the follow-ups, with continued gains observed from post to 6–24-month follow-up. With regard to the imipramine only condition, large effects were found comparing pre- with other assessments, but no further gains were observed once subjects completed treatment. The exposure condition generated the smallest treatment effect size at

TABLE 8.3
Table Represents Mean Sccores for Panic Attacks*
from 4 Outcome Studies

Study	*Treatment ns*	*Pre-treatment*	*Mid-treatment*	*Post-treatment*	*1- or 3-month Follow-up*	*6-month Follow-up*	*1-year Follow-up*	*2-year Follow-up*
I. NIMH 2 × 2 (1986)					(1 month)			
IE	*N* = 14	5.4	3.6	2.2	2.1	1.2	1.7	1.0
I	*N* = 17	4.2	2.3	1.1	1.2	1.0	1.4	1.0
E	*N* = 17	4.4	3.5	2.3	2.1	1.5	1.1	0.6
C	*N* = 14	5.6	3.7	2.2	3.6	1.3	2.2	2.1
II. IMI (1983)								
I	*N* = 7	5.4	4.5	2.1	—	—	—	—
I + PP	*N* = 8	5.6	3.4	1.6	—	—	—	—
III. PI/SST (1983)					(1 month)			
PI	*N* = 12	4.9	2.8	2.4	2.6	2.2	—	—
SST	*N* = 12	3.8	3.1	3.0	3.6	2.3	—	—
IV. CBM/NIMH (1985)								
PI	*N* = 26	3.7	3.3	1.8	1.9	1.7	1.3	1.7
GE	*N* = 22	3.5	2.9	2.0	2.7	2.0	1.5	0.4
RT	*N* = 25	4.2	2.0	1.7	1.7	1.4	1.6	2.4

Note. IE = Imipramine + Exposure; I = Imipramine; E = Exposure; C = Control (Programmed Practice); I + PP = Imipramine + Programmed Practice; PI = Paradoxical Intention; SST = Self-Statement Training; GE = Graduated Exposure; RT = Relaxation Training.

*Subjects were requested to rate the frequency and intensity of panic attacks during the past 3 days on a 9-point score ranging from 0 (no panic) to 8 (very severe frequent panic attacks). Study two used "past three weeks" as the assessment period.

TABLE 8.4
Treatment Effects* for Individual Modalities from 4 Outcome Studies from Pre- and Posttreatment to Follow-up Phases (N = 174)

Study		*Post*	*1–3-Month F.U.*	*6-Month F.U.*	*1-Year F.U.*	*2-Year F.U.*
I. *NIMH 2 × 2*						
IE						
	PRE	1.40	1.54	2.28	1.80	2.27
	POST		.04	.50	.23	.57
I						
	PRE	1.73	1.57	1.74	1.45	1.40
	POST		−.06	.07	−.19	.05
E						
	PRE	.81	.88	1.13	1.42	1.63
	POST		.09	.36	.65	.90
C						
	PRE	1.49	.82	1.95	.92	1.53
	POST		−.66	.50	.00	.05
II. *IMI*						
I						
	PRE	1.79	N/A+	—	—	—
	POST		N/A+	—	—	—
I + PP						
	PRE	2.50	2.66	—	—	—
	POST		.31	—	—	—
III. *PI/SST*						
PI						
	PRE	1.22	1.11	1.76	—	—
	POST		−.08	.11	—	—
SST						
	PRE	.38	.11	.72	—	—
	POST		.32	.32	—	—
IV. *CBM/NIMH*						
PI						
	PRE	.88	.85	.92	1.15	.89
	POST		.00	.24	.25	.05
GE						
	PRE	.70	.35	.74	.98	1.76
	POST		−.31	.00	.24	.91
RT						
	PRE	1.36	1.58	1.24	1.16	.84
	POST		.20	.05	.00	−.35

Note. A minus sign denotes worsening (i.e., increased panic) between assessment phases.

*Treatment effects were derived using the formula $\frac{\text{Mean } x - \text{Mean } y}{\text{Pooled Standard Deviation}}$

+*Note.* For this assessment, n = 1, there is no standard deviation, hence, no Treatment Effect can be calculated.

posttreatment. However, it continued to exhibit incremental, and relatively steady improvement on the panic measure over the course of the follow-up. Indeed, exposure was one of the few conditions to exhibit a large treatment effect from posttreatment to the 2-year follow-up. The "control" condition, which consisted of programmed practice, demonstrated powerful treatment effects from pre- to posttreatment. However, marked fluctuations of the panic measure were observed over the 2-year follow-up. While the final end point of this condition did not differ from the other treatments, the interim trajectory was apparently marked with alternating periods of panic relapse and remission.

Analysis of Study 2, comparing imipramine and imipramine plus programmed practice, revealed large treatment effects for both conditions, although the latter yielded the greater effect. Unfortunately, due to the initially small sample and high attrition at follow-up, extended longitudinal comparisons of these treatments could not be performed.

Examining (Study 3) Paradoxical Intention versus Self-Statement Training, large effects were found for Paradoxical Intention from pretreatment onward, with relatively little change from posttreatment to the 6-month follow-up. Conversely, SST evinced only modest outcome effects, with a moderately large, delayed effect noted at the 6-month follow-up.

Analysis of treatment effects for Study 4 (Paradoxical Intention, Graduated Exposure, Relaxation Training) revealed moderate effects for PI and GE, and large effects for RT at posttreatment. PI maintained its gains over the 2-year follow-up. Exposure after exhibiting a decline at the 3-month follow-up regained its positive trajectory at the 6-month follow-up and continued to exert beneficial effects over the 2-year follow-up. RT, which initially exhibited the largest effect at posttreatment, continued to demonstrate maintenance effects up to the 1-year follow-up. A modest increase in panic, however, was observed at the 2-year assessment. Overall, graduated exposure had almost a two-fold advantage in its treatment effect, as compared with PI and RT at the 2-year follow-up.

TABLE 8.5
Treatment Groupings for the 4 Outcome Studies

Group	*Label*	*Membership*
1 =	COGNITIVE	(includes treatments PI, SST, and PI)
2 =	IMIPRAMINE	(Imipramine treatment from IMI $n = 15$)
3 =	IMIPRAMINE + EXPOSURE RATIONALE	(Imipramine + PP treatment from $n = 15$ and I + PP from $n = 62$)
4 =	MEDS + EXPOSURE	(Imipramine + Exposure from $n = 62$ study)
5 =	PROGRAMMED PRACTICE	(from $n = 62$)
6 =	RELAXATION TRAINING	(from CBM $n = 73$)
7 =	EXPOSURE	(includes exposure treatments from $n = 62$ from CBM $n = 73$)
8 =	ALL PSYCHOSOCIAL TREATMENTS - NO MEDS	(includes treatments PI, SST, PI, RT, Programmed Practice, Exposure).

TABLE 8.6
Means and Standard Deviations of Panic Rating* for Groupings from 4 Outcome Studies (*N* = 174)

GP#/Treatment	*Pre*	*Mid*	*Post*	*1–3-mo F.U.*	*6-mo F.U.*	*1-yr F.U.*	*2-yr F.U.*
1. *Cognitive*							
Mean	4.00	3.10	2.10	2.40	1.90	1.30	1.70
S.D.	2.00	2.13	2.05	2.09	1.83	1.77	2.06
n =	50	49	39	34	42	19	7
2. *Imipramine only*							
Mean	5.43	4.50	2.14	3.00	—	—	—
S.D.	1.90	2.95	1.77	—	—	—	—
n =	7	6	7	1	—	—	—
3. *Imipramine + Self-exposure Rationale (programmed practice)*							
Mean	4.68	2.67	1.32	1.18	1.00	1.43	1.00
S.D.	1.91	1.55	1.52	1.67	1.41	1.70	2.49
n =	25	24	22	17	12	14	10
4. *Imipramine plus exposure*							
Mean	5.40	3.60	2.20	2.10	1.20	1.70	1.00
S.D.	2.10	1.82	2.32	1.97	1.14	1.36	0.96
n =	14	14	13	10	10	9	8
5. Programmed practice							
Mean	5.60	3.70	2.20	3.60	1.30	2.22	2.10
S.D.	2.41	1.98	1.90	2.20	1.25	2.63	1.85
n =	14	14	12	8	7	9	10
6. *Relaxation*							
Mean	4.20	2.00	1.70	1.40	1.57	1.70	2.40
S.D.	2.04	1.24	1.65	1.31	2.04	2.19	2.15
n =	25	25	24	23	21	15	7
7. *Exposure*							
Mean	3.90	3.20	2.10	2.50	1.80	1.32	0.40
S.D.	2.43	2.18	2.14	2.47	1.82	1.76	0.63
n =	40	39	37	34	28	31	24
8. *Psychosocial treatments*							
Mean	4.20	3.00	2.00	2.30	1.80	1.50	1.20
S.D.	2.23	2.03	1.97	2.08	1.83	1.92	1.73
n =	129	127	112	103	98	74	48

*Panic ratings consist of subjects' self-reports on the frequency and intensity of panic attacks in past 3 days (0 = no panic, 9 = severe/frequent panic).

The 11 individual treatment conditions were grouped, for purposes of conducting comparative analyses. The treatment groupings are presented in Table 8.5. The means, standard deviations, and sample sizes per condition/assessment phase are reported in Table 8.6. Treatment effects were computed for the panic severity/frequency rating for each of the groupings (i.e., within-grouping effects) from pre- and posttreatment through the follow-ups. The "Cognitive" grouping exhibited pre-posttreatment improvement on the panic measure, with

TABLE 8.7
Treatment Effects of Panic Ratings for Groups from 4 Outcome Studies (N = 174) from Pre- and Posttreatment to Follow-up Phases

Grouping:	*Post*	*1–3-Month*	*6-Month*	*1-Year*	*2-Year*
Cognitive					
PRE	.95	.79	1.10	1.40	1.14
POST		−.14	.10	.41	.24
Imipramine					
PRE	1.79	—	—	—	—
POST		—	—	—	—
Imipramine + exposure rationale (programmed practice)					
PRE	1.92	1.87	1.91	1.68	1.78
POST		.06	.33	.06	.31
Imipramine + exposure					
PRE	1.47	1.61	2.37	2.08	2.70
POST		.05	.54	.27	.62
Programmed practice					
PRE	1.55	.85	2.04	1.46	1.57
POST		−.69	.53	.00	.05
Relaxation					
PRE	1.34	1.62	1.27	1.19	.87
POST		.15	.05	.00	−.40
Exposure					
PRE	.79	.73	.95	1.05	1.64
POST		−.17	.15	.29	.91
Psychosocial treatments					
PRE	1.04	.88	1.16	1.26	1.39
POST		−.15	.10	.26	.42

Treatment effects were derived using the formula:

$$\frac{\text{Mean } x - \text{Mean } y}{\text{Pooled Standard Deviation}}$$

modest fluctuations noted over the 2-year follow-up. The "Imipramine only" grouping yielded a large treatment outcome effect. Unfortunately, due to the attenuated sample at the 3-month follow-up, further analyses were not possible. The "Imipramine plus Exposure Rationale" yielded a large treatment effect at posttreatment and generally maintained its effect over the 2-year follow-up. "Imipramine plus Exposure" exhibited a similar pattern as "Imipramine plus Exposure Rationale," with large treatment effects observed at posttreatment. In addition Imipramine plus Exposure subjects evidenced moderate and continued treatment effects over the follow-up phases.

"Programmed Practice" generated a large treatment at the completion of therapy. However, there was an apparent episode of panic relapse at the 3-month follow-up. By the 2-year follow-up, subjects in this condition remained essentially unchanged from their posttreatment status. The "Relaxation" group demonstrated a large effect at posttreatment, continued improvement at the 3-month follow-up, and experienced an increase in panic at the 2-year follow-up. The "Exposure" group had the smallest posttreatment effect size. However, between the 6- and 24-month follow-up, exposure subjects experienced gradual, but steady decreases, in panic. By the 2-year follow-up, exposure subjects had the lowest panic ratings of all the groupings. Under "Psychosocial Treatments," moderate treatment effects were observed at post, with a slight increasing trend at the 1- and 3-month follow-ups. Between the 6- and 24-month follow-ups gradual, but steady, gains were observed.

Comparative treatment effects were derived for the treatment groupings from midtreatment through the 2-year follow-up, and are presented in Table 8.8, with *t*-tests at each assessment. (Given the large number of analyses performed, an alpha level of $p < .05$ was selected to provide sufficient statistical power to detect trends in the data while controlling for alpha inflation.) There were relatively few significant differences between the groupings across assessment phases. While several midtreatment differences were found in favor of relaxation training, these effects decreased at posttreatment. The 3-month follow-up yielded four significant findings with Relaxation Training being superior to Exposure, Programmed Practice, and Cognitive treatments. Imipramine plus Programmed Practice was superior to Programmed Practice. No significant differences were observed at the 6-month or 1-year follow-up. Analyses performed at the 2-year follow-up yielded two significant comparisons, with Exposure being superior to Programmed Practice and Relaxation Training. Relatively large treatment effects were occasionally observed in the analyses which did not achieve statistical significance. This was largely due to a combination of large variance and small samples, reducing statistical power. Such trends were observed for Cognitive treatments being superior to Relaxation Training, and Imipramine plus Exposure being superior to Programmed Practice.

DISCUSSION

The results from the meta-analyses revealed that the psychosocial and pharmacological treatments exerted large treatment effects on the panic measure. Overall, the interventions significantly reduced mean panic (severity/frequency) ratings by posttreatment. Differential trajectories were observed both during and after treatment across conditions. At midtreatment, Relaxation Training demonstrated the lowest panic ratings across all treatments. In addition, moderate to large treatment effects were observed in favor of Cognitive Treatment versus Imipramine, versus Imipramine alone, and comparing Relaxation Training with Imipramine.

At posttreatment, Imipramine plus Programmed Practice, Imipramine alone, and Relaxation Training appeared to exhibit a modest advantage, compared with

TABLE 8.8
Comparative Treatment Effects of Panic Ratings for Groupings across the 4 Outcome Studies and Assessments (N = 174)

	Treatment Effect					
Comparison	*Mid*	*Post*	*3-Month F.U.*	*6-Month F.U.*	*1-Year F.U.*	*2-Year F.U.*
Cognitive vs imipramine	−.63	.00				
Cognitive vs imipramine + exposure rationale	.04	.17	.26	.29	−.04	.18
Cognitive vs imipramine + exposure	−.12	−.02	.07	.24	−.15	.26
Cognitive vs programmed practice	−.14	−.02	−.27	.19	−.27	−.14
Cognitive vs relaxation training	.31**	.14	.30*	.08	−.10	−.16
Cognitive vs exposure	−.02	.00	−.02	.03	−.06	.81
Imipramine vs imipramine + exposure rationale	.96	.50				
Imipramine vs imipramine + exposure	.36	−.05				
Imipramine vs programmed practice	.35	−.05				
Imipramine vs relaxation training	1.50	.24				
Imipramine vs exposure	.57	.00				
Imipramine vs all psychosocial treatments	.72	.05				
Imipramine + exposure rationale vs imipramine + exposure	−.54	−.50	−.51	−.12	−.14	.00
Imipramine + exposure rationale vs programmed practice	−.58	−.55	−1.3**	−.16	−.27	−.37
Imipramine + exposure rationale vs relaxation training	.50	−.25	−.14	−.19	−.08	−.34
Imipramine + exposure rationale vs exposure	−.25	−.42	−.58	−.27	−.03	.48
Imipramine + exposure rationale vs all psychosocial treatments	−.16	−.37	−.54	−.25	−.03	−.06
Imipramine + exposure vs programmed practice	−.03	.00	−.35	−.07	−.19	−.70
Imipramine + exposure vs relaxation training	.74**	.14	.30	−.13	.00	−.48
Imipramine + exposure vs exposure	.09	.02	−.07	−.21	.07	1.11

TABLE 8.8
(Continued)

Comparison	Treatment Effect Mid	Post	3-Month F.U.	6-Month F.U.	1-Year F.U.	2-Year F.U.
Imipramine + exposure vs all psychosocial treatments	.15	.05	−.05	−.19	.06	−.07
Programmed practice vs relaxation	.72**	.17	.89**	−.09	.11	−.08
Programmed practice vs exposure	.11	.02	.19	−.16	.18	2.00**
Programmed practice vs all other psychosocial treatments	.20	.05	.33	−.15	.19	.31
Relaxation training vs exposure	−.34**	−.13	−.25*	−.05	.05	1.15*

Note. A minus sign denotes that the first listed treatment was superior (i.e., less panic).
Significance = $*p < .05$ $**p < .01$ using *t*-tests

Treatment effects were derived using the formula: $\dfrac{\text{Mean } x - \text{Mean } y}{\text{Pooled Standard Deviation}}$

the other modalities. The 3-month follow-up revealed that Relaxation Training was superior to Exposure, Programmed Practice, and Cognitive treatments. Imipramine plus Programmed Practice was significantly superior to Programmed Practice alone. No significant differences were observed at the 6-month or 1-year follow-ups. At the 2-year follow-up, distinct, temporal patterns were evident across conditions. Some treatments exhibited an improving trajectory (Exposure, Imipramine plus Exposure) whereas others displayed alternating patterns of worsening and remission in panic (Programmed Practice, Relaxation Training). A trend was noted at the 2-year follow-up in favor of Cognitive treatment and Exposure, which were superior to Relaxation Training, and Imipramine plus Exposure, which was inferior to Exposure alone and superior to Programmed Practice.

Of clinical interest was the observation that Exposure, while exerting the smallest treatment effect at outcome, demonstrated the lowest panic rating at the 2-year follow-up. Conversely, Programmed Practice, which was equivalent to Exposure at posttreatment, exhibited a pattern of worsening, followed by restoration to posttreatment levels of panic at the 2-year follow-up. The Cognitive treatment grouping had a moderate treatment effect at the completion of therapy with mild fluctuations noted over the follow-up. By the 2-year assessment, cognitively treated subjects had not only maintained their initial gains, but had evinced continued improvement.

The combined Imipramine plus Exposure condition appeared to yield synergistic effects, with large treatment effects found at posttreatment and across the 2-year follow-up. The Relaxation condition also exhibited large effects at posttreatment and at 3-, 6-, and 12-month follow-ups. However, there was a noticeable decline at the 2-year assessment. Overall, the psychosocial modalities exhibited moderate to large effects at posttreatment, with a slight decline at the first follow-up, followed subsequently by an improving trend from the 6- to 24-month follow-ups. Unfortunately, there were no follow-up data available for the imipramine-only condition, thereby precluding comparative analyses of the long-term functioning of these subjects. With regard to Imipramine plus Programmed Practice, these subjects appeared to fare relatively well over the long-term follow-up with minor fluctuations in panic ratings (i.e., moderate increase at the 1-year follow-up).

Methodologically, several issues remain unresolved, which temper the drawing of firm conclusions. The presence of large standard deviations indicates marked variability on the panic measure, upon which these analyses are based. The panic measure's temporal stability was examined by Michelson and Mavissakalian (1983) for short (4 weeks), moderate (10 weeks) and extended (16 weeks) periods. Test-retest reliabilities were .69 for 4 weeks, .41 for 10 weeks, and .14 for 16 weeks. The exact reasons for the decline in reliability over time are not clear. Possibly the nature of the index (e.g., a unitary 9-point scale) may account for the finding. Another explanation is that, given the well-documented episodic nature of panic attacks, there is increased variance over longer test-retest intervals. For purposes of the present intracenter, multistudy comparison, these psychometric considerations must be duly considered in interpreting the findings.

The positive results achieved with Imipramine plus Programmed Practice and Imipramine plus Exposure may be largely a result of imipramine allowing subjects to reduce cognitive avoidance while being extensively exposed, either with the therapist, or on their own, to phobic situations. The efficacy of the exposure outings may be enhanced by imipramine.

The so-called "cognitive" treatments employed in the study were either paradoxical intention or self-statement training. More potent cognitive therapies such as those devised in our center, as well as the exemplary work of Aaron T. Beck and his colleagues, which address deeper, metacognitive structures have found that these more sophisticated forms of cognitive therapy exert enhanced therapeutic effects, compared with more superficial cognitive strategies. Indeed, part of the existing difficulty in appraising the potential value of cognitive treatments for panic stems from differences and variations of the cognitive procedures employed. Schwartz's (1982) excellent review of cognitive therapies notes that cognitions may be viewed as *simple habits* of thought with minimal organization and depth; *cognitive structures, plans,* or *strategies* with considerable organization and depth; or *unconscious cognitions,* which are also organized and of great depth.

Few reviewers of cognitive studies have made practical distinctions among cognitive techniques, and draw conclusions as though Ellis's Rational Emotive Therapy, Beck's Cognitive Therapy, and Meichenbaum's Self-Statement Training are indistinct. Hollon and Kriss (1984) suggest that treatments may be more or less metacognitive in nature and that different cognitive behavioral treatments may have different loci of effect. Specifically, differences may exist among cognitive therapies in efficacy for modifying *knowledge structures, cognitive processes,* or *cognitive products.*

Some theorists, such as Beck & Emory (1985), and Guidano and Liotti (1983), suggest that cognitive procedures operating at the level of changing cognitive products (e.g., thoughts or self-statements alone, compared with focusing on larger structures of schemata) are operating at the lowest level and the one least likely to be efficacious in treating complex anxiety disorders. In this vein, cognitive procedures which are not metacognitive may be inadequate therapeutic strategies for panic and agoraphobic disorders, with their complex metacognitive elements. Thus, the efficacy of these cognitive treatments is probably an underestimate of their potential treatment effects if more sophisticated and in-depth cognitive therapies were utilized.

With regard to Relaxation Training, this treatment exhibited potent antipanic effects up to the 1-year follow-up, which is theoretically and clinically compatible with its primary aim, that is, self-control of psychophysiological reactivity. Relaxation Training subjects appeared to use their skills initially, although by the 2-year follow-up, they may have decreased their use of RT, thus experiencing an increase in panic. While Exposure evinced modest outcome effects initially, it exerted the most potent long-term benefits at the 2-year follow-up. These results strongly suggest that *combining* Graduated Exposure with Cognitive Therapy or Relaxation Training should yield synergistic outcome and maintenance effects. Presently, we are examining the relative and combined efficacy of Cognitive Therapy plus Exposure, Relaxation Training plus Exposure compared with Exposure alone to address this issue for agoraphobics with panic attacks.

From a theoretical perspective, the findings from the meta-analyses raise several questions for the biological model of panic. First, the psychosocial treatments were effective in reducing panic attacks, even over the course of the 1-year follow-up. Since these modalities are not known to affect basic biological mechanisms purported to be responsible for panic, such as the oft-cited lactate research and similar formulations, it remains for advocates of these biological models to explain these beneficial effects (cf. Telch, this volume). Similarly, the half-life of imipramine is relatively short, with complete drug washout being achieved after 3 to 4 weeks. Hence, prolonged therapeutic effects of imipramine over the course of the 2-year follow-up suggest that cognitive factors, and not biological processes, account for the decreases in panic. Subjects' reattributional experiences of cognitive and somatic cues as nondangerous may be primarily responsible for these long-term benefits (Clark, this volume; Beck, this volume). Powerful cognitive mediational processes regarding safety, threat, prediction (see Rachman, this volume) and control, may be associated with the positive effects of the medication on panic. It should also be noted that a number of medication-treated subjects in these studies required and received interim treatment during the follow-up. Hence, the somewhat positive picture portrayed by these data must be considered in light of their differential relapse and interim treatment. Conversely, the efficacy of Relaxation Training, Exposure, and Cognitive strategies in reducing panic suggests they may offer powerful tools in terms of interoceptive reconditioning (van den Hout, this volume) increasing cognitive control (Beck, this volume), prediction, and fostering new cognitive schemata regarding the dangerousness, predictability, and control of panic (Rachman, this volume).

Methodological issues limit the generalizability of the findings. Two of these issues are the differential patterns of attrition and interim treatment during the follow-up and possible random variations of the panic measure, combined with the limited window of assessment (i.e., panic was assessed only within the past 3 weeks at each follow-up evaluation). For example, at the 2-year follow-up, subjects were requested to report their panic attacks during the past 3 weeks. No weekly or monthly ratings of panic frequency or severity were collected during the period between the first and second-year follow-up, leaving an 11-month period during which panic status was not evaluated. Given the problems of reliability in retrospective recall of even major life events, contemporaneous assessment of panic is required to track the temporal progressions of panic both during and after treatment. Future studies of panic should consider monitoring the rate, severity, and duration of panic attacks on a more frequent (i.e., daily) basis.

STUDY 2

Cognitive, Behavioral, and Physiological Correlates of Panic

The second issue in panic to be addressed in this chapter refers to the Michelson, Mavissakalian, & Marchione (1985) report previously described. An expanded sample of 73 subjects meeting DSM–III criteria for agoraphobia with panic attacks completed tripartite assessments at pre-, mid- and posttreatment. Subjects were randomly assigned to either Cognitive (Paradoxical intention—PI), Behavioral (Graduated Exposure—GE), or Psychophysiological (Progressive Deep Muscle Relaxation Training—RT) treatments.

Panic was assessed using several methods. Subjects rated the episodes of unexpected panic during the previous 3 days, with regard to their frequency and intensity on a 9-point anchored scale with 0 = no panic, 2 = mild panic, 4 = moderate panic, 6 = severe panic and 8 = very severe panic. This item was taken from the Subjective Symptom Scale. Next, subjects completed a self-rating questionnaire designed to assess DSM–III criteria and rated the severity and frequency of their panic attacks over the previous 3 weeks. Using this same questionnaire, subjects rated the severity of 10 specific panic symptoms out of the 12 listed in DSM–III (Item 5: dizziness, vertigo, or unsteady feelings; and Item 6: feelings of unreality were collapsed; and Item 8, hot and cold flashes were deleted. Thus, four measures were derived from the panic scale: (1) overall severity; (2) number of panic symptoms endorsed; (3) a mean symptom score was derived by averaging the 10 individual ratings; and (4) panic frequency. The final measure of panic was the presence of spontaneous panic attacks during the previous week. Spontaneous panic attacks were operationally defined as panic attacks occurring at home without obvious environmental provocation. The assessment also included the following measures:

Global Assessment of Severity is a 5-point scale rated by the clinician which ranges from a score of 1, representing no complaints and normal activity to 5, indicating that normal work or social activities have been either radically changed or prevented.

Self-Rating of Severity is a 9-point analogue scale rated by the subject in answer to the following question: "How would you rate the present state of your phobic symptoms on the scale below?" The scale ranged from 0, meaning no phobias present, to 8 or severely disturbing and disabling phobias present (Marks & Mathews, 1979).

The *Fear Questionnaire* (Marks & Mathews, 1979) was used as a measure of phobic severity. In addition, subjects rated their five most severe agoraphobic situations on a 9-point scale of phobic anxiety and avoidance, following the practice introduced by Marks and Gelder (1965) and later modified by Watson and Marks (1971). The scale ranges from 0, indicating no phobic anxiety or phobic avoidance, to a maximum rating of 8, representing very severe, continuous anxiety, and complete phobic avoidance. The scores of the five situations were averaged to yield a mean clinical measure of *Phobic Anxiety and Avoidance* (PAA). Anxiety was assessed using the *Taylor Manifest Anxiety Scale* (Taylor, 1953). Depression was evaluated, using *The Beck Depression Inventory* (Beck, Ward, Mendelsohn, Mock, & Erbaugh, 1961). General symptomatology was measured, using the abbreviated *Hopkins Symptom Checklist* (Derogatis, Lipman, Rickels, Uhlenhuth, & Coul, 1974).

A direct measure of agoraphobia was obtained, using a Standardized Behavioral Avoidance Course (S–BAC) (Michelson, Mavissakalian, & Marchione, 1985), which consisted of a 1-mile walk beginning at the front door of the clinic, proceeding to a crowded urban center, and ending at a congested bus stop. Subjects were requested to walk the course alone for as far as they could go and to return only when their level of anxiety became intolerable. The behavioral course was divided into 20 steps, with performance scored by assigning the number of the last step completed. In addition, at *each* step, subjects rated their anxiety on a 9-point Subjective Unit of Discomfort Scale (SUDS). The SUDS scores of the completed steps were averaged to yield a mean value per assessment as well as a peak SUDS value for the entire course.

During the Standardized Behavioral Avoidance Course, a continuous record of heart rate was obtained, using the Exersentry Model EX3. Heart rate data were generated on a continuous basis. Heart rate monitoring began with a 5-minute sitting baseline, followed by a 5-minute walking baseline during which subjects walked at their normal pace with a research assistant within the hospital. The S–BAC came last. The heart rate variables selected for study included mean heart rate sitting—baseline 1, mean heart rate walking—baseline 2, mean heart rate for the entire S–BAC and peak heart rate during the S–BAC. The first two measures, sitting and walking baselines, provided a relative baseline for resting and general activity levels of arousal. The mean heart rate for the entire behavioral course provided an overall gauge of in vivo, phobic psychophysiological arousal. The peak heart rate provided an index of the maximum severity of psychophysiological reactivity during the S–BAC.

Subjects were trained to recognize and report their thoughts during the S–BAC. These verbalizations were recorded, using a small, nonobtrusive recorder, and later transcribed and independently coded. The primary coding categories utilized were: (1) Negative, Self-Defeating Statements, (2) Positive, Coping Statements, and, (3) Neutral, Task Irrelevant Statements. Interrater reliabilities were computed for 25% of the data and indicated acceptable reliability (≥ 85%) across all categories. A State-of-Mind Index (cf. Schwartz & Michelson, in press) was also derived, using the formula:

$$\frac{\text{Positive Cognitions}}{\text{Positive + Negative Cognitions}}$$

This transformation yielded a ratio of positive to negative cognitions which excluded background "cognitive noise" (i.e., neutral statements).

An a priori operationalized measure of Improvement (Michelson, Mavissakalian, & Marchione, 1985) was used to classify subjects' overall level of therapeutic gain, using the following criteria: Decrease of ≥ 2 on the *Global Assessment Scale;* Decrease of ≥ 2 on *Self-Rating of Severity;* Decrease of ≥ 2 on *Phobic Anxiety and Avoidance,* Decrease of ≥ 2 on mean SUDS. Subjects were given one point for each criterion they met and assigned to either low (0–1), medium (2) or high (3–4) Improvement categories using pre-post computations.

Recognizing that even significant improvement does not necessarily reflect absolute level of functioning, four a priori criteria were utilized to classify subjects' level of end state [low, (0–1), medium (2), high (3–4)] functioning (Michelson et al., 1985). One point was assigned for each of the following: A score of ≤ 2 on the *Global Assessment Scale;* A score of ≤ 2 on the *Self-Rating of Severity;* A score of ≤ 3 on the *Phobic Anxiety and Avoidance;* and an S–BAC score of 20 with a SUDS score of < 3, indicating completion of the S–BAC with minimal or no anxiety. This operationalized definition of end state functioning has the merit of combining measures of clinician and subject-rated severity, clinical ratings of phobic anxiety and avoidance, and behavioral performance.

During the S–BAC, subjects rated their anxiety level, using the 9-point scale at each of the 20 steps during the 1-mile test. Subjects with peak SUDS values of 7 to 8 were classified as "Panickers," 5–6 as "Fearful," and 0–4 as "Anxious." The use of peak SUDS provided a clinically salient index of subjects' maximum (i.e., panic) in vivo anxiety. To test the internal validity of the classification procedure, the peak SUDS variable, used to assign subjects to the three categories, was analyzed. As expected, both the peak and mean SUDS measures evinced statistically significant incremental differences between subjects classified as Anxious, Fearful, and Panicked. This finding provides empirical support for the differential validity of the classification procedure.

Analyses of variance were performed on the clinical, behavioral, physiological, and cognition measures at pre-, mid-, and posttreatment assessments comparing the three (Panicked, Fearful, Anxious) groups. Assignment of subjects to anxiety groups was performed *separately,* using the classification procedure previously described at each assessment. The results of these analyses are presented in Table 8.9.

The majority of the significant analyses of the clinical measures revealed a pattern of group differences between the Anxious, compared with the Fearful and Panicked groups, and between the Anxious and Panicked groups. A significant incremental (Anxious < Fearful < Panicked) difference was observed only for the *Phobic Anxiety and Avoidance* measure at posttreatment. Analyses of variance of the physiological measures yielded only one significant finding with peak heart rate at mid-treatment being significantly *lower* (20 b.m.p) for the in vivo Panickers than either the Anxious or Fearful subjects. Significant differences were found between the three groups on the number of steps completed during the Standardized Behavioral Avoidance Course at mid- and posttreatment. (Panickers terminated the course at an earlier point.) Therefore, analyses of covariance were also performed on the heart rate measures, controlling for the number of steps completed on the S–BAC. Subjects reporting in vivo panic did not manifest statistically significant or clinically apparent elevations in heart rate, compared with subjects reporting only mild or moderate in vivo anxiety. Panickers exhibited significantly lower mean and peak heart rates on the S–BAC during the course of treatment.

Analyses of variance, performed on the cognition measures, revealed statistically significant differences between Panickers and Anxious subjects on negative cognitions at mid- and posttreatment. Both Fearful and Anxious groups were significantly different from Panickers at pretreatment on negative cognitions. In all cases, Panickers exhibited the highest percentage of catastrophic, self-defeating, and negative cognitions during the S–BAC. No significant differences were observed with regard to positive cognitions. The Ratio cognition index revealed that Anxious subjects were significantly more positively balanced in their internal dialogue, compared with their Fearful and Panicked counterparts.

Chi-squares were performed at posttreatment and at the 3-month follow-up comparing the three pretreatment anxiety groups to ascertain the predictive influence of anxiety (panic) level on outcome and maintenance. The proportion of

TABLE 8.9
ANOVA's of the 3 Anxiety Levels at
Pre-, Mid-, and Postassessments

Measure	*Pre*	*F-Ratio*	*Mid*	*F-Ratio*	*Post*	*F-Ratio*
CLINICAL						
Panic attack, severity—past 3 weeks						
anxious	5.0	1.0	3.5	3.4**	2.5	7.6***
fearful	5.9		4.1		2.8	
panicky	5.4		5.1	1 > 3	4.8	1,2 > 3
Panic attack—mean rating of symptoms—past 3 weeks						
anxious	3.1	1.4	1.9	7.6***	1.2	13.8***
fearful	3.7		2.1		1.7	
panicky	3.9		4.0	1,2 > 3	3.2	1,2 > 3
Panic attack—number of symptoms endorsed—past 3 weeks						
anxious	7.4	1.0	6.5	3.1**	5.1	7.1***
fearful	7.8		7.2		6.8	
panicky	8.4		9.1	1 > 3	8.7	1 > 3
Panic attack, frequency—past 3 weeks						
anxious	6.8	1.0	3.6	5.9***	4.5	<1
fearful	10.7		12.3		2.4	
panicky	11.9		18.0	1 > 2,3	6.1	
Spontaneous panic attacks in past week (1 = yes 2 = no)						
anxious	1.1	1.3	1.5	1.0	1.6	3.0**
fearful	1.0		1.4		1.7	
panicky	1.1		1.2		1.2	3,1,2
Global assessment of severity						
anxious	4.2	12.9***	3.6	1.1	2.5	10.0***
fearful	4.6		3.8		3.2	
panicky	4.9	1 > 2,3	3.9		3.8	1 > 2,3
Self-rating of severity						
anxious	6.1	<1	3.2	2.0	2.2	13.6***
fearful	6.7		4.0		2.6	
panicky	6.2		4.2		4.5	1,2 > 3
Phobic anxiety and avoidance						
anxious	7.6	1.6	3.0	12.4***	1.9	21.5***
fearful	7.9		4.6		3.7	
panicky	7.8		5.1	1 > 2,3	5.3	1 > 2 > 3
Fear questionnaire, agoraphobia						
anxious	24.1	10.4***	14.3	5.9***	8.1	11.7***
fearful	34.1		21.7		12.1	
panicky	32.4	1 > 2,3	22.9	1,2,3	20.2	1,2 > 3
Fear questionnaire, social						
anxious	13.7	4.4***	11.0	3.4**	9.1	<1
fearful	17.3		15.5		11.9	
panicky	21.1	1 > 3	13.6	1 > 2	9.7	
Fear questionnaire—total						
anxious	51.4	6.9***	37.8	4.7***	26.5	5.4***
fearful	68.9		50.9		34.5	
panicky	71.5	1 > 2,3	54.7	1,2,3	44.5	1 > 3

TABLE 8.9
(Continued)

Measure	*Pre*	*F-Ratio*	*Mid*	*F-Ratio*	*Post*	*F-Ratio*
Fear survey schedule						
anxious	125.1	3.1**	101.5	<1	81.2	1.8
fearful	145.2		102.1		88.1	
panicky	160.1	1 > 3	117.2		107.6	
Beck Depression Inventory						
anxious	13.7	3.6**	8.9	1.0	6.4	<1
fearful	15.8		10.4		6.2	
panicky	20.1	1 > 3	12.9		9.5	
Taylor Manifest Anxiety Scale						
anxious	26.0	4.4***	22.2	1.9	17.8	3.5**
fearful	30.6		25.1		20.0	
panicky	33.5	1 > 3	29.9		27.4	1 > 3
Hopkins Symptom Checklist—total						
anxious	110.6	3.5**	94.1	4.5***	86.7	2.7
fearful	125.6		96.9		87.3	
panicky	131.0	1 > 3	117.4	1,2 > 3	104.3	
BEHAVIORAL						
Number of steps completed—S-BAC						
anxious	13.6	1.9	16.9	4.0**	18.9	26.3***
fearful	9.7		15.0		13.6	
panicky	10.1		10.0	1,2 > 3	7.9	1 > 2 > 3
Mean SUDS completed steps—S-BAC						
anxious	1.6	42.3***	1.2	28.4***	0.8	67.2***
fearful	3.9		3.2		3.1	
panicky	5.3	1 > 2 > 3	4.4	1 > 2 > 3	4.8	1 > 2 > 3
Peak SUDS						
anxious	2.1	234.8***	1.6	145.5***	1.3	134.8***
fearful	5.8		5.1		5.1	
panicky	7.5	1 > 2 > 3	7.5	1 > 2 > 3	7.2	1 > 2 > 3
PHYSIOLOGICAL						
Mean heart rate—sitting						
anxious	95.7	<1	90.2	<1	87.9	<1
fearful	99.7		88.9		94.0	
panicky	94.3		86.8		88.6	
Mean heart rate—walking						
anxious	117.7	<1	111.5	<1	107.6	<1
fearful	124.9		113.0		113.7	
panicky	119.3		106.9		111.3	
Mean heart rate—S-BAC						
anxious	123.7	<1	122.0	2.1	121.2	<1
fearful	130.1		126.6		125.2	
panicky	127.2		111.4		119.1	
Peak heart rate—S-BAC						
anxious	136.5	<1	137.4	3.6**	137.1	1.2

(Continued)

TABLE 8.9
(Continued)

Measure	*Pre*	*F-Ratio*	*Mid*	*F-Ratio*	*Post*	*F-Ratio*
fearful	141.2		141.0		138.4	
panicky	140.5		117.7	3 > 1,2	127.3	
Heart rate last step						
anxious	128.6	<1	125.1	1.6	125.0	<1
fearful	135.5		128.2		126.3	
panicky	131.0		112.5		119.5	
COGNITIVE						
Percentage of negative statements						
anxious	.18	4.9***	.12	4.6***	.14	4.4**
fearful	.35		.19		.22	
panicky	.37	1 > 2,3	.30	1 > 3	.29	1 > 3
Percentage of positive statements						
anxious	.26	1.9	.26	<1	.35	1.0
fearful	.22		.29		.25	
panicky	.18		.33		.29	
Ratio = (positive / positive + negative statements)						
anxious	.62	5.4***	.78	6.1***	.68	2.7
fearful	.42		.59		.52	
panicky	.39	1 > 2,3	.51	1 > 2,3	.50	

Note. $^{**}p \leq .05$, $^{***}p \leq .01$.

(pretreatment) Anxious, Fearful, and Panicked subjects who met the operationalized criteria for low, medium, and high Endstate functioning and Improvement was analyzed. The three groups were not significantly different on Endstate functioning at post or follow-up or on Improvement at posttreatment. A significant difference was found in favor of the Panicked group on Improvement at the follow-up. The superior Improvement and enhanced Endstate functioning of the Panicked group might have been a function of the attenuated range among the Anxious and Fearful Subjects on the SUDS measure, which is used in computing Endstate and Improvement. Therefore, the data were reanalyzed, removing the SUDS variable from both the Endstate and Improvement composite measures. The analyses revealed that the three groups were not significantly different at either post or follow-up assessments on Endstate or Improvement measures. Indeed, Panicked subjects fared as well as their Anxious and Fearful counterparts with regard to treatment outcome.

DISCUSSION

Prior to reviewing the results of these analyses, a brief discussion of the classification procedure, upon which the foundation of the analyses is built, is provided. In the present study, the classification of subjects offered several methodological advantages. The assessment was standardized, using a quasinaturalistic (i.e., in vivo) monitoring of tridimensional functioning, permitting simultaneous assessment of behavior, physiology, and cognition. Subjects also reported their in vivo anxiety levels at frequent intervals on an ongoing basis.

The results from the mean and peak SUDS analyses provide empirical support for the differential validity of the specific groupings of Panickers, Fearful, and Anxious subjects. Examination of the four panic measures in Table 8.9 indicated significantly greater panic attacks, panic severity, panic symptoms, and panic frequency among the Panicked group, indicating good convergent validity. Therefore, the validity of using peak in vivo anxiety, as a model for studying the tripartite correlates of panic, appears well founded.

The clinical measures, which represent concomitant, but not purely tripartite domains, reflected the least number of differential effects. Panickers exhibited higher levels of fear, phobias, global severity, depression, anxiety, panic symptoms, panic frequency, and general symptomatology from pre- to posttreatment. These findings suggest that Panickers experience greater symptomatology and increased severity across clinical measures of psychological and psychiatric functioning, a finding corroborated by Norton, Harrison, Hauch, and Rhodes (1985).

Regarding the tripartite assessment, a number of interesting findings were revealed. The behavioral measure (S–BAC steps completed) yielded between-group differences at midtreatment with Panickers having terminated the phobic test significantly earlier than either Anxious or Fearful subjects. Incremental differences were found at posttreatment. By the posttreatment assessment, where the novelty of the S–BAC had been reduced, the differences between Anxious and Fearful subjects were equivalent to the differences between Fearful and Panicked subjects. Overall, these results revealed the powerful mediating influence of in vivo anxiety on phobic avoidance, and that panic appears to represent one end (albeit a severe dimension) of an anxiety continuum.

The psychophysiological analyses yielded an interesting and counterintuitive finding. Specifically, Panickers demonstrated significantly *lower* peak and mean heart rates at midtreatment. These findings indicate that panic frequently occurs in the absence of marked psychophysiological reactivity, relative to mild or moderate anxiety states. Therefore, it is logical to presume that cognitive mediational processes (Chambless, this volume), not associated with physiological reactivity, may play an important role in panic. Cognitive appraisal of danger, threats to well-being, controllability, predictability, and valence apparently modulate the panic experience (Rachman, this volume). While heart rate is generally regarded as one of the more reliable and clinically sensitive psychophysiological measures in anxiety disorders research, it is possible that some subjects may not be cardiological reactors and might exhibit their reactivity in terms of changes in skin resistance or electromyography. However, given the relatively large sample employed in this study, the findings suggest that heart rate reactivity may not differentiate in vivo panic from either mild or moderate anxiety states.

The cognitive analyses revealed several significant differences between Panickers and other subjects. Panickers and Fearful subjects reported more negative ideation at pretreatment. No between-group differences were found for positive ideation. The Ratio cognition index indicated that at pre- and midtreatment, Anxious subjects had a significantly greater proportion of positive thoughts than the other groups. Panickers experienced a significantly greater percentage of negative thoughts at mid- and posttreatment. Most importantly negative, self-defeating, and catastrophic ideation appear to be closely associated with in vivo panic (Beck, this volume; Chambless, this volume). Moreover, higher levels of anxiety were associated with a greater frequency of negative cognitions. Unfortunately, cause-and-effect relations regarding the exact sequence of events, that is, the relationship between maladaptive cognitions and panic, cannot be easily discerned from these data.

An interactive cognitive–physiological–behavioral loop, with an upward spiraling progression, may be a likely model in the development, maintenance and occurrence of panic. The sequence and relative contribution of cognition appears to play an important if not primary role, warranting further investigation. The theoretical and clinical importance of these findings attest that negative, rather then positive, ideation differentiates Panickers from subjects with moderate or mild anxiety. The "power of nonnegative thinking" may be an appropriate axiom regarding the role of cognition in panic, as reported in depression research. The exploratory analyses examining the predictive utility of pretreatment panic revealed that Panickers fared as well as Anxious subjects on Endstate functioning and Improvement at posttreatment and follow-up. Hence, exhibiting in vivo panic at pretreatment did not appear to influence treatment outcome or short-term maintenance.

Step-wise, orderly, hierarchical progressions with equidistant gradations were observed across the three anxiety groups on clinical, behavioral, and cognitive measures. The only exception to this observation was the absence of the psychophysiological differences between the three conditions.

These findings highlight the cognitive correlates and possible determinants of panic and support several recommendations regarding future research. First, the data provide the impetus for programmatic research into the specific cognitive mediational processes, schemata, and products as they relate to panic. Second, studies examining information processing, decision-making, problem solving, attributional processes, selective attention, and memory biases among subjects experiencing panic are needed. Lang (this volume) has provided a significant beginning in this regard. Also, research by Mathews and McCleod (1986) reveals biases and selectivity in cognitive processing among anxiety subjects. A critical finding of their research is that relevant cognitive processes for activation of fear structures can operate outside of awareness. The failure of subjects to identify antecedents of so-called "spontaneous panic attacks" might be explained by these findings. Similarly, studies by Baragh (1982) and Baragh and Pietromonacco (1982) indicate that verbal material can be processed without awareness and also affect subsequent cognitive processing. In addition to laboratory research, ambulatory in vivo tripartite monitoring of panic would provide important naturalistic data on possible cognitive, behavioral, and physiological antecedents, concomitants, and sequelae of panic. A third recommendation follows from the importance of cognition in panic. Promising cognitive-behavioral interventions should be systematically investigated on a short and long-term basis.

Behavioral theories, in attempting to provide a more complete account of anxiety disorders, are increasingly incorporating cognitive and psychophysiological mediational processes as explanatory mechanisms and treatment adjuncts. Recent conceptualizations of anxiety disorders suggest that cognitive interventions aimed at cognitive errors, and misattributions may be of significant benefit in ameliorating panic (Beck, this volume; Clark this volume). The conception of anxiety disorders in terms of tripartite response systems, and evidence that these systems change differentially in response to treatment prodecures raises the possibility that treatments with specific actions may be usefully combined, especially as unitary treatment approaches can no longer be presumed to produce generalized effects across all systems.

Cognitive interventions have only recently been added to the therapists' armamentarium in the treatment of panic. Despite the growing recognition of the importance of cognitive processes in the etiology and maintenance of panic, there have only been a few empirical studies of the efficacy of these techniques for panic, typically using agoraphobic subjects. While there is a voluminous literature consisting largely of methodologically excellent studies of analogue populations that demonstrate the effectiveness of cognitive behavior therapy in regard to anxiety management (Barrios & Shigatomi, 1980), there is a paucity of studies evaluating cognitive therapy for panic disorder.

Anxiety management appears to be a worthy area of research in the treatment of panic. As noted by Rachman (1980), myriad factors influence emotional processing, with cognitive factors being among the most crucial. Catastrophic ideation can result in high levels of emotional distress, leading to marked psychophysiological arousal, and thereby continuing the cognitive–physiological–behavioral loop. Cognitive therapy, relaxation training, and related anxiety management modalities can be directed to modifing the most crucial factors in panic and therefore offer much promise in its amelioration. Moreover, identification of individual differences, response typologies, and panic profiles across the three response systems would enhance both the conceptualization and treatment of panic.

ACKNOWLEDGMENT

This manuscript was supported in part by the National Institute of Mental Health (MH 36299).

9

Combined Pharmacological and Psychological Treatments for Panic Sufferers

Michael J. Telch
University of Texas at Austin

INTRODUCTION

Biological models and treatments of panic disorder and agoraphobia have enjoyed a tremendous surge in popularity, as evidenced by both the amount of recent media coverage and empirical research devoted to the topic. A recent overview of progress in psychiatry published in the *Journal of the American Medical Association* was devoted almost exclusively to the topic of panic (Freedman & Glass, 1984). Several different lines of empirical findings have been cited to support the thesis that panic disorder stems from an underlying biological dysfunction. These include (a) research pointing to the effectiveness of several classes of medications in suppressing panic (Sheehan, 1982), (b) panic provocation studies suggesting that sodium lactate precipitates attacks in panic disorder patients but rarely in controls (Appleby, Klein, Sachar, & Levitt, 1981; Liebowitz et al., 1984; Pitts & McClure, 1967), (c) the unusual age-of-onset distribution (Sheehan, 1982), and (d) the higher concordance rate in monozygotic than in dizygotic twins (Crowe, Pauls, Slymen, & Noyes, 1980). A review of these data is beyond the scope of this chapter and the reader is referred to Shear (this volume) for further information. A critical analysis of the empirical findings that support biological models of panic may be found in an excellent discussion and critique of these models by Margraf, Ehlers, and Roth (1986a).

Klein (1980) has been most influential in illuminating the relationship between panic and agoraphobia. He asserted that agoraphobia is almost always *preceded* by one or more episodes of spontaneous panic. While some individuals may experience recurrent panic attacks with no significant consequences, the majority of those afflicted develop strong apprehension and avoidance of situations that they believe might bring on an attack.

Within this biological perspective, treatment is focused on the elimination of panic attacks through pharmacotherapy. As Klein (1984) notes, "By means of the various medications available to us, we have obtained complete removal of panic attacks in well over 95% of the patients we treated in a recent series" (p. 32). Proponents of the biological approach have indicated that nonpharmacological treatments (i.e., psychotherapy and behavior therapy) are of little value *alone* in the treatment of agoraphobia, since they fail to address the underlying biological disorder (Sheehan, 1982). Psychological treatments that encourage the patient to confront fear-provoking cues, are viewed as potentially helpful adjuncts to medication for those refractory cases who continue to exhibit some avoidance behavior despite having their panic attacks blocked.

This chapter critically examines the empirical evidence for the combined use of pharmacological and psychological approaches in treating agoraphobia and panic. Proposed mechanisms of action for combined drug and psychological treatments will be presented, along with a discussion of methodological and conceptual issues. Limitations in the use of pharmacotherapy will be highlighted with special attention directed toward innovative psychological strategies that target panic as the major focus of treatment. The chapter concludes with a brief discussion of recommendations for clinical practice.

RATIONALE FOR COMBINING PSYCHOLOGICAL AND PHARMACOLOGICAL APPROACHES

Given the complexity and multifaceted nature of the agoraphobia syndrome, combining treatment modalities which address separate symptom clusters (i.e., phobic avoidance/anxiety, spontaneous panic attacks, dysphoric mood) seems warranted. Exposure-based procedures exert their most pronounced effect on behavioral avoidance and anticipatory anxiety but have not demonstrated strong antipanic or antidepressant effects (Zitrin, Klein, & Woerner, 1980). Patients undergoing exposure therapy to reduce phobic avoidance and anxiety may show limited progress or an increased risk for relapse if they continue to experience recurrent panic or a markedly depressed mood (Sheehan, 1983).

Several classes of antidepressant medication, i.e., tricyclics and monoamine oxidase (MAO) inhibitors and alprazolam, a new triazolo benzodiazepine, have been found to be beneficial in the treatment of agoraphobia and panic (Klein, 1984; Sheehan, 1985). Klein and Fink (1962) first reported that imipramine blocked spontaneous panic but had little effect on anticipatory anxiety. This form of pharmacological dissection led Klein and others to propose a qualitative distinction between panic and anticipatory anxiety. More recently, Sheehan

(1982) has echoed Klein's position by referring to panic as *endogenous* anxiety and distinguishing it from anticipatory anxiety or *exogenous* anxiety. Advocates of the pharmacological approach claim that these medications possess strong antipanic properties that are independent of their antidepressant effects (Klein, 1984; Liebowitz, 1985a; Sheehan, 1985; Zitrin, Klein, Woerner, & Ross, 1983. There is a debate over the mechanism of action of these medications in treating agoraphobia (Marks, 1983; Telch, Tearnan, & Taylor, 1983; Telch, Agras, Taylor, Roth, & Gallen, 1985), that will be discussed in detail later in this chapter.

While antidepressants such as imipramine and phenelzine appear to be beneficial in suppressing panic and elevating mood, their effects on phobic avoidance and anticipatory anxiety in the absence of exposure are limited. Alprazolam, on the other hand, may have potent antipanic effects and some beneficial effect on anticipatory anxiety, but provide limited benefit for phobic avoidance or depressed mood. For instance, in our clinic, patients are often seen who had been or who were currently on either imipramine or alprazolam, but continued to report disabling travel restrictions and anticipatory anxiety.

Since pharmacological and psychological approaches may affect different symptom clusters within the panic syndrome, their considered combination may provide more effective treatment for some patients.

STUDIES ON COMBINED APPROACHES

A number of controlled studies have reported on the efficacy of combining antidepressant medication with a psychological treatment in treating agoraphobia with panic. The pharmacological treatments most commonly studied have been the tricyclic imipramine (Klein, 1967; Marks et al., 1983; Michelson & Mavissakalian, 1985; Sheehan, Ballenger, & Jacobsen, 1980; Telch, Agras, Taylor, Roth, & Gallen, 1985; Zitrin, Klein, & Woerner, 1978, 1980; Zitrin et al., 1983) or the MAO inhibitor phenelzine (Lipsedge et al., 1973; Mountjoy, Roth, Garside, & Leitch, 1977; Sheehan, Ballenger et al., 1980; Solyom et al., 1973; Tyrer, Candy, & Kelly, 1973). Studies examining the effectiveness of the new triazolo-benzodiazepine alprazolam in treating agoraphobia/panic have begun to appear (Marks, 1984; Sheehan, 1985). However, these studies will not be reviewed here, as they do not deal with the combined use of alprazolam with psychological treatments.

The psychological treatments that have been employed in conjunction with pharmacological treatment have included: therapist-assisted in vivo exposure (Marks et al., 1983; Mavissakalian & Michelson, 1986a; Telch et al., 1985; Zitrin et al., 1980), imaginal exposure (Zitrin et al., 1978, 1983), self-directed exposure homework (also referred to as "programmed practice") (Marks et al., 1983; Mavissakalian & Michelson, 1986a) supportive psychotherapy (Klein,

1967; Sheehan, Ballenger et al., 1980; Zitrin et al., 1978) and relaxation training (Marks et al., 1983). Although the nature of the psychological interventions has varied among the different studies, all of the interventions included the common element of encouraging patients to confront fear-provoking cues outside of the therapy session. This exposure practice has been proposed as the crucial therapeutic factor in the treatment of agoraphobia with panic (Mathews, Gelder, & Johnston, 1981). The review is not exhaustive, but provides a sampling of research findings. (For a more comprehensive review of the pharmacological treatment literature pertaining to agoraphobia, see Marks (1983) or Telch, Tearnan and Taylor (1983).

In the first controlled double-blind investigation of the use of imipramine in the treatment of agoraphobia with panic, Klein (1964) randomly assigned 13 agoraphobics to receive imipramine or placebo. Patients in both groups also received psychotherapy throughout a 5-week treatment. Daily dosage for imipramine began at 75 mg for the first week and was increased 75 mg each week up to a maximum dosage of 300 mg. Imipramine was significantly superior to the placebo on psychiatrist's ratings of overall improvement. These findings were replicated by Klein (1967), using a slightly larger sample size.

In a more elaborate double-blind trial, Klein and his associates (Klein, Zitrin, & Woerner, 1977; Zitrin et al., 1978, 1983) tested the relative efficacy of imipramine and behavior therapy (primarily systematic desensitization), imipramine plus supportive therapy, and placebo plus behavior therapy, in a 26-week study. The patient population consisted of agoraphobics with panic attacks, simple phobics without panic attacks, and mixed phobics with circumscribed phobias and panic attacks. Psychological treatment (imaginal desensitization or supportive therapy) was given to all patients and consisted of 26 weekly sessions each lasting 45 minutes. Medication (imipramine or placebo) was administered throughout the course of treatment. Dosage was started at 25 mg day and increased by 25 mg every other day up to 150 mg/day. Further increases up to a maximum dose of 300 mg day were used for those patients who continued to report panic attacks. The mean dosage for patients receiving imipramine was 180 mg/day with a range of 10 to 300 mg.

The authors hypothesized that imipramine would exert a beneficial effect only for the patient groups reporting spontaneous panic. As predicted, imipramine was found to be superior to placebo for the agoraphobic and mixed phobics with spontaneous panic, but not for the simple phobics without panic. The authors concluded that the imipramine effect was due to the clinical feature (i.e., spontaneous panic) that was common to the agoraphobics and mixed phobics, but absent in the simple phobic group.

In addition to the problem of inferring pretreatment differences from treatment effects, the simple phobic group scored almost as high as the other two groups on the authors' panic rating scales and also showed significant improvement on panic following treatment. It seems either that the scales were not measuring panic or that the authors erred in assuming that the simple phobics did not experience it. Moreover, the failure to include an imipramine-only group weakens the authors' conclusion regarding imipramine's mechanism of action. However, the results do support the thesis that imipramine may facilitate the effects of psychological treatments that encourage exposure to feared situations.

Combining different types of phobics (i.e., agoraphobic, social phobics, and specific phobics), Solyom et al. (1973) conducted a double-blind trial, comparing phenelzine and placebo, in conjunction with brief psychotherapy. Both groups were compared to a third group of patients who received flooding in imagination. Patients in the phenelzine and placebo groups received 45 mg/day over a 3-month period and participated in 6 biweekly supportive psychotherapy sessions. Patients in the flooding condition received 12 hours of imaginal exposure to feared situations over the same 3-month period.

All three treatment groups showed significant short-term reductions in phobic ratings. However, the decrease in phobic ratings for the phenelzine-plus-psychotherapy group was significantly greater than for the placebo-plus-psychotherapy group. Contrary to Zitrin et al. (1978), patients classified as agoraphobic improved about as much as those with specific phobias. The results of a 2-year follow-up revealed that *all of the patients* in the phenelzine condition relapsed once the drug was discontinued, whereas in the same time period only 10% of the patients receiving flooding relapsed (Tyrer & Steinberg, 1975). The authors suggested that despite the high rate of relapse, the initial symptom suppression achieved through phenelzine may enhance patient's motivation to remain in treatment and thus justify its combined use with behavior therapy.

In a double-blind study designed to evaluate the combined use of imipramine and group in vivo exposure to feared situations, Zitrin et al. (1980) randomly assigned 76 agoraphobic women to receive group exposure plus imipramine or plus placebo. Medication (imipramine or placebo) was started 4 weeks prior to group exposure in an attempt to suppress patients' panic attacks prior to the start of exposure therapy. Medication was continued throughout exposure therapy and continued for 12 weeks after the termination of group exposure. Dosage levels were increased and adjusted in a similar fashion as in the first Zitrin et al. (1978) study. Group in vivo exposure consisted of 10 weekly sessions of 3 to 4 hours duration.

Both groups improved considerably by the end of treatment. However, the group exposure plus imipramine group was significantly superior to the group exposure plus placebo group on patient, therapist, and assessor ratings of overall improvement, severity of illness, spontaneous panic, and primary phobia. Both groups showed significantly greater improvement after 26 weeks than after 14 weeks. Unfortunately, the design of the study does not permit a determination of whether the greater improvement after 26 weeks was due to a delayed effect of the medication, a longer period of self-directed exposure, or a combination of the two. The results do suggest that imipramine may enhance the potency of group exposure therapy with agoraphobics.

In a double-blind study comparing an MAO inhibitor with a tricyclic antidepressant, Sheehan, Ballenger et al. (1980) treated 87 severe agoraphobic outpatients suffering from panic attacks with imipramine (150 mg/day), phenelzine (45 mg/day) or placebo. Patients in all groups received six hourly sessions of supportive group therapy biweekly throughout a 3-month treatment period. During group therapy, patients were encouraged to approach phobic situations gradually and were provided with social reinforcement for successful performance. The results indicated that patients in the phenelzine and imipramine conditions achieved a significantly lower degree of illness, and lower social and work disability and avoidance behavior than patients receiving the placebo. Phenelzine was found to be superior to imipramine on only 2 of the 13 scales (i.e., Symptom Severity and Avoidance Scale and the Work and Social Desirability Scale). Unfortunately, no data were reported on the effects of treatment on panic.

In a well-executed factorial study, Mavissakalian and Michelson (1986a) compared the relative and combined effectiveness of pharmacotherapy (imipramine versus placebo) and behavior therapy (prolonged in vivo exposure versus discussion) in treating 62 patients meeting DSM–III criteria for agoraphobia with panic attacks. The patients in all four experimental conditions also received programmed practice (i.e., systematic behavioral instructions for self-directed exposure) similar to that employed by Marks et al. (1983). All four treatment groups showed significant pre- to posttreatment improvement. Therapist-assisted exposure resulted in little added benefit to the programmed practice that all patients were instructed to engage in between sessions. These results are consistent with Marks et al. (1983), who showed that therapist-aided exposure added little to systematic self-directed exposure homework. Further support for the role of self-directed exposure comes from the authors' finding that the amount of practice predicted improvement on specific phobia measures.

With respect to imipramine, their results indicated an imipramine effect on several outcome measures. However, given that all imipramine patients also received programmed practice for self-directed exposure, the imipramine effect is really better thought of as a combined imipramine plus exposure effect. Of particular theoretical interest was the absence of an imipramine effect on panic. While a dose–response relationship was found for degrees of phobia, neither imipramine dose, nor plasma imipramine levels, was related to panic blockade. The results of the study lend further support for the hypothesis that imipramine facilitates the effects of exposure; however, they also raise questions about imipramine's mechanism of action. In particular, the negative findings with respect to panic blockade are not consistent with the biological view of panic as a purely metabolic dysfunction that is remedied through pharmacotherapy (Sheehan, 1982). A more thorough discussion of operative mechanisms in the pharmacological treatment of panic is presented later in this chapter.

Several studies have reported findings with respect to the facilitative effects of combining antidepressants and exposure therapy. In a well-controlled 2 × 2 study of 45-agoraphobia outpatients, Marks et al. (1983) compared (a) imipramine plus therapist-aided exposure; (b) imipramine plus therapist-aided relaxation; (c) placebo plus therapist-assisted exposure, or (d) placebo plus therapist-assisted relaxation. In addition, all patients were given a manual with structured, self-exposure homework assignments. Improvement was observed on nearly all of the outcome measures, and the gains were maintained at 1-year follow-up. However, there were no significant differences between imipramine and placebo groups, despite achieving imipramine plasma levels that are usually considered to be therapeutic. Therapist-assisted exposure proved to be superior to therapist-assisted relaxation.

In discussing the results from this study, Marks (1983) hypothesized that the effects of imipramine on agoraphobia are primarily antidepressant in nature and that the absence of a drug effect in the present study was due to patients' low initial depression scores. This study has been faulted for low imipramine dosage and the inclusion of patients who had previously not responded to antidepressants (Liebowitz, 1985a). A reanalysis of Marks's data by Raskin, Marks, and Sheehan (1983) revealed that imipramine was superior to placebo on a several outcome measures. However, a 2-year follow-up study showed that about two-thirds of the patients remained improved or much improved on phobias and spontaneous panic, with no differences between the four treatments (Cohen, Monteiro, & Marks, 1984).

In a study comparing the relative and combined effects of therapist-aided exposure and phenelzine, Solyom, Solyom, LaPierre, Pecknold, and Morton (1981) assigned 40 agoraphobics and social phobics to one of four conditions: (1) phenelzine exposure, (2) phenelzine-no exposure, (3) placebo-exposure, and (4) placebo-no exposure. Patients in all four groups received exposure homework. All of the groups showed significant reductions in phobia ratings following treatment, but the patients who received exposure improved significantly more than those who did not receive exposure. There were no significant differences between phenelzine and placebo, nor did phenelzine enhance the effectiveness of exposure.

Solyom et al.'s results with phenelzine parallel those by Marks et al. (1983) with imipramine, in that both studies found *no* specific antiphobic effect of the drugs. There were several interesting similarities between these two investigations which might account for their negative findings regarding the putative effects of antidepressant medication. First, both studies have been criticized for low dosage levels. A second note of interest was the markedly lower depression scores in these two trials, compared with previous trials. If the primary mediating effect of imipramine and phenelzine is antidepressant in nature as Marks (1983) argues, then patients' low depression levels at the outset may have contributed to the absence of an imipramine effect.

COMBINED EFFECTS OF IMIPRAMINE AND EXPOSURE

In each of the previously cited imipramine trials, the medication was given in conjunction with a psychological treatment which included encouragement to enter phobic situations. While most studies suggest that imipramine may facilitate the effects of exposure, the absence of an imipramine-only condition raises the question as to whether the facilitative effects of combining imipramine and exposure reflect a synergism of the two treatments or simply an additive effect. To address this question, the effects of exposure and imipramine need to be assessed independently and compared with a condition that combines exposure and pharmacotherapy. Several investigators have pointed to the confounding of imipramine and exposure and the need to examine the effects of imipramine independent of exposure (Matuzas & Glass, 1983; Telch et al., 1983; Zitrin et al., 1983).

Telch et al. (1985) recently addressed this issue. Thirty-seven severe agoraphobics with panic attacks were randomized to the following conditions: (a) imipramine alone; (b) imipramine plus intensive in vivo exposure; and (c) placebo plus intensive in vivo exposure. In order to help control for the effects of exposure, patients in the imipramine group were given anti-exposure instructions which emphasized the importance of refraining from entering phobic situations for the first 8 weeks so that the medication would have time to build up in their systems. Data collected from patients' activity diaries confirmed that they were adhering to the no-practice instructional set.

The intensive in vivo exposure treatment consisted of 9 hours of therapist-assisted group exposure spread over 3 consecutive days, followed by a partner-assisted, home-based exposure program modeled after that of Mathews, Teasdale, Munby, Johnston, and Shaw (1977), and Mathews, Gelder, and Johnston (1981). The patients and their partners were provided with slightly modified versions of the Mathews et al. treatment manuals and required to meet in small groups with their partners for four 90-minute weekly sessions to discuss their progress with exposure homework.

During weeks 9–26 patients continued their medication. Patients in the two exposure conditions were instructed to continue using the skills that they had learned during the exposure treatment; no further exposure sessions were provided. The no-practice instructions given to patients in Group 1 were lifted during weeks 9–26, when they were encouraged in a general way to encounter their phobic situations. Assessments were conducted at 0, 8, and 26 weeks. The outcome measures included self-report, behavioral, and psychophysiological indices.

At the 8-week assessment, the patients who had received imipramine with the no-practice instructions showed little improvement on phobic anxiety, phobic avoidance, heart rate, or panic. Interestingly, these patients did however show a significant reduction in all three measures of depressed mood, attesting to the antidepressant properties of imipramine. In contrast, the patients assigned to the two exposure conditions (imipramine plus exposure or placebo plus exposure) displayed marked improvements on measures of phobic anxiety, phobic avoidance, self-efficacy, and depression. Comparisons between the combined imipramine-exposure and placebo-exposure conditions revealed a slight advantage for the combined imipramine-exposure group after 8 weeks. However, at the 26-week assessment, a clear superiority of the combined treatment emerged. Of interest was the finding that patients receiving imipramine with no-practice instructions showed significant improvement from weeks 9–26 on measures of phobia once the no-practice instructions were removed. This finding supports the potentiating effects of imipramine and self-directed exposure.

The potentiating effects of imipramine and exposure on patients' heart rate response during the behavioral test course was examined. Neither imipramine nor exposure produced a significant improvement in psychophysiological responding during the behavioral approach test, but the combined treatment group displayed a significant reduction in their psychophysiological response during the test walk.

A similar potentiating pattern was observed for the effects on the incidence of panic; antipanic effects were evident only for the combined exposure plus imipramine treatment.

The results for depression followed a somewhat different pattern with all three groups showing similar improvement at 8 weeks. Patients receiving either imipramine alone or exposure alone showed no further improvement on depression at the 26-week assessment, whereas the combined treatment group showed marked improvement from the 8-week to 26-week assessment. These data suggest that both exposure without imipramine and imipramine without exposure have an equally positive effect on agoraphobics' mood, and that their combination results in even greater mood changes after 6 months of treatment (i.e., Beck Depression Inventory changes from 25.3 to 4.7).

PROPOSED MODE OF COMBINED TREATMENTS

Although the the efficacy of combined pharmacological and psychological approaches in the treatment of panic and agoraphobia is well supported, much debate still exists with respect to the mechanisms governing their combined effectiveness.

Panic Suppression Hypothesis

As noted earlier, the view that spontaneous panic plays a central role in the development and maintenance of agoraphobia has become increasingly popular. One possible mechanism to account for the apparent superiority of combined pharmacological and psychological treatments is the role of panic suppression in facilitating reductions in phobic anxiety and phobic avoidance. Agoraphobics who have their panic suppressed by pharmacotherapy *and* concurrently are provided with the necessary skills, support, and encouragement to venture out into situations that they previously avoided may be more willing to "test the water."

Evidence supporting the panic suppression hypothesis of antidepressants such as imipramine and phenelzine come from investigations reporting that phenelzine and imipramine block lactate-induced panic attacks (Appleby et al., 1981; Kelly, Mitchell–Heggs, & Sherman, 1971; Liebowitz, Fyer et al., 1984). However, this research has been plagued by methodological and conceptual shortcomings (see Margraf et al., 1986b, for an excellent review of the panic provocation literature).

Data pertaining to the panic suppression hypothesis from clinic-based studies are mixed. Klein and his associates have found imipramine to be superior to placebo on clinical ratings of panic in two studies (i.e., Zitrin et al., 1978; 1980), but Marks et al. (1983) and Mavissakalian and Michelson (1986a) found no significant antipanic effect for imipramine. However, as mentioned earlier, the pharmacological effects of the medication were confounded with the effects of exposure in all of these studies.

Few studies have examined the panic-blocking effects of imipramine or MAO inhibitors, independent of exposure. In a small, pilot trial, Garakani, Zitrin, and Klein (1984) examined the effects of imipramine without psychotherapy on 10 patients with Panic Disorder but no phobic avoidance. The authors reported that the 4 patients who remained in treatment ceased to report panic attacks. Mavissakalian, Michelson, and Dealy (1983) compared the effects on 18 agoraphobics of imipramine alone or imipramine plus self-directed exposure homework. Imipramine plus exposure was significantly superior to imipramine alone on measures of panic as well as phobia and depression. Patients receiving imipramine without exposure did show a modest reduction in panic, but the absence of a placebo control makes interpretation of the within-group panic changes problematical. Their analysis of the relationship between panic attacks and imipramine dose/plasma imipramine levels was of particular interest. Contrary to prediction, imipramine dose and imipramine plasma levels were significantly correlated with phobic severity, but not correlated with panic.

Further disconfirmatory evidence for the panic suppression hypothesis comes from the Telch et al. (1985) study in which we examined the panic suppression effects of imipramine independently of exposure to the feared situation. Despite adequate imipramine doses, patients receiving imipramine plus anti-exposure instructions showed no significant reduction in panic attacks as measured by detailed panic diaries or clinical ratings of panic. The value of this test of the panic suppression hypothesis was weakened by the small sample size and the absence of a placebo plus anti-exposure condition. We are currently conducting a more elaborate replication of this study with a larger sample size and with the inclusion of a placebo plus anti-exposure group.

Antidepressant Hypothesis

Marks (1983) has proposed an alternative mechanism to account for the effectiveness of antidepressant medication in treating agoraphobia. Following the interpretation introduced by Rachman et al. (1979), on the effects of clomipramine with obsessive-compulsives, Marks (1983) has postulated that the beneficial effects of tricyclics and MAO inhibitors with agoraphobics are mediated by the drugs' antidepressant effects. In reviewing 19 studies employing antidepressant medications with phobic or obsessive-compulsive disorder, Marks concluded that, in general, the tricyclics and the MAO inhibitors show a treatment effect for patients with high starting levels of dysphoric mood but fail to show an effect for patient samples with low dysphoria levels. Since antidepressants have been shown to exert a broad spectrum effect on phobias, anxiety, panic, depression, and anger, it is premature to conclude that panic suppression is the central explanatory mechanism.

Two major analytical strategies have been employed to test the antidepressant hypothesis. Correlational analyses have been used to examine the relationship between depression and other indexes of treatment outcome, with the prediction being that improvement should correlate positively with initial starting levels of depression. With the exception of the work of McNair and Kahn (1981), studies have not found a positive relationship between starting levels of depression and treatment outcome. A second approach has been to group patients with respect to their starting levels of depression and compare treatment response between the depressed and nondepressed subsamples (Rachman et al., 1979). This approach has also been used by Marks (1983) and has yielded some support for the hypothesis that depressed patients show a more favorable response to antidepressants than nondepressed patients. However, lack of common measures across studies hinders interpretation. In addition, four of the studies included in Marks' analyses focused on obsessive-compulsive populations. It is quite possible that the role of depression in governing treatment may differ between agoraphobics with panic and obsessive-compulsives.

Data from Telch et al. (1985) fail to support Marks' antidepressant hypothesis fully. Despite high mean starting levels of depression (i.e., Beck Depression Inventory score of 25, Zung Self-Rating Depression Scale score of 67), patients receiving imipramine in the absence of exposure showed marked improvements on depression at the 8-week posttest (i.e., Beck score of 15, Zung score of 54) with no significant improvement on measures of phobia or panic. These data suggest that elevation of agoraphobics' mood through pharmacological channels is not sufficient to bring about changes in panic-related symptomatology.

Dysphoria Efficacy Hypothesis

The final mechanism to be considered involves the possible facilitative effect of mood elevation on patients' self-directed exposure. Telch et al. (1985) have proposed that elevation of mood brought about by antidepressants such as imipramine may enhance the effects of exposure through several possible channels. First, alleviation of dysphoric mood may increase the likelihood that agoraphobics will engage in self-directed exposure either between therapy sessions or following the termination of therapy. Anecdotally, patients frequently report bouts of depression as being a serious obstacle in their efforts to practice. Stabilization of mood through antidepressant pharmacotherapy may help eliminate this obstacle, thus increasing the total *amount* of patient-initiated exposure.

A second way in which depressed mood may interfere with self-directed exposure is through the patient's cognitive appraisal of performance accomplishments during actual practice sessions. Mood states have been shown to influence peoples' judgments of self-efficacy. Elevated mood raises perceived self-efficacy, whereas depressed mood lowers it (Kavanaugh & Bower, 1985). Agoraphobics who practice under conditions of despondent mood may find that negative self-evaluative thoughts which typically accompany depression serves to undermine the adequate processing of self-efficacy. In summary, the proposed dysphoria efficacy mechanism asserts that depressed mood, if present, may attenuate the beneficial effects of exposure on the patient's sense of mastery by reducing the amount of self-initiated exposure and/or by attenuating the effects of exposure through negative self-evaluative processes. The addition of antidepressant medication to a psychological treatment may reduce the efficiency or operation of these dysphoria-induced inhibitory channels.

LIMITATIONS IN THE USE OF PHARMACOTHERAPY

Fear of Taking Medications

A substantial number of panic sufferers are highly fearful of taking medications (Telch et al., 1983), and even those who are willing to undergo pharmacological treatment, express some fear or concern about taking medication. For some patients, these concerns have little disruptive effect and the skilled physician is able to increase gradually and reassuringly dosage to desired levels. For other patients, however, their reluctance to take medication can be disruptive even to the point of triggering panic attacks. In these cases, even the skilled physician may find it impossible to raise the patient's dose up to desired levels. An illustration of agoraphobics' fear of medication comes from an interesting comparison between the side-effects to placebo reported by agoraphobics and bulimics. Using identical physicians and medication protocols, agoraphobics reported significantly more disruptive placebo side-effects than did bulimics. Moreover, most of the bulimics were able to be placed on the maximum dose of placebo, but few of the agoraphobics reached the maximum (Agras, personal communication).

Physical Side-effects and Their Consequences

The physical side-effects of pharmacotherapy deserve careful consideration. In the case of the tricyclics such as imipramine, anticholenergic side-effects, such as dry mouth, constipation, and agitation are common and can be disruptive for some patients. In the case of the MAO inhibitors, postural lightheadedness, constipation, delay in urination, delay in ejaculation and orgasm, muscle twitching, sedation, fluid retention, insomnia, and excess sweating are quite common (Sheehan, Claycomb, & Kouretas, 1980). Patients who are taking MAO inhibitors must also adhere to some stringent dietary restrictions, avoiding all foods containing cheese, all fermented food (e.g., aged meats), liver, red wine, and certain medications. The side-effects of alprazolam tend to be less than with the tricyclics and the MAOs. However, sedation and headaches may prove problematic for some patients (Sheehan, 1982). Moreover, both physical and emotional drug dependency makes alprazolam a particularly difficult medication to withdraw (Levy, 1984; Noyes et al., 1985).

Physical side-effects may also reinforce the panic sufferers' concerns about taking medication. The occurrence of one "true" physical side-effect may produce heightened anxiety in predisposed patients, leading to other disruptive symptoms (e.g., palpitations) which the patient attributes to the physical effects of the drug.

One consequence of pharmacotherapy and its side-effects is patient attrition. Dropout rates for the antidepressant trials with agoraphobics have typically averaged between 25% and 40%, figures that are well above the dropout rates found for drug-free behavioral treatments (Barlow & Mavissakalian, 1981). Medication side-effects may also contribute to inadequate dosage levels. As mentioned earlier, patients experiencing subjective discomfort associated with their medication taking (whether due to physical or psychological factors) are often reluctant to increase their dose level despite reassurance from their physician.

Relapse and External Attribution of Success

Relapse upon termination of drug therapy is a major difficulty that has yet to be addressed adequately. In the pharmacological treatment studies, relapse rates range from 27% to 50% (Telch et al., 1983). One potential pitfall in using pharmacotherapy in conjunction with psychological treatments is the tendency of patients to attribute their treatment gains to the drug and not to their own personal efforts. In our clinic we have seen patients who have been maintained on homeopathic doses of imipramine (i.e., 8 mg.) while receiving exposure therapy. Despite making impressive gains during behavioral treatment, the mere suggestion of medication withdrawal produces a marked rise in anxiety and in some cases a return of panic. From a social-learning perspective, one would predict that such external cognitive appraisal of treatment gains would interfere with the development of a strong sense of efficacy to handle feared situations once the patient is no longer on the medication. Effective medication tapering procedures need to be incorporated into combined drug and psychological treatments to help minimize faulty attributions of outcome and maximize patients' sense of personal mastery. Research is needed to identify optimal drug withdrawal strategies. One possible area for future research is the application of ''relapse prevention'' techniques modeled after those developed by Marlatt and Gordon (1985) for addictive behaviors. The approach consists of training the patient to anticipate some of the difficulties that he or she might experience while coming off the medication (e.g., anxious mood) and to employ specific coping and problem-solving skills to manage these difficulties effectively as they rise. One might predict that such training would enhance perceptions of personal control to manage symptoms without medication.

FUTURE DIRECTIONS FOR RESEARCH ON COMBINED APPROACHES

Design Issues

Without exception, studies examining the relative and combined effects of pharmacological and psychological treatments have included comparisons with placebo plus a psychological treatment, or with an active drug, or with an active drug alone, or an active drug plus the psychological treatment. In each study a placebo plus psychological treatment condition was used to represent the psychological treatment. The major problem with this approach is that while comparisons between drug-plus-psychological treatment versus placebo-plus-psychological treatment allow the researcher to distinguish between pharmacologically mediated effects from psychologically mediated effects, this comparison does not permit the assessment of differential treatment outcome (Hollon & DeRubeis, 1981).

The placebo plus psychological treatment combination (whether psychotherapy or behavior therapy) is very different than psychotherapy or behavior therapy alone. Unlike psychotherapy alone, patients receiving placebo plus psychotherapy believe that they are getting medication in addition to psychotherapy. The effects of perceived medication taking on treatment outcome should not be overlooked. In an excellent discussion of this issue, Hollon and DeRubeis (1981) presented data suggesting that placebo-plus-psychotherapy combinations may actually underestimate the effects of psychological procedures. One possible explanation for the observed negative interaction between placebo and psychological treatments was discussed earlier in the context of attributional processes and relapse. Falsely attributing treatment potency to a drug may serve to undermine the effects of the psychological treatment.

Investigators interested in evaluating the relative and combined effects of pharmacological and psychological approaches need to consider the inclusion of a psychological treatment (no placebo) condition as part of the study design. The placebo-plus-psychotherapy condition should be viewed as a necessary element *only* for those interested in teasing out the pharmacological versus psychological effects of a medication when administered in conjunction with a psychological treatment.

Measurement Issues

As noted by Barlow (this volume) and Turner (this volume) further development in the measurement of panic is an important area for future research. The use of a minimum standard set of reliable and valid self-report measures across studies would greatly facilitate intertrial comparisons and enhance interpretation of findings.

Despite the theoretical importance given to panic blockade among advocates of pharmacological treatments, the majority of the pharmacological trials did not include measures of panic (Telch et al., 1983). Moreover, the assessment of panic in most studies relied on retrospective ratings of panic frequency and/or intensity. Patient self-monitoring of ongoing panic episodes has been employed in several studies using "panic diaries" (Taylor et al., 1986; Taylor, Telch, & Havvik, 1982; Telch et al., 1985), and this type of assessment offers two advantages over retrospective ratings. First, ongoing monitoring of panic helps to alleviate some of the potential pitfalls of retrospective ratings (e.g., reporting bias, memory decay). Second, patient monitoring of panic episodes provides an opportunity to collect more precise information on symptom profiles and contextual factors associated with each attack. This information can then be used to classify panic episodes into theoretically interesting categories, such as cued versus uncued and expected versus unexpected (Barlow, this volume).

In addition to panic occurrence, the assessment of patients' cognitive appraisal of panic may serve as an important index of treatment outcome as well as a useful means to test hypotheses concerning onset and recovery processes. Several distinct panic appraisal dimensions need to be considered. These include: (1) perceived distress associated with specific panic sensations; (2) maladaptive beliefs concerning the anticipated adverse consequences of having a panic attack; (3) beliefs concerning the likelihood of panic occurrence in specific situations; and (4) self-efficacy in effectively coping with panic if/when it occurs. Several instruments are now available to assess these panic appraisal dimensions. Chambless and her colleagues (Chambless, Caputo, Bright, & Gallagher, 1984) have reported on the Agoraphobic Cognitions Questionnaire (ACQ) and The Body Sensations Questionnaire (BSQ), which address dimensions (1) and (2) listed herein. Telch (1985) has developed the Panic Appraisal Inventory (PAI) which addresses dimensions (2), (3), and (4).

The use of psychophysiological measures for process and outcome purposes deserves more attention. Ambulatory heart rate monitoring has been employed in several studies to assess patients' panic episodes in their home environment (Freedman, Ianni, Ettedgui, & Puthezhath, 1985; Taylor, Telch, & Havvik, 1982; Taylor et al., 1986). Psychophysiological assessment in pharmacological trials with panic sufferers may help elucidate mechanisms of drug action and should be extended to other psychophysiological modalities in addition to heart rate.

A discussion on future directions in the area of assessment cannot end without recommending the need for long-term follow-up of patients who have undergone combined pharmacotherapy and psychological treatment. Relapse has often been reported as a problem with the use of pharmacotherapy with panic sufferers (Sheehan, 1982). On the other hand, several reports have established the durability of treatment gains for agoraphobics undergoing behavioral treatments (Marks, 1971; McPherson, Brougham, & McLaren, 1980; Mumby & Johnston, 1980). Unfortunately, there is little information on the long-term status of patients after receiving combined pharmacotherapy and psychological treatment. The longest-term follow-up to date for panic sufferers treated with pharmacotherapy and psychological treatment was reported by Cohen et al. (1984). They followed the patients originally treated in the Marks et al. (1983) study and found no differences between patients treated with imipramine and placebo at a 2-year follow-up. Studies are needed to establish the long-term benefits and/or risks associated with adding pharmacotherapy to psychological treatments for panic.

Treatment Issues

Critical questions with respect to (a) the optimal sequencing of drug and psychological treatments, (b) medication prescription parameters, (c) psychological treatment parameters, and (d) the tailoring of treatments to relevant patient characteristics need to be addressed.

The question of how best to sequence combined drug and psychological treatments for panic has not been systematically studied. Although several studies (e.g., Mavissakalian & Michelson, 1986; Sheehan et al., 1980) initiated drug and psychological treatment simultaneously, most studies began drug therapy 2 to 4 weeks before initiating psychological treatment. In none of the studies reviewed was a period of psychological treatment initiated prior to the start of medication. Several reasons have been offered for including a period of pharmacotherapy before initiating psychological intervention. First, providing a medication adjustment period prior to starting exposure may help to reduce any disruptive effects of medication side-effects on the psychological treatment. This procedure may be especially important for medications such as the tricyclics in which the side-effects can be quite marked or when the psychological treatment involves exposure to fear-provoking situations. The use of psychological interventions initiated prior to the start of drug therapy which focus on patient education and reassurance about medication, are worth considering.

A second reason for initiating drug therapy prior to psychological intervention is that it would provide ample time to activate the presumed therapeutic effects of the drug (e.g., panic blockade). The facilitation of pharmacotherapy on exposure may be attenauted if exposure is begun before the pharmacological effects of the drug are present. This attenuation may account for the failure to find a drug-exposure facilitation in some studies (i.e., Marks et al., 1983; Solyom et al., 1981). Research examining the effects of different sequencing strategies are needed to help clarify how best to combine drug and psychological treatments.

Other medication-related parameters deserve further study. Much uncertainty still exists with respect to the relationship between dosage and treatment response. Several investigators have reported favorable treatment response among certain panic sufferers who were taking extremely low doses of imipramine in conjunction with a psychological treatment (Zitrin et al., 1978). In a retrospective analysis, Mavissakalian and Perel (1985) found support for a dose–response relationship among agoraphobics with panic treated with imipramine and exposure. Optimal treatment response was found among those patients on doses of 150 mg/day or more. One should use caution against drawing conclusions from retrospective analyses of dose–response, since doses are confounded with a host of patient factors (e.g., hypochondriasis) that may affect treatment outcome. Prospective studies are needed in which panic sufferers undergoing the same psychological treatment are randomized to different fixed doses and treatment response assessed separately for each of the major symptom complaints (i.e., panic, phobia, and depression).

In addition to questions about medication dose, further research is needed to address questions such as (a) the optimal duration of pharmacotherapy when used in conjunction with a psychological treatment, (b) the therapeutic rationale that patients should receive for the drug (i.e., the drug will block your panic attacks versus the drug will help you overcome your phobias), and (c) medication fading procedures that reduce the likelihood of relapse.

Future Directions in Psychological Treatment

The efficacy of psychological approaches which encourage active exposure and mastery over external fear-provoking cues has been demonstrated in the treatment of agoraphobia with panic (Mathews et al., 1981). Approximately two-thirds of those who undergo treatments of this type show moderate to marked improvement, based on observed changes on standard self-report rating scales of anxiety and avoidance (Jansson & Ost, 1982). However, the clinical meaningfulness of these improvements has been questioned (Hallam, 1985). Moreover, a sizable proportion of patients undergoing exposure-based therapies continue to exhibit some degree of psychological dysfunction and behavioral impairment (Barlow, O'Brien, & Last, 1984).

One exciting area for future research on psychological approaches is the development and refinement of psychological strategies that specifically target panic as the focus of treatment. Relevant treatment targets include: (a) reducing patients' subjective distress associated with specific panic-related physical symptoms (e.g., tachycardia, depersonalization); (b) cognitive restructuring techniques that correct erroneous beliefs concerning the catastrophic consequences of panic (e.g., people will think I'm crazy, I will have a heart attack); and (c) increasing the patient's sense of mastery in preventing, stopping, or attenuating panic.

Barlow (this volume) presented preliminary results from 16 panic patients undergoing a combined panic-focused treatment consisting of relaxation and cognitive restructuring. The results revealed a marked reduction in panic frequency that equaled or surpassed the panic suppression effects typically achieved through pharmacotherapy with imipramine. Similarly, Beck (this volume) has described a successful cognitive therapy for panic consisting of several distinct components: (a) education focusing on the nature of panic; (b) training in the use of panic management techniques (e.g., relaxation, breathing, and distraction techniques); (c) induction of panic, and (d) graded exposure.

Clark, Salkovskis, and Chalkley (1985) have developed a cognitive-behavioral treatment for panic that focuses on the reattribution of panic sensations in terms of stress-induced hyperventilation. Following the reattribution process, patients are trained in a method of controlled respiration that is incompatible with hyperventilation. Although the treatment focuses primarily on hyperventilation, patients are also encouraged to rehearse more appropriate responses to bodily symptoms and to use them to thwart an impending attack. This treatment approach was evaluated in two uncontrolled trials (see Clark, this volume). Patients receiving the panic treatment exhibited significant reductions in panic frequency. Nor surprisingly, the results suggested that the treatment approach had its most pronounced effect on patients who perceived their panic symptoms to be similar to the sensations produced through voluntary hyperventilation.

I have been piloting techniques in which data obtained through assessment of patients' cognitive appraisal of panic are used to tailor enactive experiences to the patient's specific panic cognitions. For example, a patient who is most distressed over sensations of dizziness or unsteadiness during a panic episode is instructed to twirl in circles to bring on the disturbing sensation of dizziness. A patient who fears that during a panic attack that he or she will be forced to ask a stranger for help, first observes the therapist enacting a panic attack in a public setting and then asking someone for help. With firm encouragement and reassurance from the therapist, the patient then enacts a panic attack in public and practices asking someone for assistance. In this way, direct mastery experiences are used to provide disconfirmatory evidence regarding the catastrophic consequences of panic. With respect to panic control, several strategies including behavioral (i.e., training in controlled breathing) and cognitive (i.e., paradoxical self-statement training—"come on panic, hit me with your best shot") are employed to increase patients' perceived efficacy to manage panic episodes. Panic induction is employed in the latter stages of treatment to provide further disconfirming evidence that panic sensations can be cognitively appraised and behaviorally managed in a more adaptive fashion.

The use of adjunct psychological therapies in conjunction with exposure needs further study. Arnow, Taylor, Agras, and Telch (1985) found that the effects of exposure could be enhanced by providing agoraphobics and their partners with marital communication skills. Strategies along these lines that help the panic patient manage dysfunctional mood and interpersonal conflict are just a few areas that may prove useful.

The duration of psychological treatment that is typically employed in clinical trials with panic sufferers deserves comment. Unlike in clinical practice where psychological treatments including exposure therapies are delivered for 6 months or more, the studies examining the efficacy of combined drug and psychological treatments employed relatively brief periods of psychological treatment ranging from 1 to 12 weeks. While moderate to marked improvement usually occurs in the majority of patients, it is not surprising that with such brief treatments a sizable proportion of patients continue to exhibit some disability after the termination of psychological treatment. This question arises: "How effective are the exposure-based therapies when delivered more intensively and over a significantly longer time frame?" Studies examining the efficacy of stronger "doses" of exposure-based therapies are needed.

CONCLUDING REMARKS

In reviewing the current status of research on the combined use of pharmacological and psychological approaches in treating agoraphobia and panic several concluding comments appear warranted. With respect to clinical efficacy, there is sufficient evidence demonstrating that certain classes of antidepressant medications, namely the tricyclics and MAO inhibitors, can exert a significant therapeutic effect on panic-related symptoms when administered in conjunction with psychological approaches that encourage the patient to encounter fear-provoking cues. However, the efficacy of these medications in the absence of exposure to fear-provoking situations has not been adequately demonstrated. There is insufficient evidence to conclude whether the superiority of the combined treatment is the result of a true "potentiating effect" or the result of an "additive effect." This question cannot be answered until we have data from studies in which the efficacy of the medication is assessed independently of the effects of exposure. It is important to note that the conclusion with respect to the superiority of the combined approach over exposure alone is limited to the period in which patients are still on medication. Continued superiority of the combined approach over exposure alone has not been demonstrated after patients have been withdrawn from medication.

With respect to mechanisms of action, the data are far from conclusive. The view proposed by biologically oriented theorists that the primary mode of action of the drugs is through the blocking of panic, has become increasingly less tenable. While medications such as imipramine can produce antipanic effects, antipanic effects have not been demonstrated consistently.

The hypothesis that antidepressants exert their beneficial effect on agoraphobia primarily through an antidepressant mode of action has not fared well empirically. Most studies have shown no relationship between patients' starting levels of depression and treatment response. Moreover, it has been shown that under conditions in which patients' exposure to fear-provoking situations is kept at a minimum, imipramine produces improvements in depressed mood with little or no changes in phobia or panic.

In light of the empirical evidence, it appears that the tricyclics and MAO inhibitors may serve to potentiate the effects of exposure to fear-provoking cues. The mechanisms governing this potentiation are still unclear. Earlier, I have proposed that the alteration in dysphoric mood brought about by the drug may potentiate the effects of exposure by increasing the likelihood that patients will engage in self-directed practice and by correcting the devaluation of self-observed gains during exposure. Direct tests of this hypothesis are under way. However, it should be pointed out that the search for a unitary mode of action of these drugs on the agoraphobia/panic syndrome may be misguided. Multiple pharmacological effects on panic/anxiety, depression, and avoidance are all possible and may vary from individual to individual. These effects must then be considered as interacting with a host of physical, psychological, social, and environmental factors.

What are the recommendations for clinical practice with respect to the combined use of pharmacological and psychological approaches in treating agoraphobia and panic? Mavissakalian (in Mavissakalian & Michelson, 1986a) has strongly recommended the combined use of imipramine and programmed practice as an efficacious and cost-effective treatment for agoraphobia with panic. He suggests that therapist-assisted sessions can then be added for the more refractory cases.[1] While this recommendation follows from the current knowledge of combined approaches, it fails to consider adequately the drawbacks and long-term consequences of the use of pharmacotherapy with panic sufferers, namely (a) the sizable number of patients who are unwilling to take medication, (b) the problems associated with side-effects, and (c) the problem of relapse and the potential for misattribution of success to an external source. These drawbacks, coupled with little data to support any long-term benefits after patients have been withdrawn from medication, suggest that a more appropriate recommendation may be to begin with a structured program of self-directed exposure, adding therapist-guided exposure if necessary. Concurrent psychological treatment focusing on other sequalae of the disorder, namely panic management, interpersonal conflict, mood disturbance, and low self-esteem can be addressed if needed. Pharmacological treatment can then be selectively used for those patients' whose dysphoric mood or panic fail to respond to psychological intervention.

Earlier in this chapter I suggested that one rationale for the use of pharmacotherapy in treating agoraphobia and panic is that is addresses facets of the disorder (i.e., panic and depressed mood) that have not been adequately addressed by exposure-based therapies. In the last decade we have witnessed significant advances in our understanding of the onset and maintenance of agoraphobia and panic. Hopefully these theoretical advances will lead to the development of more potent psychological treatments.

ACKNOWLEDGMENTS

The author would like to express appreciation to Dr. Susan Mineka and Dr. David Cohen for their helpful comments on the manuscript.

[1]In a recent communication, Dr. Michelson indicated that he no longer agreed with this recommendation.

10

Cognitive Models and Treatments for Panic: *A Critical Evaluation*

John Teasdale
MRC Applied Psychology Research Unit
Cambridge, England

The cognitive approach to panic, as presented by Clark and by Beck in this volume, appears to offer a compelling integrative account that is consistent with much of what is known about this disorder. It has also generated a treatment which appears remarkably effective, essentially eliminating panic attacks in a condition which has not previously responded well to psychological treatments. These are very considerable achievements. However, there is a danger that the rightful respect and enthusiasm that this work has generated may inhibit critical examination of possible limitations in theory and evidence. Confronting these limitations will, in the long run, best serve the field and facilitate the emergence of a valid psychobiological account of panic disorder. It is in this spirit that this chapter addresses the following questions:

1. Is the cognitive model of panic disorder really saying anything new or different from other points of view?
2. Just how convincing is the evidence for the cognitive approach to panic, compared to alternative accounts?
3. How persuasive is the evidence for the clinical effectiveness of cognitive treatments for panic?

IS THE COGNITIVE MODEL OF PANIC DISORDER REALLY SAYING ANYTHING NEW?

Fear of fear

A concept of "fear of fear," in which symptoms of fear become the source of further fear and anxiety, has a venerable pedigree, both in the psychological and more general literature. A similar concept lies at the heart of the Clark and Beck cognitive models of panic. Do such models increase understanding beyond the well-worn "fear of fear" concept? Clark (this volume) suggests two important differences between his proposed cognitive model and the fear-of-fear hypothesis. First, he suggests, the simple statement that panic results from a fear of fear predicts that panic patients would always panic when they notice themselves becoming anxious. However, this is not the case, there being many occasions on which panic patients notice that they are fairly severely anxious but do not panic. Clark's cognitive model accounts for such variation by specifying that individuals only panic when they notice themselves becoming anxious if they interpret the bodily symptoms of anxiety as indicating an impending and immediate disaster. (As we shall note, it is important to remember that while the cognitive model *can* account for such variation in occurrence of panics, there does not exist, at present, systematic empirical evidence that this explanation is actually true.) A second difference between the fear-of-fear and cognitive hypotheses, Clark suggests, concerns the triggering of panic. Panic is always triggered by an anxiety response in the fear-of-fear hypothesis; in the cognitive model other sources, such as exercise, can provoke the bodily sensations whose misinterpretation trigger panic.

Gains in Precision

Clark's points illustrate the most important advantage that present cognitive models have over more general suggestions that fear of fear is in some way an important factor in the origins or maintenance of panic and severe anxiety. These cognitive models specify, relatively precisely, the processes mediating the escalation of fear and anxiety to panic. The essential requirement is that bodily sensations be cognitively interpreted as indicative of an *immediate impending disaster*. By inserting this cognitive interpretative step between fear as the trigger and greater fear as the outcome, and by specifying its nature fairly closely, cognitive models offer the possibility of increasing the precision of explanation by an order of magnitude. A general notion that "fear of fear" is in some way involved in producing panic gives no direction as to what should be measured to examine the validity of this notion; nor does it suggest what should be done to treat panic. By contrast, the greater precision inherent in the cognitive models at once directs researchers to the type of measures needed to examine the models, and suggests the key target of interventions. So, for example, it focuses investigations on the thinking of panic patients while they are experiencing attacks, or on the effects of manipulating cognitive set on the interpretation of bodily sensations. Similarly, it directs clinical expertise and ingenuity toward devising interventions that alter the misinterpretations hypothesized to play such a central role. At this level, it is clear that the extra precision of the cognitive models has already "bought" considerable benefits, which would not have been easily reaped from more nebulous fear-of-fear concepts.

The ultimate advantage in specifying models precisely is that they can be shown, in sum or in part, to be wrong. In this way hypotheses can be refined over time, and treatment effectiveness and efficiency can be concomitantly improved.

Precise Enough?

Given the benefits of precision, one may ask whether the current cognitive approaches to panic actually go far enough in that direction. Indeed, in discussing these models Seligman (this volume), has expressed concern that the terms used in the cognitive accounts of panic are, essentially, layperson's terms and are not tightly related to the language of behavioral and cognitive science. According to Seligman, concepts such as "catastrophic disaster," while conveying clearly a meaning at one level, lack the precision characteristic of the concepts of cognitive and behavioral science. Further, because these ideas are not couched in the traditional terms of experimental psychology, application of relevant knowledge that has accumulated within that discipline is not easy. The history of behavior therapy provides a good example of the benefits that can be gleaned by casting clinically relevant theories in terms shared with the more academic discipline.

In response to Seligman, Beck has proposed a distinction between "clinical theories," which are expressed in everyday language and serve to guide clinicians in understanding and treating their patients, and the type of theories more characteristic of academic psychology, which aim to improve basic understanding. Ideally, of course, there would be a close link between the two. In practice, it may be that progress in both areas proceeds most rapidly by a series of "successive approximations" of theories of increasing precision, starting with accounts expressed in relatively loose terms and tightening the theories in the areas where they seem to work. In the case of cognitive approaches to depression, Beck's "clinical" cognitive theory has been much more productive in generating effective clinical procedures than the more "scientific" reformulated learned helplessness model. Beck's model has also generated considerable productive experimental enquiry. However, in depression, for the field to move off its present plateau, something more precise, ideally linked to experimental paradigms, is required; notions, such as "negative view of the future" or "dysfunctional basic assumption," lack the precision required to work experimentally toward greater understanding of psychopathology and increased effectiveness and efficiency of treatments.

As far as panic is concerned, evidence reviewed in this volume suggests that the degree of precision with which cognitive models of panic have been expressed is right for the field at this moment; model builders have been heuristic in generating research that has added to our knowledge, and in suggesting very promising treatments. In the future, such models are likely to benefit from closer integration of their concepts with those of cognitive and behavioral science.

A major difficulty here is that mainstream cognitive psychology has largely ignored the links of cognition to affect and behavior. There may be little in the way of theory or experimental procedures that is immediately applicable to panic. Thus, it will be important to avoid attempting prematurely to apply paradigms from more basic experimental psychology that are not wholly appropriate. It is possible, for example, that the attributional reformulation of the learned helplessness model of depression has had relatively little impact on clinical practice and understanding simply because the attributional framework did not mesh well with the clinical phenomena of depression. Nonetheless, there are hypotheses and methods anchored in laboratory studies that do have the promise of potential application to panic, for example Bower's associative network approach to affect and cognition (Bower, 1981; Bower & Cohen, 1982), and Lang's information-processing model of emotion (Lang, this volume). Integration of attempts to understand panic disorders with more basic cognitive and behavioral science should not only refine understanding of the clinical condition but also encourage the development of more relevant basic science.

JUST HOW CONVINCING IS THE EVIDENCE FOR THE COGNITIVE MODEL OF PANIC COMPARED TO ALTERNATIVE APPROACHES?

One of the most attractive features of the cognitive model of panic is that it appears to account plausibly for much of what we already know about this disorder. As this evidence has already been marshaled elegantly by Clark and others in this volume it will not be repeated here. Certainly, a basic requirement of any account of panic is that it be consistent with existing knowledge. The cognitive model survives this test well. As already noted, the model often does this by offering a plausible account rather than one for which empirical evidence can actually be presented. But a hypothesis must do more than account for what is known, if it is to claim much support. It is necessary to account for existing evidence better than rival hypotheses, and to survive experimental tests which deliberately pit the predictions of the favored hypothesis against those of competing alternatives. How does the cognitive model of panic fare in this situation? I shall address this question first with respect to alternate hypotheses that place little emphasis on the role of psychological factors in the escalation of panic, and then with respect to alternative psychological accounts.

Comparison with a More Biological Account

One of the main tasks of an account of panic is to explain why initially mild to moderate levels of anxiety escalate to severe panic in some people but not in others. In the cognitive models of panic the key step in this escalation is the misinterpretation of the bodily sensations of mild anxiety (or from other sources) as evidence of immediate impending catastrophe. This interpretation produces intense symptoms of anxiety which, in turn, support further catastrophic interpretations, which escalate the process. An alternative account is as follows: (a) Those who suffer panic attacks differ from those who do not (either permanently or temporarily) in possessing a biologically unstable autonomic nervous system (possibly related to reduced efficiency of central adrenergic alpha-2-autoreceptors, as suggested by Clark in his chapter); (b) as a result of this, when confronted with a situation perceived as threatening, the initial autonomic response is not damped down by homeostatic mechanisms, as it would normally be, and consequently there are violent surges in sympathetic activity; (c) These surges are interpreted as indicative of imminent bodily catastrophe, but this is a secondary phenomenon which plays little role in the escalation of the panic. In this account, the key factor responsible for the escalation of panic is some form of biological deficiency in central sympathetic control. Catastrophic interpretations occur but they do not play the role of escalating the process which the cognitive model assigns to them. How do such a model and the cognitive model stand in the light of the evidence?

Support for the cognitive model requires three conditions to be true with respect to the catastrophic interpretations which figure so centrally in it: (a) Such interpretations should be demonstrable within naturally occurring panic attacks; (b) Experimentally instigating such interpretations should produce panic-like states; (c) Reducing the extent to which naturally occurring bodily sensations are interpreted catastrophically should reduce the frequency of naturally occurring panic attacks. What is the evidence on these points, and do the cognitive and more biological accounts make differential predictions with respect to them?

Evidence reviewed throughout this volume provides consistent support for the notion that patients report the occurrence of catastrophic interpretations during panic attacks, and Clark (this volume) reports a study that suggests that such patients show a relatively specific tendency to misinterpret bodily sensations in this way. Such evidence meets the first requirement of support for the cognitive model. It is also quite consistent with the more biological model, which does not dispute that such interpretations occur, but simply suggests that they are an epiphenomenon, rather than playing any functional role in the escalation of panic. Evidence under this heading provides no differential support for cognitive hypotheses.

There are obvious ethical and practical difficulties in attempting to induce directly catastrophic interpretations of bodily sensations experimentally. The experimental evidence most relevant to this issue comes from studies investigating the effect of cognitive set on response to biological inductions. Normal subjects, given a negative interpretation of the bodily sensations resulting from hyperventilation, reported that this was a more unpleasant experience than subjects given a positive interpretation (Clark, this volume). Similarly, van den Hout (this volume) found that subjective anxiety was greater in normal subjects given lactate with an expectation of anxious apprehension than in subjects receiving it with an expectation of pleasant excitement. The finding that cognitive set can powerfully affect the affective reaction to induced bodily sensations supports a central aspect of the cognitive model.

The more biological account can cope with such evidence, simply by dismissing it as irrevelant, as follows: It is interesting, but hardly surprising, that it is possible to show experimentally that cognitive set *can* modify the affective reaction to induced bodily sensations; however, this evidence is quite irrelevant to the etiology of spontaneously occurring panic attacks: The fact that your nose bleeds if I punch it does not mean that most spontaneously occurring nose bleeds are the results of physical assault! Thus, again, evidence under this head, while consistent with the cognitive model, can also be accommodated within the more biological account.

The cognitive and more biological accounts make clearly different predictions concerning the effects of reducing the tendency to make catastrophic interpretations of naturally occurring bodily sensations. As far as the cognitive model is concerned, reducing this tendency will eliminate the key element in the escalation of panic, and so the frequency of panic attacks should be drastically reduced. As far as the more biological account is concerned, such interpretations are epiphenomenal and so modifying them should have little effect on frequency of panic attacks. The necessary evidence on this issue would be provided by evaluating the effects of interventions that modify catastrophic interpretations without also affecting other factors that could plausibly account for any beneficial effects observed. Evidence for the effects of cognitively targeted treatments will be reviewed in detail later.

Briefly, there is promising, but not conclusive, evidence that cognitive treatments are very effective in reducing panic. However, the treatments are not sufficiently "pure" for these effects on panic to be unambiguously attributed to cognitive changes produced by the treatments. The clinical need to develop robust treatments and the scientific need to evaluate interventions that include only cognitive change procedures operate in opposite directions and make the traditional outcome trial a relatively weak source of evidence in this key area.

The strategy of examining experimentally the effects of tightly controlled interventions in patients, advocated by Teasdale and Fennell (1983) for studies of cognitive change in depression, may provide better evidence. In certain cases, panic attacks occur in a restricted range of situations, and it would obviously be easier to apply this strategy in such cases. Salkovskis, Warwick, Clark, and Wessels (1986), for example, report a case where panic occurred during the last hour of renal dialysis sessions. This patient responded rapidly, and permanently, to a demonstration that his panic symptoms were a result of hyperventilation, rather than signs of imminent death. However, as it was primarily a clinical intervention, this demonstration also included training in respiratory control. Consequently, its effects cannot be unambiguously attributed to cognitive change alone. Phobic disorders with panic represent some of the more obviously situation-specific opportunities for studying panic, and Rachman's ingenious use of enclosed spaces with claustrophobics (chap. 10) represents a bold step toward getting the precise control necessary for experimental inquiry. However, as noted elsewhere in this volume, it is uncertain whether the processes underlying situational panics are the same as those underlying more "spontaneous" panic attacks.

An alternative strategy, which both van den Hout and Clark suggest in their chapters, is to examine whether the panic-like states induced in patients by sodium lactate or carbon dioxide can be eliminated by experimental instructions designed to decatastrophize the interpretation of the experimentally induced bodily sensations. Unfortunately, there is no published evidence on the results of such investigations. We have incidental comments such as those from a study by Rapee (1986), reported in Barlow's chapter (this volume): "A number of subjects reported that although physical symptoms were the same they did not panic because they knew what was causing the symptoms and they felt they were in a safe environment." Barlow also reports an unpublished study by Rapee which found that patients given detailed instructions concerning the symptoms to expect from inhalation of carbon dioxide did not panic as much as those given the customary instructions. If one accepts the validity of such inductions as analogues of panic, then this is promising evidence in support of the cognitive account. However, if we restrict consideration solely to published material on the effects of "pure" cognitive interventions designed to decatastrophize the interpretation of bodily sensations then, certainly as far as noninduced panics are concerned, at present there really is no convincing evidence to support the cognitive model over the more biological alternative hypothesis considered here.

In summary, on a strict evaluation of the evidence we have considered in this section it is not possible at present to prefer the cognitive account over the biological alternative. That said, the trend of the evidence looks as though it will flow in favor of the cognitive model, and we can hope that evidence from the crucial experiments will be available in the near future. Nonetheless, at the moment, the cognitive model lacks this vital support over the alternative hypothesis.

Comparison with an Interoceptive-Conditioning Fear-of-Fear Model

Van den Hout (this volume) has outlined an alternative psychological account of the escalation of panic, based on the interoceptive conditioning of a fear or anxiety response to stimuli associated with anxiety responses as conditioned stimuli. As a result of repeated associations between stimuli associated with initial fear or anxiety responses and subsequent continuing fear or anxiety responses, classical conditioning of a fear response to fear-produced stimuli occurs. Such conditioned fear of fear could provide the positive feedback mechanism that produces the rapid escalation of fear and anxiety characteristic of panic.

In comparing the conditioned fear of fear model with a more cognitive approach, van den Hout chooses to concentrate on the similarities of the two approaches. In view of the often sterile outcome of previous attempts to confront cognitive and conditioning approaches, this is an understandable decision. However, for our purpose it will be useful to contrast the cognitive and interoceptively conditioned fear of fear approaches as alternative hypotheses that account for the escalation of panic.

With respect to the three sources of evidence considered in the previous section, the position of the interoceptive model is analogous to that of the biological alternative: (a) Catastrophic interpretations exist but are considered secondary epiphenomena; (b) The demonstration that cognitive set affects the affective reaction to bodily sensations in normals is irrevelant to the issue of the etiology of naturally occurring panics; and (c) There is as yet no conclusive evidence that purely cognitive attempts to reduce catastrophic interpretations affect naturally occurring panic.

A major source of support for the interoceptive model comes from the effects of repeated prolonged administrations of lactate or carbon dioxide to panic patients. As van den Hout (chap. 13) indicates, it is a direct prediction from the interoceptive conditioning account that repeated and prolonged exposure to fear-eliciting bodily sensations should lead to the extinction of interoceptively conditioned fear, and consequently, of panic. Van den Hout (this volume) reports a study in which panic patients showed clear habituation of their subjective anxiety response to repeated exposure to inhalation of carbon dioxide. This study supports a direct prediction of the interoceptive account. How does the cognitive model deal with such evidence? One way would be to suggest that habituation of the bodily response to carbon dioxide occurs so that, with repeated exposures, there are fewer bodily sensations available to provoke catastrophic interpretations. The difficulty with this interpretation is that, so far as I am aware, there is no evidence that such habituation actually occurs. Alternatively, it could be argued that the interoceptive fear response extinguishes over trials, and therefore, there are fewer bodily sensations available to fuel catastrophic misinterpretations. This argument accepts, at least partly, the role of interoceptive fear conditioning but suggests that, in addition, the cognitive misinterpretation of conditioned fear responses is necessary for panic. This explanation suffers from a lack of parsimony in requiring both cognitive and conditioning components in the explanatory account.

Finally, the cognitive model could always account for such data by proposing that repeated exposure to carbon dioxide actually works by changing (implicitly) the catastrophic interpretation of the sensations induced; the fact that the patient survives each trial is cumulative evidence that the feared catastrophe does not occur and this leads to a cognitive shift in the interpretation of such sensations. Indeed, Beck (chap. 6) makes just such a suggestion. Beck's approach illustrates, at once, both the power and weakness of the cognitive model. The power is that it offers a way to account for the similar effects of apparently diverse procedures by suggesting that they share in common an effect at the cognitive level. The difficulty is that the cognitive approach can explain too much: If change depends on modifying the underlying cognitions by "corrective information" then there is a vast range of procedures which, if effective, can be seen as providing such information. It is not sufficient to show that procedures which are effective in reducing panic are also effective in changing cognition, because, as we have seen, cognitive change could be a consequence, as much as a cause, of change.

This is a central problem for cognitive models, generally. For example, one way in which apparently widely diverse psychological treatments may be effective in reducing depressive symptoms is by the shared effect of increasing the perceived controllability of the symptoms and effects of depression (Teasdale, 1985). The most powerful means of achieving this shift in perception appears to be discovering that symptoms of depression can be reduced by executing certain coping responses. How, then, can the effects of the shift in perception be disentangled from the effects of the coping responses used to achieve that shift? A similar problem arises in the case of the cognitive model of panic; Beck states in his discussion of cognitive treatment for panic that "without the actual exposure, all of the preliminary briefing would be useless." This problem is a central issue in interpreting both the outcome studies of cognitive treatments for panic and the nature of the cognitive account. It will be discussed again, after outcome studies and Lang's views have been considered, as both bear on this issue.

For the moment, we should note that the most decisive evidence in discriminating between the cognitive and conditioning accounts would be a demonstration that a "purely cognitive" informative intervention was effective both in reducing the frequency of spontaneous panic attacks and in eliminating the catastrophic interpretation of symptoms of panic. As in the contrast with the biological account, the crucial evidence is not yet available, so there is no firm basis for preferring the cognitive account.

COMPARISON WITH LANG'S AFFECTIVE NETWORK APPROACH

Lang's affective associative network model is described in Chapter 12. It aims to elucidate the interaction between physiological patterns, reports of emotional experience, and affective behavior, in terms of information processing and memory organization. Within the affective associative network, there are representations of stimuli, responses, and meaning. The network is activated when input stimuli match representations in the network, and the result of such activation is an emotion production. Such a match can occur with representations of stimuli, emotional responses, and meaning. Activation from these different sources can summate.

In the example provided by Lang, a degraded snake phobia-related stimulus (a sinuously shaped stick) can elicit a phobic emotion production if representations of autonomic and somatic responses within the phobic network have previously been activated by physical exertion. This would not necessarily require the stick to be (consciously) interpreted as a snake, as more appraisal-based hypotheses would suggest. It is on this point that Lang draws a distinction between his network model's account of panic and more appraisal-based accounts, such as Clark's cognitive model of panic attacks. In appraisal-based accounts an essential link between bodily arousal and affective reaction is a (usually conscious) interpretative step, in Clark's model one involving interpretations of impending catastrophe. Representations of catastrophic interpretations in Lang's model form part of the panic network structure, along with representations of responses such as elevated heart rate, and of stimuli related to panic-inducing bodily sensations, such as breathlessness and dizziness.

However, activation of the representations of catastrophic interpretations is not seen as having the pivotal necessary role in producing panic that more purely appraisal-based theories suggest; in Lang's scheme, activation of representations corresponding to bodily sensations or emotional responses can have direct effects in producing panic in addition to any contribution they may make to the activation of catastrophic interpretations. Most often, panic is probably the result of the summation of the activation of the different types of representation. In allowing the "appraisal"-based and more directly response-elicited activation to contribute independently to the production of fear by fear-related stimuli, Lang's view in many ways encompasses both the interoceptive and the more purely interpretative cognitive accounts of panic. The importance of distinguishing between these three accounts lies in their implications for methods of treating panic.

Lang suggests that a purely appraisal-based account would predict the effectiveness of exclusively verbal "corrective information," such as: "Mr. Doe, our physical examintion reveals that you have no heart ailment. However, you do have a tendency to hyperventilate when life gets tough. In the future, just breathe into this brown paper bag whenever you get nervous and all will be well." According to Lang's model, interventions directed only at the "meaning" representations in the panic network are unlikely to have much effect, as they leave untouched the ability of stimulus and response representations to activate emotion productions directly. In order to change the latter, procedures more related to repeated prolonged exposure to fear-related stimuli may be necessary. Within appraisal-based accounts, there is an acceptance that purely verbal interventions may be of limited effectiveness unless backed up by experiental evidence, witness Beck's statement, already noted, that "without the actual exposure, all of the preliminary briefing would be useless."

From the point of view of these accounts, such experiences are seen as necessary confirmatory evidence to validate the change at the meaning level, which is the prime focus of treatment. The difference between this and Lang's position (and the interoceptive conditioning account) is that a single experience may be sufficient to confirm for the patient an alternative explanation for his or her symptoms at the "meaning" level. This experience is unlikely to have much lasting effect on more direct associative links between representations of responses and response-related stimuli and panic production. The type of evidence that would most strongly support an appraisal-based model, of the type proposed by Clark and Beck, over the position take by Lang would be the demonstration that purely informational interventions, either alone, or backed up by single confirmatory experiences, could produce lasting change in panic frequency. Although clinicians can provide accounts that suggest the existence of dramatic "revelatory" changes, consistent with effects at the "meaning" level, there is, as yet, no convincing published evidence on this issue. Once again, it seems that in the present state of evidence, it is not possible to prefer conclusively models of the type advocated by Clark and Beck over the alternative hypotheses. At present, this appears to be true both for the biological and psychological alternative hypotheses that have been considered.

Lang's affective associative network theory suggests that activation of representations of meaning, responses, and stimuli can all contribute to an emotion production. In applying his model to panic, Lang implies that the relative contribution of "meaning" representations, and the possibility of changing these by "rational" verbal interventions, is slight. However, the extent to which this is true will clearly depend on the structure of the panic associative network; the relative contributions of the different types of representation may vary from one panic sufferer to another, or within an individual over time. It may be that in the early stages of the disorder the contribution of meaning representations is relatively high, misinterpretations of bodily sensations playing a major role in the production of panic. At this stage, mainly informational interventions may have a useful role to play both in treatment and prevention. With repeated experience of panic attacks, direct associative links are likely to be formed between stimulus-and-response representations and panic production, so that the relative contribution of these increases, and susceptibility to purely informational interventions decreases. It is one of the attractions of Lang's model that it provides a framework to examine the relative contribution, and interrelationship, of these different types of representation and their associations. The task of finding ways to assess the relative contribution of these different representations for a given individual poses an important challenge for future research.

HOW COMPELLING IS THE EVIDENCE FOR THE CLINICAL EFFECTIVENESS OF COGNITIVE TREATMENTS FOR PANIC?

In assessing the effectiveness of cognitive treatments for panic it is useful to distinguish between the questions of whether clinically useful results are produced and whether these results can be attributed to the cognitive changes which the designers of the treatments sought to achieve.

Clinical Utility

To date, there have been three evaluative studies of cognitive treatments for panic. Clark, Salkovskis, and Chalkley (1985) selected patients who perceived a similarity between the effects of overbreathing and naturally occurring panic attacks, and administered to them a cognitively oriented respiratory-control treatment. Little change occurred over a baseline period, but substantial reductions in panic attack frequency were observed during the first few weeks of treatment during which the cognitively oriented respiratory control treatment was the only treatment modality. Salkovskis, Jones, and Clark (1986) obtained substantial reductions in panic attack frequency in a subsequent evaluation of this treatment in an unselected group of panic patients. Neither of these studies included a wait-list control group nor a comparison treatment group. Clark (this volume) argues that it is unlikely that the results were the result of spontaneous remission, as there was little change in the baseline period. This point is well taken. Nonetheless, until the results of trials including wait groups and/or groups receiving established alternative treatments are available, the clinical effectiveness of this procedure cannot be conclusively determined. The same is true of the study reported by Beck (Chap. 10), in which, in an uncontrolled series of 28 patients, the initial mean frequency of panic attacks of 4.5 per week was dramatically reduced to zero by the end of the 16 weeks of cognitively oriented treatment. Thus, the present verdict on the clinical effectiveness of these treatments has to be promising but not proven.

The dramatic effectiveness of these cognitively oriented treatments for panic, which appear capable of eliminating the problem altogether, stands in interesting contrast to the effects of cognitive therapy for depression. Trials of this treatment have generally found that a sizable proportion of depressed patients still show residual symptomatology at the end of treatment. It is, of course, quite consistent with cognitive models of panic that treatments that break into the positive feedback vicious cycle that is hypothesized to be responsible for the escalation of fear should "burst the bubble" and eliminate the problem. On this view, it would be quite possible for patients in whom panics had been entirely eliminated still to show considerable residual anxiety related to other sources, but this residue would not be reflected in the measure of panic attacks. The discrepancy between the results of cognitive treatments for panic and depression may be because the measure of panic attack frequency only reflects *extreme* levels of fear and anxiety (which are eliminated), whereas most measures of depression span the *range* of severity.

It has been suggested (Teasdale, 1985) that "depression about depression," based on unduly negative interpretations of depression and its effects, may be an important factor maintaining clinical depression, in some ways parallel to the role of fear of fear in cognitive accounts of panic. In patients in whom such "depression about depression" is the major factor maintaining the condition, breaking into the maintaining cycle would be expected essentially to eliminate depression, in many ways analogous to the findings for panic. Such a process has been suggested to underly the rapid, beneficial effects sometimes seen with a variety of psychological treatments which share the common features of (a) providing patients with credible explanations for their depression, and (b) combining this with validating experiences in which patients learn that they can control their symptoms by executing coping responses that they have been taught (Teasdale, 1985). Rapid improvements would be expected in patients for whom "depression about depression" were the sole or major maintaining factor. For others, in whom persisting life problems or wider psychosocial difficulties were additional maintaining factors, further treatment directed at these problems would be required in order to achieve sustained elimination of depression.

Effective Therapeutic Processes

If, on further investigation, cognitive treatments for panic are found to be effective in trials including wait-list control groups, it will not be possible to conclude that they are effective by virtue of their effects on catastrophic interpretations. Equally, evidence for the effectiveness of these treatments would not provide very strong support for the validity of the underlying cognitive model of panic. The treatments are packages of a number of different components, some of which, it could be plausibly argued, have their effects through processes other than cognitive change. For example, the treatment developed by Clark and his colleagues, based on the assumption that the catastrophic misinterpretation of the bodily effects of hyperventilation is central to the escalation of panic, includes training in respiratory control to prevent hyperventilation and its consequent bodily effects. However, it is possible that cognitive models of panic are wrong and direct effects of hyperventilation-induced hypocapnia, rather than the cognitive misinterpretation of these effects, are the major factor in the production of panic. In this case, the beneficial effects of the treatment package would be attributed simply to the training in respiratory control eliminating hyperventilation, the components of the package directed at cognitive reappraisal of the effects of hyperventilation being irrelevant.

Determining, relatively precisely, the components and processes responsible for reduction of panic frequency is of central importanace both to the task of improving the effectiveness and efficiency of clinical treatments and to testing central predictions of cognitive models of panic, as described in a previous section. In other areas, such as the cognitive therapy of depression, there seems only a limited possibility of gaining such information from clinical trials, as the treatment packages are so complex, and the populations to which they are applied demonstrate considerable heterogeneity in their presenting problems. By contrast, evaluation of the clinical effects of cognitive treatments for panic, particularly that developed by Clark and his colleagues and based on reappraisal of the effects of hyperventilation, offers more hope of providing useful information on therapeutic components and processes. This potential exists because the procedures are specified relatively precisely and remain relatively constant from patient to patient, offering a realistic possibility of conducting "disassembly" studies in which the effects of removing different components of the total package can be assessed. A further great advantage in this area is that it is possible to select patients homogeneous for the hypothesized central etiological processes, as Clark et al. (1985) did when they included in their study only those patients who perceived a similarity between the effects of overbreathing and naturally occurring panic attacks. So, for example, it should be possible to assess the relative contributions of cognitive reappraisal and the direct effects of training in respiratory control by a comparison of groups of patients receiving training in respiratory control alone and those receiving, in addition, procedures directed at cognitive reappraisal. It would be necessary, of course, to check that no implicit cognitive reappraisal occurred in the first group. The combination of such "disassembly" studies with the type of short-term, tightly controlled studied advocated in a previous section offers a good chance of elucidating both effective therapeutic components, and testing more basic theoretical predictions. Hopefully, this would allow further refinement in effectiveness and efficiency of what already appear to be dramatically effective treatment procedures.

SUMMARY

1. Cognitive models of panic, by stating, relatively precisely, the conditions under which fear will escalate to panic, are saying something useful beyond the well-worn "fear of fear" concept. The level of precision is not at a level that is characteristic of theories in behavioral and cognitive science, nor are the terms

used by cognitive models of panic shared with these disciplines. Nonetheless, cognitive models of panic have already proved heuristic in generating useful research and extremely promising treatment procedures.

2. Cognitive models of panic offer attractive integrative accounts that are consistent with much of what is known about this disorder. However, when compared with alternative hypotheses, both biological and psychological, cognitive models do not receive strikingly greater support from the experimental evidence currently available. On the key issue on which these rival hypotheses make differential predictions, the effects of "purely cognitive" interventions on panic, the relevant experimental evidence simply is not yet available.

3. The evidence for the clinical effectiveness of cognitive treatments for panic looks extremely promising, but any more definite conclusion must await the results of trials that include control groups.

4. As yet, there is no conclusive evidence that the promising results of cognitive treatments for panic are the result of cognitive change procedures rather than other components of the total treatment package. Nonetheless, the precision with which the procedures can be specified, and the possibility of selecting patients homogeneous with respect to presumed etiology, suggests that future attempts to "disassemble" the total package to identify effective components would be worthwhile.

11

Cognitive Mechanisms in Panic Disorder

Dianne L. Chambless
American University

Examination of cognitive factors pertaining to panic disorder (PD) requires drawing on the research conducted on closely related anxiety disorders, such as agoraphobia with panic attacks and generalized anxiety disorder (GAD). One reason is purely pragmatic: There is almost no such research on patients with PD alone. The second reason is more empirical. To date, there is little evidence to support the assumption that PD, agoraphobia with panic, and GAD are clearly delineated conditions (see, for example, Hallam, 1978; Thyer, Himle, Curtis, Cameron, & Nesse, 1985; Turner, Beidel, & Jacob, this volume).

An emerging literature highlights the importance of considering cognition in our understanding of panic. As documented by Heide and Borkovec (1983) and Clark (this volume), the triggers for panic at times involve sensations that are not only innocuous but also ones that many people would consider pleasant, such as relaxation. Consequently, to predict the occurrence of panic, we must understand how the person with panic construes his or her experience. Physiological indexes do not consistently discriminate panic from nonpanic states, nor does high physiological arousal consistently precipitate panic (Freedman, Ianni, Ettedgui, Pohl, & Rainey, 1984; Taylor et al., 1986). Moreover, Ehlers, Margraf, Roth, and Birbaumer (1985) have preliminary data indicating that providing panic patients false feedback supposedly showing tachycardia is sufficient to trigger heightened levels of anxiety in this group, but not in normal controls. Such data demonstrate the importance of expectations in panic (See also Clark, this volume; Ehlers, Margraf, & Roth, 1986; Rapee, 1986; van den Hout, this volume).

A variety of methodologies has been employed in research on cognitive factors in panic and anxiety. Some investigators have gathered clients' reports of characteristic maladaptive thoughts through interviews or questionnaire assessment methods. Others have used questionnaires or diaries to search for attributional processes thought to be common in such clients. Finally, borrowing from basic cognitive psychology, anxiety researchers have conducted exquisitely controlled laboratory analogue studies of information processing in the presence of anxiety-provoking cues. Many psychological phenomena of study have been found to operate under a very narrow range of conditions. It is noteworthy, therefore, that with such a wide range of empirical approaches, anxiety investigators have consistently found significant evidence of cognitive factors. Although no one study is perfect, the combined weight of this set of studies is considerable.

From research conducted largely in the last 5 years, we seem safe in concluding that anxious patients are characterized by thoughts that harm will befall them, by their tendency to perceive harm is possible where others might not, and by their selective attention to stimuli associated with harm over less-threatening stimuli. At issue is whether these cognitive factors predispose one to develop anxiety, or whether they are simply correlates of chronic anxiety. Similarly, it would appear that at least some cognitive correlates of anxiety change with effective treatment, but it is not clear whether such changes are necessary if treatment is to be efficacious. In the remainder of this chapter, the evidence for these general assertions will be examined in some detail.

STUDIES OF SELF-REPORTED THOUGHTS

Following Beck's theory (this volume) of the association of thinking patterns with dysphoric affect, a number of investigators have examined the hypothesis that anxiety is related to characteristic maladaptive thoughts. The seminal paper is that by Beck, Laude, and Bohnert (1974), the results of which were not pursued by other researchers for nearly a decade. Thirty-two patients with a diagnosis of anxiety neurosis were interviewed concerning thoughts and images associated with their anxiety. In each case the patients reported anticipating or visualizing that social and/or physical harm would befall them. Although it is unclear how these patients would be diagnosed according to current schemes, almost all of them reported acute anxiety attacks.

A number of criticisms can be raised about this early effort: The patients could have been influenced in their reports by the orientation of the interviewers, and 20 were referred for treatment specifically to Beck, whose approach was no doubt well known. Cognitive aspects of these patients' anxiety may have been especially salient, since Beck was the referral of choice. Finally, the data for these 20 patients were not collected in a systematic fashion. Despite the methodological limitations of this preliminary study, its findings have proved to be robust. The patterns described by Beck et al. have repeatedly surfaced in more recent and rigorous research.

Hibbert (1984b) replicated the findings of Beck et al., using a more standardized approach. Reliable interview findings were that 100% of 25 patients with GAD or PD reported characteristic maladaptive thoughts before an exacerbation of their anxiety. Contrary to the findings of Beck et al., only 32% of Hibbert's subjects reported mental imagery (versus 90% in the Beck et al. study), and only one subject found imagery to be a powerful factor. Subjects with PD reported that some of their physical symptoms of anxiety were more severe than those of the GAD subjects. The PD clients also expressed more concern with illness, death, and loss of self-control. Subjects with panic attacks attributed their thoughts of physical illness to the disturbing nature of their physical symptoms. Such findings are similar to those of Pollard (1985), and of Chambless and Beck (1986), who found that the frequency of a given somatic symptom, and the degree to which the symptom was feared, were both correlated with the frequency of logically related cognitions among agoraphobics with panic attacks. For example, clients with higher frequencies of chest pains or greater fears of heart palpitations reported more often thinking, "I'll have a heart attack."

Although these studies have provided consistent descriptions of thoughts of anxious patients, they do not reveal whether such thoughts are a general feature of psychological disturbance, or whether they are particular to chronic anxiety states. In a study of 303 clients applying for treatment, Chambless and Gracely (1986) studied the ability of a self-report cognitive measure tapping "fear of fear" (fear of panic attacks) to discriminate among those with agoraphobia with panic, GAD, PD, obsessive-compulsive disorder, social phobia, and major depressive or dysthymic disorder. A sample of 23 psychometrically defined normal control subjects was also included. The possibility of demand effects was reduced, although not eliminated, by obtaining the data in questionnaire form before an intake interview.

Previously demonstrated to be reliable and valid, the Agoraphobic Cognitions Questionnaire (ACQ: Chambless, Caputo, Bright, & Gallagher, 1984) contains two empirically derived factors: frequencies of thoughts, when anxious, of physical harm (e.g., a stroke) and of loss of control (e.g., insanity). Chambless et al. found higher thought frequency to predict higher chronic anxiety and a higher frequency of panic attacks.

On the physical harm factor, the agoraphobics and clients with PD reported higher thought frequencies than all other clients. Clients with GAD differed only from the normal control subjects and the clients with panic. On the loss of control factor, clients with PD and GAD differed only from the normals, whereas agoraphobics had higher ratings than depressives and normals. Consistent with Hibbert's report, these findings indicate that clients with panic are distinguished by fears that their anxiety will lead to physical harm, such as heart attacks. Although fear of loss of control discriminated those with PD from normals, it does not appear to be a distinguishing feature of panic per se, as opposed to chronic neurotic problems, since clients with PD did not score significantly higher than those with depression or other anxiety disorders. Since the degree to which depressed clients were anxious as well is unknown, it is possible that the loss of control factor is only high in depressed clients experiencing chronic anxiety. Further research controlling for level of anxiety among depressives would be required to answer this question.

Supportive data for the hypothesis that maladaptive thinking is related to anxiety were reported by Last, O'Brien, and Barlow (1985). In this study cognitive assessment was carried out during in vivo exposure sessions. Verbalizations were recorded by tape recorder for content scoring by independent assessors, and anxiety ratings were taken at the end of each session. Within subject correlations between anxiety and negative thoughts across sessions for six agoraphobics were quite high. For most subjects there was an inverse relationship between positive thoughts and reported anxiety as well.

An important consideration in evaluating research on self-reported thoughts is the degree to which clients' reports may reflect experimental demand, although this concern is reduced in the case of comparisons among clinical samples. This issue has been addressed in a study by Sewitch and Kirsch (1984). Seventy undergraduate students were given training in reporting cognitions associated with episodes of anxiety under one of three experimental sets. In the threat condition, subjects were told that thoughts of threat typically preceded anxiety, whereas in the loss condition, subjects were told that thoughts of loss were the most common precipitant of anxiety. In pilot work the experimenters had determined that both rationales were equally credible. During training for the third and neutral condition, subjects were given examples of thoughts theoretically unrelated to anxiety. Subjects were asked to record their thoughts immediately prior to anxious feelings for a 24-hour period in a free response format.

Blind ratings of these diaries indicated that a demand effect operated. Threat thoughts were significantly more frequent in the threat instructions group than the other groups, and loss thoughts less common. However, in all three conditions threat thoughts were the most common antecedent of anxiety, with loss thoughts being reported no more often than neutral thoughts. Although the demand effect was significant, there also appears to be a true relationship between threat thoughts and the occurrence of anxiety. The authors note, however, that thoughts of threat and loss were frequently mixed, and that for some subjects, loss seemed to be an important factor in their anxiety response. These observations are consistent with the frequent report of panic attacks beginning at the time of a loss or separation (e.g., Chambless & Goldstein, 1981).

Taken together, the results of these studies provide strong support for the association of characteristic maladaptive thoughts with anxiety among clients with panic. Although these findings cannot answer the important question of causation between cognition and anxiety, the consistency of the results yielded by a variety of methodological approaches is impressive.

STUDIES ON ATTRIBUTION

As the attributional style of patients with PD has not been empirically examined, we must extrapolate from the research on agoraphobics and individuals with GAD. Riskind and Castellon (1986) examined thought records obtained from 12 clients with major depressive disorder and 12 with GAD, all of whom were in cognitive therapy. All records had been obtained without reference to the study. These written records were scored blindly for attributional patterns with a content analysis system. The characteristic attributional style for depression (perceiving negative events to be global, stable, and internal in cause) was found for the depressed but not for the GAD clients. These findings indicate that attributional styles among the neurotic disorders differ.

Brodbeck and Michelson (in press) administered the Attributional Style Questionnaire (revised to include two health-related items) to 23 agoraphobics with panic and 20 matched control subjects. Agoraphobics were found to attribute positive outcomes to limited-effect causes and negative ones to global causes, whereas the opposite pattern was found in normals. These results held for health-related items and affiliation-related items, but not for achievement. These data are consistent with the clinical picture of agoraphobics' particular concern with illness and the stability of important interpersonal relationships (e.g., Chambless & Goldstein, 1981).

In addition, agoraphobics scored as more external on Rotter's locus of control scale. Since depression is a common feature of agoraphobia and was not taken into account in the analyses, interpretation of these data is problematical. Attribution was also examined after subjects were exposed to manipulated failure or success on an anagram-solving task. Few differences were observed between subject groups. Agoraphobics in the failure condition were found to rate their performance as more personally significant and as having more impact on other areas of their lives. However, there were no differences on globality, stability, or locus of causality.

In another study on agoraphobia, Fisher and Wilson (1985) obtained findings somewhat similar to those of Brodbeck and Michelson. Seventeen agoraphobics and 11 normal controls were shown videotapes, two of which depicted a woman in phobic situations. Subsequently subjects rated the emotions they thought the woman would experience and causes of these emotions on attributional scales. While there were no differences in the emotions attributed to the woman, agoraphobics viewed causes of emotion as more internal and global; the difference in internality ratings stemmed from agoraphobics' rating fear, but not other emotions, as deriving from more internal causes. On the Helplessness Questionnaire, agoraphobics made more internal attributions for negative, but not for positive events. Agoraphobics perceived the internal causes of negative events as more consistently present, more important, and as influencing more life situations.

Because depression scores were higher among agoraphobics, and this difference was not considered in data analyses, it is once again difficult to interpret these data. In contrast to the findings of Brodbeck and Michelson, agoraphobics did not score as more external than the controls on a locus of control questionnaire.

On the whole, these studies indicate that when anxiety is mixed with depression, some elements of the depressive attributional style are found, albeit inconsistently. Castellon and Riskind's study suggests that if depression had been controlled in other studies, this style would not have been found among anxious patients. This is not an important point for the clinical picture, which is typically mixed. Not making this distinction does confound our efforts to arrive at a theoretical understanding of anxiety. A characteristic attributional style for anxiety has yet to be identified.

RESEARCH ON THREAT AND AFFECT APPRAISAL

Butler and Mathews (1983) presented subjects with ambiguous scenarios to interpret by rank-ordering provided explanations according to their probability. One explanation for each scenario yielded a threatening interpretation. Responses of 12 patients with major depressive disorder, 12 with GAD, and 12 normal controls were compared. Both patient groups rated ambiguous scenarios as more threatening than the control group. Subjects subsequently rated the subjective cost of 20 threatening items concerning physical or social harm as well as the subjective probability of 36 hypothetical events. The 36 items varied as to whether they referred to self or others, and to positive or to negative happenings. Subjective cost was highest for the depressives, followed by the patients with GAD; both patient groups gave higher ratings than the controls. On probability ratings, there were no differences among the groups on positive events, but patient groups gave higher estimates than controls for negative events. Anxious clients were higher than normals only on their appraisal that they were likely to be harmed, particularly where their health was concerned. Depressives rated harm as more likely to happen to others as well as to themselves.

The results of this investigation seem to indicate considerable similarity among anxious and depressed patients in threat appraisal. However, it is important to note that the depressed patients in this sample were equal on measures of anxiety to the GAD patients; the latter were more depressed than normals but less depressed than those with major depressive disorder. Consequently it is not surprising that the groups were almost indistinguishable. Although the results would have been clearer if depression had been controlled, the data suggest that anxiety states are associated with an inflated rate of estimations of harm and the perception that ambiguous events may be harmful. The authors suggest that when one is anxious, anxiety-related memories are accessed, inflating the perception of present risk, and increasing anxiety even further in a circular fashion.

McNally and Foa (in press) extended Butler and Mathews's work to the consideration of agoraphobia. Subjects were asked to respond to ambiguous scenarios which could be interpreted as indicative of internal (arousal-related) threats or external threats. Open-ended responses were collected as well as subsequently obtained rank orderings of several provided explanations, one of which was a threat interpretation. Responses to nine agoraphobics with panic applying for treatment were compared with those of nine normal controls. The experimenters also included nine agoraphobics with panic who had been treated with cognitive behavior therapy. Contrary to prediction, both internal and external events were interpreted as more threatening by the untreated agoraphobics, although there was a trend for internal events to be more so. Similar results were obtained for the forced rankings. In light of the small sample and the demonstrated salience of arousal-related events on other measures, this trend is probably meaningful.

Subjects were also asked to rate the subjective cost and probability of 20 unpleasant events of either an internal (arousal-related) or external nature (e.g., being short of breath versus being mugged). On the composite threat measure (threat = cost × probability), untreated agoraphobics rated only the arousal events as more threatening than did controls. The various measures of cognitive bias were then correlated to measures of psychopathology, such as the Beck Depression Inventory, the ACQ, the Agoraphobia Factor on the Fear Questionnaire, and the Anxiety Sensitivity Index, with significant results. Internal arousal threats were especially correlated with these measures with *r*s ranging from 0.50 to 0.84.

Although depression levels were not controlled in this investigation, the authors believed that the pattern of elevated ratings for internal arousal-related versus external events indicates greater specificity of cognitive bias among agoraphobics than was demonstrated by the patients with GAD in Butler and Mathews study. The methodology of the Butler and Mathews study and the McNally and Foa study do not allow ascertainment of whether the heightened threat perception is due to present mood or to a more enduring characteristic of people who develop disorders of anxiety and/or depression. However, further unpublished research by Butler and Mathews is reported (cited in Mathews & MacLeod, 1985) to demonstrate that such a bias is particularly characteristic of those with high trait, as opposed to state, anxiety.

It is noteworthy that treated agoraphobics did not differ on any analyses from normals. Given the small samples, it is difficult to know whether this is due to sample differences, or whether treatment changed the clients' perceptions. These findings are in contrast to those of Chambless, Goldstein, Gallagher, and Bright (1986) with self-reported thoughts. Thirty-one agoraphobic clients with panic, 6 months after beginning treatment, scored significantly lower on the ACQ than at pretest; however, they were still significantly different from a normal control group. This discrepancy may be due to the nature of the normal control groups used in the two studies. McNally and Foa's control group was not tested for psychopathology, whereas Chambless et al. used only normal subjects who passed a number of screening measures for psychological disturbance. The "supernormal" group in the latter study, therefore, may have had particularly low rates of cognitive distortion. Both studies indicate that this sort of surface cognitive phenomenon is amenable to change with treatment.

In a rather different type of research Fisher and Wilson (1985) assessed cue utilization by agoraphobic clients with panic. Subjects were induced to form, without awareness, facial expressions reflecting anger, happiness, and fear. Since agoraphobics are notably focused on their internal states (Belfer & Glass, 1982), the authors expected they would be more sensitive to these manipulations than normal subjects. Prior research on this task indicated that subjects who rely on internal cues in assessing their moods are especially influenced by these engineered facial expressions. Contrary to hypothesis, agoraphobics reported themselves as fearful, compared with the normals, regardless of the affect condition. These data might be interpreted as indicating that agoraphobics construe many types of arousal as fear, as hypothesized by Goldstein and Chambless (1978). However, it is difficult to draw this conclusion because the agoraphobics were higher on fear at baseline, and baseline fear was not controlled in the comparative data analyses.

The results of these studies, if replicated with controls for depression, indicate that anxiety states are accompanied by or fostered by a strong tendency to perceive ambiguous situations as threatening. In the case of those with panic, this sensitivity seems especially heightened in the case of internal, arousal-related sensations. Such findings suggest that perceptual patterns may be important in creating or maintaining anxiety states, a theme that will be explored in the next section. Using a different methodological approach, attribution researchers obtained data consistent with those of investigations described in the previous section on self-reported thoughts: Hypersensitivity to arousal-related events seems to be associated with the experience of panic attacks and higher levels of somatic symptoms in clients with panic.

STUDIES ON INFORMATION PROCESSING AND RECALL

Borkovec, Robinson, Pruzinsky, and DePree (1983) have suggested that self-reportable phenomena such as worry (and by extension, maladaptive cognitions) may be a "surface reflection of deep-structure schemata" (p. 10). A schema is a hypothetical construct, frequently evoked in basic cognitive psychology and in studies of social cognition (e.g., Alba & Hasher, 1983; Fiske & Taylor, 1984). Schema theorists believe people organize memory and assimilate new information according to pre-existing structures (schemata), which are, in turn, based on prior experience. Subjects generally cannot report the presence of schemata, but a considerable body of research supports the theory that they nonetheless influence cognitive processes (see reviews by Alba & Hasher, 1983; Fiske & Taylor, 1984). If schemata related to anxiety are not readily reportable, they require a different kind of methodology to detect than has been described heretofore.

Different approaches have been employed by anxiety researchers to test for the operation of schemata. Goldfried, Padawer, and Robins (1984), for example, used multidimensional scaling of ratings of social interactions by socially anxious and nonanxious college students. Socially anxious students were found to organize their perceptions of social situations according to a dimension of degree of evaluation, whereas socially nonanxious students did not. The bulk of the research on cognitive schemata has involved studies of memory or attentional bias and will be discussed in the next section.

Studies of Memory Bias

Martin, Ward, and Clark (1983) studied the relationship of neuroticism as measured by the Eysenck Personality Questionnaire to memory bias in 40 female undergraduates. The subjects, none of whom was severely depressed, first rated a list of positive and negative adjectives pertaining to themselves and a list of similar adjectives pertaining to others in counterbalanced order. Subsequently they were asked to remember as many words from each separate list as possible. Partialing out depression scores, the investigators found neuroticism to be significantly correlated with the number of negative, but not positive, words recalled about the self. Neuroticism did not predict the number of positive or negative adjectives recalled pertaining to others. The frequency of intrusions (including words not on the original lists) was also measured. Neuroticism was significantly correlated with the intrusion of negative words only. Finally, the occurrence of migrations (bringing in words belonging to the other list) was examined. Subjects low on neuroticism were more likely to bring in positive items from the list describing others to the list describing themselves. In all cases correlations remained significant with depression scores partialed out.

Drawing on signal detection theory, the authors found neuroticism to be significantly correlated with d' but not with β. They interpreted these findings to mean that the obtained effects were indicative of a stronger memory trace for negative words pertaining to the self, a shift in sensitivity rather than a shift in criterion. They conclude that the effects of neuroticism are probably on initial processing of information for storage rather than on subsequent retrieval. Since the effects were obtained while depression was controlled, the authors believe they are due to a stable personality trait rather than to mood. The Eysenck neuroticism factor reflects both trait anxiety and depression (e.g., Chambless et al., 1984); consequently, if depression is controlled, that personality trait may be chronic anxiety. However, state anxiety was not measured or controlled in this study, and it is possible that the obtained effects were accounted for by current anxious mood.

Nunn, Stevenson, and Whalan (1984) studied recall of phobic versus neutral material by nine agoraphobics and nine controls matched for age, sex, and verbal ability. Subjects listened to four presentations of a list of 10 phobia-related and 10 neutral words. Following each presentation, they were asked to recall as many words as possible, with the list of words being randomized after each presentation. Agoraphobics recalled more phobic words and controls more neutral words.

In a second part of the experiment, subjects listened to five passages of prose: two neutral and three phobia-related. Before they were asked to recall the material, a complex distractor task was interpolated. Controls and agoraphobics recalled comparable amounts of neutral material, but agoraphobics recalled more phobic material. Unfortunately the effects were not uniform across passages, and since the passages were always presented in the same order, order effects were confounded with content effects. The results are comparable, however, with those from the word lists where order effects were controlled. These results are consistent with interpretations of either biased attention or retrieval; however, it is also possible that enhanced performance by the phobics was simply due to their greater familiarity with phobic material. Consistent with the findings of the Martin et al. study, these data indicate that anxious clients are particularly attuned to negative stimuli. They do not, however, touch on the question of present mood versus enduring structure, as no attempt was made to control for the generally higher levels of anxiety and depression typical of agoraphobics.

Information Processing

In a series of progressively more elegant studies, Mathews and colleagues have attempted to demonstrate the operation of danger schemata in anxious patients (MacLeod, Mathews, & Tata, 1986; Mathews & MacLeod, 1985; Mathews & MacLeod, 1986). They have proposed that "anxiety is associated with a bias in processing information related to threat, due either to differences in type or extent of such schemata, or to the ease with which they can be activated" (Mathews & MacLeod, 1985, p. 563). In the first study, the Stroop color-naming task was used to examine the extent to which processing time would be allocated to threat cues by 24 out-patients with a diagnosis of "anxiety state" and 24 control subjects matched for age and sex.

Subjects were asked to name the color in which words were printed. Lists of physical or social threat-related words were taken from the descriptions of Hibbert (1984b) and Beck et al. (1974), and two sets of nonthreat words were chosen on the basis of frequency matching with the threat words. Four blocks of word lists were thus constructed. Control subjects named the colors of all kinds of words with equal rapidity, whereas anxious patients were significantly slower in responding to threat words in particular. Only those patients most concerned about physical threat were significantly slower when such words were presented, whereas those primarily anxious about physical threat and those primarily anxious about social threats were both slower on social threat as compared with neutral words. (Patients were asked to designate their primary area of concern; however, this does not mean those whose chief concern was physical harm were not also anxious about social threat. Data to answer this question were not collected.) Signal detection analyses indicated that these results were not due to greater word recognition by the anxious subjects.

Disruption on the color-naming task was significantly correlated with state anxiety for the anxious patients when depression and trait anxiety were partialed out, whereas correlations of depression and trait anxiety with disruption were reduced to nonsignificant levels when state anxiety was controlled. Thus current anxious mood appears to have influenced ability to perform on the Stroop test. However, the patients primarily concerned with physical harm were differentially affected by physical harm cues; current mood effects can not account for such differential sensitivity.

Mathews and MacLeod suggest that the interference effects were due in part to the activation of personal danger schemata which matched the content of the threat stimuli. That is, they hypothesized that anxious subjects were slower in response to threat words on the Stroop test because these words caught and held their attention, and in the process impeded task performance. An alternative hypothesis is that the disorganizing effects of anxiety impaired performance. Since subjects filled out the mood questionnaires before completing the Stroop test, the possibility remains that when subjects were exposed to threat-related cues during the test, changes in mood, with disruptive effects on performance, might have led to this pattern of effects. Threat words were massed into blocks according to predominant theme, rather than being interspersed with one another and with neutral words. This style of presentation enhances the likelihood that anxious mood would intensify during the process (Mathews, personal communication).

Recognizing the problems in interpreting the results of Mathews and MacLeod (1985), MacLeod et al. (1986) employed a different methodology in continuing to assess danger schemata. In this study the responses of 16 patients with GAD, 16 patients with a primary diagnosis of depression, and 16 normals on a visual-detection latency task were compared. Subjects were asked to signal when they detected a probe (a dot) on a computer screen while they were reading aloud the top of a pair of words on the screen. Threat or neutral words and the probe were presented in variable order on the top (attended) or bottom half of the computer screen. Both physical and social threat words drew more attention from anxious people (i.e., probes were detected more quickly in the half of the screen with a threatening word, regardless of whether the threatening word was in the attended position) than did neutral words. Normal controls selectively attended to neutral words when they were present. The anxious patients' predominant area of concern (social versus physical harm) had no effect in this study, in contrast to that of Mathews and MacLeod (1985). Depressed subjects showed no bias in either direction.

The disruptive effects of anxious mood cannot account for these findings, in that anxiety *facilitated* probe detection where threat cues were concerned. Nor can it be argued that the response to the probe (pushing a hand switch) was particularly familiar or related to an operative danger schema and was thus more readily activated in anxious patients. Both the probe (a dot on a computer screen) and the response were neutral. Consequently these results support the hypothesis that danger schemata in anxious patients serve to divert attention toward threatening stimuli. The authors cite unpublished research in their laboratory by Mogg, who determined that anxious patients demonstrated no enhanced recall of threatening material compared with nonanxious controls. They suggest that depression may be marked by selective *recall,* whereas anxiety is characterized by enhanced *attention* to dysphoria-producing cues. Normal subjects may show a protective bias against negative cues; however, this result requires replication.

Further pursuing the results of their 1985 study, Mathews and MacLeod (1986) attempted to determine whether the effects of threat-related cues were due to conscious or preconscious attentional biases. Sixteen subjects with generalized anxiety disorder and 16 matched controls completed a dichotic listening task in which they verbally shadowed a story on the dominant channel, while on the unattended channel threat or nonthreat words were randomly presented. Subjects were further asked to monitor a video screen and to press a hand switch when cued by the monitor. Reaction time for the anxious patients was significantly slower when threat-versus-nonthreat words were presented in the unattended channel, whereas there were no differences for the controls. There was a nonsignificant trend for shadowing errors (errors in repeating the words in the story on the dominant channel) to show the same effect.

Subsequent recognition of threat and nonthreat words was not above chance, indicating that the shadowing task prevented conscious attention to the unattended channel, and that the bias operated at a preconscious level. Nevertheless, one might argue that had the subjects been asked immediately whether they were aware of the words in the nonattended channel, recognition might have been higher, especially in the case of threat words for the GAD patients. Consequently the authors ran an additional group of eight controls and eight patients, stopping subjects in the middle of the listening task to detect ability to report the words in the nonattended channel. Recognition continued to occur at chance levels, buttressing the interpretation that biases were operating preconsciously.

Anxious patients did not rate themselves as more anxious before beginning the dichotic listening task or after listening to each story. Current mood effects may not, therefore, account for task disruption; however, the authors question the sensitivity of the mood measure. In light of prior negative findings on depression (MacLeod et al., 1986), it seems unlikely that the GAD patients' higher levels of depression led to the increased response latency. The authors conclude that anxious patients' danger schemata lead to a preattentive shift of information-processing resources toward threat cues. The results of this investigation, if replicated, are extraordinarily important to our understanding of anxiety states. If danger cues outside of awareness can affect cognitive processes, might anxiety itself not be instigated by unconsciously perceived cues? These data are congruent with the speculation that so-called spontaneous panic attacks may actually be attacks triggered by stimuli operating out of conscious awareness.

SUMMARY AND CONCLUSIONS

On the whole, the studies reviewed, when extrapolated to Panic Disorder, indicate that PD patients believe harm is more likely to befall them than is normal, and that they think about the possibility of harm, especially somatic harm, more frequently. They are particularly attentive to the presence of cues that might indicate harm, and, when presented with such cues, may suffer disrupted functioning without even being aware of the presence of the perceived threat. When preconscious cues lead to heightened arousal, the arousal itself may then result in further arousal, perhaps in the extreme case, to panic that seems to "come out of the blue." The notion that GAD and PD are disorders in which patients do not respond to specific stimuli may well be in error. The triggers for increased anxiety may be diffuse and often internal (see also in this volume Barlow; Turner et al.; van den Hout), and we cannot assume they are not there because the patient cannot report them. The challenge is to demonstrate empirically such subtle processes.

Additional research is required to tease out whether the demonstrated differences between anxious patients and other subjects are due to current mood or to enduring characteristics of these individuals. This is a difficult problem to resolve, and longitudinal research may be required. Short of that, however, current research designs could be strengthened by statistical controls for state effects. Moreover, more would be gained from research efforts if researchers were more attentive to sorting out the effects of depression from those of anxiety in preparing their studies and analyzing their data.

A rather different issue is how to change not only surface, accessible to consciousness, maladaptive cognitions but also how to alter deeper structures (i.e., schemata). Explicitly cognitive therapeutic interventions have generally focused on the former which, the data indicate, can be reduced, if not eliminated. Whether schemata change during present types of treatment, and if so, how, remains an open question. Nor do studies to date tell us whether these cognitive structures result from the experience of high anxiety states or, rather, lead to anxiety. This issue is difficult, if not impossible, to resolve. In any case, it is highly probable that such schemata, once formed, serve to maintain the anxious person in an aroused state and/or vulnerable to anxiety under conditions of stress.

12

Fear, Anxiety, and Panic: *Context, Cognition, and Visceral Arousal*

Peter J. Lang
University of Florida

Psychological analyses of panic states and panic disorders generally emphasize the role of physiological symptoms as precursors of the subjective state of anxiety, and as the explanation for reports of fear, loss of control, or impending doom. Beck, Emery, and Greenberg (1985, p. 136) see the "attribution of causality in panic attacks" as critical to their development. In the view of emotion pioneered by Schachter and Singer (1962), and later developed by Lazarus (1975) and Mandler (1975, 1984), as well as Beck, emotional states begin with an appraisal of one's own physiological state in the context of current environmental stimulation. That is to say, human beings are presumed by Schachter to have "evaluative needs," vis-à-vis their bodily sensations. These sensations are considered to be unidimensional (i.e., different levels of arousal) and by themselves, to serve no direct, affect-cueing function.

The meaning of the arousal, and thus the emotional state experienced, depends on an analysis of context. For example, a condition of rapid heart rate, oxygen debt, and muscle weakness does not lead to emotional expression if the subject has just completed his weekly aerobic workout at the gym. However, the same physical state would be differently appraised, and fear experienced, if it occurred immediately after a pistol-brandishing mugger emerged from the gloom of a deserted alley.

The appraisal view assumes that emotions are the products of conscious, rational analysis (or sometimes, of an *unconscious* process which is "like" conscious, rational analysis). Certainly this is the way we prefer to explain most of our behavior (e.g., why we went into medicine rather than engineering, or why we choose the salad, rather than the beef, that we really like better).

However, it may be asked, is it not in the particular case of emotional reactions that these "rational" explanations work least well?

One is reminded here of a humorous skit of comedian, Jack Benny, who made great fun of his own supposed miserliness: A mugger appears out of the gloom and asks, "Your money or your life?" Benny stands mute for several long seconds. Exasperated by the delay, the mugger again poses the fateful query, "Your money or your life?" Benny, with equal exasperation, finally explains his silence: "I'm thinking!"

The humor in Benny's bit lies in his reason for the absurd delay. In these circumstances of intense fear, he carefully appraises the comparative value of his money—and life itself! Most of us feel that we do not do much "thinking" when confronted by a strong emotional prompt; we respond seemingly without thought.

IS RATIOCINATION THE COGNITION IN EMOTION?

From the perspective of appraisal theory, the subjective reports of panic and their behavioral sequelae are the result of misattributions. It begins with physiological arousal, perhaps stemming from life problems that are novel to the patient or even from some psychologically innocuous activity. The arousal includes a synchrony of physiological changes—hyperventilation (CO_2/O_2 imbalance), lactate increases, accelerated heart rate, and other cardiovascular symptoms, which cannot be accounted for by any obvious external event. In the absence of an external rationale, the symptoms are construed to be the result of physical or mental illness. Their mysterious appearance, and the lack of control over their expression, implies "impending physical or mental disaster." This interpretation occasions yet more arousal, which acts only to confirm the patient's fears. A vicious cycle of physical symptoms, invidious explanation, and further emotional arousal ensues, which is the essence of panic.

Such an explanation is readily appreciated by professionals and laity alike. It has the force of a good story, and does not ask us to believe in any cognitive mechanism beyond those that have been familiar to playwrights and novelists for centuries. Above all, it can be readily comprehended by the patient, whose cooperation can then be enlisted in lending substance to the scenario. The expectation is that when the patient learns new, less distressing explanations for his wayward physiology, *mutatis mutandis,* the panic condition is alleviated.

Despite these virtues, there are problems with this approach. If everything operates rationally, why is the condition seldom ameliorated by the doses of "objective" information, usually provided by family and friends, or the consulting physician? For example, "Mr. Doe, our physical examination reveals that you have no heart ailment. However, you do have a tendency to hyperventilate when life gets tough. In the future, just breathe into this brown paper bag whenever you get nervous. That will help balance the gases in your respiratory system, and reduce these symptoms. But in any event, remember if they do occur that they are normal physical responses and have no implications for your physical or mental health.'' The failure of patients to embrace such instructions easily is for some the defining criterion of panic disorder. (Clark & Beck's results described in this volume suggest, nevertheless, that in the proper hands it might work!). Furthermore, why at the outset does the patient select egregious explanations of his or physiological state, rather than alternatives such as those described, which are both more rational and more benign? Also, can we be so sure that external stimuli have minor significance in panic, just because patients do not attribute to them a causal role? Finally, isn't this process (like Benny's ''thinking'') too slow to develop, considering patient reports of abrupt panic states, appearing spontaneously and without aura?

These questions have frequently been raised by critics of the appraisal explanation of emotion and anxiety (e.g., Berkowitz, 1983; Leventhal, 1980; Zajonc, 1980; Zillman, 1983), and have received thoughtful responses from this view's supporters (e.g., Mandler's, 1984, extensive response to Zajonc, concerning the speed of appraisal processes.). These questions will not receive detailed reexamination here. Rather, appraisal theory will be considered in the general context of scientific explanation in psychology. The fundamental issue: Is this the best way to explain anxiety, or is it an inherently limited level of discourse? Subsequent to this analysis, an alternative approach will be outlined, and some preliminary data presented.

INTENTIONAL SYSTEMS

Appraisal theories assume as a given that emotional behavior is the product of what Daniel Dennett (1978, following Brentano) calls an intentional system. It is furthermore presumed that a scientific understanding of its mechanism can be achieved in the system's own terms. Intentional explanations are framed in the vernacular of goals and plans. The system is described as having wishes, desires, and needs that can be realized or thwarted; it appraises and chooses; the specification of these ''variables'' and their logical relationships accounts for its observed behavior.

For example, we might describe the behavior of a chess-playing computer as indicative of its ''desire'' to win. We might infer that it is ''appraising'' the situation on the chessboard and ''selecting'' certain methods to achieve this goal (although we may balk at inferring the machine is ''satisfied'' with a successful capture). Indeed, if you are playing chess with a computer, *or a person,* this is a very useful way to conceive of the psychology of your opponent.

Appraisal theories appear to have a second implicit postulate. They presume that this intentional stance regarding a system's mechanism is not, in the case of human behavior, merely a theory. What are considered to be inferred parameters and no more than a convenient posture for working with the chess-playing computer, are held to exist substantively in the human mechanism. That is to say, such things as desires, wishes, goals, and plans, are irreducible psychological variables. Intentional explanation is an ineluctable explanation because human desires and wants are real motivators, and syllogistic analysis is the prototype of thought. This approach is buttressed by what is held to be an unanswerable argument: "Can you not see within your own conscious experience, the reality of these concepts and processes?"

Despite the conviction that intentional explanation may be the only "psychological" approach, cognitive theorists of most every persuasion accept, nevertheless, the view that the human intentional system can also be understood from a *physical stance*. Predictions about the output of a mechanism can be based, at least in principle, on its actual physical state. These "hardware" explanations, as Dennett (1978) pointed out, are most often enlisted to explain malfunctions, that is, "The computer doesn't work, because its not plugged in" or "It's putting out gibberish, because the power supply has overheated and melted a circuit board." Such physical stance interpretations of human panic are currently under intense investigation by researchers. One view holds that panic attacks (a malfunction in human behavior) occur because of a buildup in lactate (Carr & Sheehan, 1984a; Klein, 1981; Pitts, 1969). The physiological state directly prompts symptoms, which are relieved by direct modification of the physical system (through administration of a drug, e.g., imipramine). From this perspective, the patients' cognitions (goals and appraisals) are secondary, if not epiphenomena.

While explanations of behavior disorder from the physical stance are deceptively simple, and promise easy treatments, they frequently flounder when used as a basis for analyzing behavior in the essentially intact and functioning human organism. It is analogous to trying to understand the chess-playing strategy of the computer through analysis of its active hardware. All would agree that the computer's behavior depends on its physical state (and furthermore, that its physical state and the engineering of its architecture can be described in detail); even so, a thousand technicians, let loose with as many oscilloscopes and circuit testers, will not be able to say exactly what the machine is doing. In brief, the system is simply too complex for functional, physical analysis. In order to understand its chess game, we would have to know the machine's program.

THE COMPUTER METAPHOR: MENTATION AS SOFTWARE

With this limitation of the physical stance in mind, let us return to the question of the psychological assessment of intentional systems. Let us also make a tentative assumption at the outset, that anxiety and panic are not wholly symptoms of gross physical malfunction, but are system design outputs which include specific language, overt actions, and patterns of somato-visceral physiology.

It is basic to the logic of explanation that a phenomenon cannot be elucidated in its own terms. Thus, Molière's physician is a figure of fun, because he "explained" the effect of a sleeping drug, as attributable to its "soporific action." To say that a situation is frightening because it is appraised as "fearful" has, at the least, similar explanatory limitations. To an extent, all traditional analyses of mentation have this problem of circularity. Watson (1924) attempted to free us from the wheel by rejecting mental phenomena as outside the domain of scientific psychology. This behavioral revolution focused research on the field of conditioning, which culminated in the development of potent behavioral methods for the analysis and treatment of anxiety disorders.

While the focus on behavior has been salutary, the limitations of traditional conditioning theory in explaining complex pathologies have become increasingly apparent. The method of cognitive behavior therapy and analysis is an effort to respond to this problem (e.g., Beck, 1976; Mahoney, 1974; Miechenbaum, 1974). However, in some ways this approach has represented a step backwards, as it revived the subjective conception of behavioral causality. Furthermore, until very recently, the cognitive-behavioral approach has ignored a major "second revolution" in experimental psychology, based on a wholly new way of comprehending mentation, which is geared to the complexity of human behavior and potentially free of phenomenological bias. It is this novel, third way of explaining intentional systems that is the focus of this presentation.

The proposed concept of mentality is based on the metaphor of the computer. It assumes that the human brain is an organized, logical, information-processing system. The system is designed to control the pattern, sequence, and timing of behavior. All complex behavior is presumed to be consequent on cognitive processing (whether emotional or not). However, *cognition is defined here as computation.* Mental processes such as stimulus evaluation, semantic categorization, or syllogistic reasoning (traditional contents of phenomenological analysis) are products of this computation, but other outputs, such as skilled performance or avoidance behavior, may lay equal claim. Cognition, as computation, is not identical with conscious thought, nor with unconscious mentation, construed to be an alternate form of conscious thought. From this perspective, behavior is understood as a production of an information processing system. To understand the action of the system, we need to know the information data base for individual productions, for example, What is the pertinent conceptual content in associative memory? How is it coded and organized?, and we want to understand the "program," that is, the logical sequence of information transactions that leads to an output. The purist form of this approach is that practiced by workers in artificial intelligence, whose task is actually to build, in whole or part, intentional systems.

The proposed radical cognitive approach is not envisioned as a necessary, universal view for psychology. The perspective described here is simply a pragmatic stance from which, it is proposed, a natural science of cognition and behavior (including emotional behavior) can be realized. Judgment is suspended on the substantive validity of human experience. However, the language code of subjective report is not presumed to be the basic code of cognition: While phenomenological reports are held to be products of cognitive work, they are not assumed to be a priori isomorphic with the processing that produced them.

Contemporary appraisal theories are all derived from the original work of William James (1884). When James proposed that emotional "feelings" were a perception of physiological changes in the body, he was not trying to explain emotional *behavior,* rather he intended to explain the nature of emotional *experience.* Contemporary appraisal theorists, such as Mandler (1984), have frankly pursued the same goal, and the philosophical legitimacy of such an endeavor is beyond question. It is suggested, however, that what may be a suitable topic for disinterested, scholarly inquiry is not necessarily appropriate to the task of improving the assessment and treatment of human psychopathology. In this latter case the final goal cannot be the elucidation of phenomenological experience; it must be the understanding and modification of the measurable behaviors (verbal, physiological, overt action) which are the objective pathological state.

EMOTIONAL MEMORY AND EMOTIONAL EXPRESSION

A limitation inherent in the cognitive approach advocated here is that an all-embracing theory of human behavior, cradle to the grave, or of psychopathology, from assessment to treatment, is not immediately obvious. As was suggested earlier, theories of human subjectivity have the virtue of being "ready made," with a historically well-understood logic and language of intentions, appraisals, wishes, and wants. The more austere effort, to define the program behind the behavior, is more data-dependent even in its first steps, and thus must begin with more limited scope. The present approach considers mechanisms of information processing and memory organization which elucidate the interaction between physiological pattern, reports of emotional experience, and affective behavior. The focus here is on how the brain processes images. In the present context, images are considered to be perceptual-motor information structures. They are memory structures which integrate environmental inputs, semantic information, and action patterns, and are the cognitive format of effective expression. It is argued that image processing and/or the organization of emotional memories differ significantly among anxiety disordered patients. The primary goal of the subsequent theoretical presentation and research description is to elucidate these differences—to help develop a more parsimonious foundation view for the cognitive analysis of anxiety disorder, including panic states.

It is proposed that emotional responses be construed primitively as action dispositions, that is, efferent programs which mobilize the organism for flight and attack. In less complex animals, and for the most part in humans, emotional behavior is context bound. Theorists such as Seligman (1975) and Ohman (1979) have even argued that there are phylogenetic dependencies between certain stimuli (e.g., heights, snakes, and spiders) and fear or avoidance behavior. Whatever their genesis in past experience or heredity, most emotions appear to be expressed in specific stimulus environments.

In the present view, information about stimuli *and* about responses are represented in associative memory. Furthermore, following a current view of memory organization (e.g., Anderson & Bower, 1974), an emotion information structure is conceived to be a conceptual network. A network contains representations of stimuli (the context of action), responses (verbal, gross motor, and visceral), and meaning (internuncial propositions, connecting stimulus and response concepts from one unit structure with other information networks). Networks are seen as varying in *coherence,* that is, associative strength and number of associative links between concepts. For example, we might presume that most people have a knowledge schema (a kind of conceptual network) for restaurants. It includes concepts such as WAITER, MENU, CASHIER, ORDERING, which are highly interrelated and strongly associated. Thus, activation of a small subset of concepts has a high probability of activating the whole schema, with its associated restaurant behaviors. Coherence determines reliability of response pattern and specificity of context activation. Among the anxiety disorders, the emotion-memory schema of a simple phobia would have the highest network coherence.

When an affective network is activated, an emotion production results. An emotion production is an efferent pattern, determined by the network's defining action disposition. In the case of simple phobia, an emotion production invariably takes the form of an avoidance response. Emotion productions occur when input cues match concepts in the network. The instigating match can occur with concepts of any type. Thus, the appearance of an alive snake, matching all stimulus concepts, readily prompts phobia network activation and avoidance response production. However, a degraded stimulus (e.g., a sinuously shaped stick) might prompt the same fear production, if some of the response information in the network were already activated. This might occur, for example, if sympathetic arousal had been initiated by physical exertion during a wholly unrelated physical task.

In a similar manner, one affective state can synergistically enhance another. Zillman (1983), for example, has shown in the laboratory that prior sexual arousal can potentiate aggression; Barlow, Sakheim, and Beck (1983) have shown that a fear context can enhance subsequent sexual tumescence. The present model presumes that these effects are mediated by the fact that two emotions share response structure. The prior affect provides matching response information, which both increases the probability of the second emotional response and augments its intensity.

To summarize, the present view assumes that information regarding responses is represented in associative memory. Furthermore, when response concepts are activated, they not only prompt behavioral productions, but also activate other associated conceptual units, that is, stimulus concepts, other action representations, and semantic elaborations. Thus, for example, context-dependent and mood-dependent memory may be explained in terms of a mediating response code (Lang, 1985). Mood dependencies occur when semantic material has become associated during acquisition with the central representation of a particular affective response disposition, (i.e., a specific pattern of somato-visceral activity). The semantic material (words, lists, sentences) has a retrieval advantage, if it is subsequently called for coincident with reactivation of the response program (the mood) that was operating during learning. If mediation through response information is assumed, the stimulus circumstances that prompt the mood could be quite different from those that served this function in the original acquisition context. Furthermore, response concepts are *not dependent on interpretive appraisals* for their mediating effect, that is, on their conversion into response outputs which are subsequently "perceived" interoceptively (or exterocepetively through distance receptors, as in biofeedback). Response concepts would directly cue stimulus or semantic concepts in the same schema, and even in related networks, because the response information is itself centrally represented in the associative net.

Theories such as that proposed here, that postulate a network memory structure, face the problem: "If everything is interrelated, will not activation of any individual unit activate all the rest of one's stored memories, resulting in a competition for production that paralyzes the organism?" The present model certainly assumes that many concepts are activated in parallel, and that activated units are distributed widely over memory storage. In theory, response programs can be protected by elaborate computation which produces inhibition of competing pattern of activation. However, simple strength of association is assumed to be the first line of defense against cognitive chaos. The association between an affective response disposition and, for example, a list of words (as in mood dependency studies) is likely to be weak and its influence transient. A happy result!—considering how, in most circumstances, it is more useful to have the knowledge base independent of context and emotion. It is not surprising that replicable, laboratory demonstrations of such mediating effects are very rare (Bower & Mayer, 1985; Fernandez & Glenberg, 1985). On the other hand, what seem like quite minor cues—sensory, semantic, or efferent—which are part of a simple phobic's fear network, can prompt a full-blown anxiety attack with astonishing speed and reliability!

It is suggested that emotion networks vary in coherence, that is, the degree to which information units are associatively interdependent and stable, and are activated as an organized sequence, separate from other memory structures. A highly coherent network can be activated by relatively few matching cues, and the response configuration generated has high reliability. To the extent that behavior disorders are determined by such affective dispositions, their character may be similarly defined.

The memorial basis for phobic disorders resides in characteristic, specific networks of conceptual information—in effect, various fear dispositions, involving stimulus, response, and meaning information. Traditionally, we discriminate anxiety disorders in terms of the different cues which prompt distress: snakes, blood, heights, for simple phobics; various social situations for social phobics; and open spaces, supermarket lines, and distance from home, for agoraphobia. However, it is proposed (Lang, 1985) that these disorders may differ in a more fundamental way, in terms of the way affective information is organized in memory:

> It is proposed that the anxiety disorders may be distributed along a continuum of affective memory organization. The continuum is defined by the degree to which arousing, negatively valent responses (and perhaps also disruption of control) are linked associatively to coherent affect networks; or viewed from the other direction, the degree to which these affective response dispositions float in memory, and are prompted by many stimuli, transferring their excitation to great varient of other memory structures. Proceeding from most to least along the continuum of network coherence, the order of nosology is as follows: focal phobia . . . social anxiety; agoraphobia. . . . (Lang, 1985, pp. 166–167)

Panic attacks are, of course, a common feature of agoraphobia. The fact that they are unpredictable, and not reliably associated with a particular context, could contribute to the development of the kind of diffuse affective memory structure that has been hypothesized herein for agoraphobia.

IMAGERY AND FEAR

From the perspective of phenomenological investigation, images are sensory events in the mind, pictures presented to the mind's eye, which vary from the vague, fleeting, and ghostly to idetic impressions that rival the vivid world of reality—hallucinations indistinguishable from the objects they mentally represent. It is a surprising fact that despite the compelling nature of the subjective hypothesis, experimental psychology has uncovered little evidence that the self-reported prevalence of imagery in thought or the vividness of individual images relate to sensory memory (e.g., see Strosahl & Ascough, 1981). For example, several investigators have failed to find that self-described good imagers remember previously observed visual materials more accurately, or in more detail, than do people who maintain they have few if any images at all.

On the other hand, studies of psychophysiological changes in imagery almost always show a positive relationship between responses observed during perception (e.g., sense organ adjustments, patterns of visceral activation) and those observed when subjects image. Furthermore, the probability of finding this relationship is increased significantly when the subjects studied are people who say that their thinking about events or objects normally involves vivid sensory imagery. For example, researchers have examined tasks that require highly stereotyped cyclical eye movements (such as visual tracking of an oscillating pendulum or of a moving verbal display on a cathode ray tube) and demonstrated that during recall of this task, good imagers tend to regenerate eye movements that have a dominant frequency similar to that of the actual perceptual display (Brady & Levitt, 1966; Brown, 1968; Deckert, 1964; Weerts, Cuthbert, Simons, & Lang, in preparation).

The results described here are consistent with the hypothesis that sensory and response information are both coded at intake and retained within the same structure in memory. This structure is assumed here to be an associative network. Thus, when sensory information is cued by instructions to "remember what you saw," the unasked-for response information is also automatically activated. Activation of the conceptual response code, initiates the motor program, resulting in an eye movement production. A similar cognitive sequence is presumed to occur with more elaborate, emotional imagery—as when a phobic patient recalls a focal experience with the fear object. In this latter case, the associated response code would include, in addition to the responses related to stimulus intake (e.g., eye movements), a context-relevant array of affective behaviors.

In a series of experiments, we explored the effects of inducing emotional imagery through textual descriptions of affect-arousing scenes. Such imagery is, of course, determined in part by differences in formal text structure and text-processing mode, that is, the subjects set to respond and the match between text cues and hypothesized concepts in memory; as well as variations in processing instructions and individual differences in imagery ability (Lang, Kozak, Miller, Levin, & McLean, 1980; Miller et al., in press; Vrana, Cuthbert, & Lang, 1986). However, the results also showed that *the basic pattern of visceral responses evoked in script-based fear imagery* is the same as that evoked by other media, for example, a presentation of the fear context, using actors and props (McLean, 1981), and more importantly, *it is the same as that evoked in the actual, behavioral field* (Lang, Levin, Miller, & Kozak, 1983; Levin, 1982). A common associative structure appears to determine fear responding over different contexts of evocation. This finding encourages the use of the imagery paradigm in examining the memorial organization of phobia, as it varies with anxiety nosology.

SIMPLE PHOBIA, SOCIAL ANXIETY, AND AGORAPHOBIA: DIFFERENCES IN MEMORY ORGANIZATION?

Recently, the anxiety disorders research group at the University of Florida (Cook, Melamed, Cuthbert, McNeil, & Lang, 1987) has undertaken a study of imagery response differences among anxiety diagnoses. An imagery assessment battery was devised, adapted from a paradigm employed successfully with normal subjects (e.g., Lang et al., 1980). Subjects are instructed to imagine that they are active participants in a series of situations, each of which is prompted by a verbal script that describes both context and response. The scenes imaged are either personal (phobic situations and other aversive, pleasant, and neutral scenes), that are derived from individual, structured interviews, or standard (common fearful situation, active but nonaffective scenes, and neutral scenes), that are the same for all subjects. Six dependent variables are recorded in connection with each image: heart rate and skin conductance, and subjects' scaled appraisals of their feelings along dimensions of arousal–calm, pleasure–displeasure, dominance (control)–submission (controlled), plus ratings of scene vividness.

Data obtained from all anxiety patients in the experiment (Simple Phobia = 13; Social Phobia = 14; Agoraphobia = 11) are presented in Fig. 12.1. In general, visceral responses related positively to the patient's appraisal of his or her arousal. That is to say, phobic imagery was described as the most arousing (and the most unpleasant!), and phobic scenes also prompted the largest heart rate and skin conductance responses; positive, relaxing situations were appraised as least arousing and showed little heart rate or conductance change. This association between feelings and physiology was not consistent across diagnostic groups: all diagnoses reported a similar experience of distress while imaging phobic scenes, but agoraphobics showed significantly less visceral response than simple phobics. Mean heart rate and skin conductance responses for each diagnostic group are presented in Fig. 12.2. Both social phobics and agoraphobics showed a greatly reduced response relative to the simple phobics. This pattern of group differences observed for phobic images was not found reliabily with nonphobic material.

A possible explanation for these findings is that diagnostic groups differed in imagery ability. It will be recalled that response amplitude in the image is hypothesized to be determined in part by the subject's ability to regenerate the contextual response code. To assess subjects' general experienced vividness and prevalence of imagery, patients were administered the Questionnaire on Mental Imagery (Sheehan, 1967), prior to the experiment. Groups did not differ significantly in average questionnaire scores. When this scale was considered in the analysis of subjects' visceral response during phobic imagery, an interaction was observed between diagnosis and imagery score. These data are described in Fig. 12.3. "Good" imager simple phobics tended to be more responsive than "poor" imager simple phobics. This relationship was also present among the socially anxious, although somewhat less pronounced, and had been observed previously for fear imagery in normal subjects (Miller et al., in press). Nevertheless, this questionnaire assessment of imagery ability was completely unrelated to visceral activation for agoraphobics.

The finding of reduced responses for agoraphobia is counterintuitive, particu-

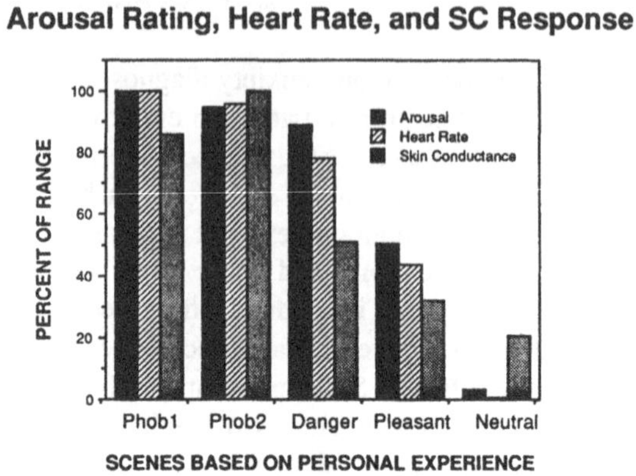

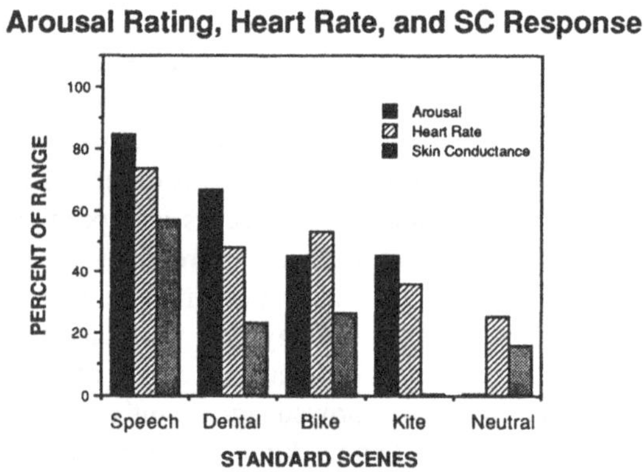

FIG. 12.1A. Arousal rating, heart rate, and skin conductance responses of anxiety patients during imagery of scenes based on personal experience.

FIG. 12.1B. Arousal rating, heart rate, and skin conductance responses of anxiety patients during imagery of standard scenes.

larly for subjects who report that they experience vivid images. Agoraphobics are arguably more severely anxious than those experiencing other phobic disorders, and are expected to show more rather than less sympathetic activation (e.g., Lader & Wing, 1966). Consistent with this view, agoraphobics did have the highest mean heart rates at this assessment (these group mean differences were not, however, significant, and covarying for base value did not alter imagery response scores). Questionnaire results were also in line with expected group differences in severity. That is to say, agoraphobics had significantly higher scores than the other two groups on self-report measures of "feeling of insecurity" and anxiety-related muscle tension (Fenz & Epstein, 1965), as well as on the Marks and Mathews (1979) agoraphobia scale. Furthermore, they showed signif-

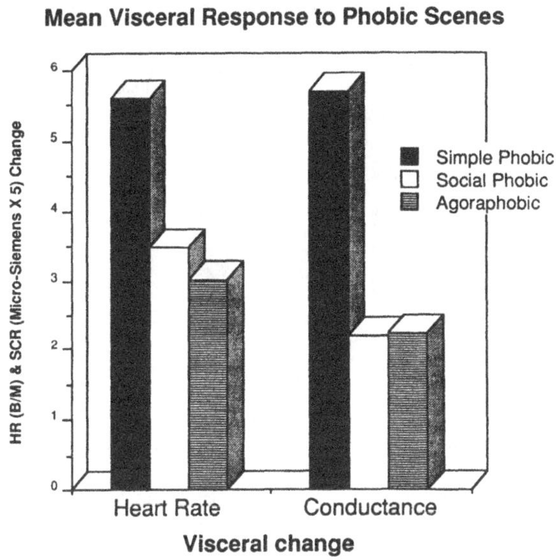

FIG. 12.2. Mean visceral responses of simple, social, and agoraphobic patients during imagery of phobic scenes.

icantly higher scores on the Fear Survey Schedule (Wolpe & Lang, 1964) and the Beck Depression Inventory (Beck, 1976) than did the simple phobic group. The questionnaire results do no suggest that the imagery differences observed here were due to sampling errors, that is, that these agoraphobics were less severely ill than the other patient groups, or than agoraphobics in general.

The data indicating a reduced imagery response in agoraphobia are, nevertheless, clearly at odds with appraisal theory (e.g., Margraf, Ehlers, & Roth, 1986a; Beck & Clark, this volume). This view emphasizes the potency of fear cognitions (e.g., in the "vicious circle" of fearful thoughts and arousal), implying their visceral consequences of fearful images should be greater than for other disorders. Similarly, it argues that agoraphobics are more sensitive than other anxious patients to their own physiology.

This latter hypothesis could be construed to mean that greater concordance between affective appraisal and physiology should be observed for this diagnosis. However, agoraphobics did not generally show this effect, even for affective reports directly appraising the phobic scenes.

System Concordance. Concordance measures are presented in Fig. 12.4. They are based on within subject correlation (Pearson *r*), over the 10 scenes assessed, either between the two visceral responses, or between an appraisal dimension and a visceral measure. Differences in the group means of these correlations were tested. For concordance within the viscera, a decending order

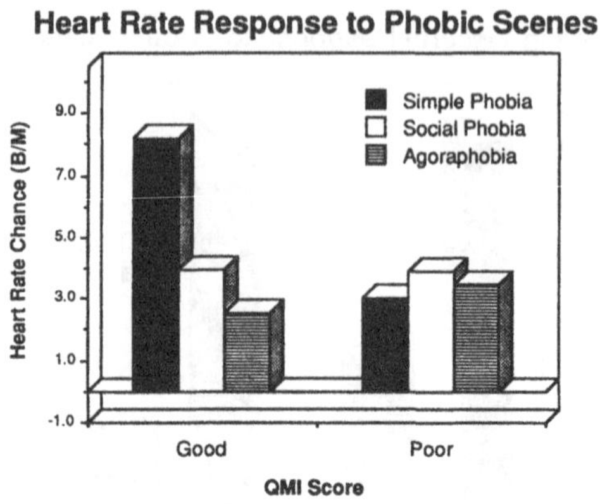

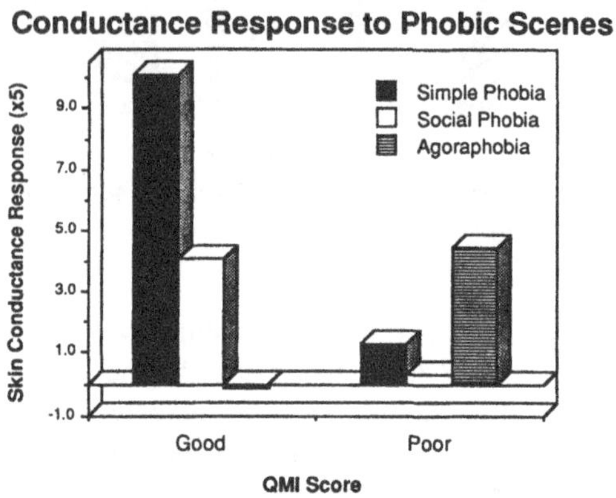

FIG. 12.3A. Heart rate responses of simple, social, and agoraphobic patients (classified as good or poor imagers) during imagery of phobic scenes.

FIG. 12.3B. Conductance responses of simple, social, and agoraphobic patients (classified as good or poor imagers) during imagery of phobic scenes.

of magnitude was observed. Thus, simple phobics showed the highest average correlations, followed by the socially anxious subjects, with agoraphobics showing the lowest relationship between measures. "Good" imager simple and social phobics were somewhat more concordant than the sample as a whole; this imagery ability effect was not found for agoraphobics. Concordance estimates between arousal report and physiology did not differ greatly over diagnoses for the total group. However, diagnosis did interact with imagery ability. "Good" imagers showed a reduction in concordance over diagnostic groups (similar to that within visceral measures), with agoraphobics being the least concordant.

Only within affective report measures (e.g., arousal versus pleasure) did

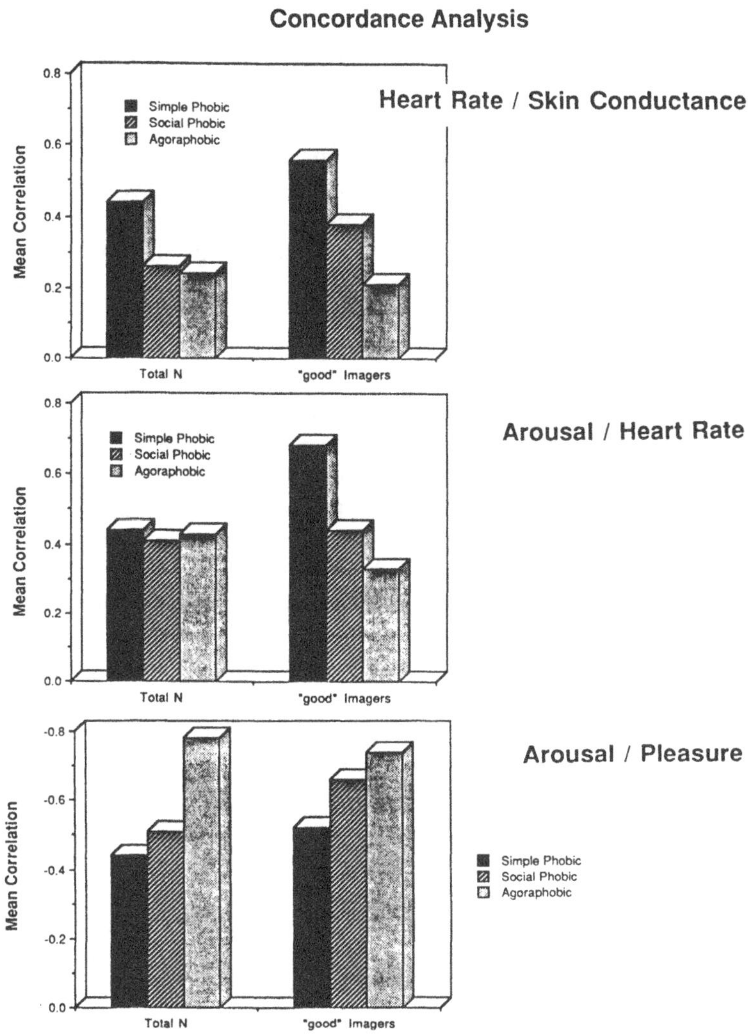

FIG. 12.4. Concordance analysis of imagery responses for simple, social, and agoraphobic patients: mean within subject correlations (Pearson's *r*) over all scenes for *heart rate/skin conductance, arousal/heart rate,* and *arousal/pleasure.*

agoraphobics tend to be more concordant than the other diagnoses. This finding is consistent with the appraisal theory hypothesis that agoraphobics find arousal especially distressing (i.e., "fear of fear"). However, the preliminary data suggest that this could be a wholly semantic phenomenon—that it is based on an association between the semantic concepts of arousal and distress, and not on a direct association between feelings of distress and actual visceral arousal, objectively measured.

These findings are preliminary, and await cross-validation with a larger sample. Also, alternative explanations must be considered. One possibility is that the results obtained here for imagery accurately reflect differences in visceral responding that would also be observed in the actual, behavioral field. That is to say, agoraphobics are simply less responsive, physiologically, than are persons with other anxiety diagnoses. As we have already noted, this explanation is neither consistent with other data from the present experiment, nor with previous studies of agoraphobia. A second possibility is that agoraphobics were simply less cooperative, that is, because of their "greater" fear, they did not actively participate in the imagery. It is not clear to what variable one should appeal in evaluating this "motivational" issue. If one considers verbal report decisive, it can be confidently answered that there was no difference between groups in the reported vividness of phobic imagery. Furthermore, this assessment context did not prompt frightened subjects to be less responsive in general. Simple phobics with a "greater" fear did not respond less. In fact, for the former diagnosis the correlations between phobic visceral response and measures of general pathology were positive and (even in this small sample) frequently significant. Only for agoraphobics were such relationships wholly absent. While it is possible that agoraphobics are all dissemblers and simple phobics are all honest folk, this hypothesis seems less parsimonious than the suggestion, entertained at the outset, of differences in memory organization.

Panic and Agoraphobia. All of the agoraphobia patients studied in this experiment had a history of panic attacks. These attacks were all described as severe and unpredictable. The context of the attack and the re-experiencing of the physiological responses (hyperventilation, heart rate increase) was the invariable script of the phobic scene. Present data suggest that the patient's description of the attack as unpredictable reflects not only its spontaneity of occurrence, but also a real isolation of the response program from meaning concepts or semantic representations of stimulus context. The patients' visceral memory of the attack is apparently not organized in a way that permits retrieval through instructions. If it cannot be imaged, it cannot be recollected, "worked through," or habituated in memory. Passivity, true "helplessness," is a logical, unameliorating sequel. Such patients would be difficult treatment cases; "corrective information" (Foa & Kozak, 1986) could be acquired only in the behavioral field.

The scenario that we have presented presumes agoraphobia to be a postpanic state. It is consistent with a concept of fear and avoidance as sequelae to a spontaneous, sudden disruption of the physiology (i.e., as suggested by Klein, 1981; Sheehan, 1982, and others). It also accommodates evidence (see Rachman, this volume) that panic behavior can have a higher probability of occurrence in specific environments. It does not require that the conscious appraisal of a cue's affective relevance is necessary for emotional behavior to occur.

The trigger for panic could be a physiological response, an environmental event, or both. The present model permits the following hypothesis: Physiological responses which are "like" those found in anxiety (but are instigated by nonpsychological factors) might occur in conjunction with independent, subactivation threshold, affective stimuli; their combination could produce an affective state that would not be consequent on either cue, presented alone. That is to say, the probability of activating an affective network is related to the number of matching cues, irrespective of their origin. We presume that a chance conjunction (physiological and psychological) might combine to initiate panic.

In a less dramatic way, this phenomenon of synergistic cues augmenting an affective state was evoked in a recent study of the startle response (Spence, Vrana, & Lang, in press). Auditory startle stimuli were presented to normal subjects, prompting a reflex eye blink, while they viewed a series of slides that varied in affective quality. Subsequent examination of blink latency and amplitude revealed that, relative to neutral slide content, startle responses were systematically larger and faster when subjects viewed aversive content (mutilated bodies) and smaller when the slides attended to were positive (attractive nudes of the opposite sex). Furthermore, in a subsequent review of the large body of slide material viewed in the experiment, subjects reported aversive slides to be significantly more unpleasant, if startle stimuli had been presented during the initial viewing (even though subjects did not remember which slides had been accompanied by startle). It is significant that the perceived arousal value of the background stimulus was not the critical variable in this result (both the nude and the mutiliation scenes were equal on this dimension); the effect seems to depend on similarity in the valence of the *response* to acoustic startle and to a different, *but also aversive visual stimulus.*

CONCLUSIONS: A RESEARCH AGENDA

The present consideration of information-processing factors in phobic disorders is certainly not intended to be definitive. Similarly, the experiments described here are presented as illustrations of this approach, rather than as *the* pathfinding paradigms for such investigation. It is the writer's hypothesis that response information is represented in associative memory, with the same conceptual status as encoded stimulus or "meaning" concepts. However, this view certainly needs to pass through a more extended gantlet of basic experiments before it can be applied with confidence in practical settings. Little is known about what sort of response information might be encoded, that is, what aspects of a response program are active at a conceptual level and could serve a mediating role. While generalized arousal may be conceptually relevant, as appraisal theories suggest, valence (e.g., approach-avoidance behavior) accounts for much more variance, even in studies of affective language. In a theory more tuned to the "feed forward" of response concepts in determining emotional behavior, rather than "feedback" and secondary conscious appraisal, directional response information may be much more important than undifferentiated activation.

The present approach highlights the potential role of both context and response state in determining emotional memory. Simple phobia appears to be a highly explicit context learning; the special character of the agoraphobic response may lie in the fact it is not context-bound. If different anxiety disorders imply different patterns of memory organization or different associative mediators, then simple phobics and agoraphobics might respond in singular ways on context and mood-dependent learning tasks.

Finally, returning to the opening theme, it is suggested that the appraisal theory approach is question begging, in the sense that it presumes that behavior and physiology must be organized in the terms of direct experience. From this perspective, everyperson's mental life is both a metaphysical fact and the theory of one's behavior. It is argued here that the deep structure of cognition might be other than traditional mentalism suggests. It is proposed that the constraints of an artificial intelligence-oriented view might actually prove to be a liberating posture, leading to both a more parsimonious and more powerful conception of cognition in anxiety. This does not imply that the patient's "story" of his or her behavior is wholly irrelevant to our enterprise. Individuals do organize their behavior into narrative schemata, and clearly, they are differentially responsive to narratives as stimuli. While affective language and action are not as coordinated as appraisal explanations imply; natural language is nevertheless, a powerful system for encoding data, organizing information, and modulating output. For example, the formal story grammar of an imagery script (and of its representation in memory) may contribute importantly to image response production, in addition to the rules of match and activation considered here. All these problems will need to be addressed by researchers, if a practical model of anxious behavior is to be achieved. In summary, we are still at the very beginning of the study of cognition in psychopathology. Basic research in cognitive science has defined a path. As was demonstrated by the introduction of behavioral methods into the clinical domain, a more powerful treatment technology can be the reward of persistent scientific rigor, not only in the critical approach to data but in the development of theoretical models.

13

The Explanation of Experimental Panic

Marcel A. van den Hout
University of Limburg

INTRODUCTION

Panic disorder (PD) is a poorly understood yet serious clinical condition that is characterized by the occurrence of unpredictable panic attacks (APA, 1980). Those who feel that a scientific approach to the dynamics of panic is worthwhile should not take this element of unpredictability too literally, however. Doing so would imply that there are no prior events to which the attacks are functionally related, and that is tantamount to saying that the attacks defy scientific understanding.

Theoretical defeatism can be avoided by assuming that panic attacks are not necessarily related to environmental cues and by postulating that the attacks result from processes *within* the organism. This is where the rationale for pharmacological panic provocation comes in. If a given provocation test reliably provokes panic in PDs but not in controls, one is said to have a specific, exclusive laboratory model of panic. The scientific merit of such a model is that it serves to generate hypotheses regarding the dynamics of clinical phenomena.

A satisfactory explanation of how and why panic provocation works must meet certain general criteria. Such criteria are formulated in the next section. The main findings on pharmacological panicogenesis are then given. As it has been repeatedly demonstrated that carbon dioxide inhalation and sodium lactate infusion reliably induce panic in most PD sufferers but not in normal individuals, and as these interventions represent the most elaborated provocation tests, the focus here will be on these models. In a following section, physiological and psychological hypotheses regarding the nature of carbon dioxide-induced and lactate-induced anxiety are elaborated. One's attention will be drawn to the fact that, at present, there is no biological theory that covers the etiology of carbon dioxide- or lactate-induced anxiety (Fyer & Gorman, 1986; Gorman, Liebowitz, Fyer et al., 1985; Liebowitz, Gorman et al. 1985). One major argument is that while carbon dioxide inhalation and lactate infusion apparently have dissimilar physiological effects, they still produce comparable behavioral responses. This does not make carbon dioxide and lactate tests "uninformative" as Woods, Charney, Goodman, and Henninger (1986) claim. On the contrary, it will be argued that carbon dioxide and lactate share some characteristics that readily explain their panicogenic power. Finally, a psychological hypothesis will be judged against the standards set down earlier.

CRITERIA FOR THE EXPLANATION OF EXPERIMENTAL PANIC

Given that a pharmacological intervention produces panic in most PDs but seldom in normals, the provocation test can be assumed to activate a pathogenic mechanism, the identification of which is a crucial scientific endeavor. The author suggests that an explanation of experimental panic should meet the following criteria:

1. The hypothesis regarding the underlying mechanism of one provocation test should not be inconsistent with findings from other tests.
2. The hypothesis should be supported by data outside the realm of provocation tests, which show that the pertinent mechanism is either present or easily activated in PDs only.
3. PDs should loose their vulnerability to the test as soon as the hypothetical mechanism is inactivated or eliminated.
4. Controls should turn from nonresponders into responders as soon as the hypothetical mechanism is experimentally established or activated.
5. Theoretically deduced new provocation tests, whose only common characteristic with known ones is the capacity to activate the hypothetical underlying mechanism, should produce higher anxiety in PDs than in controls.

When these five criteria are satisfied, one will be able to claim that we understand how panic provocation works. These stringent criteria should be used to judge pharmacological explanations of experimental panic and also to determine the explanatory power of psychological accounts of panic provocation tests.

LACTATE- AND CARBON DIOXIDE-INDUCED SYMPTOMATOLOGY IN PANIC PATIENTS AND CONTROLS

Sodium Lactate Studies

Efforts at panic provocation by sodium lactate infusion started in 1967 with the Pitts and McClure (1967) experiment, and in the last several years there has been an upsurge of interest and research in the area. An overview of the results of eight published lactate studies using placebos and normal controls is given in Fig. 13.1.

The picture that emerges is clear: A majority of panic patients react to the infusions with panic attacks, while only a minority of normal controls do. The incidence of panic in panic patients ranges from 26% to 100%, with an average of approximately 75%. This variance may be due in part to the ambiguous nature of the term "panic," the crucial dependent variable in these experiments. In the New York/Columbia experiments, the criteria typically describe panic as "a crescendo of extreme apprehension or fear and DSM-III physical panic symptoms." In individual cases, one may have doubts as to whether the fear is "extreme" or if its development may be described as a "crescendo."

One lactate study that failed to show clear-cut differences between patients and controls was reported by Ehlers, Margraf, Roth et al. (1986). Though PDs reported much higher anxiety during lactate infusion(s) than normals, they also began with much higher baseline anxiety. The increase in anxiety after the infusions was comparable in patients and normals. From this study it is impossible to decide whether the similarity and anxiety increase in PDs and controls was due to ceiling effects of high baseline values in PDs.

The question whether lactate-induced panic is specific to PD or whether it is a feature of other neurotic subgroups was addressed in three studies. The results are shown in Fig. 13.2.

The incidence of lactate-induced panic in nonpanicking neurotic controls was 2 out of 13 generalized anxiety disorder patients (Lapierre, Knott, & Gray, 1984), 1 out of 7 obsessive-compulsives (Gorman, Liebowitz, Fyer et al., 1985), and 1 out of 15 social phobics (Liebowitz, Fyer et al., 1985). All in all, the effects of lactate appear to be diagnostically specific.

Other noteworthy features of the lactate model include that the incidence of lactate-induced panic can be reduced by antidepressant medication (Kelly, Mitchell–Heggs, & Sherman, 1971; Rifkin, Klein, Dillon, & Levitt, 1981). Also, during the infusion, there is an increase in Autonomic Nervous System activation reflected in, among other things, heart rate, blood pressure, and galvanic skin conductance. Biochemical observations include a hypocalcemia but no consistent rise in epinephrine or norepinephrine (Shear, 1986).

One physiological effect of lactate is of particular interest. In 1967, Pitts and

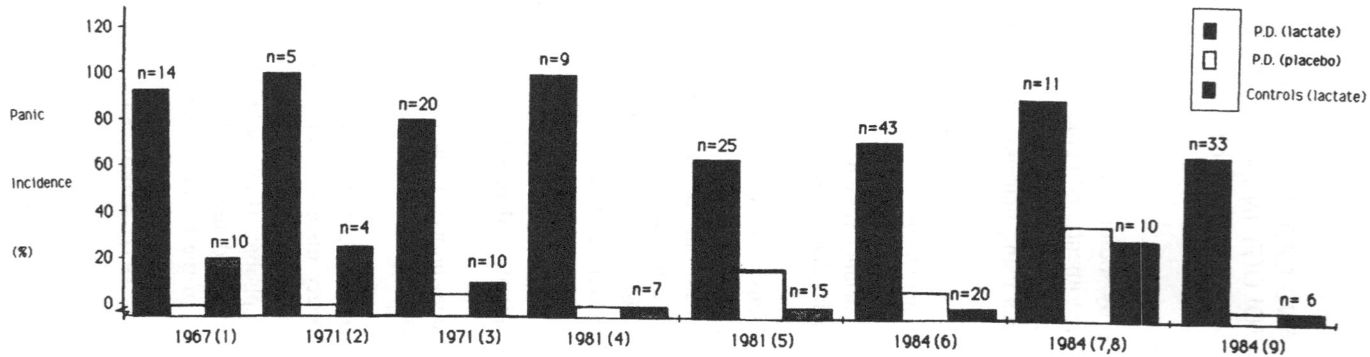

FIG. 13.1. Panic incidence after lactate and placebo in panic patients, and after lactate in normal controls. Data are from Pitts and McClure, 1967 (1); Fink, Taylor, and Volavka, 1971 (2); Kelly et al., 1971 (3); Rifkin et al., 1981 (4); Appleby, Klein, Sachar, and Levitt, 1981 (5); Liebowitz et al., 1984 (6); Rainey, Frohman et al., 1984 (7); Freedman, Ianni, Ettedgui, Pohl & Rainey 1984 (8); and Fyer et al., 1984 (9).

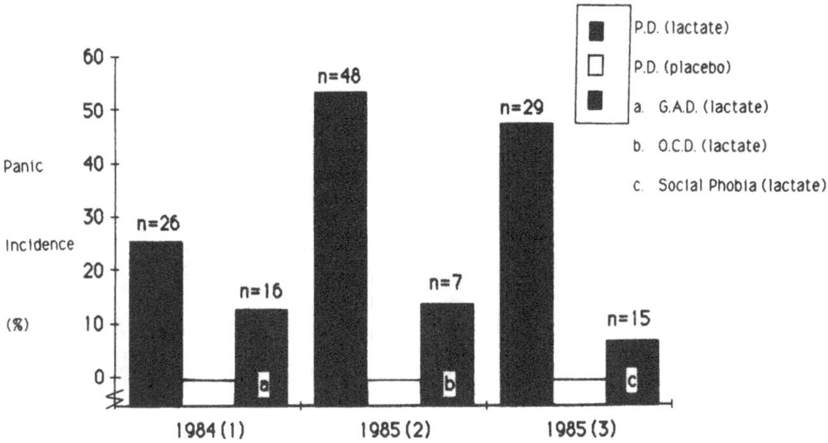

FIG. 13.2. Panic incidence after lactate and placebo in panic patients and neurotic controls. Data are from Lapierre et al., 1984 (1); Gorman, Liebowitz et al., 1985 (2); and Liebowitz, Fyer, Gorman et al., 1985 (3).

McClure assumed that sodium *d,l*-lactate would result in a metabolic acidosis. However, it was later pointed out—and rightly so—that exogenous lactate is actually a weak base and that its infusion produces a rise in pH (alkalosis) (Grosz & Farmer, 1969). Indirect evidence by the same authors showed striking similarities between symptomatology after lactate and after an alkalosis that was induced by HCO_3 infusion (Grosz & Farmer, 1972). Recently, Liebowitz, Gorman et al. (1985) found direct evidence of a lowered plasma pCO_2 (hypocapnia) and of a heightened pH (alkalosis) during lactate infusion. Interestingly hypocapnia/alkalosis seems to link lactate to the hyperventilation theory of panic. Lactate-induced alkalosis in consistent with evidence being gathered from various sources to indicate that hyperventilation is at least partly responsible for many panic symptoms (Garssen, van Veenendaal, & Bloemink, 1983). The panicking subject blows off much more carbon dioxide than is needed for his metabolism, and as with lactate infusion, overventilation results in an alkalosis.

35%CO_2/65%O_2 Inhalation

Inhalation of hypercapnic/hyperoxic mixtures have been used in psychiatry ever since Meduna (1955), who claimed that the procedure had beneficial effects in "psychoneurosis." The procedure was then adopted by J. Wolpe (1958), who believed that the immediate effects of carbon dioxide were antagonistic to anxiety and that carbon dioxide inhalation might be used to inhibit "pervasive" anxiety reciprocally. Four studies were carried out to determine whether carbon dioxide inhalation did result in a diminution of anxiety, but no evidence was found. (Griez & van den Hout, 1982; van den Hout & Griez, 1982a; Ley & Walker, 1973; Slater & Levy, 1966).

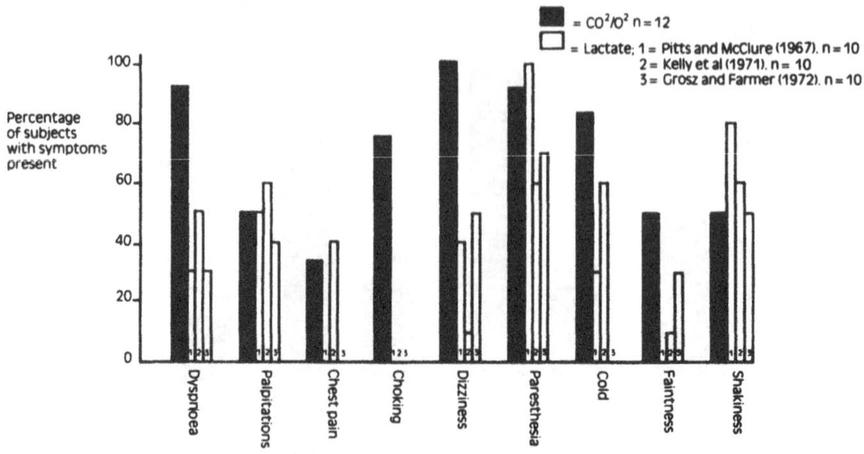

FIG. 13.3. Bodily sensations after 35% carbon dioxide inhalation and sodium lactate infusion. *Note.* From "Panic Symptoms after Inhalation of CO_2" by M. A. van den Hout and E. Griez, 1984, *British Journal of Psychiatry, 144,* p. 503–507. Reprinted by permission of the British Journal of Psychiatry.

Carbon dioxide, it should be stressed, rapidly produces an intense urge to ventilate and a wide range of short-lived physical symptoms, including dizziness, blurred vision, and shakiness. Clinical observations have found some patients becoming highly anxious after carbon dioxide, with peripheral signs *after* exhalation (Griez & van den Hout, 1983). We were struck by the similarity between carbon dioxide effects and panic symptomatology as defined by DSM-III; these observations were the impetus for a further series of experiments focusing on panicomimetic aspects of 35% carbon dioxide inhalation.

We explored the similarity between panic symptoms and carbon dioxide symptoms in a placebo-controlled experiment (van den Hout & Griez, 1984). Twenty normal subjects received either 35% carbon dioxide or air and were asked to self-rate the presence of DSM-III panic symptoms. The match of symptoms proved quite strong. A graphic impression can be obtained from Fig. 13.3, showing DSM-III panic symptoms after carbon dioxide and after lactate.

The effects of carbon dioxide were reduced by approximately 20% through the administration of beta blockers. As for subjective anxiety occurring immediately after inhalation, non-PD subjects were hardly affected by carbon dioxide inhalation (Griez & van den Hout, 1982; van den Hout & Griez, 1982a). Panic patients, on the other hand, consistently showed quite high anxiety during carbon dioxide challenge (Griez, Lousberg, van den Hout, & van der Molen, 1987). Though panic patients also showed somewhat higher anxiety during placebo (inhalation of air), the different reactions of panic patients and normal controls cannot be accounted for statistically by a difference in general or "background"

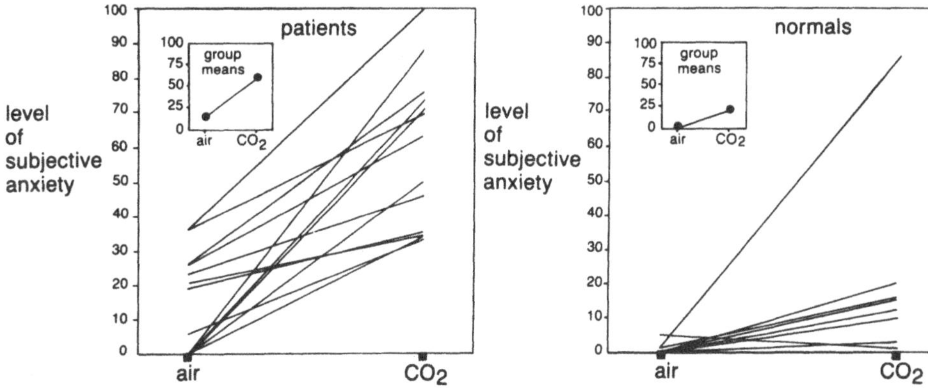

FIG. 13.4. Subjective anxiety after 35% carbon dioxide inhalation and placebo in panic patients and normal controls.

anxiety levels as reflected by placebo scores (van den Hout, van der Molen, Griez, & Lousberg, 1987a). The results are represented in Fig. 13.4.

As far as the physiological effects are concerned, carbon dioxide inhalation produces a hypercapnia and a respiratory acidosis—just the opposite effect of lactate infusion and hyperventilation. However, as demonstrated in another experiment, this is not the contradiction that it appears to be.

One vital capacity inhalation of 35%CO_2/65%O_2 results in an alveolar hypercapnia (see the high peak in Fig. 13.5) with a violent stimulation of the chemoregulatory system, which, in turn, immediately intensifies ventilation (the strongly increased respiration rate reflected in the smaller distance between the spikes immediately to the right of the high peak). Alveolar pCO_2 displays a rapid fall, resulting in a hypocapnic overshoot; the height of the spikes after the peak being lower than before the peak (van den Hout & Griez, 1985). The alevolar

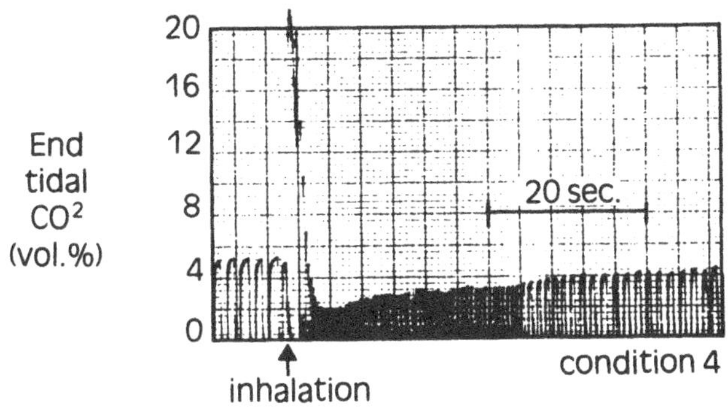

FIG. 13.5. Alveolar carbon dioxide before and after inhalation of 35%CO_2/65%O_2 (From van den Hout & Griez, 1985).

changes occurred in all subjects and comparable phenomena are reflected in the arterial plasma: a hypercapnic acidosis was followed by a pCO_2 drop/pH rise, resulting in a hypocapnic alkalosis. During the changes in blood gases, electrolyte changes are apparent: a biphasic change in ionized calcium (an initial rise followed by a drop beneath the baseline) and an inverted U pattern of potassium (Griez & van den Hout, 1984). Apart from dizziness, the other DSM-III physical panic symptoms emerged during the rapid fall in pCO_2 and remained during the alkalotic/hypocapnic overshoot phase.

To what extent are the results of the $35\%CO_2/65\%O_2$ studies influenced by the hyperoxidity of the mixture? Oxygen suppresses ventilation and the hyperventilatory interoceptive and affective reactions may be masked by the 65% oxygen inhibiting the chemoreceptors. In a double-blind experiment with normal subjects, no differences were found in either pCO_2 curves or interoceptive changes after $35\%CO_2/65\%O_2$, compared with a normoxic mixture of $35\%CO_2/20\%O_2/45\%N_2$ (van den Hout, Griez, & van der Molen, 1987).

5% Carbon Dioxide Inhalation

As early as 1951, Cohen and White wrote an extraordinarily interesting paper that went virtually unnoticed for quite a while. Entitled "Life Situations, Emotions and Neurocirculatory Asthenia," the article described numerous experiments. In one such experiment, 43 patients and 27 control subjects first breathed oxygen for 12 minutes, then had a second test of 12 minutes of rebreathing expired air, during which carbon dioxide was accumulated to about 4% of inspired air. Patients developed sysmptoms which 46.5% believed to be identical to the symptoms of their illness, particularly those who reported anxiety attacks. Many symptoms developed in patients, including a feeling of fear, in contrast to the response of the control subjects.

The inconsistency of these findings is that the rebreathing of expired air anxiogenesis was produced by inducing a respiratory acidosis, that is, the very opposite physiological effect of lactate or 35% carbon dioxide. Quite accidentally, these findings were replicated by Gorman, Askanazi et al. (1984), who explored the symptomatic association between sodium lactate (metabolic alkalosis) and hyperventilation (respiratory alkalosis). As a control treatment, 5% carbon dioxide inhalation was given. "Our rationale was that if hyperventilation causes panic attacks by inducing respiratory alkalosis, then 5% carbon dioxide inhalation, which increases ventilation but does not induce alkalosis, should not be panic-inducing. We did not predict that carbon dioxide would be panic-inducing."

Whether predicted or not, 8 out of 12 PDs panicked during lactate infusion, 7 during 5% carbon dioxide challenge, and 3 during hyperventilation of room air. Ehlers, Margraf, Roth et al. (1986) found higher levels of anxiety during carbon dioxide rebreathing in patients than they did in normals. The patients also had higher baseline values, while the carbon dioxide induced *increase* in anxiety was identical for the two groups. It is likely that this lack of group difference was due to the ceiling effect of high baseline values. Woods, Charney, Loke et al. (1986) gave 5% carbon dioxide to 10 panic patients and 10 matched controls and observed that when baseline was high, comparison of pretest with posttest levels was less informative than posttest scores on mood changes. On this parameter, patients reported a much steeper increase in anxiety than did normals. Depending on the strictness of the criteria used for "panic attack," between 7 and 9 of the 10 patients panicked, compared with between 2 and 4 of the 10 matched controls. Five percent carbon dioxide breathing appears to be as sound a panic model as 35% carbon dioxide of lactate.

While lactate and 35% carbon dioxide produce a rise in pH (alkalosis), comparable psychological effects are obtained by a 5% carbon dioxide breathing-induced pH decrease (acidosis). How should we account for this apparent conflict of evidence.

Acid Base Balance in Lactate and Carbon Dioxide Challenge

At first sight, it seems plausible that if a pharmacological intervention reproduces full-blown pathology in vulnerable people but not in normals, a biological pathogenesis must be somehow involved: "Results of lactate studies suggest that panic disorder is a biological disease" (Carr & Sheehan, 1984b) and Shader, Goodman, & Gever (1982) maintain that "biological evidence of the distinctness of panic disorders from other disorders comes primarily from lactate challenge tests." Still, plausible or not, it is not necessarily correct to infer etiology from interventions that reproduce or reduce the pertinent pathology. In fact, biological hypotheses regarding carbon dioxide-induced and lactate-induced panic give rise to physiological inconsistencies.

A respiratory or metabolic *alkalosis* is produced by hyperventilation, 35% carbon dioxide inhalation/overshoot, and lactate infusion. Though alkalosis is, indeed, a common denominator, an alkalosis explanation of panic fails to account for the observations: (a) during 35% carbon dioxide inhalation, patients are most panicky before hypercapnia is "shot over" into an alkalotic hypocapnia (van den Hout & Griez, 1985), and that (b) hyperventilation provocation (e.g., during routine electroencephalogram screenings) in PDs rarely produces full-blown panic. More importantly, hyperventilation seems far less panicogenic than prolonged and acidifying 5% carbon dioxide breathing (Gorman, Askanazi et al., 1984).

Rapid and sudden *pCO_2 and pH changes* have been suggested as biological mechanisms underlying panic. These changes are in line with clinical impressions from Lum (1981) and data from 35% carbon dioxide studies. On the other hand, it is inconsistent with the lactate evidence (Liebowitz, Gorman et al.,

1985) showing that pCO_2/pH changes occur immediately but that panic occurs several minutes later. Furthermore, during hyperventilation, central and peripheral symptoms become manifest well after the pCO_2 drop has taken place.

Acidosis. Data are in line with the 5% carbon dioxide provocation studies but they are incompatible with the hyperventilation literature. Data from 35% carbon dioxide studies tend to be a little ambiguous because arterial acidosis does, indeed, occur; however, it is only for a short period of time following inhalation. At first sight, the acidosis theory also seems to run counter to lactate findings, but recently several authors have claimed that lactate findings can be linked with an acidosis theory.

Another explanation assumes the occurence of *pH disequilibria* between CNS and serum. Sodium lactate is metabolized into bicarbonate (HCO_3^-) and the pH rises. This alkalosis in venous blood has been documented. In venous blood also hypocapnia ensues (Liebowitz, Gorman et al., 1985). Where does this hypocapnia come from? Is it a direct result of lactate metabolism, or is it partly an indirect effect as Lieberman, Gorman, and colleagues infer? The reasoning of Gorman, Askanazi et al. (1984) is that HCO_3^- binds to H^+, forming carbonic acid, which dissolves into H_2O and carbon dioxide. The latter freely enters the cerebrospinal fluid, and in the CNS, a *hypercapnia* and *acidosis* will ensue. The central hypercapnia implies a violent chemoreceptor stimulation, producing an increase in ventilation. The peripheral hypocapnia is, therefore, also the result of a somewhat paradoxical hyperventilation.

There are at least two objections to the pH disequilibria hypothesis of Gorman and his coworkers. First, it was experimentally observed that the lactate-produced alkalosis is usually not accompanied by an increase, but by a *decrease,* in respiratory rate (van der Molen, van den Hout, & Griez, 1986). It is somewhat unlikely that the assumed central hypercapnia produces profound hyperventilation by reducing respiratory rate and increasing respiratory volume with peripheral hypocapnia as a net effect. Second, the disequilibrium explanation is offered to link 5% carbon dioxide to lactate, but it does nothing to explain clinical panics. On the contrary, the disequilibrium view rests on HCO_3^- or pCO_2 increases, while in panic patients—both at rest and during panic—HCO_3^- and pCO_2 are typically lowered.

In summary, acid-base changes are the most prominent physiological effects of lactate and carbon dioxide challenges. A major problem is that although they produce comparable behavioral effects, 5% carbon dioxide, 35% carbon dioxide, and lactate do so with different, or even opposite, effects on pH. It is, therefore, difficult to formulate a comprehensive hypothesis that assumes that an abnormal sensitivity to specific acid-base changes is the basis for experimental panic.

Methodologically, the occurrence of comparable behavior after challenges with diverging central nervous system effects is very informative. It suggests that it is not necessary to postulate a specific neurophysiological abnormality that is triggered by lactate and/or carbon dioxide.

Interoceptive Fear in Panic Disorder

With the very introduction of the term ''agoraphobia'' in 1872, Westphal suggested that agoraphobics suffer from *Angst vor dem Angst*. A concise paraphrase in modern terms would be that panic patients become frightened by the perception of interoceptive sensations that happen to be part of the anxiety response; that is, they suffer from an interoceptive phobia. A Pavlovian conceptulization would be that during intense anxiety (the UR) produced by any given US, the organism is exposed to various interoceptive stimuli that are part of the anxiety response.

Intense anxiety in itself can be an aversive event (Eysenck, 1968), and because of its temporal association with physical sensations, the latter may acquire CS characteristics (i.e., the capacity to elicit anxiety, the CR). As the CS is part of the CR a positive loop may ensue. As an example, palpitations may, once felt, produce anxiety, increasing heart rate and stroke volume, intensifying the saliency of the CR, increasing the strength of the CR, etc. Schematically, it would appear as:

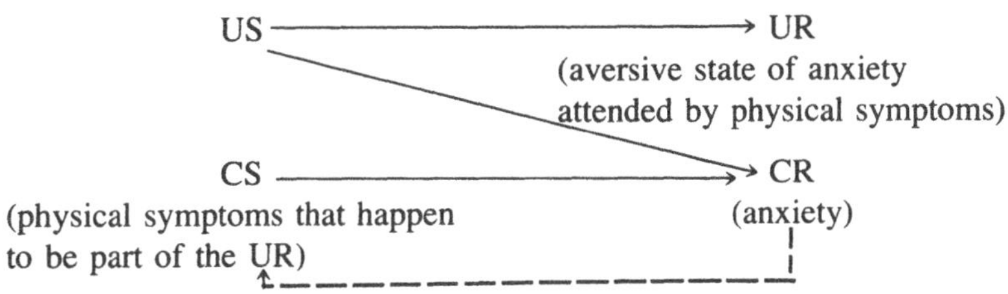

There are at least two major problems with this model. The first concerns *overprediction*. The model implies that everyone experiencing an UR of the kind indicated will become an interoceptive phobic, and this is not the case. Several hypotheses could be tested regarding the conditions under which UR experiences promote the indicated CS–CR link. One could, for example, claim that interoceptive fears are more likely to arise if the experienced UR was not predicted, if the physical symptoms are perceived as uncontrollable, or if the symptoms are, in themselves, highly aversive (e.g., feelings of suffocation). Attribution may very well play a role here and the UR may more likely promote interoceptive fears if the subject cannot attribute the UR to the US. One should note that the factors mentioned here are common in acute hyperventilation, so that generally speaking, it can be hypothesized that excessive hyperventilation, as part of the UR, predisposes one to the development of the CS–CR association.

A second theoretical problem concerns the *maintenance of interoceptive fears*. Exteroceptive phobias may, in large part, be maintained by nonexposure and the anxiety-reducing effects of avoidance. The anxiety reduction theory does not, however, seem applicable to panic disorders. PDs are quite regularly exposed to feared cues and yet the CR does not extinguish. An explanation may be found in the aversive nature of the CR. The introceptive fear may persist, not because avoidance prevents the extinction that occurs during nonreinforced exposure, but because each exposure to the interoceptive cues is reinforced by the aversiveness of the CR.

There is a cognitive version of the interoceptive fear hypothesis which, in many respects, is not unlike the behavioral one. It is assumed that pathological anxiety results from the subject's overestimating the probability and severity of a feared event and underestimating his coping resources and rescue factors. Panic patients tend to believe that various internal sensations are omens of "impending doom." Thus, interoceptive cues are misinterpreted in a catastrophical and fear-arousing way (cf. Clark, this volume; Clark, 1986a; Clark & Salkovskis, 1985).

For purposes of this discussion, it is not essential to concentrate on the different predictions that can be made from the behavioral and cognitive accounts of panic. Both approaches share the idea that *PDs become frightened by the perception of bodily sensations that are typically part of the anxiety response.*

Interoceptively Cued Fear as an Explanation of Pharmacological Panic Genesis

Criterion 1: The Hypothesis is Consistent with Findings from Various Challenges

In normal subjects, 35% carbon dioxide inhalation and lactate infusion induce a wide range of bodily sensations that also occur during clinical panic attacks. A graphic representation is given in Fig. 13.2. Woods, Charney, Loke et al. (1986) demonstrated that during 5% carbon dioxide challenge comparable symptoms occur in normal subjects who do not tend to get anxious.

The data on carbon dioxide and lactate challenges indicate that physical panic symptoms occur, independent of any subjective anxiety. Thus, the findings are compatible with the idea that these challenges are panicogenic in PDs because *they trigger interoceptive fears.*

Criterion 2: Data Outside the Realm of Challenge Test Show Interoceptive Fears to be Specific to PDs

Are there indications from sources other than challenge tests that interoceptive fears are characteristic of PDs?. Reiss, Peterson, Garsky, & McNally (1986) tried to validate a construct they called "anxiety sensitivity," which is assumed to encompass the belief that the experience of anxiety causes illness, embarrassment, or additional anxiety. Agoraphobics scored much higher than either non-panicking neurotics or normal controls. In two independent samples of normals, scores on the anxiety index were shown to be distinct from general anxiety. Though these results are in line with the present hypothesis regarding the specificity of interoceptive fear to panic patients, it should be noted that the panic sample consisted of only nine patients, all of whom were agoraphobics. More-

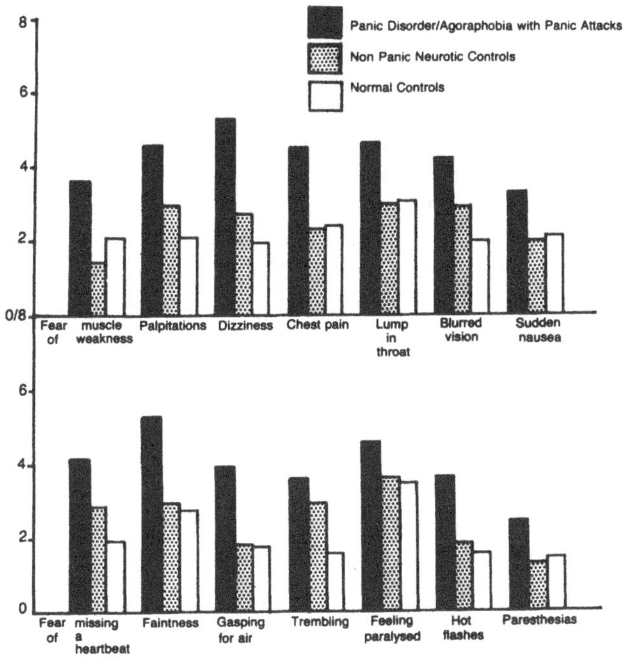

FIG. 13.6. Fear of bodily sensations: mean scores of panic patients, nonpanic neurotic controls, and normal controls. *Note.* From "Specificity of Interoceptive Fears to Panic Disorders" by M.A. van den Hout, G. M. van der Molen, E. Griez, and H. Lousberg, 1987, *Journal of Psychopathology and Behavioral Assessment, 9,* p. 99–106. Reprinted by permission.

over, the trait that was measured was a "fear of the state of fear," rather than a "fear of the physical symptoms that happened to occur during fear."

Assuming that it is interoceptive fear that is triggered by lactate or carbon dioxide challenge, van den Hout et al. (1987c) reasoned that interoceptive fear should also become manifest from self-reports. Groups of 29 panic patients, 29 nonpanicking neurotic controls, and 30 normal controls indicated how fearful they were of each of 14 bodily sensations that are often part of the anxiety response. Nonpanicking neurotics tended to score a little higher, but not significantly more than normals, while on all but one item, PDs scored significantly higher than the other two groups.

These findings closely match those of Chambless, Caputo, Bright, and Gallagher (1984). In a study with a large number of subjects, but without a nonpanicking neurotic control sample (93 agoraphobics and 15 to 20 normals), it was shown that agoraphobics scored considerably higher on fear of bodily sensations. These findings strongly suggest interoceptive fears to be specific to panic patients.

Support for the idea that catastrophic misinterpretations of bodily sensations mediate interoceptive fears comes from a particularly well-controlled study (Salkovskis, this volume) in which panic patients, nonpanicking neurotic controls, and normal controls were asked to interpret several ambiguous situations and symptoms. In a paper-and-pencil task, PDs systematically gave catastrophic interpretations to ambiguous interoceptions that are concomitants of anxiety. Normal and nonpanicking controls either did not or did so to a much lesser degree. Of particular interest with regard to the specificity issue is the fact that catastrophizing ideation in PDs occurred only when bodily anxiety sensations were involved. Ambiguous social events or nonanxiety-related physical symptoms did not elicit frightening cognitive elaboration.

In summary, the interoceptive fears of anxiety concomitants are characteristic of PDs. This cross-validates the idea that carbon dioxide and lactate are panicogenic since they expose a subgroup of neurotics to feared cues.

Criterion 3: Challenge Vulnerability in PD Wanes when Interoceptive Fears are Experimentally Reduced

There are indications that successful treatment with antidepressants or behavioral therapy for agoraphobic fears blocks the response to lactate infusion (Kelly et al. 1971; Rifkin et al. 1981; Shear, 1986). However, it is not clear whether the therapies block experimental panic by reducing the interoceptive fears or by some other means. Still, one may be able to judge whether or not the psychological model meets the present criterion. Repeated and prolonged exposure in vivo reduces phobic fears. If panic disorder represents an interoceptive fear that can be activated by carbon dioxide or lactate, one can expect repeated and prolonged administrations of lactate or carbon dioxide to vulnerable individuals to produce less anxiety as the number and duration of administrations increases. Bonn, Harrison, and Rees (1973), using lactate infusion to induce maximum anxiety in 33 anxiety neurotics during six 20-minute sessions, found that "the phobophobic element which was so frequently elicited from these patients was substantially reduced." This study, however, was uncontrolled in that it did not use challenge-by-challenge ratings, did not use a placebo control condition, and did not include a normal control sample.

We carried out a carbon dioxide experiment under all of these necessary conditions, which provided a robust confirmation of this hypothesis (van den Hout, Griez et al., 1987). In this study, 14 panic patients and 8 controls received a series of 35% CO_2/65%O_2 inhalations (6 sessions; 10 inhalations per session) as well as air inhalations (3 sessions; 10 inhalations per session). The order was: carbon dioxide (3 sessions), air (3 sessions), carbon dioxide (3 sessions) or air (3 sessions), carbon dioxide (3 sessions), carbon dioxide (3 sessions). Subjects reported anxiety on a 100-point scale after each inhalation and all scores for a given session were averaged. There was a clear habituation effect in the patient

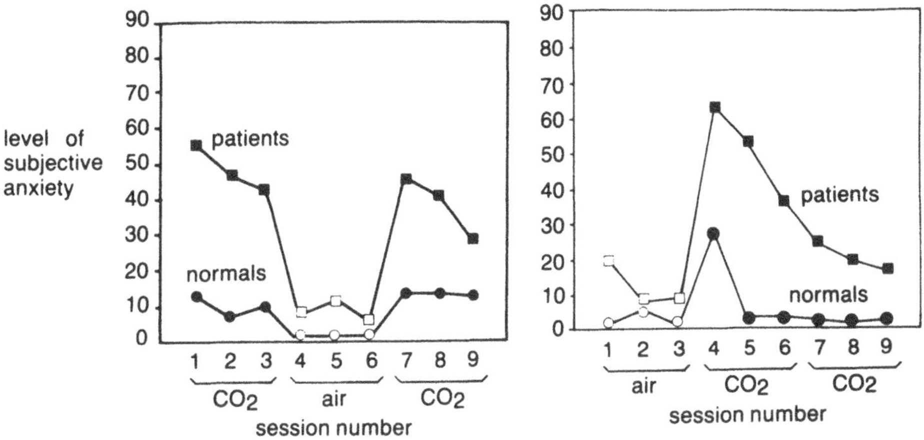

FIG. 13.7. Reduction in CO_2 induced subjective anxiety in 13 panic patients over the course of 6 CO_2 inhalation sessions. *Note.* Figures 13.7 and 13.8 reprinted with permission from *Behavior Research and Therapy, 24,* G. M. van der Molen, M. A. van den Hout, E. Griez, and H. Lousberg, "Cognitive Determinants in Lactate Induced Anxiety." Copyright 1987 Pergamon Journals Ltd.

groups. Normals did not report any distress after air and only very little, transient anxiety after carbon dioxide inhalation. Data are given in Fig. 13.7.

These findings support to a behavioral account of lactate or carbon dioxide-induced panic, but it would be interesting to take the investigation a step further to see whether the reduction of interoceptive fears, independent of the challenge (e.g., through cognitive interventions), also reduces one's vulnerability to the challenge.

Criterion 4: Challenge Vulnerability Occurs in Controls when Interoceptive Fears are Experimentally Induced

Panic attacks are often attended by hyperventilation; deliberate hyperventilation reproduces a wide range of physical panic symptoms (Garssen, van Veenendaal, & Bloemink, 1983). From a cognitive perspective, there is nothing intrinsically frightening about experiencing hyperventilation symptoms but the latter become frightening only when they are interpreted in a catastrophic way. In a recent study by Salkovskis and Clark (1986b) normals who were made to misinterpret hyperventilation-induced symptoms in a catastrophic way became highly anxious. Normals who were made to interpret the same symptoms in a positive way did not report any anxiety. Although the ecological validity of the hyperventilation provication test is greater than that of lactate provocation, the latter intervention is a more accepted and probably more powerful experimental panicogenic agent.

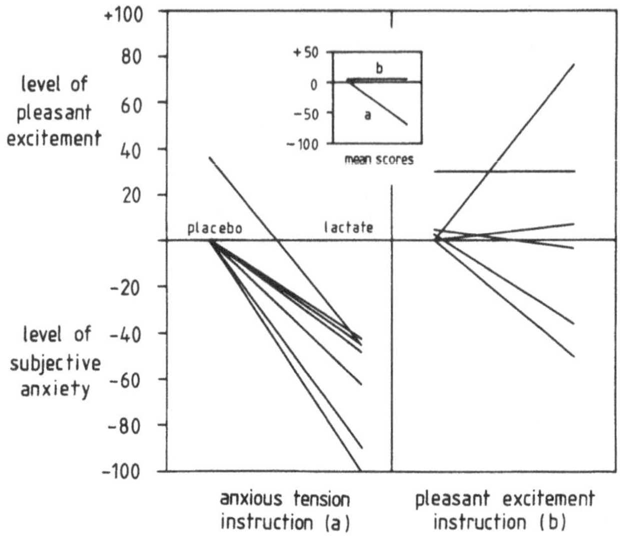

FIG. 13.8. Affective responses to lactate infusion and placebo in two differently instructed groups of normal controls (From van der Molen, van den Hout, Griez, & Lousberg, in press).

It is therefore also of interest that, with lactate too, normals can be changed from nonresponders into responders by manipulating their cognitive set. In a recent study (van der Molen, van den Hout, Griez, & Lousberg, in press) 13 normal volunteers were given sodium lactate and glucose in a randomized order. Seven of the subjects were told that the infusions would be anxiogenic, and the other 6 were told to expect pleasant excitement, as when watching a movie. Affective changes were indicated on a scale ranging from +100 (a very high level of pleasant excitement) to −100 (extreme, subjective anxiety), with 0 indicating the mood before the infusion. The results of the double-blind study are presented in Fig. 13.8.

The induced expectation did not affect mood in the placebo conditions, but had a powerful effect on the lactate challenges: The subjects in Group A expected to experience anxiety and reported sharp increases in subjective anxiety, but the subjects in Group B showed no systematic change. The average subjective anxiety indicated on the 100-point scale by the Group A subjects was 65. This figure closely matches the level of subjective anxiety reported by PDs after 35% carbon dioxide inhalation (van den Hout et al., 1987), 5% carbon dioxide inhalation (Ehlers, Margraf, Roth et al., 1986), and lactate challenge (Ehlers, Margraf, Roth et al., 1986). The findings strongly suggest that lactate is panicogenic because it triggers interoceptive fears: When normals without any psychiatric history become fearful of interoceptive changes, their lactate responses become indistinguishable from those of PDs.

Criterion 5: A Nonpharmacological Intervention Resulting in Perceived Bodily Changes is Anxiogenic in PDs.

The model endorsed here predicts that PDs will respond anxiously to any perceived increase in arousal and that perceived arousal will spiral up via a positive feedback loop to even higher levels of arousal (cf. the model on p. 247). Pharmacological panic-provocating agents are inadequate to record signs of psychophysiological loops as the measures are confounded by the direct effect of the administered substance.

A test of whether PDs react anxiously to nonpharmacologically induced, perceived bodily changes and also display a positive feedback pattern on psychophysiological measures was carried out by Ehlers Margraf, Roth, Taylor, & Birbaumer (1986). Twenty-five PDs and 25 matched controls received true heart rate feedback, followed by false feedback of an abrupt heart rate increase equal to 50 b.p.m. over 30 seconds. On all psychological and psychophysiological variables, there were significant group (patients versus controls) by condition (true versus false feedback) interactions. Results are given in Fig. 13.9.

For the cardiovascular and electrodermal variables, only PDs showed the pattern that is necessary for positive feedback; they responded to perceived arousal with further arousal. Consistent with the interoceptive fear theory, this study indicates that PDs react anxiously to any perceived increase in arousal, regardless of whether the perception is the result of pharmacological or nonpharmacological intervention.

CONCLUSIONS, CONJECTURES, AND FUTURE RESEARCH

The repeated and well-documented observation that lactate and carbon dioxide provocation tests produce high anxiety in PDs but not in controls is an important contribution to the experimental psychopathology of anxiety. The evidence reviewed here indicates that pharmacological panicogenesis can be explained adequately from a psychological perspective. It is not necessary to postulate that carbon dioxide or lactate in PDs trigger an as yet "unidentified" metabolical disorder.

Given that cognitive/behavioral theories provide sound explanations of experimental panic, the question remains: How does the theory deal with the real thing, that is, the clinical condition of PDs? Two issues that need to be resolved are: (1) Why does one associate panic episodes so closely with agoraphobic avoidance, and (2) How can one explain the "spontaneous" nature of panic attacks?

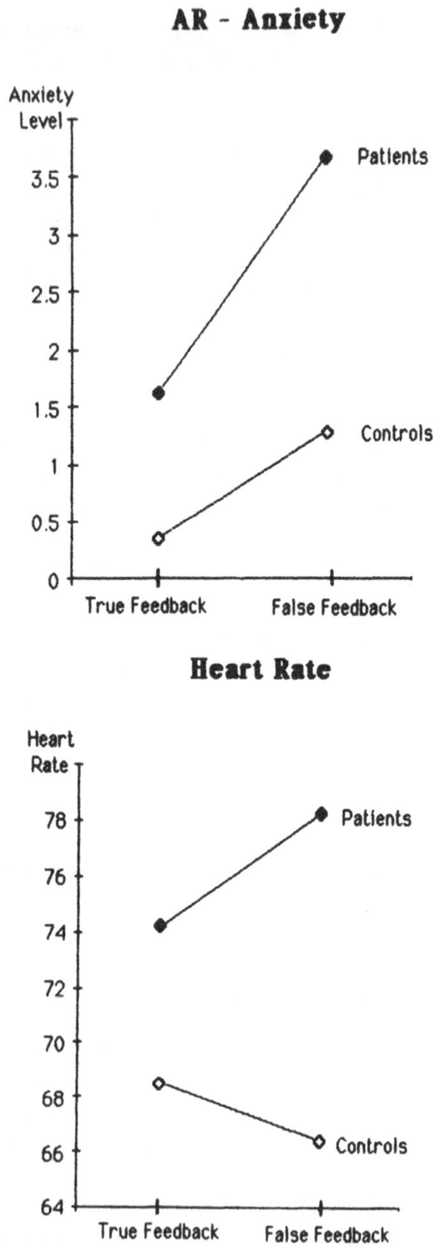

FIG. 13.9. Subjective and cardiac responses in panic patients and controls during true and false heart-rate feedback. (From Ehlers, Margraf, Roth, & Birbaumer, 1986).

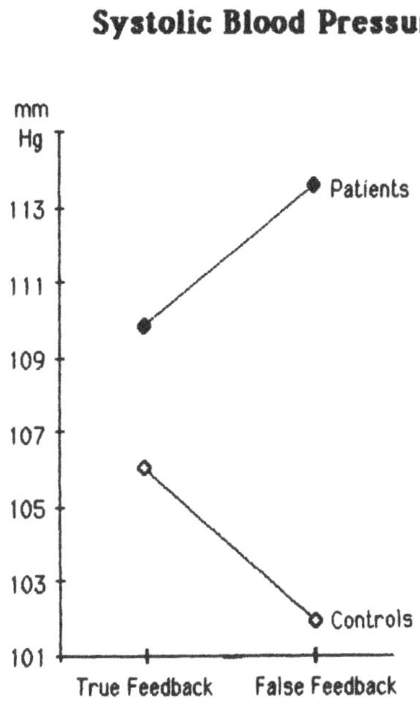

FIG. 13.9 (*Continued*)

As to the prodromal role of panic episodes in the development of agoraphobic avoidance, it appears that an interoceptive fear theory in itself is insufficient. The idea is that agoraphobic cues, because of their temporal association with aversive panic, become conditioned stimuli lacks specificity. Why does the experience of panic typically induce agoraphobic, but no other phobic avoidance? And why does agoraphobic avoidance apparently not follow such aversive events as renal colics?

A partial explanation of the panic–agoraphobia link may be that the respiratory alkalosis present during panic interacts with learning processes. It is interesting to note here that the acquisition of electrodermally conditioned responses is facilitated and extinction inhibited during the premenstrual phase when pCO_2 is typically lowered (van der Molen, van den Hout & Merckelbach, unpublished data; Villa & Beech, 1978). Investigation is presently under way to determine whether these findings can be replicated with a group in which alkalosis is experimentally induced. Furthermore, a variation on the Garcia effect (Garcia & Koelling, 1972) may exist. That is, breathing difficulties are common during panic attacks, and agoraphobic cues are typically situations from which excape is difficult. There may be a "prepared" connection (see Seligman, this volume) between feelings of suffocation and agoraphobic/claustrophobic cues. If true, one would expect avoidance to occur readily when a subject is experimentally made to experience breathing difficulties in an agoraphobic, rather than in a nonagoraphobic, situation. On the other hand, a combination of agoraphobic cues with a UCS that is different, but just as aversive as breathlessness, would likely produce little avoidance.

If hyperventilation is involved in the positive loop of interoceptive fears, the panic attack will, by a homeostatic mechanism, display a self-limiting course: During hyperventilation pCO_2 will drop and pH will rise to the degree that the chemoreceptory system is no longer stimulated. Continued breathing through the voluntary movement of chest muscles is rather tiring and will stop, due to fatigue. After a hyperventilatory period, both the chemoreceptor and the volitional impetus for ventilation decreases; pCO_2 and pH will be restored and interoceptive fear cues will disappear. Any ongoing operant behavior or escape may be adventitiously reinforced by the termination of the attack which, in any event, will run its own, time-limited, course. Agoraphobic behavior may thus result from superstitious conditioning (Thyer, 1986).

Regarding the "spontaneous" nature of clinical panic, the interoceptive fear model assumes that panic attacks are triggered, and thus preceded, by bodily sensations. Indeed, Ley (1985) demonstrated that, at least in the perception of PDs, bodily feelings precede the anxiety attack, while Hibbert (1984b) showed that this sequence of events is specific to panic and does not occur in nonpanicking neurotics. A second inference would be that clinical panic results from the subject increasing his focus on bodily feelings. This would imply that relaxation, meditation, and similar expercises would trigger panic specifically in PDs. Indeed, clinical evidence suggests that patients suffering from nonsituational anxiety are especially prone to relaxation-induced anxiety (Heide & Borkovec, 1984). However, it has not been documented that PDs are the only anxiety patients who are vulnerable to relaxation.

Finally, though interoceptive fear models of panic suggest that pharmacological panicogenesis does not require one to postulate pathophysiological disorders underlying PD, the model is not incompatible with the hypothesis that many PDs share biological pecularities that predispose them to their clinical condition. Perhaps PDs have relatively low interoceptive thresholds, or relatively marked fluctuations in arousal, or a predisposition to overbreathe rather strongly during stress. Such predispositions would certainly increase the likelihood of the subject's developing interoceptive fears.

In principle, provocation studies may elucidate biological vulnerabilities, provided however, that the intervention in normal subjects does not give rise to somatic symptoms. Yohimbine studies are of interest in this context. This alpha 2 adrenergic receptor antagonist is more anxiogenic in PDs than in controls. Normals do not report significant greater increase in physical sensations after Yohimbine than after placebo. Nevertheless, there is at least a trend for normals to notice more symptoms after Yohimbine than after placebo; the baseline post-test increase after Yohimbine exceeding the placebo effect on 8 out of 11 symptoms (Charney, Henninger, & Breier, 1984). From the present perspective it is predicted that normal subjects, like PDs, are able to tell Yohimbine from placebo on the basis of induced interoceptive changes. Normals are likely to ignore these minor symptoms. To PDs, the symptoms may be frightening. If Yohimbine or any other substance could be proven to produce no interoceptive changes in normals, and still be anxiogenic in PDs this effect would be hard to explain in the manner proposed here, and we may have a cue about biological peculiarities characteristic of PDs. Considering the robustness of the recent data on interoceptive fears, one would expect a substantial proportion of the general population having the particular biological predisposition to be a symptomatic. By the same token many PDs may be symptomatic without having the biological predisposition. There is a vast amount of fascinating research yet to be done on how biological and environmental factors interact to produce the interoceptive fears that so clearly characterize panic disorder.

14

Panics and Their Consequences: *A Review and Prospect*

S. Rachman
University of British Columbia

The consequences of panic can constitute a more serious problem than the panic itself. Most panics are distressing, but the consequences can be disabling. The average duration of a panic is about 20 minutes (Taylor, Shiek, Agras et al., 1986), and the consequences can endure for years. Panics can be followed by a compression of the person's activities within intolerable limits, and in severe instances lead to the adoption of a housebound existence.

Of course, this gloomy description assumes that the claimed connection between panic and subsequent avoidance is valid. One purpose of this chapter is to scrutinize the evidence and arguments on which this major assumption is founded, and then to add some new evidence. The consequences of panic will be considered within the framework of a three-system analysis (Lang, 1968): (a) behavioral consequences, (b) cognitive consequences, and (c) psychophysiological consequences. As most of our knowledge concerns the cognitive consequences, that aspect is the central part of this chapter.

BEHAVIORAL CONSEQUENCES

There are disagreements between proponents of the biological theory and the cognitive-biological theory of panic, but both sides appear to share the assumption that there is a close and necessary connection between the occurrence of panic and the development of extensive avoidance behavior.

This plausible view of the generation of avoidance behavior appears to rest mainly on the evidence of clinical reports, and the general expectation that fear will be followed by avoidance behavior—as is often the case (see Rachman,

1978). However, the clinical reports are retrospective, incomplete, and nonrepresentative, and should be treated with reserve. It is likely that in a proportion of cases, perhaps even the majority, the occurrence of panic is indeed followed by the development of avoidance behavior; however, because of the weaknesses in the clinical reports, and especially the fact that they are not representative of all of the people who experience panics, there is a tendency to exaggerate the frequency with which panics are followed by the emergence of avoidance behavior. There are important exceptions.

The evidence to support the idea of a connection between the panic and the emergence of avoidance behavior is referred to by Klein, Rabkin, and Gorman (1985), Uhde, Roy-Byrne, Vittone et al. (1985) and indirectly in much of the literature on agoraphobia (e.g., Mathews, Gelder, & Johnston, 1981; Thorpe & Burns, 1983). It would appear that many patients trace the onset of their agoraphobic avoidance behavior to an experience of panic (e.g., Thyer & Himle, 1985, report that 79% of 28 agoraphobic patients attributed their agoraphobia to panics). Even at this point one reservation should be noted: There are other examples of the development of agoraphobic avoidance behavior that are not related to the occurrence of panics. Uhde et al. (1985) stated that 97% of their sample of 38 cases of panic disorder developed "avoidant behavior after, rather than before their first panic attacks" (p. 560). Overwhelming as this figure is, it may be inflated, and caution is advisable because of the retrospective and incomplete nature of the data. As the authors noted, "it is possible that there is a substantial proportion of such patients with only panic attacks who never come to psychiatric attention and never become involved in research studies" (p. 560). (Note in passing, that there are other routes to research studies.) Also of interest is the comment that all of their patients who had panic attacks, without agoraphobia, were men. Other examples of panic without avoidance may have been excluded because Uhde et al. deleted from their analysis all those patients who were unable to "recall in detail the exact time, place, situation and characteristics of their first panic attack" (p. 559). These cases were classed as "atypical" and excluded.

In view of the regrettable lack of experimental investigations of panic-related avoidance, and of agoraphobia as a whole (see Rachman, 1984b), it is not at all surprising that there is little information on the connection between panic and avoidance to supplement the persuasive but flawed clinical evidence. In the course of carrying out some experimental investigations into psychologically provoked panics (described fully on p. 269), we took the opportunity of compiling some incidental information on the connection between panic and avoidance (Rachman & Lopatka, 1986a).

Several weeks after they had participated in an experiment on the induction of panic, 26 subjects (including the 10 who had reported having a panic in the experimental setting) were contacted and asked if they would agree to return for one further test. They were also asked to rate on a 0–100 scale how willing they were to participate in this additional test. All of the 24 subjects who were successfully approached agreed on the telephone to return for an additional test, but only 13 actually turned up for the retesting. There was no difference in return rate for those who had or had not panicked (roughly 50% of each group returned). If we assume that the subjects' failure to turn up for the retesting, despite having agreed to do so on the telephone, is an indirect, if weak, index of avoidance behavior, it appears that having experienced a panic did not increase avoidance behavior. There was no difference either in expressed willingness to return; those who completed the procedure without panicking reported an average of 68% willingness to return, compared with 76% for those who had panicked. However, a comparison of returners with nonreturners showed that the latter had higher predicted fear (60%) than the returners (47%, $p = .05$). The observed connection was that between predicted fear and subsequent avoidance, not between panic and avoidance.

Given the plausibility of the connection between panic and subsequent avoidance, it might come as a surprise to learn that this connection is open to challenge. Starting from the acknowledgment that there very likely is a connection between panic and subsequent avoidance in a proportion of cases, possibly the majority, we have then to consider how to interpret this information in the light of the important exceptions which can be identified, and the minor failure described herein. It has already been pointed out that agoraphobic avoidance can develop without a report of previous panic. Avoidance behavior of other kinds can also develop in the absence of panic, and indeed in the absence of a specific frightening experience (Thorpe & Burns, 1983).

So, panics are not always followed by avoidance, and avoidance is not always preceded by panic.

1. Many agoraphobic patients report the development of avoidance behavior after an experience of panic(s) (Klein, Rabkin, & Gorman, 1985; Thyer & Himle, 1985).

2. A significant minority report the development of avoidance behavior after events in which no panic occurs. For example, Thorpe and Burns (1983) reported that 23% of their large sample of agoraphobics dated the onset of their problems to a bereavement.

3. Panics are reported by patients with psychological problems that are not agoraphobic. Barlow et al. (1985) imply that many patients with mixed phobias or depression, including those who have unpredictable panics, do not display a broad pattern of avoidance.

4. There are numerous instances of patients who experience panic but do not subsequently display avoidance behavior. The following four examples are sufficient to illustrate the general point. As noted, Barlow et al. (1985), found that the great majority of their patients with mixed psychological problems had panicked,

but presumably did not develop avoidance behavior (e.g., panic without agoraphobia, major depression). Uhde et al. (1985) emphasize the connection between panic and subsequent avoidance, but also note that some patients, all of them men, continued to show normal approach behavior despite having experienced some panics. In a study on the relationship between impaired mobility and cognitions, Craske, Rachman, and Tallman (1986) found that 9% of the 34 social phobics in their sample reported having had significant panics. In that same study a surprisingly high number of people *without* apparent psychological problems also reported having experienced panics (22% out of 346 made such reports; see No. 5).

5. Panics are reported by people who are free of any significant psychological problems (and are presumably free of disabling avoidance behavior). In keeping with the Craske et al. (1986) finding, Norton, Harrison, Hauch, and Rhodes (1985) found that 64 out of 186 normal subjects reported having experienced at least one panic within the past year. Although they do not specifically address the question of whether or not their respondents displayed extensive avoidance behavior, in the absence of such information, and in the absence of any diagnosed psychological problem, it is not unreasonable to presume that few of these people had developed significant avoidance.

It would appear then that extensive avoidance behavior can arise in the absence of panic experiences, and on the other side of the matter, panic experiences are not necessarily followed by the emergence of avoidance behavior. Not for the first time, we are obliged to face up to the puzzling questions of why avoidance does or does not emerge (e.g., Gray, 1981; Seligman & Johnston, 1973) and why in many clinical instances the avoidance behavior persists for prolonged periods (Rachman, 1978). I shall return to these questions presently, but as an opening, it is suggested that the occurrence, or nonoccurrence, of panic-related avoidance will be found to be determined in part by (a) the predictability of the panic(s), (b) the operation of safety signals, and (c) the person's interpretation of the nature of the threat associated with the panic.

Given the growing interest in distinguishing between predicted and unpredicted panics, it might be wise to incorporate this distinction when attempting to address the question of how panic and avoidance are related. As yet there is no experimental, or indeed clinical evidence on panic that can guide us. However, it is possible to make deductions from what is known about the importance of predictability in panics, and to relate this to what is known about the emergence of avoidance behavior. What follows is a prospect of what the relations between predictability, panic, and avoidance, are likely to be. The moderating influence of safety signals is acknowledged.

It is probable that there is a strong correlation between predictability of panic (or intense fear) and subsequent avoidance. When a person predicts that a panic (or intense fear) is likely to be experienced, he or she probably will take steps to avoid the situation or circumstances in which that panic might occur. There is also likely to be an intensity variable operating, in that predictions of intense panics are more likely to evoke avoidance and more intense avoidance at that.

We can also postulate that the onset, or increase, of avoidance behavior is far more probable after an unpredicted panic than after a predicted panic. Related to this postulate, it is probable that after a predicted panic there will be no change in avoidance, or even a decrease in such behavior.

We can also expect to find a temporal variable. It is postulated that avoidance behavior will develop/increase more rapidly after unpredicted panics. Furthermore, such increases/onset can occur after few panics, or indeed after a single panic.

On the other hand, we can assume that decreases in (panic-related) avoidance behavior will occur gradually and slowly. Furthermore, these decreases will occur after repeatedly disconfirmed predictions of panic. (It will be noted here that this implies an asymmetry between the onset/increase in panic-induced avoidance, and the decrease of such behavior once established.)

All of these postulated relationships between prediction, panic, and avoidance are subject to the influence of safety signals, such that the introduction of a new safety signal or the strengthening of an existing signal will be followed by a decrease in avoidance behavior. Furthermore, the withdrawal or weakening of a safety signal will be followed by an increase in avoidance behavior. The concept of safety signals is discussed by Gray (1981), Seligman and Johnston (1973), Seligman and Binik (1977) and Rachman (1984a).

We can now turn to a consideration of what happens after a predicted no-panic; that is, what are the consequences of a disconfirmed expectation of panic? One might think that disconfirmed predictions of panic, the so-called over-predicted no-panic experiences, will rarely be followed by avoidance behavior, and this may turn out to be the case. However, there are some reasons for expecting that the relationship will not be that straightforward. In our research on laboratory-induced panic states, we have come across evidence of excessive cautiousness among our subjects, of a kind that is consistent with the cautiousness among clinical patients reported by Butler and Mathews (1983). It was observed that anxious and depressed patients overrated the probability of the occurrence of aversive events. We have picked up indications of this excessive cautiousness, and of the rapid development of such cautiousness, even after a single panic. It is as if the person decides that it is best to avoid a risk. Conceivably, this kind of cautiousness, and reduction of risk taking, plays a part in the postulated asymmetrical relationship between the emergence and the extinction of avoidance behavior.

The postulates regarding the relationships between prediction, panic, and avoidance, can now be listed.

1. Experience of panic will increase the prediction of future panics.
2. Predictions of expected panic will be followed by more intense avoidance behavior.

3. The onset/increase of avoidance behavior is more probable after an unpredicted than a predicted panic.
4. After a predicted panic there will be no change in avoidance behavior, or a decrease in such behavior.
5. There is an asymmetry between the development and the reduction of panic-related avoidance behavior, such that:
   (a) Avoidance behavior will develop/increase rapidly after unpredicted panics.
   (b) After disconfirmed predictions of panic, decreases in (panic-related) avoidance behavior will occur gradually and slowly.
6. The introduction or strengthening of a safety signal will be followed by a decrease in avoidance behavior.
7. The weakening or withdrawal of a safety signal will be followed by an increase in avoidance behavior.

The thrust of these postulates can be summed up as an attempt to formulate some answers to the basic questions of why and when panics are followed by avoidance behavior.

Avoidance behavior will develop or strengthen if the person predicts that there is a high probability of experiencing a panic, if unpredicted panics occur, if a safety signal is weakened or withdrawn. In contrast, avoidance will be weakened if the person predicts that there is a low probability of having a panic, if the panics are accurately predicted, if predictions of panic are repeatedly disconfirmed, if safety signals are introduced or strengthened.

Perceived control probably plays an important part in determining panic-related avoidance. As a pointer in this direction, a clinical study of the avoidance behavior of agoraphobic patients revealed that after panic, patients reported significant reductions in perceived control (Rachman, Craske, Tallman, & Solyom, 1986).

Cognitive factors are bound to play a part in determining avoidance. Presumably the *content* of the associated cognition is critical. If the person fears that his or her panic may prove fatal, then strong and specific avoidance patterns are appropriate (e.g., avoid being alone or far from medical assistance). If he or she fears that the panic will be embarrassing (e.g., social fears) there is less urgency in the need to avoid. Strictly speaking, we should not expect *broad* patterns of avoidance to emerge in all cases of panic (see the discussion of exceptions to the connection of panic leading to avoidance). A cognitive interpretation of panic, such as Clark's (1986a and this volume), allows and even requires a set of *specific* connections between panic and avoidance. A person whose main panic cognition is a fear of a heart attack may continue to use public transport and department stores but strongly avoid demanding physical exertion, running up stairs, and so on (see Salkovskis, this volume). In these cases, conventional forms of agoraphobic avoidance are not evident, but other cognition-specific avoidance behavior should be detectable. People who panic when they fear that they are about to choke to death can travel freely, but avoid a wide range of foods and eating places, and so on. People who fear that they are going to die in their sleep, can panic during the onset of sleep, during deep relaxation, and so on (see page 266 below). The cognitions should be threat-relevant and situation-specific.

The introduction of a cognitive interpretation can help to make intelligble some of the previously puzzling discrepancies between panic and avoidance, and has the added advantage of increasing the precision of the connections between panic and avoidance. The matter cannot be resolved at present, and it should not be decided prematurely that the cognitive interpretation will salvage the original view that avoidance behavior is a major, inevitable consequence of panic. Some of the exceptions described earlier are open to a cognitive reinterpretation, but not all of them are readily explicable in cognitive terms. In addition to explaining observed avoidance behavior, a theory that incorporates the three key factors proposed here (predictability, safety signals, and cognitions) will need to be tested for its precision and predictive power.

Cognitive factors no doubt interact with the other determinants of avoidance, set out in the aforementioned seven postulates. If the central fear is of an event possibly leading to death, then avoidance behavior will be much strengthened by the unpredictability of the panics, by the (predicted) probability of their occurrence, and by the absence of safety signals. Exploration of the connections between (a) the content of the cognitions, (b) their predictability and (c) the influence of safety signals, and how they influence avoidance behavior is likely to prove enlightening.

The renewal of interest in avoidance behavior that arises from the current focus on panic, and the proliferation of assumptions and predictions, make it desirable to resume the attempts to provide a satisfactory explanation of the persistence of avoidance behavior in general. It has been argued elsewhere (see Rachman, 1976, 1978) that the Mowrer (1939) two-stage theory of fear and avoidance has much to recommend it, but is incapable of accommodating the available information on the subject. Although fear and avoidance often are closely connected, there are many instances in which fear can occur without avoidance, and avoidance can develop and be sustained in the absence of fear. Specific weaknesses of the Mowrer theory were lucidly discussed by Seligman and Johnston (1973) who drew attention to three major problems: the resistance of avoidance responses to extinction, the concomitant absence of fear, and lastly, the difficulty of specifying the relevant conditioned stimuli. It is well to remember that panic is not always or necessarily followed by avoidance behavior, nor is all avoidance behavior (even of the agoraphobic type) a product of panic. A preliminary attempt has been made to interpret some of the clinical data within the context of safety signals (Rachman, 1984a, following the suggestions implied in the writings of Gray, 1981; Seligman & Johnston, 1973; Seligman & Binik, 1977).

To sum up, the occurrence of panic-related avoidance—and the equally important nonoccurrence of avoidance after panics—appears to be determined by fear levels, the predictability of panic, cognitions associated with panic and safety, and the operation of safety signals.

THE PSYCHOPHYSIOLOGICAL CONSEQUENCES OF PANIC

There is a growing interest in the psychophysiological manifestations of panic and the introduction of ambulatory monitoring has produced useful information (e.g., Taylor et al., 1986) and promises an even larger yield in the near future. As there are no data on the psychophysiological *consequences* of panic, this section is necessarily prospective.

As far as manifestations of panic are concerned, it appears that during many or most panics, as indexed by the subject's verbal report of a panic, a steep increase occurs in heart rate (e.g., Lader & Mathews, 1968; Taylor et al., 1986). The search for endocrine changes has not been rewarding (Stokes, 1985; Uhde et al., 1985).

It is of potential importance that in a proportion of (verbally indexed) panics no increase in heart rate takes place; indeed, panics can be reported even at low levels of heart rate (e.g., Taylor et al., 1986). These examples of discordance, and also of desynchrony (Rachman & Hodgson, 1974), may be of considerable importance in the construction and evaluation of theories of panic. Examples of these phenomena are not easy to incorporate in a purely biological explanation of panic, but may be more amenable to cognitive explanations, especially those which are based on the person's interpretation (or more often, misinterpretation) of his or her bodily processes (e.g., Beck & Emery, 1985; Clark, 1986a). If the person is fearful of choking, or of going insane, there is no reason to expect cardiac accelerations. Rather a cognitive interpretation would require specific connections between verbal report and physiological reactions, perhaps along these lines: Panic patients who fear that they are losing control and going insane are more likely to react to dizziness that is say associated with a drop in blood pressure (and even deceleration of heart rate); but panic patients whose major fear is of a fatal heart attack should show a greater concordance between heart rate changes and panic. Patients who fear that a loss of control is premonitory of death or serious illness will tend to panic when they are relaxing. (Incidentally, the occurrence of relaxation-induced panics is explicable by cognitive theorists but presents a problem for proponents of exclusively biological interpretations of panic.) In short, the psychophysiology of panics should match the cognitions that are believed to play a crucial role in all experiences of panic.

In some cases respiration will be critical, in others it will be cardiac activity. Even relaxation exercises can induce a panic. In passing, the psychophysiological patterns associated with panic may provide a basis for differential predictions (Seligman, this volume) flowing from exclusively biological theories and from cognitive-biological theories. The latter allow and require a variety of (malleable) psychophysiological patterns that are connected to the prevailing cognitions. Biological theories lead one to predict a relatively uniform and unchanging pattern of psychophysiological reactions.

The differential predictions can also be stated in a broader manner. Cognitive theories lead one to expect "discordances" between the three systems of fear, but biological theories lead to an expectation of concordance (Rachman & Hodgson, 1974).

Consequences and Predictability. At least four specific psychophysiological consequences of panic can be predicted.

1. An unexpected panic is likely to be followed by an increase in tonic level of arousal. It is probable that most people who experience panics, in common with others who suffer from excessive anxiety, have high tonic levels (e.g., Lader & Wing, 1966; Margraf, Ehlers, & Roth, 1986a) and it is not too far-fetched to suppose that panics, especially unpredicted panics, contribute to these elevated levels. Consistent with this possibility, Liebowitz et al. (1984) found panic patients to be more fearful and generally aroused preassessment than nonpanic patients.

If Margraf et al. (1986a) are correct in assigning importance to the role of tonic levels of arousal in the elicitation of panics, then panics may be self-promoting. They may follow this sequence:

panic → increased level of arousal → increased probability of panic.

If no other factors entered into the picture, one could postulate, simply, that *panics promote future panics* (they do increase the expectation of future panics). But other factors, such as predictability, enter the picture and may interfere with the self-promotion of panics.

2. A second probable consequence of unpredicted panics is the development of conditioned anticipatory psychophysiological reactions. When a person reenters the situation in which he or she previously experienced a panic, these conditioned psychophysiological reactions are likely to be evoked (see Seligman, this volume). In turn, these conditioned reactions may increase the probability of the occurrence of a panic, and the intensity of any panic that does occur.

3. It is probable that the psychophysiological consequences of unpredicted panics differ from the psychophysiological consequences of *predicted* panics. The consequences of unpredicted panics will follow closely the two main predic-

tions, that is, increased tonic levels and the development of conditioned reactions that, in turn, may lead to increases in probability or intensity of future panics.

However, the consequences of predicted panics may be quite different. Given the evidence of differing psychological consequences of predicted and unpredicted panics (see Rachman & Levitt, 1985, and later in this chapter), it is reasonable to expect that the psychophysiological consequences of predicted panics will be relatively benign. Specifically, there will be little or no increase in tonic levels of arousal after a predicted panic. Secondly, there will be little or no evidence of conditioned psychophysiological reactions when the person re-enters the situation in which the predicted panic occurred (assuming, of course, that the person's current expectation of panic is held constant).

There is a third possibility here. Repeated experiences of predicted panics may be followed by *reductions* in tonic level and by the extinction of any conditioned psychophysiological reactions.

4. The repeated experience of predicted or unpredicted no-panics, by a person who has some experience of panics, will be followed by reduced levels of tonic arousal and by the extinction of any conditioned psychophysiological reactions.

None of these predictions pertaining to the psychophysiological consequences of panic have been tested, but they can easily be incorporated into the procedures which have been developed for the laboratory study of panics (see Rachman & Levitt, 1985). The inclusion of psychophysiological measurements into the study of the consequences of panic, using this laboratory procedure, is strongly recommended. Studies of the psychophysiological consequences of panics that are induced by hyperventilation (or by lactate or other substances) are similarly easy to design, and are likewise recommended.

In addition to elucidating the nature of panic, psychophysiological analyses will enable one to test differential predictions from a biological and from a cognitive theory. Biological theory leads one to expect psychophysiological patterns that are: (a) uniform, (b) stable, (c) concordant. Cognitive theory leads one to predict that the patterns will be (a) variable, (b) malleable, (c) discordant.

COGNITIVE CONSEQUENCES

In the course of carrying out preliminary testing for an experiment on the development of safety signals in mildly claustrophobic subjects, an unexpected number of the subjects experienced panic attacks in the small, enclosed room that served as our test and training laboratory. In keeping with the deliberate shift toward greater reliance on experimental analyses of phobias (e.g., Rachman, 1984b), we exploited this unforeseen opportunity to analyze panics that occur under controlled conditions.

After discovering the unexpected frequency of panics in our early claustrophobic subjects, we placed the observations on a formal basis. The panics were recorded and rated for quality and intensity, and we also asked each subject to make a prediction about the likelihood of their having a panic attack or near-panic on the next trial. This information about panics, experienced and/or expected, was then related to the experimental data on fear and safety signals (Rachman & Levitt, 1985).

We were interested in finding out as much as we could about panics that occurred under controlled conditions, and we also framed a series of specific questions. The main interest focused on the question of whether or not the presumed relationship between panic attacks and subsequent fear could be substantiated. Are panic attacks followed by increases in fear? How common are these panic attacks? Does the occurrence of a panic impede the (therapeutic) reduction of fear? Do panics retard the reduction of fear? What proportion of panics are unexpected? How often are the expectations of panic disconfirmed? Do predicted and unexpected panics have different effects on fear and avoidance? Are repeated disconfirmations followed by increases in safety? Is there a law of primacy, such that the first panic is the most damaging? Is there a law of frequency, such that the damaging effects of panics show an accumulative growth? What is the relationship, if any, between panics and habituation of fear?

The panics observed in the present study were situational rather than spontaneous, using those current if debatable terms. We included for analysis only those panics which met the Taylor et al. (1986) (and the Upjohn study) criterion of at least three ''symptoms.''

Method. The investigation of panic and its effects was carried out in the context of a study designed to promote safety signals (Rachman, 1984a) in claustrophobic subjects. During the course of pretesting, training trials, and posttesting, the subjects were required to go into a bare, dark, small room and remain there for 2 minutes. Prior to and after each test and training trial, the subjects were asked to predict, and report, the occurrence of panic and their levels of fear. They were also asked to complete a checklist of bodily reactions and cognitions that are said to characterize panics (DSM–III).

In the attempt to generate safety signals in subjects with mild claustrophobia, each person was given a number of trials during which they were required to enter the enclosed room for 2 to 4 minutes (all *test* trials lasted 2 mintues). At the end of each training trial, they chewed a colored tablet immediately before leaving the room; i.e., the consumption of the tablet was followed by departure from the aversive situation. The safety signal value of the colored tablet used in training sessions was reassessed with a posttest on the same day as the training trials, and then again with another posttest 24 to 72 hours after the training trials, and a third posttest 1 month after completion of the training trials.

Subjects. Thirteen undergraduates at the University of British Columbia were recruited from psychology courses to serve as volunteers in a study involving fear of enclosed spaces. They were paid $6 for their participation. Subjects were screened with the UBC Fear of Enclosed Spaces Questionnaire (FOESQ; Rachman, in preparation).

To be considered as a potential subject, a student had to report on the FOESQ screening device that he or she would (a) "avoid most of the time" or "always avoid" "small, enclosed rooms, without windows," or that (b) the maximum amount of time they could tolerate while in an enclosed space was less than 10 minutes, or (c) that the amount of anxiety they expected to experience while in a small, enclosed space was greater than 6.0 on a scale of 0 to 10.

Of the 331 students initially screened, 64 students were contacted and asked to participate in the study. Of these, 47 were excluded because the test situation proved not to be sufficiently fear producing. This was determined (a) by the subject's verbal reports, and (b) by the subject's "fear" and "safety" scores reported after the first trial, based on a scale from 0 to 100. If a safety score of more than 70 (100 being "totally safe") and a fear score of less than 30 (0 being "not at all fearful") were reported on the written questionnaire, the subjects was excluded. In addition, any student with a past history of any psychiatric disorders was excluded. Four subjects did not wish to participate because they were too busy, which left 13 subjects in our sample.

Of the 13 who acted as subjects in the study, 5 said they avoided small, enclosed rooms without windows, *most of the time,* and 3 said that they *always avoided* small, enclosed rooms, without windows. The average amount of time that they expected to tolerate remaining in a small, enclosed space was 7.7 minutes (mode = 5 minutes), and, the average expected anxiety score was 8.7.

Materials. The structure of the FOESQ is based on the Agoraphobia Questionnaire developed by Chambless (1982), and consists of three parts. The first is a list of 12 different situations or places (e.g., caves, crowded department stores, elevators). Subjects are asked to respond with one of the following choices: "never avoid," "rarely avoid," "avoid half the time," "avoid most of the time," or "always avoid." In the second part subjects are asked: "If you had to do it, how long could you tolerate being in the place that you have indicated you would *always avoid* or that you would be most *likely to avoid?*" In the third part they are asked: "If you had to do it, how anxious would it make you to remain in the place you would *always avoid* or be *most likely to avoid?*" The subjects are asked to place a mark along a 10-centimeter line, with 0 being "not at all anxious" and 10 being "extremely anxious." In addition to the FOESQ, the UBC Enclosed Spaces Cognitions Questionnaire (Rachman, in prep.) was also completed. On this questionnaire subjects are asked how often, while in an enclosed space, they would have each of the ideas or thoughts listed, such as "I am going to pass out" or "I am going to lose control of myself."

The subjects' pretrial estimates and posttrial reports of their fear and safety experienced during each trial of the study were collected by means of three simple questionnaires, dealing with expected and reported fear, safety, and panics (see Rachman & Levitt, 1985, for details). The subjects were also given a checklist comprised of 14 items describing the subjective physiological and psychological symptoms experienced during panic. The list contained the DSM–III items, notwithstanding their unsatisfactory nature (why 14? Why these 14? etc.), because the list is now in common use.

Design. In the majority of the analyses performed on the panic data, we compared panic with no-panic trials across subjects. That is, each trial was placed into one of two categories ("panicked" or "did not panic"), and these two groups of trials were compared on several dependent measures.

Some of the analyses were within-subject comparisons, between panic trials that were divided into groups according to a specific criterion, such as whether the panic was expected or not.

The majority of safety signal analyses were within-subject, comparing each subject's scores on several dependent measures (taken from their questionnaire responses) on the first two trials (*pretests* with each type of tablet—pink and orange), with his or her scores on later trials (*posttests* with each type of tablet plus a trial with no tablet), executed after several "training trials."

Other measures were analyzed between subjects, separating the sample into different categories according to a given variable, such as whether or not the subject panicked frequently, or whether or not he or she was a "habituator" (felt less frightened as a function of increased exposure to the small room).

Procedure. Students who were classified as sufficiently claustrophobic on the FOESQ were contacted by telephone, and asked to participate in a study involving fear of enclosed spaces.

The purpose of the study was explained and the following instructions were given: "For this study, you will be required to enter a small, dark room several times, for a period of 2 to 5 minutes on each occasion. The door will be unlocked, and you are free to leave the room before I return to knock on the door to signal the end of the trial. Each time you go into the room, I am going to give you either a pink or an orange tablet. The pink tablets are sodium fluoride, and the orange are ascorbic acid (vitamin C). These tablets contain no other drugs. Before you enter the room, I will tell you when I'd like you to chew the tablet during that particular trial. I cannot tell you the exact reasons for having you take the tablets until the end of the study, but, it has been found that some people find that taking the tablets helps to reduce their fear. On each trial, before you enter the room there will be one short questionnaire to fill out, and after you leave the room there will be two other questionnaires for you to complete." If the subjects agreed to participate, they were given a consent form which contained all of the preceding information. They were then shown the room that was to be used in the testing procedure, which was directly next door to the experimenter's office. The room was a small storage closet, measuring 1.28 meters (length) by 2.48 meters (width) by 2.75 meters (height). It had a set of cupboards on opposite walls, further reducing the width of the room to 1.28 meters.

The procedure for each trial was held constant. The subjects filled out a "Pretrial Estimate" questionnaire, and then, after receiving (in most cases) a tablet from the experimenter and instructions as to when to take it, they entered the small room. After a given interval, the experimenter knocked on the door and the subject came out, returned to the experimenter's office, and completed both a "Posttrial Estimate" questionnaire and a "Self-Report" checklist. Then the subject filled out the *next* "Pretrial Estimate" questionnaire, and went on with the subsequent trial.

There were three different types of trials: pretests, training trials, and posttests. The first and second trials were pretests, which established the subject's baseline scores. On one of these, the subjects were given the pink tablet, and instructed to take it any time they liked while in the room. On the other, the subjects were instructed to do the same, this time with an orange tablet. The order of these pretests was varied randomly from subject to subject.

The subjects then went through a number of training trials, during each of which they received instructions to take the tablet either at the point when the experimenter knocked on the door to signal the end of a trial, or if the subjects decided to leave before this point, to take it just as they were leaving the room. The number of these "training trials" varied from subject to subject, depending on the number of trials it took before they reported fear scores reduced to approximately half (as compared to their very first reported fear score). It was at this point that the first set of posttests was executed.

Some subjects, however, showed no signs of their fear diminishing (the "nonhabituators"). If, after five training trials, a subject showed no reduction of fear, training trials were stopped and the first set of posttests were conducted. The range of the number of training trials that each subject had was from 4 to 20, the average being 7.5 (mode = 5 training trials).

The first set of posttests consisted of three separate trials: one with an orange tablet, one with a pink tablet, and one with no tablet. The order of these posttests was also varied randomly from subject to subject. For the posttests with either tablet, the subjects were told that they could take the tablet whenever they liked while in the room. The experimenter later asked and made a record of when the subjects had taken the tablet. After these three posttests had been completed, the experimenter and subject arranged a second meeting. On the second meeting (a few days later), another set of three posttests were run, exactly as the first set had been on the earlier occasion.

In order to standardize between-subject comparisons, the length of all pre- and posttests periods was exactly 2 minutes, although the subjects were told that each trial period varied from 2 to 5 minutes. The training trials, however, *did* vary from 2 to 4 minutes, so that the subject could not be certain when the experimenter would return. Once the second set of posttests had been run, the subject was given a debriefing form to read in the presence of the experimenter, who answered any questions.

Results. The focus of this analysis is on panics, but before turning to those results, a summary account of the findings on safety signals will be given in order to provide a context for the data on panic. The attempt to promote the growth of safety signals was only slightly successful. All of the changes in safety were in the predicted direction but few reached acceptable levels of statistical significance. Further research on this problem is under way and the findings on the promotion of safety signals will be reported in due course.

In summary, the provision of the safety signal training was followed by a significant increase in predictions of safety, rising from 31 to 58 on a 0–100 scale. Predicted fear scores were reduced from 69 to 50. However, these results are not unequivocal (Rachman & Levitt, 1985).

Seventy-five percent of the subjects reported experiencing a panic on at least one occasion, and 66% did so on at least two occasions.

In all, 238 trials were given and panic or near-panics occurred on 67 of them. Panics (and near-panics) were defined by subjective reports; 75% of all such reports were accompanied by an endorsement of at least 3 items from DSM–III panic checklist (the same criterion as that used by Taylor et al., 1985). Thirteen of the subjects had at least 1 panic, 11 of these *S*s had at least 2 panics, and 4 of the subjects had none at all. The distribution of checklist items is shown in Table 14.1.

The number of predicted panics, unpredicted, and overpredicted was as follows: correctly predicted = 50, unexpected = 17 (total 67). In addition, there were 39 errors of overprediction in which the expected event was disconfirmed (false alarm). (Expected panics are those in which the *S* predicted at higher than 50% probability that she would have a panic on the coming trial; unexpected panics had a probability score of less than 50%.) It can be seen that in most instances the occurrence of panics was correctly predicted. The proportion of unexpected panics is relatively low. However, this tolerably high level of predicted accuracy has to be seen against the background of gross overprediction of panic.

Fear and Safety. Are panics followed by increases in (a) predicted fear and (b) reported fear?

Two one-way analyses of variance were performed in order to test these questions. It was found that panics were indeed followed by an increase in predicted fear scores, but there was a decrease in *reported* fear scores on the trial following the panic. Fig. 14.1 illustrates the findings. In summary, panics were

TABLE 14.1
Items on Panic Checklist, and Number of Times Each Item was Reported During a Panic over All Subjects who Completed this Checklist (n = 6)

Item	*No. of Times Reported (out of 67 Panic Trials)*	*No. of Subjects who Reported Item at Least Once (out of 6 Maximum)*
1. Shortness of breath	7	3
2. Choking or smothering sensations	5	2
3. Palpitations or accelerated heart rate	17	4
4. Chest pain or discomfort	2	1
5. Sweating	11	3
6. Faintness	4	2
7. Dizziness, light-headedness, or unsteady feelings	13	3
8. Nausea or abdominal distress	4	2
9. Depersonalization or derealization	18	3
10. Numbness or tingling sensations	8	3
11. Flushes (hot flashes) or chills	10	2
12. Trembling or shaking	18	3
13. Fear of dying	0	0
14. Fear of going crazy or doing something uncontrolled	4	2

followed by expectations of greater fear, but such expectations were not confirmed. Panic appears to have led to an overprediction of fear.

A similar pattern occurred with predicted safety and reported safety scores. A one-way ANOVA showed that predicted safety scores decreased significantly after panic. However, reported safety scores increased on the trial following a panic as shown in Fig. 14.2. Once again, the occurrence of a panic was followed by over-prediction. Subjects overpredicted the loss of safety after a panic.

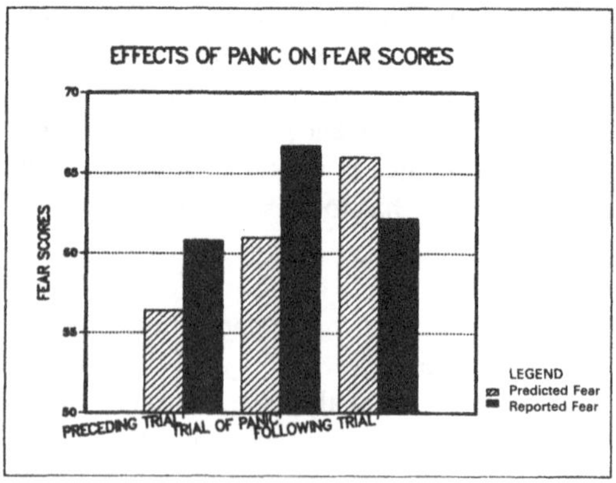

FIG. 14.1. Effects of panic on Fear scores. Predicted (▨) Fear scores rose following a panic (P = 0.015), reported (□) Fear scores decreased following a panic (P = 0.098).

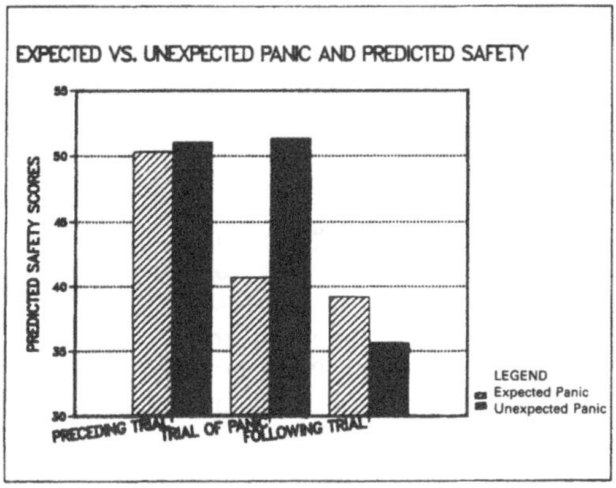

FIG. 14.2. Effects of panic on Safety scores. Predicted (▨) Safety scores decreased following a panic ($P = 0.006$), reported (□) Safety scores increased following a panic ($P = 0.004$).

Expected and Unexpected Panics. The next set of questions dealt with the problem of whether or not predicted and unpredicted panics were followed by the same or different changes in predicted and in reported fear and safety.

It turned out that *expected* panics did not have the same effect on scores on subsequent trials as did unexpected panics. When a panic was expected, there was a drop in predicted safety scores from the trial before the panic to the trial of the panic. However, there was no change in predicted safety scores on the trial following the panic. When a panic was *unexpected,* the subsequent predicted safety scores dropped sharply. This is shown in Fig. 14.3. As far as predicted safety is concerned, it was the unexpected panics that contributed most to changing these predictions.

Reported safety scores on a trial subsequent to a panic were similar to predicted safety scores, but smaller and not significant. A one-way ANOVA showed a trend for reported safety scores to increase after a trial on which an expected panic occurred. Following an unexpected panic, there was only a slight

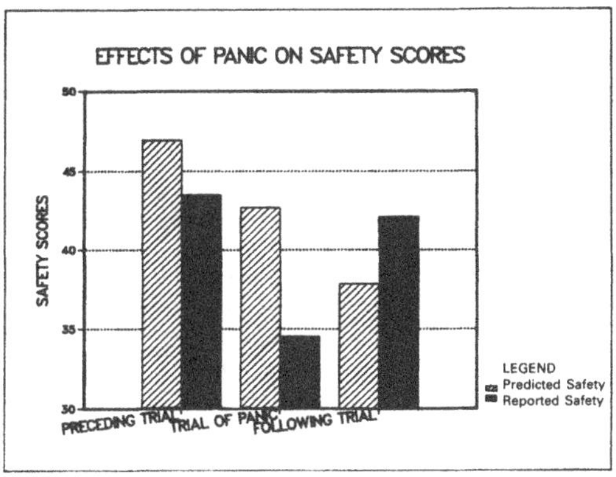

FIG. 14.3. Expected (▨) vs unexpected (□) panic and predicted safety. An expected panic has little effect on the predicted Safety scores of the subsequent trial ($P = 0.06$), but an unexpected panic leads to a sharp drop in predicted Safety scores on the following trial ($P = 0.04$).

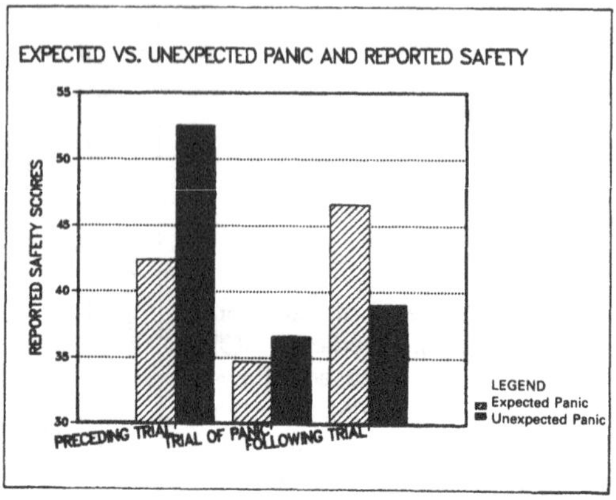

FIG. 14.4. Expected (■) vs unexpected (□) panic and reported safety. Reported Safety scores increased following an expected panic ($P = 0.15$), but showed only a very slight increase on a trial after an unexpected panic ($P = 0.125$).

increase in reported safety scores on the subsequent trial. This result is shown in Fig. 14.4.

Predicted fear scores showed a parallel pattern to predicted safety scores. When a panic was expected and then occurred, predicted fear scores increased from the trial before to the trial of the panic, but then showed only a slight increase following the occurrence of the panic. An unexpected panic, however, was followed by a large increase in predicted fear scores on following trial. This is shown in Fig. 14.5.

Panics, whether expected or not, did not have much effect on *reported* fear scores on subsequent trials. Following an expected panic, reported fear scores decreased slightly, on average. There was a tendency for reported fear scores to decrease, although not as much, following an unexpected panic. These results are shown in Fig. 14.6.

As with safety scores, so with fear, unexpected panics were followed by

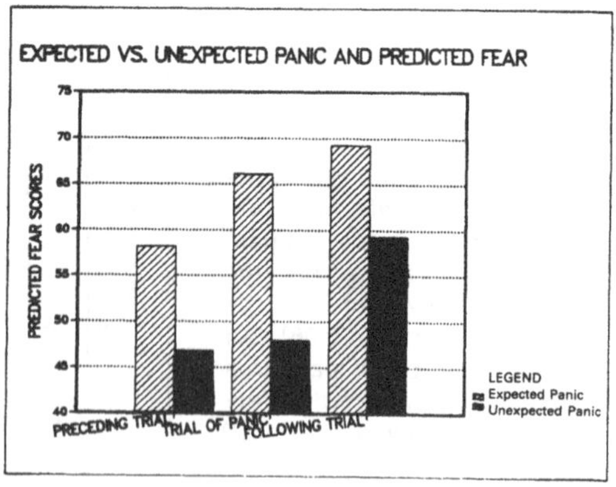

FIG. 14.5. Expected (▨) vs unexpected (□) panic and predicted fear. An expected panic had little effect on the predicted Fear scores of the subsequent trial ($P = 0.05$), but unexpected panics lead to an increase in predicted Fear scores ($P = 0.08$).

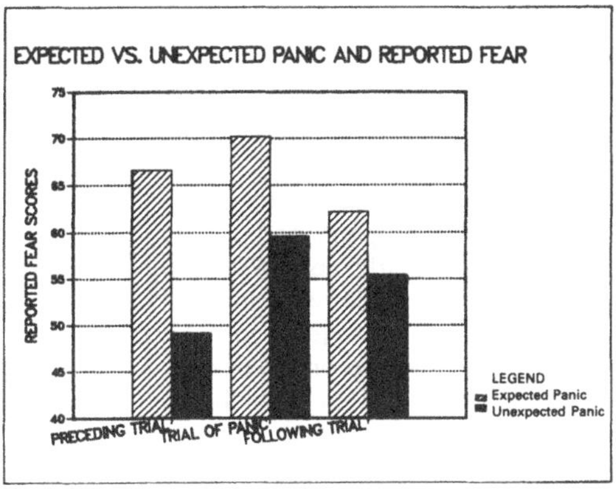

FIG. 14.6. Expected (▨) vs unexpected (□) panic and reported fear. Reported Fear scores decreased on average after an expected panic (NS), and showed a smaller decrease following an unexpected panic (NS).

overprediction. After an unexpected panic, subjects overpredicted how frightened and how unsafe they would feel on the subsequent trial.

By contrast, expected panics did not distort fear and safety predictions. Neither expected nor unexpected panics were followed by significant increases in reported fear. In order to test the idea that a predicted panic is less disturbing than one that is not predicted, we made a within-subject comparison between fear scores on predicted and unpredicted panic trials. A t-test comparing these scores was not significant. Subjects did not report less fear when the panic was predicted than when it was not predicted.

No-panic Trials. Here we were interested to find out whether confirmed predictions of "no-panic" were followed by smaller or larger changes in predicted and reported fear and safety, than were *disconfirmed* predictions of panic.

A trial in which no-panic occurred led to no significant change in predicted safety score on the following trial, regardless of whether the subject had been expecting to panic or not. This result is illustrated in Fig. 14.7.

There was a trend toward an increase in reported safety scores following a trial during which the subject had been expecting to panic but did not do so. Reported safety scores remained constant after a trial during which the subject had not been expecting to panic, and did not panic. These two one-way ANOVAs are illustrated in Fig. 14.8.

As with predicted safety, there was no change in predicted fear scores after a no-panic trial, whether the subject had expected to panic or not. This result is shown in Fig. 14.9. As illustrated in Fig. 14.10, reported fear scores remained constant before, during, and after a nonpanic trial in which the subject did not expect to panic, but there was a large drop in reported fear scores on a trial in which a panic was expected but did not in fact occur. Reported fear scores remained low on the following trial. Disconfirmed expectations of panic were followed by reductions in fear.

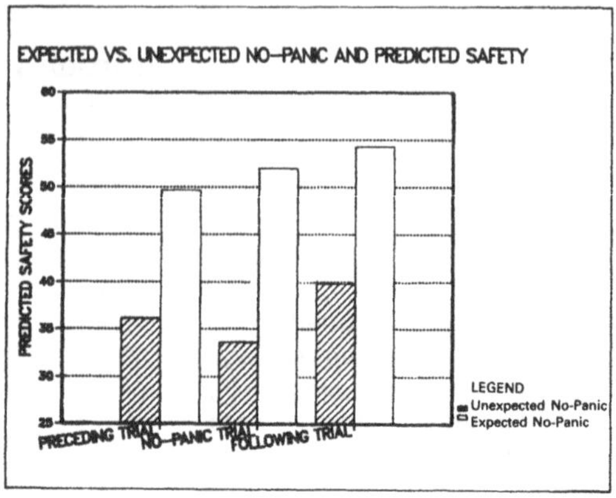

FIG. 14.7. Expected (▨) vs unexpected (□) no-panic and predicted safety. A trial upon which the *S* did not panic resulted in no significant change in predicted Safety scores on the next trial, regardless of whether the *S* had been expecting to panic or not.

Loss of Predictability. In order to test the notion that a loss of predictability is more disrupting than an absence of predictability, we compared predicted and reported fear and safety scores after a broken run of expected panics, with scores associated with plain unexpected panics. Unfortunately, the cases and instances were too few to permit formal analyses, but there appears to be a weak trend for reported fear to increase on the trial after a loss in predictability. The idea will be pursued in future research.

Predictability and Return of Fear. The same data limitations preclude drawing conclusions about the relation between predictability and the return of fear, but we detected a weak relationship such that if the last recorded panic was unexpected, then there was a larger return of fear. Similarly the later in training the first unexpected panic occurred, the larger the return of fear. These relationships are worthy of attention in future research.

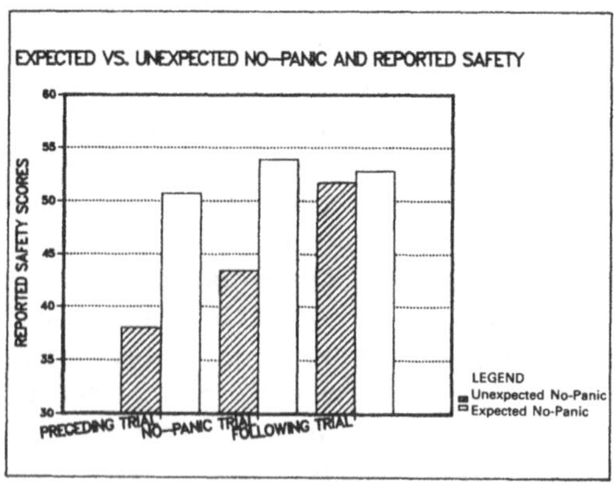

FIG. 14.8. Expected (▨) vs unexpected (□) no-panic and reported safety. A trial upon which a *S* had been expecting to panic but did not (an 'unexpected no-panic') was followed by an increase in reported Safety scores ($P = 0.098$), but there was no change in reported Safety scores following an 'expected no-panic'—a trial upon which a *S* had not been expecting to, and did not, panic (NS).

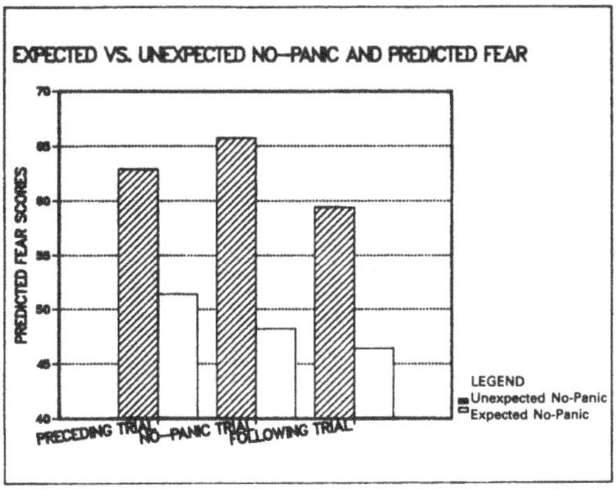

FIG. 14.9. Expected (▨) vs unexpected (□) no-panic and predicted fear. A trial upon which a *S* did not panic resulted in no significant change in predicted Fear scores on the following trial, regardless of whether the *S* had been expecting to panic or not.

Predictability and Frequency of Panics. As might be expected, there was a positive correlation (+ 0.6330, $n = 13$, $p < .025$) between average predicted panic scores and frequency of panics. The more you experience, the more you expect. Also those subjects who had few panics, had low predictions of panic on trials during which they did panic; they were more surprised by their panics than were the subjects who experienced them frequently.

Habituation

We then looked into the question of whether or not those subjects who showed little or no habituation or fear overall, reported more panics than did those subjects who showed substantial habituation of fear. The expectation was that panics might impede habituation.

Subjects who showed little or no habituation of fear across the trials experi-

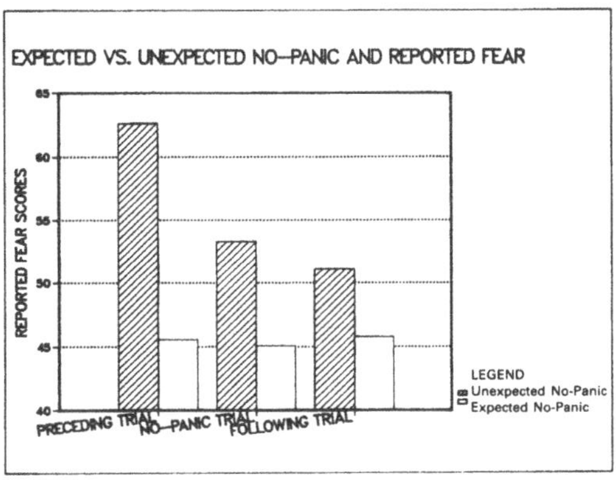

FIG. 14.10. Expected (▨) vs unexpected (□) no-panic and reported fear. There was a large drop in reported Fear scores on a trial when a *S* had been expecting to panic but did not (an 'unexpected no-panic') (P = 0.11). However, there was no change in reported Fear scores on an 'expected no-panic' trial, where the *S* had not expected to, and did not, panic (NS).

enced an average of 6.0 panics. Subjects whose fear dropped substantially over the course of the investigation—habituators—experienced an average of 2.3 panics (t = (11) = 1.6, p = .07). A t-test between the two groups was not significant.

Escape Behavior

In view of the intimate connection between fear and avoidance (and escape) behavior, we assessed whether those subjects who failed to remain in the test room for the requested 2-minute period (i.e., those who escaped prematurely) reported more panics, more or less fear, and more or less safety, overall.

In general, those subjects who failed to remain in the test room for the required period showed more panics, more fear, and lower safety scores overall. Escape behavior was associated with panics, higher fear, and lower safety, but the data were too sparse to allow conclusions.

A Primacy Effect?

On the basis of clinical and experimental evidence (e.g., Rachman & Levitt, 1985), we postulated that a primacy effect operates in the consequences of panic. We predicted that changes in fear and safety scores recorded after the *first* panic would be larger than the changes recorded after subsequent panics. Although the results were not significant, some were in the predicted direction. The average predicted fear score on the trial of the first panic was 58.2, but it then averaged 64.3 on all of the subsequent trials ($t(p)$ = 1.1, N.S.). The subjects' predicted probability of having a panic on the first panic trial averaged 46.8, and on the following panic trials their rated probability of having another panic averaged 57.5 ($t(p)$ = 2.4, p = .02). This suggests that the first panic was "more surprising" than subsequent panics, and also means that after the first panic the subjects increased their estimate of the probability of experiencing another panic.

Predicted fear and safety scores on the trial after a panic were about equal on average for the trial of the first panic and on the trials of subsequent panics. Reported fear scores on the trials after that of the very *first panic* were higher than the reported fear scores on later panic trials. The average reported fear scores were 70.0 for the trial immediately after the first panic, and only 63.2 on average after subsequent panics. There was slight evidence of a primacy effect, in that the largest increment in fear occurred after the first panic.

However, there was no evidence that the changes in the fear and safety scores recorded after the first *unpredicted* panic were larger than changes recorded after subsequent panics. It remains possible (see page 287) that it is the *first panic* that does the damage, regardless of whether it is a predicted panic or not. (However, some patients report that it was their second panic that forced them to recognize the emergence of a serious problem.) In view of our other evidence of the important role of unpredictability, no conclusions about primacy are defensible at this stage.

Frequency Effect

Given the ubiquity of habituation processes, especially in fear responding, we postulated that there is a frequency effect in panic phenomena. In particular we expected to find that the changes in fear and safety scores recorded after the first 25% of panics would be larger than the fear and safety scores recorded after the last 25% of panics. A comparison of these two samples of panics, and their consequences, failed to support this notion.

Summary. The provision of safety signal training was followed by increases in predicted safety. This connection was especially clear after disconfirmed predictions of high fear. Panics or near-panics occurred on 67 out of 238 trials, and in 75% of instances were accompanied by at least three signs from the DSM–III panic checklist. Roughly two-thirds of panics were correctly predicted, and there was a high rate of overprediction.

Panics were followed by increases in expected fear, but not in reported fear. They were also followed by overpredictions of loss of safety. Unexpected panics contributed most to these changes in prediction. Expected panics had little effect on safety and fear predictions, or on reports of safety and fear. Disconfirmed expectations of panic were followed by reductions in fear. Nonhabituators reported more panics than habituators. Escape behavior was associated with panics, high fear, and low safety.

Replication. A close replication of this study was carried out on 11 subjects, of whom 5 reported at least one panic (Rachman, Lopatka, & Levitt, 1986). The results were similar in all major respects but the cases were too few to permit formal analysis. After a panic, predicted fear increased from 77.4 to 83.8 and reported fear decreased from 85.6 to 78.4.

After a panic, the *S*s rated the probability of having another panic, on the next trial, as increased. After a no-panic they predicted a reduced probability of a repeat panic on the succeeding trial.

Safety Signal Study. The finding that the predicted probability of future panics is decreased after a no-panic experience, was repeated in a study designed mainly to assess the effects of strengthened safety signals on panic. Again, it was found that predicted panic decreased on the trial following no-panic; the probability of recurring panics was significantly increased after a panic trial. The estimates of probability were as follows are shown in Table 14.2.

A fuller account of this topic is given later. This study on safety signals was an attempt to increase the strength of such signals, and to see how powerfully

TABLE 14.2
"Probability I Will Panic on the Next Trial"

	Before the Trial	*After the Trial*	*Significance (one-tailed)*
Panic trial	56.3	62.1	($t(8) = 3.1$, $p = .008$)
No-panic trial	30.2	27.9	($t(25) = 2.55$, $p = .009$)

they can affect panic and fear. It was pointed out that in the main study, as described, the safety signal effect produced by a classical conditioning procedure, was slight. Our attempt to produce more effective safety signals was satisfactory, and reduced the frequency and dampened the effects of panic.

Given the enlargement of fear acquisition theory to include vicarious acquisition and informational acquisition—in addition to conditioned acquisition—it was decided to attempt to strengthen safety signals by the provision of information instead of relying on a conditioning procedure as before. This experimental application of the so-called "three pathways to fear" theory (Rachman, 1978) also generated some additional information on panic. (In a revision of the conditioning theory of fear acquisition, it was proposed, by Rachman, 1978, that fears can be acquired by conditioning, or by vicarious learning, or by the provision of information.) As will be seen, the results are not always consistent with the earlier findings on panic and present some problems of interpretation.

Twenty-six university students participated in the experiment, for course credit or money. They were recruited by means of the FOESQ (Rachman, in preparation), which was completed during class time, and the same selection criteria that were used in the two earlier studies were applied.

The selected subjects were given the following description:

> For this study you will be asked to enter a small room several times for a period of 2 to 5 minutes. The door will be unlocked, and you are free to leave the room; however, we would like to stay in the room for as long as you can. I will return to knock on the door to signal the end of the trial. On each trial before you enter the room there will be one short questionnaire to fill out and after you leave the room there will be three other questionnaires for you to complete.

If the subjects agreed to participate they were given a consent form to sign. Then the subject was shown the chamber that was to be used in the testing procedure—a metal cupboard (.85 m length by .42 m width by 1.8 m height, shelf 1.5 m from top) in a small storage closet which measured 1.28 m (length) by 2.48 m (width) by 2.75 m (height). It had a set of cupboards on the opposite walls, reducing the width of the room to 1.28 m.

The procedure for each trial was held constant. The subjects filled out a "Pretrial Estimate" questionnaire and then entered the small room. After a given interval of time, the experimenter knocked on the door and the subject came out, returned to the experimenter's office and completed a "Posttrial Estimate" questionnaire, a "Self-Report" symptoms checklist and a "Cognitions Questionnaire." Then the subject filled out the next "Pretrial Estimate Questionnaire" and proceeded to the next trial.

There were two different types of trials: safety training trials and posttests. The length of all pre- and posttests was a constant 2 minutes. The subjects were told that each trial would last between 2 and 5 minutes. The safety trials were varied between 2 to 4 minutes in order to ensure that the subject was not able to predict when the experimenter would return.

The subject went through a series of safety trials which consisted of either having a candle lit and relevant information provided or having the candle not lit and irrelevant information provided. (The relevant information consisted of facts about oxygen availability and consumption, all very reassuring). The subjects were randomly assigned to these conditions. The number of safety trials varied, depending on the number of trials it took before the subjects' reported fear scores reduced to approximately half of the first reported fear score. At this point the first set of posttests were conducted. (However, if after five safety training trials, a subject showed no reduction of fear, the trials were stopped and the first set of posttests were conducted.) Posttest 1 was identical to the previous safety trials. In Posttest 2, the subjects received the condition opposite to their safety trials (i.e., candle lit or not lit). Forty-eight to 72 hours later, another two posttests were carried out; these were identical to the first set, and at the end of this session *S*s completed two "credibility" questionnaires concerning the information they had been given. A third set of posttests were conducted 1 month later, following the procedure used in the first set.

Results. Of the 26 subjects who took part in the study, 11 reported at least one panic or near-panic, while 9 reported at least two. None of the subjects left the room before a trial was completed. Over the entire sample, there was a total of 246 trials—safety trials and posttests combined. Of these 246, panic or near-panic was reported on 43 of them; approximately 17%. Fifteen subjects did not report any panics (see Table 14.3).

Of all the self-reports of panic or near-panic, 93% (40/43) were accompanied by at least three endorsements on the Panic Symptom Checklist. Table 14.4 lists the distribution of the commonly endorsed items on the panic checklist, both for panic and no-panic trials, and compares the distribution of subjects' reports of their commonly endorsed *cognitions* during panic and no-panic trials.

An *expected panic* was defined as one on which the subject's predicted panic score (from the Pre-Trial questionnaire) was greater than 50 (out of 100) and the *S* then panicked. An *unexpected panic* was one on which the subject's predicted panic score was less than or equal to 50 and then panicked. Similarly, an *accurately predicted (expected) no-panic* occurred when the subject was not expecting to panic (predicted panic score less than 50) and did not. An *over-*

TABLE 14.3
Expected and Unexpected Panic and No-panic ($n = 26$), over a Total of 246 Trials

		Reported a Panic/ Near-panic	
		Yes	*No*
Predicted panic	Less than/equal to 50/100	15	156
	Greater than 50/100	28	47

predicted (unexpected) no-panic was one in which a subject's predicted panic score was greater than 50 and the subject did *not* report a panic or near-panic.

The proportion of these four types of trials is shown in Table 14.3. As can be seen, 65% (28/43) of all panics were expected, and 77% (156/203) of all no-panics were accurately predicted; 37% (28/75) of all instances of a prediction of panic were accurate, and 63% (47/75) were disconfirmed; 91% (156/171) of all instances of prediction of no-panic were accurate, and 9% (15/171) were disconfirmed; 35% (15/43) of panics were not predicted.

TABLE 14.4

Symptoms	*Panic*	*No-panic*	*t (1-tailed)*
Shortness of breath	83%	53%	$t(10) = 2.84, p = .01$
Choking or smothering sensations	42%	13%	$t(10) = 2.41, p = .02$
Palpitations or accelerated heart rate	82%	47%	$t(10) = 3.04, p = .005$
Sweating	53%	30%	$t(10) = 1.97, p = .04$
Nausea or abdominal distress	30%	6%	$t(10) = 2.23, p = .03$
Trembling or shaking	38%	16%	$t(10) = 2.28, p = .03$
Fear of going crazy or doing something uncontrolled	10%	0%	$t(10) = 1.76, p = .05$

	Cognitions		
Cognitions	*Panic*	*No-panic*	*t (1-tailed)*
I am going to pass out	48%	25%	$t(10) = 2.38, p = .02$
I am going to suffocate	60%	28%	$t(10) = 2.49, p = .02$
I am going to lose control of myself	30%	8%	$t(10) = 2.19, p = .03$
I am going to panic	63%	16%	$t(10) = 4.35, p = .00$
I am going to run out of air to breathe	78%	37%	$t(10) = 3.98, p = .002$

*(Among the 11 subjects who reported having at least one panic, the % of panic trials in which a given cognition/symptom was endorsed was compared with the % of no-panic trials on which the symptom/cognition was endorsed. Significant differences were found for the symptoms shown.)

TABLE 14.5
Fear and Safety

	Panic	*Trial After*	*p (one-tailed)*
Predicted safety	53.0	51.9	N.S.
Reported safety	44.0	49.1	$t(8) = 2.88, p = .008$
Predicted fear	54.1	54.8	N.S.
Reported fear	60.9	54.0	$t(8) = 2.51, p = .01$

We examined the consequences of a panic on fear and safety; 23% (47/203) of all no-panics were instances of an overprediction of panic, as in the main study. The trends were nonsignificant but in the same direction as in the main study with the exception of predicted fear; on the average, predicted safety decreased and reported safety increased following a panic. Predicted fear remained the same and reported fear decreased following a panic (see Table 14.5).

The analyses of the effects of all panics, all no-panics, unexpected, and expected panics, and accurate and overpredicted no-panics were conducted in the following manner. Each dependent variable (Predicted Safety, Predicted Fear, Predicted Panic, Reported Safety, and Reported Fear) was summed over all relevant trials (all trials of, e.g., a panic) and over all trials directly following it. If there was a "gap" between these two trials—that is, the relevant trial was the last trial on a day and the subsequent trial took place on a different day—the subsequent trial score was not included in this summation. (An analysis was conducted, however, in which these "gapped" scores were included in these summations. The results were found to be very similar to those found when "gapped" scores were *not* included, but we chose to report the latter as they more closely represent the phenomenon under study. Two average scores were then computed for each dependent variable for each subject: the average score on the *relevant* trial and the average score on the *subsequent* trial. These two scores were then compared by means of a dependent measures *t*-test, which indicated any consistent differences in average scores for each dependent variable between the relevant trial and the trial directly following it.)

Presumably, all of the measures remained constant because no new information was accrued. After a correctly predicted no-panic trial, nothing changed (see Table 14.6). Following an overpredicted no-panic (i.e., a trial on which the subject expected to panic but did not—a disconfirmation) predicted fear, safety, and panic all changed. After these disconfirmations, reported fear decreased, but not significantly (Table 14.6).

Effects of Safety Information on Panics

Of the 13 subjects in the experimental group (those who received the safety information and had a lit candle in the room during their "training trials"), only

TABLE 14.6
Accurate and Overpredicted No-panics

	Accurate ($n = 24$)			Overpredicted ($n = 11$)		
	No-panic Trial	*Next Trial*	*p(one-tailed)*	*No-panic Trial*	*Next Trial*	*p(one-tailed)*
Predicted safety	67.3	68.6	$t(23) = .85$,NS	52.3	59.8	$t(10) = 3.3$, $p = .004$
Reported safety	71.4	72.7	$t(23) = .45$,NS	57.4	57.5	$t(10) = .04$,NS
Predicted fear	33.3	31.3	$t(23) = 1.2$,NS	62.5	55.1	$t(10) = 2.1$, $p = .03$
Reported fear	26.5	26.1	$t(23) = .21$,NS	58.7	49.1	$t(10) = 1.2$,NS
Predicted panic	24.2	22.7	$t(23) = 1.2$,NS	64.4	51.8	$t(10) = 2.4$, $p = .02$

1 experienced at least one panic. Of the 13 subjects in the control group (who received irrelevant information and an unlit candle during their training trials), 10 experienced at least one panic. The average number of panics per person in the experimental group was .31, while the average number of panics per person in the control group was 3.0 ($t(24) = 3.7, p = .001$). It appears that *the safety information reduced the frequency of panics.*

To determine if the *effects* of panic were also suppressed by the safety information, we examined only those panics experienced by the control group on their "training trials"—that is, before they received any safety information. As most of the panics examined in the overall "panic and its consequences" analysis reported earlier, were experienced by members of the control group—mostly in the training trials as habituation occurred by the time the posttests were executed, this present analysis was very similar to the one done on all trials including both groups of subjects. We still did not find entirely the same results with respect to the effects of a panic as we found in the two earlier studies (see Rachman, Levitt, & Lopatka, submitted for publication).

Did the First Panic Produce the Largest Increment?

In the first two experiments of this series (Rachman & Levitt, 1985), we were unable to detect a primacy effect—that is, the first panic did not produce exceptional effects. However, a recent result (Rachman & Lopatka, 1986a) from an experiment on the related subject of fear summation suggested that the first of two fear responses exerted a strong "pivotal" effect. We therefore checked the affect of the first panic on predictions of future panic in the latest study of panic (Rachman, Levitt, & Lopatka, 1987).

For each subject, a difference score was calculated in which the "Predicted Panic" score reported on the trial of the panic was subtracted from the "Predicted Panic" score reported on the trial following the panic, thus indicating the relative drop (a negative difference score) or increment (a positive difference score) in the "Predicted Panic" score following a panic trial. For each subject, two scores were then computed: the change in the "Predicted Panic" score following the first panic was compared with the average change in "Predicted Panic" scores following all other panic trials. It was found that the increment in "Predicted Panic" scores following the first panic averaged +17 across subjects, while the average increment following all subsequent panics across subjects was only +2, $t(8) = 2.84, p = .01$. This analysis was conducted on data from the subjects who experienced two or more panics ($n = 9$). It appears that the first panic did produce the largest increment in the prediction of the probability of future panics.

Did Subjects Report Greater Fear on Pre-panic Trials than on Pre-No-Panic Trials?

In view of Margraf et al. (1986a) recent interpretation of pharmacologically induced panics, in which they attribute importance to the baseline level of arousal, we decided to test whether a similar basebline effect could be detected in our psychologically induced panics. Two complementary analyses produced the same outcome.

For each subject, two average "Reported Fear" scores were calculated: one for all the trials preceding a panic trial and one for all trials preceding a trial upon which no-panic occurred (a no-panic trial). It was found that among those subjects who experienced two or more panics ($n = 9$), the average "Reported Fear" score before a panic trial was 56, while the average "Reported Fear" score before a no-panic trial was 42, $t(8) = 3.03$, $p = .01$). "Reported Fear" scores were found to be higher on the trial preceding a panic trial than those preceding a no-panic trial.

For each subject, two averages were calculated: the average number of symptoms endorsed (on the list of DSM–III symptoms of a panic, which contained 14 items) on the trials prior to a panic trial, and the average number of symptoms endorsed on the trial prior to a no-panic trial. It was found that among those subjects who experienced two or more panics ($n = 9$), the average number of symptoms endorsed prior to a panic trial was 5.3, while the average number of symptoms endorsed prior to a no-panic trial was 3.0, $t(8) = 3.50$, $p = .004$). Subjects endorsed more symptoms on the DSM–III checklist on trials prior to a panic, compared with trials prior to a no-panic.

These two related sets of results are consistent with the Margraf et al. (1986a) analysis, and if they can be confirmed, will have implications for predicting panics, for the interpretation of panic inductions, and possibly for the debate about whether panics are continuous or discontinuous with fear.

Did the Subjects Improve in their Ability to Predict their Panics?

With the emergence of clear evidence that fearful subjects can learn to predict their fears with increasing accuracy (Rachman & Lopatka, 1986a,b), we reanalyzed the results from our three studies of panic to determine whether people can learn to improve the accuracy of their predictions of panic.

To answer this question, we classified each trial into one of four categories: a hit (subject expected to panic and did); a surprise (subject did not expect to panic but did); an overprediction (subject expected to panic but did not); and, an accurate prediction (subject did not expect to panic and did not). (A "Predicted Panic" score of 50 or less was considered as "not expecting to panic," while a "Predicted Panic" score of greater than 50 was considered as "expecting to panic" in creating these categories.) These four categories were then collapsed into two: accurate predictions of panic/no-panic (hits and accurate predictions); and inaccurate predictions of panic/no-panic (surprises and overpredictions). For each trial, the number of subjects who accurately predicted their panic/no-panic is plotted against the number of subjects who inaccurately predicted their pan-

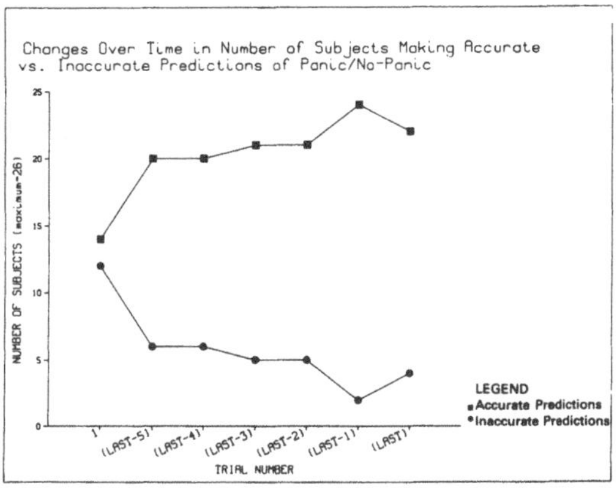

FIG. 14.11. The percentage of correct matches increased over trials.

ic/no-panic. This change in accuracy/inaccuracy in prediction of panic/no-panic over time is shown in Fig. 14.11.

The number of subjects who correctly predicted their panics increased over trials and the number who incorrectly predicted their panics/no-panics decreased. When these two categories were broken down into the four specific classes that have been mentioned, it become evident that in all three studies, it was mainly an increase in the accurate prediction of no-panic that accounted for the increase in accurate predictions of panic/no-panic, and it was mainly a decrease in the number of overpredictions of panics that accounted for the decrease in inaccurate predictions of panic/no-panic. This is partly explained by the fact that the absolute number of panics decreased over time for most subjects, and therefore, toward the end of each subject's participation he or she was not experiencing many panics to predict accurately or inaccurately.

Bodily Reactions and Cognitions During a Panic. Given the importance attached to the list of 14 symptoms incorporated in the DSM–III diagnosis of panic, we decided to check whether the ''symptoms'' endorsed after a predicted panic differed from those endorsed after an unpredicted panic. Barlow et al. (1985) concluded from their clinical study of the phenomena of panic that differences exist between these two types of panic (predicted and unpredicted) and that it is important to discover the nature of these differences. Actually, they found surprisingly few differences between the groups of patients who reported predicted and unpredicted panics. The patients who reported having had at least one unpredicted panic endorsed significantly more of the 14 symptoms than did those who reported a predicted panic, but there were no differences in severity or in patterning. Our results produced no significant difference in the number of items endorsed (a mean of 6.6 per unexpected panic, versus a mean of 5.4 per expected panic).

As our experimental design was directed at specific panic experiences, and included specific predictions of panic/no-panic, it provided us with an opportunity to determine whether predicted panics are accompanied by different "symptoms" (actually, 12 bodily sensations and 2 cognitions) than are unpredicted panics. We were also in a position to test the suggestion of Barlow et al. (1985) that, since 90% of their patients with unpredictable panic (panic disorders and agoraphobia with panic) reported loss of control and dizziness as symptoms, and since these 2 features seem to discriminate predictable from unpredictable panics so well, these factors may emerge as defining characteristics of unpredictable panic. The question was, do they emerge as defining characteristics of unpredictable panic in the present experiment? Our data (Rachman et al., to be submitted) failed to support the suggestion that dizziness and loss of control are defining characteristics of unpredictable panic. (On panic trials, choking, shortness of breath, palpitations, and trembling were reported more frequently than on no-panic trials).

Panic vs. No-panic

As far as panic cognitions are concerned, the most frequently reported were, in order: the possibility of running out of air, of suffocating, and of panicking (see Table 14.4). Thoughts of acting foolishly, being paralyzed by fear, or having a heart attack, were rarely reported. Perhaps of greater interest is the negative observation that during *no-panic* trials, 73% of the 26 subjects reported thoughts of suffocating at least once, and a similar number reported of running out of air. The question of greatest interest here is why these thoughts did *not* produce panics in these subjects on these occasions, as might be predicted by cognitive theorists (e.g., Beck & Emery, 1985; Clark, 1986a).

Of course it is unsurprising that our subjects had thoughts of suffocating or running out of air, as the experiment took place in a small, enclosed space. The cognitions were appropriate and lead one to believe that panic cognitions may well be situation-specific and threat-relevant. Accordingly, safety information should be made situation-specific and threat-relevant.

The Link Between Bodily Sensations and Fearful Cognitions

Beck (this volume) implies that there should be a logical relationship between the precipitating event and the specific sensations that are experienced during a panic episode. One can add that there should be a logical relationship between the specific cognition and the specific sensations.

We decided to examine this idea by reanalyzing the data collected in the course of testing out the influence of safety information on panics. After each test trial in a confined space, the mildly claustrophobic subjects completed the 14-item DSM–III checklist of symptoms and 10-item checklist of fearful cognitions.

Using only those trials on which a panic occurred, we matched each of the four most commonly reported cognitions, in turn, with the accompanying "symptoms" (bodily sensations), with the following result:

TABLE 14.7
Panic Trials ($N = 43$)

Cognition	*No. Panic Trials Cognition Endorsed (Max. 43)*	*Most Frequently Reported Bodily Sensations*
1. I am going to run out of air to breathe	36	Short of breath, dizziness, palpitations
2. I am going to suffocate	30	Short of breath, palpitations, dizziness
3. I am going to pass out	22	Dizziness, short of breath, palpitations
4. I am going to lose control	18	Palpitations, short of breath, dizziness

The connection between the particular cognitions and shortness of breath is as expected, but there is no obvious reason for these cognitions to be accompanied by palpitations. Why should a fear of suffocation by accompanied of palpitations? More puzzling, why should palpitations be "catastrophically misinterpreted (Clark, 1986a)" as a sign of impending suffocation?

We also matched the four most commonly reported bodily sensations (symptoms) with the accompanying cognitions, using panic trials only.

TABLE 14.8
Panic Trials

Bodily Sensation	*No. Panic Trials Sensation Endorsed (Max. 43)*	*Cognitions*
1. Shortness of breath	38	Suffocate, panic, run out of air
2. Palpitations or accelerated heart rate	38	Run out of air, suffocate, panic
3. Dizziness, light-headedness, or unsteady feelings	34	Run out of air, suffocate, panic
4. Sweating	23	Run out of air, suffocate, panic

The bodily sensations of shortness of breath and of dizziness fit well with the reported cognitions, and the situation, but the associations between palpitations and the cognitions of suffocation and running out of air are less obvious.

Overall, the results were broadly consistent with Beck's idea and our elaboration to include a link between cognitions and sensations. However, in view of the crucial role allocated to fearful cognitions in the induction of panics (see especially Beck, this volume, and Clark, 1986a, and this volume), we also checked all the panic trials for evidence of panics that may have occurred in the absence of a fearful cognition, or at least in the absence of a cognition included in our checklist. The results were consistent with the theories of Beck and Clark. We found no instances of panic without an accompanying (preceding?) fearful cognition.

Marshall (this volume) draws attention to the need to account for instances in which panics might be expected, but fail to occur. With this point in mind, we questioned whether there were instances in which the subject reported one or more of the fearful cognitions, but failed to panic.

Overall, panic trials were accompanied by more fearful cognitions and more bodily sensations than were no-panic trials, but we did uncover examples of no-panic in which subjects reported one or more of the fearful cognitions or bodily symptoms.

The pattern of fearful cognitions and of accompanying bodily sensations reported on these no-panic trials resembles the pattern on panic trials. It remains possible that the differences between panic and no-panic trials are those of intensity, but at present, we are not in a position to explain the non-occurrence of panics in these instances.

Perhaps the fearful cognitions are necessary but not sufficient. If so, then what factors glide a fearful cognition from insufficient to sufficient? Clark (1986a) would argue that appropriate bodily sensations must be misinterpreted (a catastrophic, erroneous cognition) to induce a panic.

TABLE 14.9
No-panic Trials (n = 203)

Accompanying Cognitions	*Main Accompanying Bodily Sensations*
1. I am going to run out of air to breathe (79/203 = 39%)	1. Shortness of breath (96/203 = 47%)
2. I am going to suffocate (65/203 = 32%)	2. Dizziness, light-headedness, or unsteady feelings (93/203 = 46%)
3. I am going to pass out (50/203 = 25%)	3. Palpitations or accelerated heart rate (79/203 = 39%)
4. I am going to panic (15/203 = 7%)	4. Sweating (59/203 = 29%)

As a further question, we therefore looked for examples of panics that were accompanied by fearful cognitions but not by bodily sensations. According to Clark's theory, presumably there should be no panics in the absence of relevant bodily sensations. Fully consistent, we found no instances of panic in which the subject failed to report relevant bodily sensations. All panics were accompanied by at least two bodily sensations, and usually many more. To conclude

1. All panics were accompanied (or preceded) by fearful cognitions and by relevant bodily sensations,
2. The frequencies of these cognitive and bodily reports were greater on panic trials than on nonpanic trials,
3. Evidence of direct connections between cognitions and bodily sensations was found (but some connections are not fitting),
4. No-panics occurred even in the presence of fearful cognitions and bodily sensations.

These findings are compatible with the cognitive theories of Beck (this volume) and of Clark (1986a and this volume), and can indeed be taken as supportive. The nonoccurrence of panics, even when the person had a fearful cognition, can be absorbed by the cognitive theories (e.g., inappropriate/weak thought, absence of appropriate bodily sensation), but further inquiry is obviously necessary. The potential problem of untestability does, however, arise from these anticipated counterarguments. Interestingly, these no-panics cannot be accounted for by individual differences (See Rachman et al., to be submitted for publication). In cognitive theories (e.g., Beck & Clark) it is postulated that people will be found to differ in panic-proneness; this is, of course, plausible but cannot explain the no-panics in our study because they were reported by subjects who did panic on some occasions (see previous discussion of discussion of threat relevance).

Summary

To sum up the results of the recently completed safety signal study, the estimated probability of a panic was increased after a panic experience, and reduced after a no-panic experience. Forty-two percent of the subjects experienced at least one panic in the enclosed space, and these were usually (93%) accompanied by at least three endorsements from the DSM–III panic checklist. Many of the panics (65%) were correctly predicted, but there was a very high rate of overprediction (63%). The effects of panics on predicted and reported safety and fear scores that were noted in earlier research were confirmed only in part. The differences can be attributed to the obscuring effects of the safety information, and these effects were in turn influenced by the credibility of the information (see Rachman et al., submitted for publication, for a full discussion). Although there were some differences in the bodily reactions reported to accompany the predicted and unpredicted panics, they did not support the suggestion that dizziness and loss of control are key characteristics of unpredicted panics. There were no instances of panics without an accompanying cognition. *The cognitions that were reported during the panics were threat-relevant.*

Bodily sensations showed specificity and some nonspecificity; palpitations were reported across various cognitions. There were many instances in which the fearful cognitions and bodily sensations were present but the subject did not panic.

If the *cognitions* that precede and/or accompany panics do prove to be threat-relevant (and situation-specific), as can be deduced from the cognitive theory, it will give rise to an apparent conflict with the prevailing view (as seen in DSM–III–R, e.g.) in which the unexpectedness of "spontaneous" panics is given a critical place. Phenomenologically, these are the panics that are reported to "come out of the blue." The resolution of this aspect of panic experiences promises an interesting journey.

Can We Distinguish Situational and Spontaneous Panics?

Biological theorists have attached importance to the distinction between situational and spontaneous panic attacks (increasingly referred to as "unexpected"), and the distinction is now incorporated in DSM–III–R.

As has been noted, we were unable to find support for Barlow et al.'s (1985) proposed distinction between predictable and unpredictable panics, using the items on the DSM–III checklist. Nor are there grounds, at present, to assert that predictable and unpredictable panics (or expected vs. unexpected panics, to use those terms) differ in the psychophysiological patterns associated with each.

Here we need to bear in mind the range of psychophysiological patterns associated with panic. Thus far it has not been possible to isolate a specific psychophysiological pattern that distinguishes satisfactorily between panic and no-panic, so the search for a pattern that will distinguish between *types* of panic may be a lengthy one (see, e.g., the report by Taylor et al. 1986a, p. 482, of an absence of differences in heart rate responding during situational and spontaneous panics). Nevertheless, the differences that are emerging in the cognitive aspects of expected and unexpected panics may well lead to the discovery of psychophysiological differences in due course, given that the present proposal for distinguishing between types of panic proves to be useful and provides a basis for further analysis.

A simple method for prising apart expected and unexpected panics arises from earlier research on the matching of predicted and reported fear responses (Rachman & Lopatka, 1986a,b) and the matching of predicted and reported panics (Rachman & Levitt, 1985). Subjects are asked to predict how much fear they will experience on their next exposure to a fear object situation, and then after the exposure, they report how much fear they actually experienced. The predictions and reports are made on a 0–100 visual analogue scale, and it is a simple matter to match the predicted fear score and the reported fear score. The same method has been used in assessing panics. Subjects are asked to predict the probability (0–100) of having a panic on the pending exposure, and after the exposure, they report the intensity and occurrence of the experienced panic, if any.

When prediction and report match, the panic is classed as expected; when the report exceeds or falls short of the prediction, the panic is classed as unexpected. It has proved necessary to distinguish between two types of unexpected panic: the overpredicted and the underpredicted. So, in addition to the broad division into expected and unexpected panics, subtypes emerge:

- *Expected* panics, in which prediction and report match,
- *Expected* no-panics, in which prediction and report match,
- *Unexpected* panics, in which report exceeds prediction (underpredicted),
- *Unexpected* no-panics, in which the prediction of panic is not confirmed.

This method of analysis can be made more precise by using a refined method (Rachman, Levitt, & Lopatka, 1987), in which the *degree* of unexpectedness is calculated. Rather than classifying matches into broad categories the extent of the mismatch is calculated.

Using the original, simple method, we were able to detect differences in anticipation, and differences in the consequences of panics (Rachman & Levitt, 1985). Many of these are described in the present chapter (e.g., unexpected panics tend to be more damaging). The best alternative or complementary method for distinguishing between expected and unexpected panics, and the one that is the basis for all current systems, is of course, phenomenological. Unexpected panics are those that are reported by the patient to, "come out of the blue." Many patients insist on distinguishing these experiences from other experiences of anxiety or fear, but their claims have some drawbacks when used as the main basis for making a categorical distinction between unexpected ("spontaneous") panics and expected ("situational") panics. In addition to the potential for nonvalid, retrospective reporting, their distinction may be found to rest on individual differences in the ability to identify and/or describe subtle cognitive and physiological changes, and may not be a reliable guide.

At present, the matching method appears to offer important advantages for research studies, and for restricted clinical use—restricted because of the practical problems involved in collecting predictions and reports, and the weakness of relying on retrospective estimates of predicted and reported panics and no-panics. A partial answer is to avoid reliance on retrospective estimates and to start collecting prospective data from the patients at the earliest possible time. A comparison of the matching method and phenomenological accounts will be of considerable interest.

PANIC, COGNITIONS, AND FEAR

The main points of interest in the research that we have described are the nature and frequency of panics, and their influence on subsequent fear and expectations of future fear. A second focus of interest, one that arises mainly from the stimulating writings of Mineka (1985), Mineka and Kihlstrom (1979), Seligman (1968, 1975) and Seligman and Binik (1977), is the role of predictability in determining and moderating panics. Thirdly, the research introduced a novel experimental method for analyzing panics and their consequences. Most of the following discussion is concerned with panic and its consequences, regardless of the operation of safety factors; the clarification of their influence will, in due course, lead to a fuller and more complex analysis.

The results are compatible with theories that postulate a causal connection between panics and the onset of conditional anxiety (and perhaps, of escape behavior as well). The only point at which the match fails is in the fear scores reported after a panic. Panics were followed by reductions in predicted safety and by increases in expected fear—but not by increases in *reported* fear. In this sense, the result comes very close to Klein's (1980) view, as well as that of learning theorists. It will be recalled that Zitrin, Woerner, and Klein (1981) postulated that, "as a result of these panics, they develop anticipatory anxiety" (p. 27). Yes, they do anticipate anxiety. However, their anticipation exceeds the amount of fear experienced in the event. This is not unlike agoraphobics (and other phobic subjects) whose expectations exceed the amount of fear that they experience; when they are persuaded to go shopping or to use a bus, not infrequently they express surprise at how little fear is experienced. It could be therefore, that *a main effect of panic is precisely to increase anticipatory anxiety*.

The Effects of Panic on Later Fear May be Minor. To recall a phrase used by Chambless and Goldstein (1980), panic engenders a "fear of fear, and an excessive fear of fear at that. The results contain several facets that may be of therapeutic significance, but the most obvious is the decline in fear observed after *disconfirmations* of high fear (see Seligman & Johnston, 1973). It is of great interest, too, that panics increase *expected* fear but do not seem to increase reported fear.

The finding that expected no-panics are followed by little or no change gives rise to the possibility that exposure-based treatments will produce little or no change on patients' "good days." And that in turn leads to a seemingly paradoxical idea that panic patients, especially those of the agoraphobic type, will benefit most from sessions given on their "bad days"!

The important connections between predictability and controllability of stress have been skillfully analyzed by Seligman (1968, 1975) in his classic contributions, Mineka (1985) and others, but there is nothing in the present research to contribute to that aspect of the subject because we did not measure controllability. So far we have confined our attention to predictability.

Unpredictable and potentially aversive events can be damaging and result in motivational and learning deficits, as well as emotional disturbances (Mineka & Kihlstrom, 1979; Seligman, 1968, 1975; Seligman & Binik, 1977). Broadly, organisms prefer predictability, even in potentially aversive circumstances; predictability may also serve to blunt the effects of an aversive event (Alloy & Tabachnik, 1984; Mineka & Henderson, 1985). The *loss* of predictability may produce more profound disturbances than mere lack of predictability (Mineka & Kihlstrom, 1979). Predictability may have proactive effects that become evident only when subjects experience stressors some time after acquiring predictability (Mineka & Hendersen, 1985). It should also be remembered that perceptions of prediction and control may be inflated (e.g., Alloy & Abramson, 1982) and thereby provide unfounded reassurance. In the present findings, the false predictions went in the opposite direction. The subjects overpredicted their fears, and if anything, this may have undermined rather than boosted their illusory self-confidence. Butler and Mathews (1983) found that relative to controls, anxious patients overpredict the probable occurrence of negative events, in a manner consistent with the present results.

We were not able to adduce evidence of a blunting effect, in that the fear levels reported on predicted panic trials did not differ from the levels reported on unpredicted panic trials. However, we did find evidence to support the claim that unpredicted panics were more damaging than predicted panics. Subsequent to unexpected panics, the subjects' predicted fear scores rose and their predicted safety scores dropped sharply. In a sense, this is evidence of the proactive effects of an unpredicted aversive event, even if the time intervals were short. It will be an easy matter to check these proactive effects of unpredictability over a longer period of time, and it is a task well worth undertaking.

We were unable to find evidence to support the notion that a loss of predictability had greater effects than a mere lack of predictability, but this conclusion is based on too few cases of shifts from prediction to loss. The question is an important one and remains to be addressed.

The Disconfirmation of an Expected Panic was Followed by a Significant Reduction in Fear. This potentially useful finding is consistent with Seligman and Johnston's (1973) cognitive theory of avoidance, in which disconfirmations of expected aversiveness play a central role (see also Rachman, 1983, for some clinical implications). It is not too far-fetched to consider the therapeutic value of basing a course of treatment training on systematically repeated disconfirmations of expected panics (e.g., Rachman, 1983). Additionally, the question arises as to whether we can produce a dependable procedure for increasing the patient's expectation of panic, thereby preparing the way for the disconfirming experience?

The evidence shows that unpredicted panics contribute to increases in predicted fear and to decreases in predicted safety. There is no evidence of predictability blunting the level of fear, and we could find no support for the distinct effects of a loss of predictability. The inflation of expected fear, and the reduction in safety observed after a panic, may be of considerable clinical interest.

Mismatches

The concept of mismatches between expectation and event often features in discussions of habituation and of conditioning. It is argued that mismatches are mainly responsible for the changes in responding, perhaps by virtue of the fact that a mismatch is more informative than a confirmed expectation. (The similarity between our findings on this topic, referred to in various parts of this chapter, and the Rescorla–Wagner (1972) model of conditioning has not passed unnoticed. The extent of the similarity, and its implications, will require much thought and effort (see Seligman, this volume), but should perhaps be postponed until the present work can be placed on a firmer basis.) There is a strong tendency to overpredict one's fear responses—that is, to expect to be more frightened than one turns out to be (Rachman & Lopatka, 1986a,b). Although the subjects began by overpredicting, they readily learned how to correct these errors. After a correct match between predicted and reported fear, predictions of fear remained unchanged. However, predicted fear *increased* after the subjects had made an underprediction—that is, after they had experienced greater fear than expected. By contrast, predicted fear decreased after overpredictions, these findings have been replicated and their relation to panic is under active consideration (Rachman & Lopatka, 1986b).

Although the role of matching was not directly addressed in the main study of panic (Rachman & Levitt, 1985), the data on mismatches are incidental, but not without interest. There are indications that mismatches between expectations of panics and the occurrence or nonoccurrence of panics, are indeed more influential than matches. This finding is consistent with the research on fear matching referred to herein. In the main panic study, (a) unexpected panics were followed by larger changes than expected panics, and (b) disconfirmed predictions of panic were followed by larger changes than confirmed predictions of no-panic. To put it another way:

- Unexpected panics are followed by large changes;
- Disconfirmed predictions of panic are followed by large changes;

- But confirmed predictions of panic are followed by little or no change;
- Confirmed predictions of no-panic are followed by little or no change.

These findings will need to be substantiated in fuller studies in which the analyses of mismatches are incorporated in the original design. Then it will become possible to measure the informational value of matches and mismatches, and to relate these to changes in responding. If the analysis of panics in terms of matches or mismatches proves to be successful, it will of course have wider implications.

A Note on Safety Signals. At various points in this chapter, attention has been drawn to the influence of safety signals on panic, and some elucidation is necessary (a fuller analysis of fear and safety signals is given by Rachman, 1984a). As Seligman and Binik (1977) have argued, safety signals limit fear in time and in space. Similarly, they should help to limit panics in time and in space—perhaps not as dependably or as effectively, but nevertheless. Although the influence of safety signals can more easily be incorporated into a cognitive theory of panic, they can help to explain some biological findings, such as the influence of laboratory setting and instructions on panics that are induced by biological interventions (e.g., van den Hout, this volume; Margraf et al., 1986a).

Incorporation of a safety perspective into cognitive theory may expand its explanatory value. In the presence of safety cues, bodily reactions and the ensuing cognitions that might promote a panic, can be inhibited. Predictively, the probability of a panic occurring should be reduced by the introduction of a safety signal. To take a hypothetical example, the panic-inducing effects of hyperventilation should be inhibited by mere knowledge of the availability of titrated amounts of CO_2 that will rapidly restore normal feelings. Palpitations are less likely to proceed to a panic in a hospital than in remote solitude, and so on. Note that the safety signals should be connected to the panic cognitions; specific and explicable connections are demanded of cognitive theory.

Predictively, safety signals should play a major role in shaping and maintaining the *behavioral consequences* of panic. The affected person should seek out, and develop, safety procedures and signals. Applying cognitive theory, these safety procedures should show clear and explicable connections to the panic cognitions. Panics induced by a fear of a heart attack should lead to the adoption of safety procedures that are believed by the person to reduce the likelihood of such an attack (e.g., carrying tranquilizing tablets, gentle exercise, etc.). Those which are induced by a fear of choking should lead to the selection of soft foods and liquids. Some safety signals are irrational, but presumably reflect the person's misguided belief, such as an agoraphobic woman who coped with her fear of loss of control by carrying a gag and rope that her husband was instructed to use if she behaved in a grossly abnormal manner (they were never used, or required, but she was unable to travel without them!).

The psychophysiological consequences of panic should be modified by safety signals in much the same way that is, they should be inhibited by the presence of such signals.

The influence of safety signals on the *cognitive consequences* of panic is implicit in much of cognitive therapeutic procedures, but has yet to be analyzed systematically. At this early stage, a most interesting question is why the provision of safety information appears to require validating confirmation by behavioral reheasal (including exposure).

Clinical Significance of Panic. From a clinician's point of view, the interpretation of the experimental findings depends to a degree on whether or not the panics reported by the present subjects are comparable with the panics described by patients with agoraphobic or other anxiety disorders. (A general discussion of the utility of so-called analogue research is provided by Borkovec & Rachman, 1979.) The problem can be put in the form of two questions: Are the panics in the present study comparable with "clinical panics," and if they are not, how does that affect the interpretation of these data?

The differences between clinical panics and these laboratory panics include the following. Clinical panics occur in people with diagnosed psychiatric disorders, and the present research was conducted on mildly claustrophobic subjects, i.e. we are dealing with different samples. Secondly, the laboratory panics occur under controlled and contained conditions; the training trials are discrete, planned, and limited—and are known by the subjects to be so. The subjects are not told to expect panics, but they are asked to predict the likelihood of a panic. Furthermore, those subjects who experienced panics on at least one trial, were aware of the possibility of further panics. In contrast, clinical panics are not contained, and carry a risk of significant uncontrollability. They may be more difficult to predict. In any event, the general risks to one's well-being are minimal in laboratory panics, but can be considerable if a panic occurs in the course of everyday living. Clinically, one can distinguish between spontaneous panics (see the recent findings of Taylor et al., 1986) and situational (provoked) attacks, such as the panics elicited by a trip on public transport. The panics in our study fall into the second category, and come closer to the "provoked" panics characteristic of agoraphobia, claustrophobia, etc.

The major similarity between laboratory and clinic panics is that in both cases the person reports "a sudden onset of intense apprehension, fear, or terror." As in the DSM–III system, the "most common symptoms experienced during an attack are dyspnea, palpitations, chest pain or discomfort, choking or smothering sensations, feelings of unreality, paresthesias, hot and cold flashes, sweating, faintness, trembling or shaking, and fear of dying, going crazy or doing something uncontrolled during the attack. Attacks usually last minutes; more rarely, hours" (APA, DSM–III, p. 230). These symptoms form the basis for the DSM checklist.

To assess the similarity between the panics observed in our laboratory and clinical panics, we asked our subjects to complete the DSM–III checklist of 12 symptoms as soon as they came out of the test room. (In the Barr Taylor studies of panic (Taylor et al., 1986), at least 3 of the 12 symptoms were required to meet the criterion of a panic attack.) As reported here, the results of our main study showed that in 75% of the 67 reported panics the subject endorsed at least 3 of the 12 symptoms. In the second study, 93% of the panics were accompanied by at least three endorsements.

As the DSM–III definition states, "The essential features (of panic disorder) are recurrent (anxiety) attacks that occur at times unpredictably" (p. 230), it was necessary to measure the predictability of our laboratory panics. As mentioned earlier, roughly 20% of the reported panics were unpredicted in the main study, and 35% in the last study. In terms of reported bodily "symptoms" and the proportion of unpredicted panics, the laboratory panics and clinical panics share some common features. The intensity and extensity of the bodily reactions are greater in clinical panics, and research on clinical panics will permit a comparison between the frequencies of unpredicted panics in the laboratory and the clinical phenomenon.

These *effects* of laboratory and clinical panics are likely to share important features, and data gathered in the course of carrying out a clinical trial of a behavioral treatment of agoraphobia, revealed the following: During those weeks in which the patients reported experiencing at least one panic, their sense of controllability declined in 50% of the instances (Rachman, Craske, Tallman et al., 1986). In those weeks that were free of panics, control declined by only 22%. In addition, *increased* controllability was recorded in 42% of instances during panic-free weeks (versus only a 25% increase during panic weeks).

At this stage of the research, the conservative course is to assume that the differences between laboratory and clinical panics outweigh the similarities. A test of the laboratory findings in a clinical sample must be addressed in due course. (The results of a clinical study, not available earlier, have now revealed important similarities to the laboratory findings.)

SUMMARY AND CONCLUSIONS

The advantages of studying panic as a fear phenomenon are set out and a Langian three-system analysis adopted. The *behavioral* consequences of panic often take the form of avoidance behavior but there are important exceptions. Avoidance can develop after nonpanic experiences, panics are reported by patients who do not display avoidance, and panics are reported by nonpatient samples who do not display avoidance behavior. In sum, panic and avoidance often are connected but panics can occur without avoidance emerging, and avoidance can occur without panics. These examples of the independent development of fear and avoidance recall earlier theoretical problems with the Mowrer two-stage theory. At present, it seems probable that panic-related avoidance (and the equally important *nonoccurrence* of avoidance after panic) is determined by fear levels, the predictability of panic, the cognitions associated with panic and safety, and the operation of safety signals.

The *cognitive* consequences of panic include the following: Subject to possible moderation by safety signals, panics are followed by increases in predictions of future panics. Panics are followed by increases in expected fear, but not in reported fear. They are also followed by expectations of reduced safety. Unexpected panics contribute most to these changes in prediction. Expected panics have little effect on reports or predictions of fear or of safety. Disconfirmed expectations of panic are followed by reductions in fear. Subjects correctly predict roughly one in three laboratory panics, but show a high rate of overprediction.

The *psychophysiological* consequences of panic have yet to be analyzed, but four postulates can be formulated: (a) Unpredicted panics are likely to be followed by increases in tonic level of arousal; (b) Unpredicted panics are likely to be followed by the development of conditioned psychophysiological reactions; (c) The consequences of predicted panics will be different and show little or no sign of these changes; and (d) Repeated experiences of predicted or unpredicted no-panics will be followed by reduced levels of tonic arousal and the extinction of any conditioned psychophysiological reactions.

Immediate Consequences of Panic. Most panics are distressing and some patients report that they are left exhausted and incapable for as long as 24 hours after an episode. Beck (this volume) states that, during the height of an episode, the subjects' cognitive abilities are impaired, and they find it difficult to access corrective information (Teasdale, this volume). If these suggestions are confirmed, they will bring to the fore an impediment to the full implementation of aspects of cognitive therapy, especially the distraction techniques advocated by Beck (this volume) and others. Other cognitive and perceptual consequences of panic include a possible state-dependent (Eich, 1980) loss of skill knowledge, and an unadaptively narrow focusing of attention of the type described in the four studies by Baddeley (1972).

Research. Several recommendations for further research flow from the work already completed. Starting from the premise that the consequences of panic are at least as important as the panic itself, we need to collect a great deal of information about the behavioral and psychophysiological consequences of panic. The laboratory procedure described here needs to be expanded to include psychophysiological recordings and behavioral measures. The extent to which the laboratory findings are applicable to clinical settings is an important empirical question.

As far as the reported findings are concerned, they remain tentative until replications are completed and they may need to be tailored to incorporate the influence of safety signals—an important phenomenon in its own right. A large number of behavioral, cognitive, and psychophysiological postulates are available for stepping-stones. Finally, best and most rapid progress is likely to be achieved by construing panic and its consequences as a phenomenon of the psychology of fear, rather than as a pathological condition.

15

An Appraisal of Expectancies, Safety Signals, and the Treatment of Panic Disorder Patients

W. L. Marshall
Queen's University

It has been suggested (e.g., Beck, Emery, & Greenberg, 1985; Clark, 1986a; Rachman, 1984a) that cognitive factors are relevant to the development and modification of panic disorders. Beck, Clark, and Salkovski (see chapters in this volume) propose that catastrophizing thoughts are crucial to the maintenance of these problems and that such thoughts must be changed if treatment is to be effective. These remarks are very much in the tradition of cognitive therapy, which in recent years has turned to experimental cognitive psychology for its theoretical referents and practical strategies (see chapters by Chambless and Teasdale in this volume). Rachman, on the other hand, derives his analyses from the study of basic learning processes in animals where the consideration of cognitive factors has excited interest over the past 10 years (Hulse, Fowler, & Honig, 1976). From these sources Rachman has recognized the possibility of applying what amounts to an analysis of the role of expectancies, to the understanding of the development and treatment of panics.

Michelson gives consideration to the comparative value of cognitive interventions against the more traditional behavioral therapies or pharmacological treatments. His evaluations encompass several methodologically sound studies, which vary the types of treatment offered. Telch reports one treatment study which simply compared exposure treatment with imipramine; however, his discussion of the beneficial effects of the drug are relevant to issues involved in cognitive therapy.

PANICS AND THEIR CONSEQUENCES

Rachman outlines his view of the relationships between cognitions and the physiological and behavioral features of people who experience panics. However, the cognitions which concern him are quite different from those which have been identified by other researchers whose theoretical positions have been labeled "cognitive" or "cognitive-behavioral." These latter theoreticians have focused on underlying cognitive "schema," which are said to guide the way in which people characteristically construe their world, or on cognitions (e.g., catastrophizing thoughts) which arise once the panic process is initiated. Rachman's interest is in the thoughts that individuals entertain about the possibility that a particular situation will induce a panic (predictions of panic) and about their identification of situational features which will moderate their predictions (i.e., safety signals). While this perspective on panics is novel and is sufficiently well articulated that numerous experimental tests are readily identifiable, it is still in its formative stages. In order for their value to be realized, Rachman's views will require a greater degree of specificity as research progresses. There can be little doubt, however, that Rachman's clear exposition and insightful observations will generate the kind of research that will increase knowledge and refine our treatment approaches. What follows are some observations which may lead to the kind of clarification and spcificity necessary to increase the value of Rachman's theorizing.

One of the most pressing needs, not only for Rachman's theory but also for the whole area of research and treatment, concerns a more precise specification of what is meant by "avoidance." Rachman describes postulates that define whether or not increases or decreases in avoidance will result from the confirmation or disconfirmation of expectations regarding the occurrence of panics. He does not define clearly the nature of these proposed changes in avoidance. Does he mean that all avoidant tendencies across all situations will decrease or increase? I doubt he meant this. There is likely to be considerable situational specificity of avoidance behavior, but some elements of a general disposition may be understood behaviorally in terms of generalization of learned responses or cognitively in terms of a guiding schema.

Furthermore, does the term "decreases" mean that the intensity or vigor of avoidance will be changed, or that particular instances of avoidance will be eliminated, or that the frequency with which avoidance is enacted will be reduced? Avoidance, of course, is not the only behavioral sign of anxiety. Indeed, in some patients, who at least occasionally experience panics or near-panics, avoidance is not obvious (e.g., anxious public speakers, and particularly those patients diagnosed as panic disordered without avoidance, but also perhaps even those with generalized anxiety disorder). Patients often engage in subtle avoidance (e.g., lack of eye contact), but it is important not to neglect, even in agoraphobics, the overt manifestations of anxiety as important behavioral indicators of both the nature of panics and the processes of change. These remarks are not meant to challenge the value of Rachman's theorizing, but rather to draw attention to the need to refine the theory progressively.

Rachman's point that unpredictable panics will have the most damaging effects is astute and is not likely to raise objections from anyone. The one postulate with which I have most difficulty, however, appears to be crucial to the theory. Postulate 4 states that "After a predicted panic there will be no change in avoidance behavior, or a decrease in such behavior." The truth of this claim depends on which stage in the process we are discussing. In considering the etiology of the marked avoidance behavior which characterizes panic agoraphobics, quite the opposite of this postulate seems to be true. From patients' descriptions of their etiology, extensive avoidance seems to develop as a result of the confirmation of their generalized expectancies of experiencing panics. Typically, patients describe initially experiencing spontaneous panics which evoke feelings of apprehension that the same, but also similar situations, will produce panics. These expectations are confirmed with sufficient frequency to produce a degree of generalized dread which can only be diminished by a marked curtailing of activities, resulting in the characteristically widespread avoidance seen in agoraphobia. Rachman may be correct (and his experimental data bear on this issue) that once generalized avoidance is entrenched, further confirmations of expected panics do not exacerbate the problem. Could this finding be due to ceiling effects? Avoidance is so all-encompassing that there is no possibility of further restrictions developing. Even here it is inconsistent with clinical experience to claim that such confirmations will lead to a reduction in avoidance behavior. Furthermore Marshall, Gauthier, Christie, Currie, and Gordon (1977) arranged to confirm the worst fears that our subjects held about their possible encounter with their phobic object. The results of this study revealed that confirmations of expected distress either increased avoidance or at best did not change it. While these subjects had circumscribed phobias rather than panic disorders, the findings do not encourage confidence in Rachman's postulate. In any case, this particular postulate requires modification toward greater specification of its relevance to the temporal sequence in the development of avoidance.

Postulate 5(b) also requires some minor qualifications. This postulate declares that "After disconfirmed predictions of panic, decreases in avoidance behavior will occur gradually and slowly." This statement matches the observation of the beneficial effects of certain treatment procedures (e.g., exposure-based treatments). It does not specify the optimal conditions relevant to the effectiveness of these procedures. Optimal conditions for exposure-based treatments require that the subject remain in the situation long enough for anxiety and distress to abate (Marshall & Segal, in press) presumably so that (in Rachman's terms) disconfirmation of expected distress in response to the situation can occur. Similarly, long-term, posttreatment reductions in avoidance appear to be maximized by learning coping responses during exposure (Marshall, 1985).

Rachman notes that panic patients are excessively cautious and have a reduced risk-taking style, and this is why decreases in avoidance, when they occur, do so very slowly. Perhaps he means to suggest a prepanic dispositional style, and it is this predisposition which causes them to develop their disorder while others who have occasional or isolated panics do not. In this respect Rachman's remarks sound very like Beck's suggestion that maladaptive deep cognitive schemata guide the behavior of panic patients. While it is essential, in the interest of good theorizing in this area, to point to why only a few of the many people who experience panics go on to develop a disorder, it is likely that this cautious personal style is derived from the experience of panics rather than a precursor. However it is said to have developed, several theorists, Rachman among them, are pointing to the disadvantageous nature of more enduring cognitive styles. If they are correct, these cognitive styles will need to be modified if treatment is to have lasting benefits.

The most significant moderating variable in Rachman's analysis of panic concerns the operation of "safety signals." Essentially these are features of the environment which the patient takes to indicate that he or she will be safe from the threat of a panic attack. Of course, the most significant feature of the environment which signals safety is the place to which the fearful patient escapes when threatened so that in a very important sense the so-called avoidance response is in fact an approach response to a "safety zone." There are other safety signals, not the least of which is a reassuring friend or therapist, and Rachman mentions these, but he is most concerned to point to additional signals (including information) which may enhance the feeling of safety in a patient. The provision of these additional safety signals, so Rachman suggests, will reduce avoidant behavior and he seems to intimate that such procedures could be beneficially added to therapy. However, while information which may correct erroneous, fear-evoking assumptions would clearly be valuable, serious problems may arise, as I will note subsequently, with extending this notion that information about safety signals can be utilized in treatment.

Some animal researchers (e.g., Gray, 1981; LoLordo, 1969) have suggested that avoidance behavior is maintained not simply by the negatively reinforcing effects of escape from a noxious stimulus (i.e., the UCS which might be shock in animal research or panic in human patients, or a CS which has in the past signaled the onset of the UCS), but rather by the positively reinforcing effect of attaining safety. In this view the escape chamber (and any stimuli associated with it) in avoidance training acquires incentive value by being consistently paired with a positive state.

To illustrate the experimental demonstration of this view, and to make clear its basis, I will briefly describe two series of studies involving animals. Weisman and Litner (1969) showed that a previously established Pavlovian conditioned inhibitor (CS-) of fear (i.e., a stimulus signaling a shock-free period), modified the rate of Sidman avoidance responding in an expected manner. In this particular experimental procedure, the animal was placed in a wheel chamber and was required to turn the wheel in order to avoid shocks. Rate of avoidant responding was increased during DRH schedules (i.e., differential reinforcement of high response rates) and decreased during DRL schedules (i.e., differential reinforcement of low rates of responding). In a later experiment, Weisman and Litner (1972) demonstrated that these safety signals (CS-) acquired an eliciting function, the effects of which were more powerful when acquired through avoidance training than through the usual procedures for instilling a stimulus with safety signal properties. Similarly, Beninger (1983) describes a series of experiments in which dopamine (thought to mediate incentive learning) was blocked in rats during typical avoidance training procedures. These animals acquired escape responding (as evidenced by progressively reduced latencies over trials to escape after shock onset) and they also acquired Pavlovian conditioned fear to the warning signal (as evidenced by autonomic signs of fear and tests which indicate the degree of suppression of a previously established response in the presence of the warning signal). They did not, however, acquire the usual avoidance responding, while animals whose dopamine functions were not blocked, did. Beninger takes these results to indicate that in the dopamine-blocked animals the safety signals (i.e., the stimuli associated with relief from shock) failed to be endowed with incentive value, which of course, implies that in the normally functioning rats the safety signals are incentive-laden.

In terms of the extrapolation of these observations to human phobic behavior, several points, which do not entirely agree with Rachman's view, seem to be important: (a) the presence of safety signals will strengthen rather than weaken avoidance behavior; (b) increasing the strength or number of safety signals may increase rather than decrease avoidance; and (c) extinction of the incentive value of safety signals will accelerate the rate of extinction of avoidance behavior. If the number and strength of safety signals are increased, as Rachman recommends, the phobic patient may feel more comfortable, but these procedures might also interfere with attempts to both increase the range of their activities and reduce their dependency on others. On this point it should be noted that information denying the patient's expectations of harm should he or she confront the feared situation (death or madness for the panic patient; exhaustion of the oxygen supply for the claustrophobic patient), is not an example of increasing safety signals in the same sense that animals researchers have used the term. Rather this information is aimed at moderating the power of the CS+ (i.e., the Pavlovian excitor of fear, or more simply the feared stimulus) to elicit fear. This information may facilitate the extinction of avoidance behavior through processes similar to those initiated by exposure to the feared stimulus.

The important implication of the animal literature on safety signals is that exposure to the CS+ will not be sufficient (or rather will be impeded) unless this is accompanied by procedures designed to extinguish the incentive value of the safety signals. Presumably this is a nonprogrammed effect of successful exposure procedures, but making extinction of the CS- an explicit part of therapy should both speed up the treatment process in each patient and increase the consistency of treatment across patients. Indeed, according to Weisman and Litner's (1972) analysis, the incentive value of safety signals is the most powerful factor operating to maintain avoidance behavior. For the agoraphobic, staying at home not only avoids possible confrontations with fear but also produces a positively enhanced state making staying at home (and all the other dependent behavior so characteristic of the agoraphobic's restricted mobility) a pleasurable experience somewhat independent of its fear-reducing properties. From this perspective extinguishing the incentive value of these safety signals may be seen as the first priority in treatment rather than as a secondary feature added to the usual exposure procedures.

In Rachman's (1983, 1984a) earlier version's of the safety signal hypothesis, he made far more valuable recommendations for treatment. He suggested making use of the powerful incentive-laden cues in CS+ exposure procedures. For example, the presence of certain other people serves as a safety signal for most agoraphobics, which means, in terms of the animal literature, that these people have powerful positive incentive value for these patients. Rather than forcing patients to become independent of these people during exposure treatment, the incentive value can be used constructively in therapy by placing the supportive person at the end of the proposed exposure route. By enduring the feared exposure, the patient is rewarded at the end of the procedure by access to their incentive-laden friend. While this use of access to friends as rewards seems to be an improvement over the tactic of employing these supportive friends or spouses as cotherapists (which neither extinguishes the need for them nor fully effectively utilizes their incentive value), it nevertheless serves to increase the incentive value of safety signals. In this particular case, the safety signal enhances the dependent style of the patients. Indeed, the whole issue of dependency in agoraphobics lends itself to a behavioral analysis in terms of safety signals. Clearly Rachman has drawn attention to an entirely novel way of constuing agoraphobic behavior which should lead to a very fruitful expansion of our understanding of the mechanisms of effective treatment.

One of the many important contributions of Rachman's paper, is his description of the laboratory setup of examining panic attacks. He has provided a procedure which reliably produces panics in claustrophobics and allows, therefore, a functional analysis of their problem. Rachman's delineation of an experimental strategy for investigating panic and its related processes and moderating variables, is a significant step forward in bringing the phenomenon under laboratory control. The laboratory control utilized by Rachman represents a quite different strategy and is a more naturalistic recreation of the experience, than are the strategies of panic-induction by lactate infusion (see the chapter by Hout) or hyperventilation (see the chapters by Clark and Salkovskis). If other researchers are able to replicate this protocol and secure high-frequency panic inductions, the field will be in a position to not only extend Rachman's pioneering work, but also to determine better why some people experience panics yet do not develop a disorder. This seems to be just as puzzling, if not more so, than the fact that some do. While Rachman's procedure was designed to evaluate panic processes in claustrophobics, it might be adapted easily to the examination of agoraphobics, and this would markedly increase our understanding of this pervasive disorder.

Despite my enthusiasm for this experimental procedure, I am not encouraged by the data resulting from Rachman's studies, although as more subjects are analyzed the results may become clearer. Similarly there are concerns about the way in which the data were handled, at least in some instances. Two examples will serve to illustrate these concerns. In the first place the strategy of simply converting predictions of panics (subjects were required to declare the probability of expecting a panic on the next trial) to "predicted" versus "unpredicted" is at best weak and at worst misleading. Predicted panics were those trials where the subject declared a 50% or better chance of having a panic, whereas unpredicted panics were those trials where subjects assigned a value of less than 50%. It seems an odd use of language to categorize subjects who said they had a 49% chance of experiencing a panic on the next trial, as someone for whom the possibility of a panic is unpredicted. Perhaps "least" versus "most" expected would have been better descriptors. Furthermore, I have found that in describing present anxiety states, phobic subjects differ markedly in assigning percentage values even when they agree in terms of their descriptions of the severity of symptoms. This of course, is well known to students of signal detection theory (Green & Swets, 1966) and indicates that a between-subjects analysis of this type of data is far from satisfactory. Correlational analyses of Rachman's data would have overcome this objection and would have had the further advantage of utilizing all of the data rather than reducing it to arbitrary categories.

A second concern about the data is possible floor and ceiling effects. For example, in terms of Fig. 14.5, Rachman notes that "An expected panic has little effect on the predicted Fear scores of the subsequent trial . . . but unexpected panic leads to an increase in predicted Fear scores." Looking at various figures presented throughout the text, and from my own experience in assessing subjects in fear studies, a fear score of around 65–70 out of 100 is close to asymtotic for group data. A further increase is unlikely to be statistically significant. In Fig. 14.5, a ceiling effect means that those subjects who expected a panic had little or no room to increase their fear on the subsequent trial, so it is surprising and possibly important, that they did display marginally significant ($p = .05$) increases in fear. Conversely in Fig. 14.10 there appears to be no room for the expected no-panic subjects to reduce their reported fear. There were, however, two findings from Rachman's studies which I found most exciting. His observation that panics (particularly those which were least expected) led to an increase in anticipated fear but not an actual increase in the experience of fear on the trial in question, directly confirms Goldstein and Chambless's (1978) long-revered notion that a crucial feature of panic-based disorders is a "fear of fear." These findings also support Klein's (1981) idea that anticipatory anxiety is to be distinguished from the actual anxiety or panic experienced in the feared situation.

The second finding represents a challenge to the cognitive theory presented by

Dr. Clark and Dr. Salkovskis (see chapters in this volume). According to them, the experience of a panic has the effect of altering a person's cognitions such that when fear arousal occurs, catastrophizing thoughts are generated (e.g., "I am suffocating and so I will die"), which in turn enhance fear so that it quickly escalates into a panic attack. All of Rachman's subjects experienced at least one panic during the study and yet subsequently, on trials where they reported no panics they also reported the same symptoms (e.g., suffocating) as they did on panic trials (Experiment 3). According to Clark and Salkovskis's theory, these subjects, having previously experienced a panic (particularly since it was in the same setting), and presently experiencing the same symptoms, should have catastrophized and panicked, but they did not. Again this seems to be a very important finding.

COGNITIVE, BEHAVIORAL, AND PSYCHOPHYSIOLOGICAL TREATMENTS AND CORRELATES OF PANIC

Michelson provides two reports, one of which describes the responses of agoraphobics with panics to different treatments while the other examines changes on various indexes during and after treatment of patients classified according to the degree of fear they experienced during a behavioral test.

In the first report, Michelson presents data from four previously published treatment outcome studies with some data added to the last study. In addition to describing the comparative outcome on panics for each of the four studies, Michelson also attempts to make comparisons across the studies in order to provide an evaluation over all the treatments employed. He describes "End State" functioning, a term which attempts to include a clinical rating of effective functioning into the appraisal of change. So that the benefits of treatment for the patient's day-to-day life may be inferred.

The procedures evaluated in this series included a pharmacological treatment (imipramine) with and without Graduated Exposure; a behavioral treatment (therapist-assisted, in vivo exposure—called either Flooding or Graduated Exposure); a physiological treatment (Relaxation Training); and two cognitive therapies (Paradoxical Intention and Self-Statement Training). Each of these procedures (with the exception of the imipramine-alone procedure of Study II) was accompanied by instructions to practice self-directed, in vivo exposure between treatment sessions (called Programmed Practice). This procedure matches current clinical practice, but Michelson was able to provide data indicating that the amount of Programmed Practice actually engaged in by patients predicts benefits derived from treatment. This is the first time such data have been provided, and these findings are consistent with, although not directly confirmatory of, the frequent claim that exposure is a necessary although perhaps not a sufficient component of effective treatment. Echoes of this same thesis were made by Beck (see this volume) who indicated that cognitive treatments did not produce results unless accompanied by instructions to engage in exposure.

Michelson's excellent series of treatment studies show that adding therapist-assisted, in vivo exposure to home practice provides a very powerful treatment for these patients. While reductions in panics lagged behind the dramatic improvements on all other indexes, by the end of the 2-year follow-up, panics were less frequent in the pure exposure groups than in any of the other treated subjects. This is a clear illustration of the effectiveness of strictly behavioral treatments. This is not to say that Graduated Exposure or Flooding cannot be improved, since these procedures are not to everyone's liking (some patients refuse such treatments and some drop out) nor do they uniformly benefit everyone (see Marshall & Gauthier [1983] for a discussion of these issues).

The evaluation of the other procedures in Michelson's series (and indeed the cognitive therapies described by Beck, Clark, and Salkovskis) may be seen as a way of determining how best to enhance an exposure-based strategy. For these reasons, it is unfortunate that reference is not made to Barlow's treatment program for agoraphobics (see Barlow, O'Brien, & Last, 1984), nor to his comprehensive approach to panic disordered patients (see chapter in this volume, plus Barlow, Cohen et al., 1984). In his work with agoraphobics, Barlow has shown that improvement rates with graduated in vivo exposure (both therapist-assisted and self-directed practice), are significantly enhanced by including the patient's spouse as a cotherapist. We have similarly shown that adding training in interpersonal problem solving to graduated exposure, markedly enhances outcome (Kleiner & Marshall, in press). In this respect the shift in emphasis to a view which stresses (I might say exaggerates) cognitive aspects, seems to be somewhat misplaced since Michelson's data indicate that behavioral procedures are the most demonstrably effective.

Imipramine alone produced significant immediate reductions on all indexes of distress, including panics, but these benefits were apparently rapidly lost upon withdrawal of the drug, a result which is consistent with what is known about the use of drugs (typically the benzodiazepines) in the treatment of other aspects of anxiety disorders (Rickels, Case, & Diamond, 1980). The combination of imipramine and graduated exposure produced dramatic immediate effects which endured to long-term follow-up. As noted previously, graduated exposure alone had, by long-term follow-up, reduced panics to a level below all other treatments, including the imipramine plus exposure procedure. Perhaps the combination of therapist-assisted exposure and home practice, provided clients with skills which they could enact (even without therapist contact) over a long period to increase continually control over their behavior and physiological responsiveness. No doubt cognitive theorists would attribute improvement after exposure treatment to some change in the patient's thinking, but they have yet to demonstrate that it is more than the acquisition of behavioral skills; in any case, the argument that direct cognitive intervention is necessary seems severely weakened by these data.

From a strictly cognitive perspective, one might expect those patients treated by the combination of imipramine plus exposure to demonstrate a loss of gains upon withdrawal of the drug, since improvement might well be attributed to the effects of medication. However, these patients maintained their gains which seems more readily explicable in terms of: (1) the acquisition of skills in encountering the environment; and (2) the extinction of (a) the aversive valence of certain features of the internal and external environment and (b) the positive valence of certain safety signals. Imipramine, given in the context of instructions which indicate that it will suppress panics, reassures the patient to a sufficient degree that he or she will participate readily in therapist-assisted exposure and will more vigorously follow instructions to engage in home practice. Imipramine, given with these instructions, effectively does the same as Rachman's provision of information regarding contact with the feared situation; that is, it reduces the fear-evoking properties of the CS+, albeit temporarily. Effective exposure occurs allowing fearfulness in response to the CS+ to extinguish. Similarly, the positive effects of combining relaxation training with self-directed exposure, demonstrate an effective way to ensure that effective exposure occurs. In this respect, while it supports this view to know that amount of self-exposure mediates treatment outcome, it would have been valuable to know how much self-directed practice was actually engaged in by each of the treated groups or how enthusiastically each group participated in the therapist-assisted exposure.

In any case, my understanding of Michelson's data is that the three most effective procedures were: Graduated Exposure; Imipramine plus Graduated Exposure; and Relaxation Training plus Graduated Exposure. The two cognitive treatments (Paradoxical Intention and Self-statement Training) produced effective results but appeared weaker and less stable than the other three, while imipramine alone was the least effective in the long term. These observations, it should be noted, do not deny the possibly greater effectiveness of the sort of cognitive therapy described by Beck or by Clark and Salkovskis (see chapters in this volume), who each provide data indicating very powerful changes in severly debilitated patients. Again, however, the cognitive procedures used by these therapists were engaged in the context of in vivo exposure to panic-eliciting cues, although these were restricted to the internal cues to panic. While this suggests the possibility of explaining the benefits of these cognitive procedures as due to exposure effects, it should be remembered that Michelson's imipramine-alone procedure was effective in the short term and yet did not include any elements of exposure. Exposure alone cannot, therefore, account for all the observed benefits.

In his second report, Michelson describes in far more detail the effects of treatment on various indexes. To facilitate a clearer understanding of these processes, Michelson divided his patients into one of three groups (Anxious,

Fearful, or Panickers) on the basis of their reports of anxiety subjectively experienced at the behavioral tests. Anxious subjects were those who reported the least distress while the Panickers were those whose distress was extreme. As we will see, there is good reason to doubt the bases for these classifications. If, however, these categories are accepted, at least three important observations become apparent. Panickers showed the greatest degree of improvement (at least on the "percentage improvement" measure at 3 months follow-up) even after correcting for differences in the range of anxiety scores across groups. This improvement occurred despite the fact that the Panickers exhibited a consistently broader range of symptomatology and greater severity of symptoms across all measures. Thus, the treatment procedures employed in this study (Paradoxical Intention, Graduated Exposure, and Relaxation Training all accompanied by self-directed exposure) had their greatest effect on the most severely disabled patients, a finding which challenges any claim that behavioral or cognitive/behavioral therapies are unsuitable for the most severe anxiety disorders. What is, in fact, puzzling here is the observation that, at least in terms of the end-state measure, the Fearful patients did poorest. That the Anxious subjects, who were the least distressed at the behavioral tests, profited quite markedly from treatment is no surprise, but it is difficult to see why the most severely distressed did well while the moderately distressed did not. Although this study needs replication, the fact that the number of subjects was quite large (74 agoraphobics) provides greater confidence that this is a replicable observation.

The second observation of this study concerns the finding that at midtreatment assessment, the Panickers displayed the lowest heart rates during the behavioral test. This result is particularly puzzling since these subjects reported levels of distress during the behavioral test which allowed them to be classified as Panickers. While the Panickers' heart rates were significantly lower than those of the other subjects, their heart rates were elevated relative to their own recordings taken while sitting or even while walking. It is important to note that although the Panickers were apparently more sensitive to internal cues of anxiety, and therefore quit the behavioral test earlier than other subjects, correcting for this difference in exposure did not alter the observed differences in heart rate. As a group, therefore, the Panickers responded to the test with elevated heart rates, although not as elevated as the other two groups of subjects. Now this elevation could reflect a reasonably uniform group response or it could be the result of some subjects showing a marked rise in heart rate during the test while others' were lowered. The latter response is most clearly and consistently observed in blood/injury phobics and in other phobics who have a tendency to faint during exposure to fearful situations. Some panic patients report a fear of fainting, although it is not clear that they actually do faint. It seems, therefore, that more detailed subject-specific analyses of these data are warranted.

Cognitive theorists hold that the internal signs of distress signal to these patients that they are going to have a panic, which in turn triggers catastrophizing thoughts, further elevating internal distress into a panic. If the group data presented by Michelson reflect common processes across all patients who experience panics (i.e., Michelson's so-called "Panickers"), then the chain of events proposed by cognitive theorists seems unlikely. If Michelson's Panickers detected low-level changes in internal states and registered these as distressing, they should then have catastrophized and displayed further elevations in heart rate. Apparently they did not show these latter increases in arousal expected by cognitive theorists. However, at least two interpretations may offset this conclusion. As mentioned, the group data may obscure the possibility that some of the Panickers showed markedly increased heart rates while others may have displayed marked drops. If so, then the key signal of an imminent panic attack for these patients may simply be a sudden noticeable change in arousal (i.e., either an increase or decrease). It is well documented that while most people respond to fearful stimuli with an increased heart rate, some do show a decrease (Engel, 1972; Lacey, 1956).

A more serious threat to the value of this aspect of Michelson's data is the possibility that describing these patients as Panickers may be misleading. His data (see Table 8.8 in Michelson's chapter) reveal that on the five pretreatment measures of panic taken on all subjects, the Panickers did not differ from the other two groups of subjects. To call them Panickers on the basis of their responses to the behavioral test while ignoring their panic indexes, may misrepresent more meaningful differences between these patients and the other two groups. These findings, therefore, may not represent any threat at all to a cognitive perspective. In any case Michelson did find that relative to the Anxious and Fearful subjects, Panickers entertained far more of the type of negative catastrophizing thoughts during the behavioral test that the cognitive theorists would expect.

COMBINED PHARMACOLOGICAL AND PSYCHOLOGICAL TREATMENTS FOR PANIC SUFFERERS

Telch considers the issue of combining pharmacological interventions with psychological therapies in the treatment of panic-based anxiety disorders, and he appears to be persuaded that the combined procedure is more effective than either drugs alone or behavioral treatment alone. While I do not disagree with the conclusion that the combined procedure is more effective than drugs alone, the latter aspect of his conclusion (i.e., the combined treatment is better than behavioral alone) is an overstatement of the available evidence. Marshall and Segal (1986) evaluated the evidence on both the possible facilitatory effects of drugs on behavioral therapy and the combination of the two in treating phobias and anxiety disorders, and could find no strong support for the value of either. In those studies where the combination was clearly more effective than either components alone (e.g., Zitrin, Klein, & Woerner, 1978, 1980), we criticized the choice of a very limited behavioral intervention and pointed out that a more comprehensive behavioral program might be expected to be more powerful than simple exposure and recent evidence supports the efficacy of a comprehensive program (Barlow, O'Brien, & Last, 1984; Kleiner & Marshall, in press). Michelson also presents evidence which calls into question the supposed superiority of the combination of behavioral and pharmacological treatments although his studies do indicate that this approach is very effective.

Telch reports one of his own studies which compared imipramine alone versus imipramine-plus-intensive, in vivo exposure versus placebo plus exposure. Since all subjects receiving therapist-assisted exposure were also told to engage in self-directed exposure between sessions, this study matches procedures reported by Michelson. The findings were approximately replicated, although the follow-up period was not as long in Telch's study, and at the last assessment (26 weeks after treatment commenced) the combined group was clearly superior to exposure alone. However, as Michelson showed, the anti-panic effects of exposure are slow to appear and may not be apparent this early in assessment. Perhaps most important is the fact that the therapist-assisted procedure involved only 9 hours of exposure, and there is evidence that such brief intensive therapy is far less effective than more extensive exposure (Mavissakalian & Barlow, 1981). Furthermore, as noted, utilizing such circumscribed behavioral interventions in a comparative analysis prejudices outcome against a behavioral approach.

In any case Telch's study, along with others in the literature, demonstrates only marginally greater effects for the combined procedure, and these effects, Telch says in his concluding remarks, disappear upon withdrawal of the drug. Researchers with a behavioral or cognitive approach might more fruitfully expend their energy on developing more comprehensive, and hopefully more effective therapies derived from their own views, than diverting their efforts to the determination of why it is that adding drugs to limited behavioral interventions produces marginal benefits.

However, Telch's discussion of these issues is revealing. From his consideration of the evidence, Telch quite rightly concludes that neither the panic suppression hypothesis nor the antidepressant explanation can account for the effectiveness of imipramine in the treatment of panic disorders. The panic suppression hypothesis is derived from studies demonstrating that tricyclic drugs block lactate-induced panics (Appleby, Klein, Sacher, & Levitt, 1981), whereas the antidepressant explanation claims that the tricyclics and MAO inhibitors are effective in treating agoraphobia because they relieve the associated depression (Marks, 1983). Telch, Agras, Taylor, Roth, and Gallen (1985) offer an alternative view which they call the "dysphoria-efficacy hypothesis." According to this account, the antidepressants are effective with agoraphobics because they stabilize mood, thereby removing the obstacle which dysphoric mood presents in treatment. Agoraphobics who are depressed are said to be apathetic toward treatment and this presents a serious obstacle to effective therapy. This alternative dysphoria efficacy hypothesis is elegant and fits well with current theorizing and knowledge. Accordingly it seems worthy of further investigation.

Perhaps the most interesting aspect of Telch's discussion concerns his evaluation of the evidence for and against the claim that imipramine (and presumably the other drugs which have been effective in treating panic disorders, e.g., the other tricyclics, the MAO inhibitors, and more recently alprazolam) is effective in the treatment of these patients because it suppresses panics. When imipramine has had long-term benefits it has always been in combination with exposure-based treatments. Behavioral therapists tend to emphasize exposure to external cues (e.g., crowded places, public transport, etc.), whereas cognitive therapists emphasize exposure to internal cues (physiological changes). If imipramine suppresses these internal cues, as the panic suppression hypothesis claims, then from a cognitive perspective such medication should render exposure treatment ineffective. This is so because cognitive therapists (see chapters by Beck, Clark and Salkovskis in this volume) claim that these internal cues are the triggers for the catastrophizing thoughts which they see as crucial to having panics. In treatment, therefore, these internal cues must be evoked if patients are to learn not to respond to them with panic-provoking thoughts.

While behavioral views tend to emphasize external cues, most behavioral therapists consider internal cues to be part of the stimulus complex which triggers panics. A behavioral perspective would, therefore, also consider panic suppression during exposure to be a less than optimal strategy. It has been my clinical practice to evoke deliberately both external and internal cues during exposure, a procedure which is more consistent with a behavioral perspective than graduated exposure which attempts to avoid the elicitation of anxiety during treatment. Unfortunately, the evidence does not clearly support the value of having subjects experience anxiety during exposure (Marshall, Gauthier, & Gordon, 1979). For example, Mathews and Shaw (1973) found that higher levels of anxiety during flooding therapy predicted poor treatment outcome. On the other hand (and this is consistent with both my clinical practice and some recent data [Marshall, 1985]), Mathews and Shaw showed that decrements in anxiety during exposure were positively correlated with improvements.

Consistent with the idea that anxiety must be evoked for treatment to be effective, Chambless, Foa, Groves, and Goldstein (1979) found that brevital suppression of peripheral anxiety (which eliminates the prime internal cues) reduced the effectiveness of exposure therapy with agoraphobics. This finding fits well with their (Chambless & Goldstein, 1982) notion that these patients are exquisitely sensitive to internal signs of anxiety. There is also support in this observation for the claims of cognitive therapists that the evocation of internal sensations is critical in treatment since it facilitates, and may even be essential to, the modification of catastrophizing thoughts. The evidence that the antidepressant drugs, while effectively treating panic disordered patients, do not do so via a panic suppression mechanism, lends support to the already overwhelming evidence that exposure to both the internal and external cues to distress is a necessary (but apparently not optimally sufficient) condition for the effective treatment of these patients.

SUMMARY

Rachman has provided an elegant, well-defined theory, and described an experimental strategy to investigate this theory which lends itself to the study of other aspects of panic. The theory is in need of refinement and clarification, and the data generated by the theory seem open to alternative interpretations as do some inferences from his theory. However, overall, Rachman's paper is likely to be seminal in advancing our understanding of panics and related disorders.

Michelson's excellent series of treatment evaluations permit a comparison of procedures derived from various orientations. My understanding of this data is that exposure-based strategies are a necessary basic ingredient in all effective treatments of panic disorders with other elements simply serving to maximize the benefits of behavioral approaches. Although Telch concludes that drugs plus exposure represents the optimal treatment package, I think Michelson's long-term, follow-up data oppose this view but do not deny the value of such an approach. As to the basis of the facilitatory effects of drugs on exposure treatment, it seems possible that the role of exposure to internal versus external cues in behavior change among these patients can be evaluated by employing drugs which have primarily peripheral, dampening effects.

As to the role of cognitions in the etiology, maintenance, and change in Panic Disorders, the present three papers offer somewhat confusing data. No doubt Rachman is correct in pointing to a set of cognitions which differs from those said to mediate panics by Beck and the other cognitive theorists; however, the role they play in enhancing the benefits of exposure therapy remains undetermined.

Finally I would draw attention to the need for a more detailed examination of the responses of individual subjects to experimental preparations such as Rachman's, as well as to treatment. One of the distinguishing features of a behavioral approach was a concern for each individual's response. There was an assumption that each individual is unique and that what is true for one person may not be true for another, depending on their learning histories. For various reasons this emphasis on the individual, and on discerning idiosyncratic processes, seems to have been minimized as behavior therapists seek to fit their research and treatment into the mainstream of clinical literature. This literature is dominated by traditional views which cluster people rather than behavior. This is not mean to deny the value of studies which compare groups of subjects but rather to claim that the neglect of individual differences in favor of group differences may impede the fuller understanding of these problems. Groups are formed either on the basis of some shared characteristics which subjects bring to the study (e.g., agoraphobia) or as a result of random allocation of subjects having this shared characteristic.

In evaluating the outcome of research it might also be informative to group subjects in terms of their responses to the experimental manipulation. In Rachman's paradigm, this might allow a clearer understanding of why it is that under certain, well-defined conditions, some subjects have panics while other do not. In Michelson's and Telch's treatment studies, such a strategy might help us understand why some patients benefit and some fail in response to any particular procedure. This approach to the analyses of research data is meant to be additional to the usual procedures, in order to facilitate greater understanding. Furthermore a concern for individual patterns of responding may also encourage much needed research into the question of why it is that some people experience panics without developing avoidance and why it is that some people who experience panics do not develop any disorder at all! Hopefully future research will address these issues.

16

Competing Theories of Panic

Martin E. P. Seligman
University of Pennsylvania

I will outline the strength of the cognitive views of panic, point to one glaring weakness and one concealed mystery, outline a Pavlovian theory, and make four recommendations for future research.

Two introductory remarks are in order. First, the therapeutic results described by Clark (this volume) and Beck (this volume) are extremely promising, and need to be pursued with vigor. Second, we are participating in a debate between two models of psychopathology, with panic disorder as the centerpiece. One model, biomedical, claims essentially that panic is a disorder of the body, is biochemical, with genetic vulnerability, and appropriately treated by drug therapy. The other, cognitive-behavioral, claims that it is a disorder of the mind, based on misinterpretation, with a cognitive diathesis, and suitable for psychotherapy. The present discussion is confined to psychological approaches to panic.

THE COGNITIVE-BEHAVIORAL MODEL STRENGTHS

This model has four basic strengths. First, it has put forward a theory (the catastrophic misinterpretation of bodily sensations) that probably subsumes the biological claims about etiology. It claims that all chemicals that produce panic probably do so by instigating the bodily sensations that give rise to these misinterpretations in those people who are disposed to make such misinterpretations. While this argument needs to be worked out point for point, I suspect that it is valid (see Clark, this volume).

Second, a method has been developed for bringing panic into the laboratory.

By placing informed claustrophobic volunteer subjects into confined spaces, Rachman (this volume) was able to produce panic reliably in the laboratory. This will allow us to investigate the properties of panic in situ. This exercise is essential in our attempts to obtain a detailed understanding of its mechanism. We can now begin to determine the consequences of an unexpected panic, and ask how relabeling diminishes the probability of a panic occurring. We can also ask if prior helplessness magnifies later panic, and if its sequential properties fit the Rescorla–Wagner model of Pavlovian conditioning. Such undertakings, I cannot resist mentioning, are what research psychologists are best qualified to carry out, and this type of work has been unwisely devalued and neglected.

Third, the cognitive-behavioral model raises the possibility of bringing panic under experimental control. Clark (this volume) reports that instructional set changes the probability of panic symptoms being experienced in the laboratory. To the extent that experimental variables increase and decrease panic in the laboratory, we will be in a position to understand and test its mechanism in nature. This will help us to answer the question of "How?", not just "Where?". This strategy also will help to clarify the argument about continuity and discontinuity. To the extent that only DSM–III-certified patients are studied, it is easy to assume—without evidence—that panic disorder is discontinuous from panic in nonpatients. By looking at the limits of the extent to which panic can be produced in the laboratory among nonpatients, we can find out if panic "disorder" is sui generis, or merely more severe than panic among nonpatients.

Fourth, the cognitive-behavioral model has generated a therapy that follows from the theory and shows remarkable promise. Not only does it appear to be effective, but in most cases it seems to produce total cure (Beck, this volume; Clark, this volume).

It has usually been the case that effective therapy precedes understanding of etiology, and I believe that panic therapy also follows this rule. I do not believe that the mechanism of panic is understood. And this is because the theory is unsatisfactory; it is not an ordered psychological theory, but merely a grab bag of intuitions.

COGNITIVE-BEHAVIORAL MODEL WEAKNESSES

Is There a "Cognitive" Theory?

There are three salient problems with the cognitive theory of panic. So far it has failed to make differential predictions, predictions that differentiate it from other psychological theories of panic and from biological theories of panic. Second, its terms are not tied to terms from cognitive and behavioral sciences. They sound like the terms used in cognitive psychology, but are deceptive because they are ordinary language terms, not anchored in any scientific corpus. Third, although the theory sounds simple, it is unparsimonious, and it is hard to count its many premises. These are the same problems that have plagued Beck's (1976) Cognitive Theory of Depression. We have learned from our research into depression of the great need for specificity and parsimony in theorizing, and this lesson should be taken seriously at the outset of theorizing about panic.

Differential Predictions

There are three competing psychological theories of panic, and more generally, of the anxiety disorders: Cognitive, Pavlovian, and Lang's propositional theory (this volume). My suspicion is that Lang's theory will ultimately fare best, because it comfortably bridges information processing and conditioning, is parsimonious and seems to be rigorous. Lang has not, however, explicitly elaborated the theory with reference to anxiety disorders, and I am not facile enough with his theory to do so. I will, however, describe Pavlovian theory since it has been neglected and because it comfortably explains, with more rigor and parsimony, most of what the cognitive theory explains. I do so because it is necessary to determine the differential predictions of the cognitive and Pavlovian approaches, to test between them, and ultimately to add or subtract sufficient premises to arrive at a concise theory that encompasses the facts and allows one to test its predictions.

Pavlovian Accounts: Simple Phobia with Trauma

In Pavlovian theory, a conditioned stimulus (CS), for example, a kitten is paired in time with a traumatic unconditioned stimulus (US), like being bitten, which produces an unconditioned response (UR), fright. Later, seeing cats produces the conditioned response (CR) of fear, and avoidance results.

Simple Phobias without Trauma

About 50% of people with simple phobias have no remembered trauma from the time their fear originated (Ost & Hugdahl, 1981). Here, Pavlovian theory postulates a spontaneous panic. The CS is cats, and US is some biological substratum, for example, "lactate," the UR is spontaneous panic, and the CR is fear of cats. By the preparedness premise (Seligman, 1971), cats do not need to be contiguous with panic, just in the general temporal vicinity.

Agoraphobia with Panic

The CS is the agora, the US is "lactate," the UR is spontaneous panic, and the CR is the fear of the agora. Again, preparedness is invoked to explain the lack of explicit pairing of agora and panic, avoidance occurs, and safety signals (CSs paired with no panic) explain the etiology and maintenance.

Panic Disorder

The CSs are specific bodily sensations, for example, heart palpitations, the US is "lactate," the UR is the first spontaneous panic attack, and the CR is panic caused by the palpitations (van den Hout, this volume).

The Pavlovian account is parsimonious, rooted in behavioral science, and well tested in its general propositions, but not in this manifestation. In addition, like the cognitive account, it subsumes the biological data by the parallel moves. It explains the occurrence of panic attacks when lactate or other agents are given to susceptible individuals by claiming that the biochemical agent produces the CS of bodily sensations. The effects of therapeutic drugs are explained by claiming elimination of either the CS of bodily sensations or the CRs of panic directly. The bulk of the cognitive therapy data is explained by exposure of the individual to extinction trials, in which the CS occurs but the US–UR of lactate panic does not. A Pavlovian explanation claims that the effect of information and interpretation is merely to make the extinction trials more salient or effective. It explains the sequential effects of expected and unexpected panic that Rachman (this volume) reports, by invoking the Rescorla–Wagner model (Kamin, 1969; Rescorla & Wagner, 1972) in which only unexpected USs produce conditioning.

In addition to accounting for much of the existing biochemical and cognitive data, the Pavlovian model generates a host of differential predictions. To name a few:

1. Cognitive misinterpretation is not necessary to produce panic in susceptible individuals; merely the perception of the bodily sensations.
2. Sequences of expected and unexpected panics in the Rachman procedures should follow the mathematical laws specified by the Rescorla–Wagner model or other related models. This unpacks into dozens of subpredictions.
3. Mere exposure to the bodily sensations without the US–UR is sufficient to produce extinction; reinterpretation has no effect except insofar as it makes exposure more salient.
4. It is necessary to have a biologically induced panic (US–UR) on the first few acquisition trials in order to acquire a panic disorder.

What are the differential predictions of the cognitive view? First it should be said what they emphatically are *not:* They are not the three predictions that Clark makes (That panic disordered patients will interpret bodily sensations more negatively than other anxiety disorder patients; that drugs produce panic by producing bodily sensations of panic; and that treatments that change interpretations of bodily sensations will do better than treatments that do not). These predictions differentiate the cognitive theory from the biomedical theory, but not from the Pavlovian theory. Pavlovian theory makes virtually identical predictions (The CS of bodily sensations is more fear evoking in panic patients, because it has been followed by panic; drugs that produce panic produce the CSs of relevant bodily sensations; treatments that extinguish the CR will fare better, and will be accompanied by the epiphenomenal report of less misinterpretation of the CS.) It is essential that the cognitive theorists address themselves to differential prediction, not merely prediction per se. Among the predictions that proponents of the cognitive view might invoke are the converse of the foregoing 1–4:

1. Cognitive misinterpretation, which is not a mere epiphenomenon of Pavlovian conditioning, is necessary for panic. Panics will occur only when the sensations are perceived *and misinterpreted,* not on trials in which they are perceived but not catastrophized about.
2. The Rescorla–Wagner type predictions will not obtain, except insofar as they are deducible from cognitive premises (as yet unstated).
3. Mere exposure to extinction contingencies will not produce decrements in panic, except insofar as exposure changes misinterpretation for the better.
4. Panic disorder can begin without biologically induced first panic attacks.

We need to sharpen the differences, not dull them. Any call for an integrative model now is premature and anesthetic. The call for differential predictions—both between the biomedical model and the psychological ones, and among the psychological ones—is intended to tell us what premises need to be added to the Pavolvian model or subtracted from the cognitive model to accommodate the facts.

UNANCHOREDNESS OF COGNITIVE THEORY

I have for the last decade found cognitive theory frustrating to work with. The attributional style reformulation of the learned helplessness theory of depression was my attempt to translate into rigorous and testable terms, Beck's cognitive theory of depression (Seligman, 1980). What I found frustrating in the cognitive theory of depression is present in the same form in the cognitive theory of panic. It is unparsimonious and its terms, despite appearances, are not anchored in cognitive psychology.

Take "catastrophic misinterpretation" for example. What does it mean? I understand it in the everyday sense, but not in any scientific sense. Neither word is from relevant corpuses, such as information-processing or decision theory. Can they be translated into receiver operating characteristic functions, into a biased search for confirmation, into inaccurate perceptions of contingency? How many premises are needed to unpack this central notion? How many basic terms are there? This is not to say that the unpacking cannot be done, and even parsimoniously done, but just that it has not been done. After a decade, it has still not been done for the cognitive theory of depression. The cognitive theory of panic should not repeat the same error. Its proponents should go out of their way at the outset to use few and rigorous terms, which have meaning in other scientific endeavors. Unless they do so, the theory will remain mere clinical intuition, with the appearance of a theory.

THE MYSTERY: ACCOUNTING FOR THE IRRATIONAL WITH THE RATIONAL

Before turning to some recommendations, I want to point out a central weakness in both the cognitive and Pavlovian theories of the anxiety disorders: Neither theory clearly distinguishes the rational from the irrational, the conscious from the unconscious. There are, I believe, two distinguishable processes, obeying different laws, which are blurred by both theories. Let us approach this concretely.

A person who has had panic disorder for a decade may have had about 1,000 panic attacks. In each one, on the cognitive account, he misinterpreted his racing heart as meaning that he was about to have a heart attack, and this was disconfirmed. Under the laws of disconfirmation that I know, he received ample evidence that his belief was false, and he should have given it up. On the Pavlovian account, he has had 1,000 extinction trials in which the CS was not followed by the US–UR (being followed by the CR of panic is an extinction trial if the original US–UR do not also appear). His panics should have extinguished long ago. Proponents of both theories would advise trying to extinguish panic by providing disconfirmation of the expectation. But neither theory explains why the belief did not extinguish in the face of disconfirmation long ago. What is it about cognitive therapeutic procedures which makes them effective disconfirmations, and about the Pavlovian exposure procedures that make them effective extinction procedures?

I have considered this problem in the domain of conditioning (Seligman, 1970, 1971; Seligman & Hager, 1972), and suggested that there were two different processes, obeying different laws. These processes are blurred by the similarity of procedure of pairing a CS with a US. I argued that when biologically arbitrary CSs and USs are paired, "unprepared" conditioning takes place. When a tone is paired with food, what gets learned in this (evolutionarily) arbitrary relationship has the following properties:

1. It is rational. Close temporal proximity of CS and US is required for conditioning to occur, and the relationship is mediated by an expectation that the US will follow the CS.
2. Learning is gradual. By tracking the real contingencies of the world, it builds up in strength, when the CS is followed by the US (confirmation).
3. It extinguishes readily and gradually, when the CS is followed by no US (disconfirmation).
4. It is a conscious, or in more modern terms, a controlled, rather than automatic process.
5. It is carried out by higher brain centers.

On the other hand, when a biologically related CS and US co-occur, a different process is engaged. When a taste is paired with gastrointestinal illness (the sauce bernaise phenomenon), or heart palpitations with panic, a different process governs conditioning. Such evolutionarily "prepared" conditioning has the following properties:

1. It is irrational. Temporally highly degraded relationships will be learned about. It is not mediated by expectations, appraisals, judgments or the like. It is a blind association, of the sort that Thorndike, Pavlov, and Skinner all sought.
2. It is learned in one trial. Survival is often at stake.
3. It does not extinguish readily, and once acquired does not, in general, track the contingencies of the world.
4. It is not conscious, or subject to conscious persuasion. Being told that the stomach flu has caused an illness and not the sauce bearnaise, does not weaken one's aversion to the sauce.
5. It is carried out by lower brain centers. Taste aversion conditioning can occur under anesthesia, and perhaps to CSs that are below thresholds of awareness (Ohman, 1986).

No Pavlovian account of anxiety disorders can fit the data without such a preparedness premise. Similarly, any cognitive account which does not distinguish these two processes is incomplete. As cognitive theory stands, basic distinctions of this sort are not made. Beliefs, expectations, thoughts that you are aware of and those of which you are not aware are talked about in the same way, as if they obeyed common laws. Labeling them both "cognitions" does not clarify the mechanism; on the contrary, it obfuscates the problem, and conceals that there is a mystery here. The cognitive account has the same problem in depression. Depressive behavior does follow rationally from the premise that the future is hopeless. But why the person holds this premise with such tenacity and defends it with such vigor in the face of so much disconfirming evidence, is not explained. The neurotic paradox will not be labeled away. It re-emerges when we confront the etiological question in depression and when we ask why the panic victim still believes he or she will have a heart attack in spite of 1,000 extinction trials. In the fields of perception and memory, "having" the perception or "having" the memory does the work. But "having" the cognition or "engaging" in the ideation is not all there is to ideations and cognitions. It is *believing* the cognition that is responsible for the cognitive disorders. (Recall the fatuousness of reinforcing yourself, by engaging in the coverant "well done" to yourself.) And the psychology of belief—rational (Baron 1985), but especially, irrational—is still *terra incognita*. A cognitive psychology that incorporates and explores a preparedness premise may begin to illuminate the neurotic paradox.

RECOMMENDATIONS

First, there is theoretical work to be done. Cognitive theory should be stated in more rigorous, anchored, and parsimonious terms. The terms should be linked, wherever possible, to the terms of information-processing and decision theory. Where this is not possible, weaknesses of information-processing and decision approaches will be made salient and the more general problem of linking hot and cold psychology will be focused. Similarly, Pavlovian and Lang's theories should be stated explicitly as they apply to the anxiety disorders, and differential predictions spelled out.

Second, the use of laboratory models of panic and the experimental control over panic should be encouraged. Here is the road to insight into the etiology of panic disorder.

Third, animal models of panic should be encouraged. As van den Hout (this volume) has pointed out, rats probably do not "catastrophically misinterpret" their bodily sensations, but they do classically condition. In addition to testing between these two theories, a good animal model will illuminate the etiology, brain physiology, therapy—both somatic and psychotherapy—vulnerability, and prevention of panic disorder.

Finally, the question of whether panic disorder is discontinuous, a phenomenon in a class by itself, or continuous with normal psychological processes, only more severe, must be reopened. Some theorists assume that because many panic disorder patients are vulnerable to lactate-induced panic, that it is discontinuous. But the finding that varying the instructions to normal people (e.g., "a few people pass out when they hyperventilate") may induce panic attacks in the laboratory, along with the finding that putting nonpatients in enclosed spaces can produce panic, strongly suggests that the "disorder" may only be the severe end of a psychological continuum. If the study of panic is prematurely confined to the study of panic disorder patients in their natural setting, or even in the laboratory, we may come to find therapies that work, but I doubt that we will understand the mechanism or the etiology of panic or of Panic Disorder.

ACKNOWLEDGMENT

Supported by NIMH grant MH19604.

References and Author Index

Abramson, L. **[297]**

Ackerman, S. H., Hofer, M. R., & Weiner, H. (1975). Age at maternal separation and gastric erosion susceptibility in the rat. *Psychosomatic Medicine, 37,* 180–187. **[68]**

Ackerman, S. H., & Sachar, E. J. (1974). The lactate theory of anxiety: A review and re-evaluation. *Psychosomatic Medicine, 36,* 69–81. **[39]**

Agras, W. S. **[13, 17, 24, 27, 29, 42, 43, 52, 64, 67, 87, 174, 176, 177, 178, 181, 182, 185, 239, 317]**

Alba, J. W., & Hasher, L. (1983). Is memory schematic? *Psychological Bulletin, 93,* 203–231. **[212, 213]**

Alexander, A. B. **[114, 115]**

Alloy, L., & Abramson, L. (1982). Learned helplessness, depression and the illusion of control. *Journal of Personality & Social Psychology, 42,* 1114–1126. **[297]**

Alloy, L., & Tabachnik, N. (1984). Assessment of covariation by humans and animals: The joint influence of prior expectations and current situational information. *Psychological Review, 91,* 112–149. **[297]**

American Psychiatric Association. (1980). *Diagnostic and statistical manual of mental disorders (DSM–III),* (3rd ed.). Washington, DC: Author. **[20, 37, 51, 71, 112, 126, 138, 237, 300]**

American Psychiatric Association. (1987). *Diagnostic and statistical manual of mental disorders,* (3rd ed., rev.) (DSM–III–R). Washington, DC: Author. **[1]**

Anderson, D. J. **[38, 43, 60, 87]**

Anderson, D. J., Noyes, R., & Crowe, R. R. (1984). A comparison of panic disorder and generalized anxiety disorder. *American Journal of Psychiatry, 141,* 572–575. **[27, 114]**

Anderson, J. R., & Bower, G. H. (1974). A propositional theory of recognition memory. *Memory and Cognition, 2* (3), 406–412. **[225]**

Anderson, S. **[3, 14, 27, 41, 43, 52, 60, 72, 80, 81, 167, 176, 238, 240, 241, 245, 246, 267]**

Annable, L. **[38, 57, 72]**

Anthony, J. C. **[20, 46]**

Appleby, I. L. **[3, 14, 27, 40, 41, 43, 52, 60, 72, 80, 81, 167, 176, 238, 240, 241, 245, 246, 267]**

Appleby, I. L., Klein, D. F., Sachar, E. J., Levitt, M. (1981). Biochemical indices of lactate-induced panic: A preliminary report. In D. F. Klein & J. G. Rabkin (Eds.), *Anxiety: New research and changing concepts* (pp. 411–423). New York: Raven Press. **[72, 80, 81, 167, 176, 240, 317]**

Arnow, B. A., Taylor, C. B., Agras, W. S., & Telch, M. J. (1985). Enhancing agoraphobia treatment outcome by changing couple communication patterns. *Behavior Therapy, 16,* 452–467. **[185]**

Ascough, J. C. **[227]**

Askanazi, J. **[3, 18, 80, 244, 245, 246]**

Baddeley, A. (1972). Selective attention and performance in dangerous environments. *British Journal of Psychology, 63,* 537–546. **[302]**

Ball, G. **[58]**

Ballenger, J. D. **[32, 51, 169, 170, 172, 183]**

Balter, M. B. **[20]**

Baragh, J. A. (1982). Attention and automaticity and the processing of self-relevant information. *Journal of Personality and Social Psychology, 43,* 425–436. **[164]**

Baragh, J. A., & Pietromonaco, P. (1982). Automatic information processing in social perception: The influence of trade information presented outside of conscious awareness on impression formation. *Journal of Personality and Social Psychology, 43,* 437–449. **[164]**

Barlow, D. H. **[14–18, 20, 22, 24–26, 29, 33, 41, 46, 53, 56, 67, 68, 115, 124, 125, 208, 317]**

Barlow, D. H. (in press). *Panic, anxiety, and the anxiety disorders.* [Title tentative] New York: Guilford Press. **[12, 13]**

Barlow, D. H., Blanchard, E. B., Vermilyea, J. A., Vermilyea, B. B., & DiNardo, P. A. (1986). Generalized anxiety and generalized anxiety disorder: Description and reconceptualization. *American Journal of Psychiatry, 143,* 40–44. **[112–114]**

Barlow, D. H., Cohen, A. S., Waddell, M. T., Vermilyea, B. B., Klosko, J. S., Blanchard, E. B., & DiNardo, P. A. (1984). Panic and generalized anxiety disorders: Nature and treatment. *Behavior Therapy, 15,* 431–439. **[27, 51, 58, 129, 313]**

Barlow, D. H., & Mavissakalian, M. R. (1981). Directions in the assessment and treatment of phobia: The next decade. In M. Mavissakalian & D. H. Barlow (Eds.), *Phobia: Psychological and pharmacological treatment* (pp. 199–245). New York: Guilford Press. **[179]**

Barlow, D. H., O'Brien, G. T., & Last, C. G. (1984). Couples treatment of agoraphobia. *Behavior Therapy, 15,* 41–58. **[184, 313, 317]**

Barlow, D. H., Sakheim, D. K., & Beck, J. G. (1983). Anxiety increases sexual arousal. *Journal of Abnormal Psychology, 92,* 49–55. **[225]**

Barlow, D. H., Vermilyea, J., Blanchard, E., Vermilyea, B., DiNardo, P. A., & Cerny, J. (1985). The phenomenon of panic. *Journal of Abnormal Psychology, 94,* 320–328. **[20, 22, 32, 33, 44, 45, 112, 117, 118, 261, 289, 290, 294]**

Baron, J. (1985). *Rationality and intelligence.* New York: Cambridge University Press.

Barrios, B., & Shigatomi, C. (1980). Coping skills training for the management of anxiety: A critical review. *Behavior Therapy, 10,* 491–522. **[165]**

Beck, A. T. **[86, 96, 97, 99, 106, 122, 207]**

Beck, A. T. (1984a). Cognitive therapy, behavior therapy, psychoanalysis, and pharmacotherapy: A cognitive continuum. In J. Williams & R. Spitzer (Eds.), *Psychotherapy research: Where are we and where should we go?* (pp. 114–134). New York: Guilford Press. **[93]**

Beck, A. T. (1976). *Cognitive therapy and the emotional disorders.* New York: International Universities Press. **[7, 93, 95, 223, 231, 323]**

Beck, A. T. (1970). Role of fantasies in psychotherapy and psychopathology. *Journal of Nervous and Mental Disease, 150,* 3–17. **[95]**

Beck, A. T., & Emory, G. (with Ruth Greenberg). (1985). *Anxiety disorders and phobias: A cognitive perspective.* New York: Basic Books. **[7, 18, 48, 71, 73, 122, 135, 155, 219, 266, 290, 305]**

Beck, A. T., Laude, R., & Bohnert, M. (1974). Ideational components of anxiety neurosis. *Archives of General Psychiatry, 31,* 319–325. **[3, 66, 95, 97, 206, 214]**

Beck, A. T., & Sokol-Kessler, L. (1986, October). *A test of cognitive dysfunction in panic attacks.* Paper presented at the research conference, University of Pennsylvania, Philadelphia. **[99]**

Beck, A. T., Ward, C. H., Mendelsohn, M., Mock, J., & Erbaugh, J. (1961). An inventory for measuring depression. *Archives of General Psychiatry, 4,* 561–571. **[157]**

Beck, J. G. **[225]**

Beech, H. R. **[255]**

Beidel, D. C. **[40, 48, 49]**

Beirne, G. J. **[126]**

Belfer, P. L., & Glass, C. R. (1982, November). *Agoraphobic anxiety and fear of fear: A cognitive attentional model.* Paper presented at the meeting of the Association for the Advancement of Behavior Therapy, Los Angeles. **[212]**

Beninger, R. J. (1983). The role of dopamine in locomotor activity and learning. *Brain Research Reviews, 6,* 173–196. **[309]**

Berkowitz, L. (1983). Aversively stimulated aggression. Some parallels and differences in research with animals and humans. *American Psychologist, 38,* 1135–1144. **[221]**

Berkson, J. (1946). Limitations of the application of fourfold table analysis to hospital data. *Biometric Bulletin, 2,* 47–53. **[5, 6]**

Binik, Y. **[263, 265, 296, 297, 299]**

Birbaumer, N. **[205, 253, 254]**

Birmacher, B. **[57]**

Blanchard, E. B. **[14–17, 20–23, 27, 29, 32, 33, 41, 44–46, 51, 53, 58, 67, 112, 114, 117, 118, 129, 261, 289, 290, 294, 313]**

Blazer, D. G. **[6]**

Bloemink, R. **[63, 115, 241, 251]**

Bloom, P. A. **[76]**

Blowers, G. H. **[43, 239]**

Bohnert, M. **[3, 66, 95, 97, 206, 214]**

Bonn, J. A., Harrison, J., & Rees, W. L. (1973). Lactate infusion in the treatment of "free-floating" anxiety. *Canadian Psychiatric Association Journal, 18,* 41–46. **[250]**

Bonn, J. A., Harrison, J., & Rees, W. L. (1971). Lactate induced anxiety: Therapeutic application. *British Journal of Psychiatry, 119,* 468–470. **[18, 80]**

Borkovec, T. D. **[29, 30, 205, 256]**

Borkovec, T. D. (1985). Worry: A potentially valuable concept. *Behaviour Research & Therapy, 23,* 481–482. **[44]**

Borkovec, T. D., & Rachman, S. (1979). The utility of analogue research. *Behaviour Research & Therapy, 17,* 253–261. **[300]**

Borkovec, T. D., Robinson, E., Pruzinsky, T., & DePree, J. A. (1983). Preliminary exploration of worry: Some characteristics and processes. *Behaviour Research & Therapy, 21,* 9–16. **[212]**

Boulenger, J.-P. **[3, 54, 63, 72]**

Boulenger, J.-P., Marangos, P. J., Patel, J., Uhde, T. W., & Post, R. M. (1984). Central adenosine receptors: Possible involvement in the chronic effects of caffeine. *Psychopharmacology Bulletin, 20,* 431–435. **[54]**

Bower, G. H. **[178, 225]**

Bower, G. H. (1981). Mood and memory. *American Psychologist, 36,* 129–148. **[192]**

Bower, G. H., & Cohen, P. T. (1982). Emotional influences on learning and cognition. In M. S. Clark & S. T. Fiske (Eds.), *Affect and cognition* (pp. 291–331). Hillsdale, NJ: Lawrence Erlbaum Associates. **[192]**

Bower, G. H., & Mayer, J. D. (1985). Failure to replicate mood-dependent retrieval. *Bulletin of the Psychonomic Society, 23*(1), 30–42. **[226]**

Boyd, J. H. **[6, 20, 46]**

Boyd, J. H., Burke, J. D., Gruenberg, E., Holzer, C. E., Rae, D. S., George, L. K., Karno, M., Stoltzman, R., McEvoy, L., & Nestadt, G. (1984). Exclusion criteria of *DSM–III:* A study of co-occurrence of hierarchy-free syndromes. *Archives of General Psychiatry, 41,* 983–989. **[5]**

Brady, J. P., & Levitt, E. E. (1966). Hypnotically induced visual hallucinations. *Psychosomatic Medicine, 28,* 351–353. **[228]**

Breggan, P. R. (1964). The psychophysiology of anxiety with a review of the literature concerning adrenalin. *Journal of Nervous & Mental Disease, 139,* 558–568. **[18]**

Brehm, S. S. **[47]**

Breier, A. **[3, 54, 60, 61, 72, 85, 86, 257]**

Breier, A., Charney, D. S., & Heninger, G. R. (1985). The diagnostic utility of anxiety disorders and their relationship to depressive disorders. *American Journal of Psychiatry, 142,* 787–797. **[45, 51, 57]**

Bright, P. **[19, 41, 44, 46, 120, 182, 207, 211, 212, 213, 249]**

Brodbeck, C. E., & Michelson, L. (in press). Problem-solving skills and attributional styles of agoraphobics. *Cognitive Therapy and Research.* **[209, 210]**

Brougham, L. **[182]**

Brown, B. B. (1968). Visual recall ability and eye movements. *Psychophysiology, 4,* 300–306. **[228]**

Brown, W. T. **[63]**

Burke, J. D. **[5, 20, 46]**

Burns, D. D. (1980). *Feeling good: The new mood therapy.* New York: New American Library. **[135]**

Burns, L. **[260, 261]**

Butler, G., Cullington, A., Hibbert, G., Klimes, I., & Gelder, M. G. (in press). Anxiety management for persistent generalized anxiety. *British Journal of Psychiatry.* **[113]**

Butler, G., & Mathews, A. (1983). Cognitive processes in anxiety. In J. Teasdale & S. Rachman (Eds.), *Cognition and mood. Advances in Behaviour Research & Therapy, 5,* 51–62. **[46, 118, 210, 211, 263, 297]**

Butler, K. F. **[47, 54, 60]**

Cameron, O. G. **[40, 62, 63, 72, 128, 205]**

Candy, J. **[169]**

Caputo, G. C. **[19, 41, 44, 66, 120, 182, 207, 213, 249]**

Carr, D. B. **[3]**

Carr, D. B., & Sheehan, D. V. (1984a). Evidence that panic disorder has a metabolic cause. In J. D. Ballenger (Ed.), *Biology of agoraphobia* (pp. 99–111). Washington, DC: American Psychiatric Press. **[54, 222]**

Carr, D. B., & Sheehan, D. V. (1984b). Panic anxiety: A new biological model. *Journal of Clinical Psychiatry, 45,* 323–330. **[54, 245]**

Case, W. G. **[313]**

Catalan, J., & Gath, D. H. (1985). Benzodiazepines in general practice: For a decision. *British Medical Journal, 290,* 1374–1376. **[87]**

Cerny, J. A. **[20, 21, 22, 32, 33, 44, 45, 112, 117, 118, 261, 289, 290, 294]**

Chalkley, A. J. **[72, 80–84, 89, 114, 120, 128, 184, 200, 202]**

Chambless, D. L. **[84, 212, 311]**

Chambless, D. L. (1982). Characteristics of agoraphobics. In D. L. Chambless & A. J. Goldstein (Eds.), *Agoraphobia* (pp. 1–20). New York: Wiley. **[270]**

Chambless, D. L., & Beck, A. T. (1986). *Catastrophic cognitions and fear of somatic symptoms: A factor analytic study.* Manuscript in preparation. **[207]**

Chambless, D. L., Caputo, G. C., Bright, P., & Gallagher, R. (1984). Assessment of fear of fear in agoraphobics: The Body Sensations Questionnaire and the Agoraphobic Cognitions Questionnaire. *Journal of Consulting & Clinical Psychology, 52,* 1090–1097. **[19, 41, 44, 66, 120, 182, 207, 213, 249]**

Chambless, D. L., Caputo, G. C., Jasin, S., Gracely, E., & Williams, C. (1985). The Mobility Inventory for Agoraphobia. *Behaviour Research & Therapy, 23,* 35–44. **[19]**

Chambless, D. L., Foa, E. B., Groves, G. A., & Goldstein, A. J. (1979). Flooding with brevital in the treatment of agoraphobia: Countereffective? *Behaviour Research & Therapy, 17,* 243–251. **[318]**

Chambless, D. L., & Goldstein, A. J. (Eds.). (1982). *Agoraphobia: Multiple perspectives on theory and treatment.* New York: Wiley. **[105, 318]**

Chambless, D. L., & Goldstein, A. J. (1981). Clinical treatment of agoraphobia. In M. Mavissakalian & D. H. Barlow (Eds.), *Phobia: Psychological and pharmacological intervention* (pp. 103–144). New York: Guilford Press. **[208, 209]**

Chambless, D. L., & Goldstein, A. J. (1980). The treatment of agoraphobia. In A. Goldstein & E. Foa (Eds.), *Handbook of behavioral interventions.* New York: Wiley. **[296]**

Chambless, D. L., Goldstein, A. J., Gallagher, R., & Bright, P. (1986). Integrating behavior therapy with psychotherapy in the treatment of agoraphobia. *Psychotherapy, 23,* 150–159. **[211, 212]**

Chambless, D. L., & Gracely, E. J. (1986). *Fear of fear and the anxiety disorders.* Manuscript submitted for publication. **[207]**

Charney, D. S. **[45, 51, 57, 238, 245, 248]**

Charney, D. S., & Heninger, G. R. (1986). Abnormal regulation of noradrenergic function in panic disorders: Effects of clonidine in healthy subjects and patients with agoraphobia and panic disorder. *Archives of General Psychiatry, 43,* 1042–1054. **[86]**

Charney, D. S., & Heninger, G. R. (1985a). Noradrenergic function and the mechanism of action of antianxiety treatment. I. The effect of long term Alprazolam treatment. *Archives of General Psychiatry, 42,* 458–467. **[57, 60, 62]**

Charney, D. S., & Heninger, G. R. (1985b). Noradrenergic function and the mechanism of action of antianxiety treatment. II. Effect of long term imipramine treatment. *Archives of General Psychiatry, 42,* 473–481. **[57, 60, 62]**

Charney, D. S., Heninger, G. R., & Breier, A. (1984). Noradrenergic function in panic anxiety: Effects of Yohimbine in healthy subjects and patients with agoraphobia and panic disorder. *Archives of General Psychiatry, 41,* 751–763. **[3, 54, 60, 61, 72, 85, 86, 257]**

Charney, D. S., Heninger, G. R., & Jatlow, P. I. (1985). Increased anxiogenic effects of caffeine in panic disorders. *Archives of General Psychiatry, 42,* 233–243. **[72]**

Charney, D. S., Heninger, G. R., & Sternberg, D. E. (1982). Assessment of alpha 2 adrenergic autoreceptor function in humans: Effects of oral Yohimbine. *Life Science, 30,* 2033–2041. **[61]**

Chaudhry, D. R. **[51, 56, 128]**

Chouinard, G., Annable, L., Fontaine, R., & Solyom, L. (1982). Alprazolam in the treatment of generalized anxiety and panic disorders. A double-blind placebo-controlled study. *Psychopharmacology* (Berlin), *77,* 229–233. **[38, 57, 72]**

Christie, M. M. **[307]**

Cisin, I. H. **[20]**

Clancy, J. **[179]**

Clancy, M. **[38, 43, 60, 87]**

Clark, D. M. **[80, 83, 89, 111, 112, 114, 116, 121, 124–128, 130, 135, 194, 200, 213, 251]**

Clark, D. M. (1986a). A cognitive approach to panic. *Behaviour Research & Therapy, 24,* 461–470. **[58, 71, 74, 111, 117, 118, 120, 248, 266, 290–293, 305]**

Clark, D. M. (1986b). Cognitive therapy for anxiety. *Behavioural Psychotherapy, 14,* 283–294. **[83, 120]**

Clark, D. M. (1979). *Therapeutic aspects of increasing PCO_2 by behavioural means.* Unpublished thesis. University of London. **[71, 80, 114, 125]**

Clark, D. M., & Beck, A. T. (1986). Cognitive approaches. In C. Last & M. Hersen (Eds.) *Handbook of anxiety disorders.* New York: Pergamon Press. **[122]**

Clark, D. M., & Hemsley, D. R. (1982). The effects of hyperventilation: Individual variability and its relation to personality. *Journal of Behaviour Therapy & Experimental Psychiatry, 13,* 41–47. **[72, 80, 126]**

Clark, D. M., & Salkovskis, P. M. (1986a). A cognitive–behavioural treatment for panic attacks. In W. Huber (Ed.), *Proceedings of the SPR: European conference on psychotherapy research.* Louvain-la-Neuve, Belgium: Louvain-la-Neuve University Press. **[129, 131]**

Clark, D. M., & Salkovskis, P. M. (1986b). *Cognitive therapy for panic attacks: Treatment manual.* Unpublished manuscript. **[123, 129–131]**

Clark, D. M., & Salkovskis, P. M. (1985). Cognitive and physiological processes in panic attacks. *Paper presented at the 15th annual meeting of the European Association for Behaviour Therapy,* Munich. **[248]**

Clark, D. M., Salkovskis, P. M., & Chalkley, A. J. (1985). Respiratory control as a treatment for panic attacks. *Journal of Behaviour Therapy & Experimental Psychiatry, 16,* 23–30. **[72, 80–84, 89, 114, 120, 128, 184, 200, 202]**
Clark, D. M., Salkovskis, P. M., Koehler, K., & Gelder, M. G. (1987). *Interpretation of ambiguous internal and external events by panic and other anxious patients.* Manuscript in preparation. **[88]**
Claycomb, J. B. **[172, 179, 183]**
Clinthorne, J. **[20]**
Cobb, J. **[176]**
Cohen, A. S. **[27, 51, 58, 129, 313]**
Cohen, A. S., Barlow, D. H., & Blanchard, E. B. (1985). The psychophysiology of relaxation-associated panic attacks. *Journal of Abnormal Psychology, 94,* 96–101. **[14, 15, 16, 17, 29, 41, 67, 124, 125]**
Cohen, B. S. **[80, 125, 126, 239, 241]**
Cohen, M. E., & White, P. Q. (1951). Life situation, emotions and neurocirculatory asthenia (anxiety neurosis, neurostenia, effort syndrome). *Psychosomatic Medicine, 13,* 335–357. **[244]**
Cohen, P. T. **[192]**
Cohen, S. D. **[84, 87, 127, 169, 170, 172, 173, 176, 182, 183]**
Cohen, S. D., Monteiro, W., & Marks, I. M. (1984). Two-year follow-up of agoraphobics after exposure and imipramine. *British Journal of Psychiatry, 144,* 276–281. **[173, 182]**
Coleman, D. J. **[27]**
Cook, E. W., III **[228, 229]**
Cook, E. W., III, Melamed, B. G., Cuthbert, B. N., McNeil, D. N., & Lang, P. J. (1987). Emotional imagery and the differential diagnosis of anxiety. Manuscript in preparation. **[228]**
Cook, M. **[48]**
Coryell, W. H. **[179]**
Costello, A. **[48, 49]**
Coul, L. **[157]**
Covi, L. **[38]**
Cox, B. J. **[20, 117, 118]**
Craske, M. G. **[264]**
Craske, M. G., Rachman, S. J., & Tallman, K. (1986). Mobility, cognitions and panic. *Journal of Psychopathology & Behavioral Assessment, 8,* 199–210. **[19, 262]**
Craske, M. G., Sanderson, W., & Barlow, D. H. (1987). How do desynchronous response systems relate to the treatment of agoraphobia: A follow-up evaluation. *Behaviour Research & Therapy, 25,* 117–122. **[18]**
Crowe, R. R. **[27, 38, 43, 51, 56, 60, 87, 114, 128]**
Crowe, R. R. (1985). The genetics of panic disorder and agoraphobia. *Psychiatric Developments, 2,* 171–186. **[49]**
Crowe, R. R., Noyes, R., Pauls, D., & Slyman, D. (1983). A family study of panic disorder. *Archives of General Psychiatry, 40,* 1065–1069. **[20]**
Crowe, R. R., Pauls, D., Slyman, D. J., & Noyes, R. (1980). A family study of anxiety neurosis. *Archives of General Psychiatry, 37,* 77–79. **[64, 167]**
Cullington, A. **[113]**

Currie, D. W. **[307]**
Curtis, G. C. **[40, 62, 72, 128, 205]**
Cuthbert, B. N. **[228]**

Dalton, J. W. **[80, 114]**
Damas-Mora, J., Davies, L., Taylor, W., & Jenner, F. A. (1980). Menstrual respiratory changes and symptoms. *British Journal of Psychiatry, 136,* 492–497. **[85]**
Danielson, E. **[240]**
Davidson, M. **[48]**
Davidson, R. J. **[27]**
Davies, L. **[85]**
Davies, S. O. **[3, 14, 27, 41, 43, 52, 60, 72, 80, 81, 167, 176, 238–241, 245, 246, 267]**
Davis, J., Nasar, S., Spira, N., & Vogel, C. (1981). Anxiety: Differential diagnosis and treatment from a biological perspective. *Journal of Clinical Psychiatry, 42,* 4–14. **[57]**
Dealy, R. **[142, 176]**
Deckert, G. H. (1964). Pursuit eye movements in the absence of moving visual stimulus. *Science, 143,* 1192–1193. **[228]**
Deltito, J. A., Perugi, G., Maremmani, I., Mignani, V., & Cassano, G. B. (1986). The importance of separation anxiety in the differentiation of panic disorder for agoraphobia. *Psychiatric Developments, 3,* 227–236. **[57]**
Dempsey, J. A. **[126]**
Dennett, D. C. (1978). *Brainstorms.* Montgomery, VT: Bradford Books. **[221, 222]**
Dent, H. R. **[122]**
Dent, H. R., & Salkovskis, P. M. (1986). Clinical measures of depression, anxiety and obsessionality in non-clinical populations. *Behaviour Research & Therapy, 24,* 689–691. **[122]**
DePree, J. A. **[212]**
Derogatis, L. R., Lipman, R. S., Rickels, K., Uhlenhuth, E. H., & Coul, L. (1974). The HSCL: A self-report inventory. *Behavioral Sciences, 19,* 1–15. **[157]**
DeRubeis, R. J. **[180, 181]**
de Silva, P. (1986). Obsessional-compulsive imagery. *Behaviour Research & Therapy, 24,* 333–350. **[122]**
Detre, T. P. (1985). Is the grouping of anxiety disorders in DSM–III based on shared beliefs or data? In A. H. Tuma and J. D. Maser (Eds.), *Anxiety and the anxiety disorders* (pp. 783–786). Hillsdale, NJ: Lawrence Erlbaum Associates. **[38]**
Devereux, R. B. **[52, 57, 63]**
Diamond, L. **[313]**
Dickman, W. **[53]**
Dillon, D. **[3, 14, 27, 41, 43, 52, 58, 60, 72, 80, 81, 167, 176, 238–241, 245, 246, 250, 267]**
Di Nardo, P. A. **[20–22, 27, 32, 33, 44, 45, 51, 58, 112, 114, 117, 118, 129, 261, 289, 290, 294, 313]**
Di Nardo, P. A., O'Brien, G. T., Barlow, D. H., Waddell, M. I., & Blanchard, E. B. (1983). Reliability of DSM–III anxiety disorder categories using a new structured interview. *Archives of General Psychiatry, 40,* 1070–1074. **[20, 22, 23, 46, 53]**
Dorward, J. **[20, 117, 118]**
Downing, R. W. **[38]**

Easton, D., & Sherman, D. G. (1976). Somatic anxiety attacks and propranolol. *Archives of Neurology, 33,* 689–691. **[62]**

Eaton, W. W. **[47]**

Ehlers, A. **[3, 13, 17, 24, 27, 29, 41–43, 52, 64, 113, 123, 167, 181, 182]**

Ehlers, A., Margraf, J., & Roth, W. T. (1986). Experimental induction of panic attacks. In I. Hand and H.-U. Wittchen (Eds.), *Panic and phobias: Empirical evidence of theoretical models and longterm effects of behavioral treatments* (pp. 53–66). New York: Springer–Verlag. **[205, 239, 244, 252]**

Ehlers, A., Margraf, J., Roth, W. T., & Birbaumer, N. (1985, September). *Perceived heart rate changes and hyperventilation as anxiety triggers in panic patients.* Paper presented at the 15th annual meeting of the European Association for Behaviour Therapy, Munich. **[205]**

Ehlers, A., Margraf, J., Roth, W. T., Taylor, C. B., & Birbaumer, N. (1986). *Anxiety induction by false heart rate feedback in patients with panic disorder.* Unpublished manuscript. **[254, 253]**

Ehlers, A., Margraf, J., Roth, W. T., Taylor, C. B., Maddock, R. J., Sheikh, J., Kopell, M. L., McClenahan, K. L., Gossard, D., Blowers, G. H., Agras, W. S., & Kopell, B. S. (1986). Lactate infusions and panic attacks: Do patients and controls respond differently? *Psychiatry Research, 17,* 295–308. **[43, 239]**

Eich, E. (1980). The cue-dependent nature of state-dependent retrieval. *Memory & Cognition, 8,* 157–173. **[302]**

Elsworth, J. D. **[52]**

Emery, G. **[7, 18, 48, 71, 73, 122, 135, 155, 219, 266, 290, 305]**

Engel, B. T. (1972). Response specificity. In N. S. Greenfield & R. A. Sternbach (Eds.), *Handbook of psychophysiology.* New York: Holt, Rinehart, & Winston. **[316]**

Epstein, S. **[230]**

Erbaugh, J. **[157]**

Ettedgui, E. **[14, 25, 42, 52, 64, 182, 205, 240]**

Evans, I. M. (1972). A conditioning model of a common fear pattern-fear of fear. *Psychotherapy: Theory, research and practice, 9,* 238–241. **[39]**

Eysenck, H. J. (1968). A theory of the incubation of anxiety/fear responses. *Behaviour research & therapy, 6,* 309–321. **[247]**

Eysenck, H. J., & Eysenck, S. B. G. (1968). *Manual for the Eysenck Personality Inventory.* San Diego: Educational and Industrial Testing Service. **[48]**

Eysenck, S. B. G. **[48]**

Faravelli, C. (1985). Life events preceding the onset of panic disorder. *Journal of Affective Disorders, 9,* 103–105. **[39]**

Farmer, B. B. **[241]**

Fennell, M. J. V. **[194]**

Fenz, W. D., & Epstein, S. (1965). Manifest anxiety: Unifactorial or multifactorial composition? *Perceptual and Motor Skills, 20,* 773–780. **[230]**

Fernandez, A., & Glenberg, A. (1985). Changing the environmental context does not reliably affect memory. *Memory & Cognition, 13,* 333–345. **[226]**

Fink, M. **[23, 37, 40, 168]**

Fink, M., Taylor, M. A., & Volavka, J. (1971). Anxiety precipitated by lactate. *New England Journal of Medicine, 281,* 1429. **[240]**

Fischler, I., & Bloom, P. A. (1979). Automatic and attentional processes in the effects of sentence contexts on word recognition. *Journal of Verbal Learning & Verbal Behaviour, 18,* 1–20. **[76]**

Fisher, J. **[29]**

Fisher, L. M., & Wilson, G. T. (1985). A study of the psychology of agoraphobia. *Behaviour Research & Therapy, 23,* 97–107. **[209, 212]**

Fisher, S. **[38]**

Fishman, S. M., Sheehan, D. V., & Carr, D. B. (1985). Thyroid indices in panic disorder. *Journal of Clinical Psychiatry, 46,* 432–433. **[3]**

Fiske, S. T., & Taylor, S. E. (1984). *Social cognition.* New York: Random House. **[212, 213]**

Florio, L. **[6]**

Foa, E. B. **[211, 318]**

Foa, E. B., & Kozak, M. J. (1986). Emotional processing of fear: Exposure to corrective information. *Psychological Bulletin, 99*(1), 20–35. **[234]**

Foa, E. B., & Kozak, M. J. (1985). Treatment of anxiety disorders: Implications for psychopathology (pp. 421–452). In A. H. Tuma & J. D. Maser (Eds.), *Anxiety and the anxiety disorders.* Hillsdale, NJ: Lawrence Erlbaum Associates. **[65]**

Fontaine, R. **[38, 57, 72]**

Fowler, H. **[305]**

Fox, P. O. **[47]**

Frances, A. J. **[51, 52, 56–58, 63, 64]**

Freedman, D. X., & Glass, R. M. (1984). Psychiatry. *Journal of the American Medical Association, 252,* 2223–2228. **[167]**

Freedman, R. R. **[72, 80, 240]**

Freedman, R. R., Ianni, P., Ettedgui, E., Pohl, R., & Rainey, J. M. (1984). Psychophysiological factors in panic disorder. *Psychopathology, 17,* 66–73. **[205, 240]**

Freedman, R. R., Ianni, P., Ettedgui, E., & Puthezhath, N. (1985). Ambulatory monitoring of panic disorder. *Archives of General Psychiatry, 42,* 244–255. **[14, 25, 42, 52, 64, 182]**

Freud, S. (1940a). The justification for detaching from neurasthenia a particular syndrome: The anxiety-neurosis. *Collected Papers* (Vol. 1). London: Hogarth Press (Original work published in 1894). **[71]**

Freud, S. (1940b). Obsessions and phobias: Their psychical mechanisms and their aetiology. *Collected Papers* (Vol. 1). London: Hogarth Press. (Original work published in 1895). **[84]**

Friedman, K., Shear, M. K., & Frances, A. J. (1987). DSM–III personality disorder in panic disorder patients. *Journal of Personality Disorders, 1,* 132–135. **[56, 57]**

Friedman, M. **[29]**

Frohman, C. E. **[240]**

Frohman, R. **[58]**

Fuller, T. C. **[51, 56]**

Fyer, A. J. **[2, 3, 14, 18, 27, 41, 43, 52, 54, 60, 63, 72, 80, 81, 125, 126, 167, 176, 238–241, 244, 245, 246, 267]**

Fyer, A. J., Gorman, J. M., Liebowitz, M. R., Levitt, M., Danielson, E., Martinez, J., & Klein, D. F. (1984). Sodium lactate infusion, panic attacks and ionized calcium. *Biological Psychiatry, 19,* 1437. **[240]**

Fyer, M. **[3]**
Fyer, M., & Gorman, J. (1986). *Pharmacologic provocation of panic: Sodium lactate infusion*. Paper presented at the World Psychiatric Association Regional Symposium, Copenhagen. **[238]**

Gallagher, R. **[19, 41, 44, 66, 120, 182, 207, 211–213, 249]**
Gallen, C. C. **[67, 87, 169, 174, 176–178, 181, 317]**
Gallo, J. **[51, 56]**
Garakani, H., Zitrin, C. M., & Klein, D. F. (1984). Treatment of panic disorder with imipramine alone. *American Journal of Psychiatry, 141*, 446–448. **[87, 176]**
Garcia, J., & Koelling, R. A. (1972). Relation of cue to consequence in avoidance learning. In M. E. P. Seligman & J. L. Hager (Eds.). *Biological boundaries of learning* (pp. 10–16). New York: Appleton. **[255]**
Garside, R. F. **[169]**
Garssen, B., van Veenendaal, W., & Bloemink, R. (1983). Agoraphobia and the hyperventilation syndrome. *Behaviour Research & Therapy, 21*, 643–649. **[63, 115, 241, 251]**
Garvey, M. J., & Tuason, V. B. (1984). The relationship of panic disorders to agoraphobia. *Comprehensive Psychiatry, 25*, 529–531. **[40]**
Gath, D. H. **[87]**
Gauthier, J. **[307, 313, 318]**
Gelder, M. G. **[84, 88, 113, 127, 130, 157, 170, 174, 184, 260]**
Gelder, M. (1986). Panic attacks: New approaches to an old problem. *British Journal of Psychiatry, 149*, 346–352. **[2]**
George, L. K. **[5]**
Gever, J. **[245]**
Ghoneim, M. M. **[38, 43, 60, 87]**
Gibbons, F. X., Smith, T. W., Ingram, R. E., Pearce, K., Brehm, S. S., & Schraoeder, D. J. (1985). Self-awareness in a clinical sample. *Journal of Personality and Social Psychology, 48*, 662–675. **[47]**
Gibson, H. B. (1978). A form of behaviour therapy for some states diagnosed as "affective disorder." *Behaviour Research & Therapy, 16*, 191–195. **[80]**
Gitlin, B., Martin, J., Shear, M. K., Frances, A. J., Ball, G., & Josephson, S. (1986). Behavior therapy for panic disorder. *Journal of Nervous & Mental Disease, 173*, 742–743. **[58]**
Gittelman, R., & Klein, D. F. (1985). Childhood separation anxiety and adult agoraphobia (pp. 389–402). In A. H. Tuma & J. D. Maser (Eds.), *Anxiety and the anxiety disorders*. Hillsdale, N.J.: Lawrence Erlbaum Associates. **[56]**
Glass, C. R. **[212]**
Glass, R. M. **[167, 174]**
Gledhill, N., Beirne, G. J., & Dempsey, J. A. (1975). Renal response to short term hypocapnia in man. *Kidney International, 8*, 376. **[126]**
Glenberg, A. **[226]**
Gliebe, P. A. **[80, 114]**
Gliklich, J. **[63]**
Goetz, R. R. **[3]**
Gloger, S. **[63]**

Gloger, S., Gruenhaus, L., Birmarcher, B., & Troudart, T. (1981). Treatment of spontaneous panic attacks with chlomipramine. *American Journal of Psychiatry, 138,* 1215–1217. **[57]**

Goldfried, M. R., Padawer, W., & Robins, C. J. (1984). Social anxiety and the semantic structure of heterosocial interactions. *Journal of Abnormal Psychology, 93,* 87–97. **[213]**

Goldstein, A. J. **[105, 208, 209, 211, 212, 296, 318]**

Goldstein, A. J., & Chambless, D. L. (1978). A reanalysis of agoraphobia. *Behavior Therapy, 9,* 47–59. **[84, 212, 311]**

Goodman, M. **[245]**

Goodman, W. K. **[238, 245, 248]**

Gordon, A. **[307, 318]**

Gordon, J. R. **[180]**

Gorman, J. M. **[3, 14, 27, 41, 43, 52, 54, 60, 72, 80, 81, 167, 176, 238–241, 246, 260, 261, 267]**

Gorman, J. M. (1984). The biology of panic. In D. F. Klein (Ed.), *Psychiatry update: The APA annual review.* Washington, DC: American Psychiatric Press. **[60]**

Gorman, J. M., Askanazi, J., Liebowitz, M. R., Fyer, A. J., Stein, J., Kinney, J. M., & Klein, D. F. (1984). Response to hyperventilation in a group of patients with panic disorder. *American Journal of Psychiatry, 141,* 857–861. **[18, 80, 244–246]**

Gorman, J. M., Fyer, A. F., Gliklich, J. (1981). Mitral valve prolapse and panic disorder: Effect of imipramine (pp. 167–174). In D. F. Klein & J. G. Rabkin (Eds.), *Anxiety: New research and changing concepts.* New York: Raven Press. **[64]**

Gorman, J. M., Fyer, A. F., Gliklich, J., King, R., & Klein, D. F. (1981). Effect of sodium lactate on patients with panic disorder and mitral valve prolapse. *American Journal of Psychiatry, 138,* 247–249. **[63]**

Gorman, J. M., Fyer, A. J., Ross, D. C., Cohen, B. S., Marinez, J. M., Liebowitz, M. R., & Klein, D. F. (1985). Normalization of venous pH, pCO_2, and bicarbonate levels after blockade of panic attacks. *Psychiatry Research, 14,* 57–65. **[125, 126]**

Gorman, J. M., Goetz, R. R., Fyer, M., King, D. L., Fyer, A. J., Liebowitz, M. R., & Klein, D. F. (in preparation). *The mitral valve prolapse-panic disorder connection.* **[3]**

Gorman, J. M., Levy, G. F., Liebowitz, M. R., McGrath, P., Appleby, I. L., Dillon, D. J., Davies, S. O., & Klein, D. F. (1983). Effect of acute beta-adrenergic blockade on lactate-induced panic. *Archives of General Psychiatry, 40,* 1079–1082. **[43]**

Gorman, J. M., Liebowtiz, M. R., Fyer, A., Dillon, D., Davies, S., Stein, J., & Klein, D. F. (1985). Lactate infusions in obsessive-compulsive neurosis. *American Journal of Psychiatry, 142*(7), 864–866. **[238, 239, 241]**

Gorman, J. M., Martinez, J. M., Liebowitz, M. R., Fyer, A. J., & Klein, D. F. (1984). Hypoglycemia and panic attacks. *American Journal of Psychiatry, 141,* 101–102. **[2, 3]**

Gorman, J. M., Shear, M. K., Devereux, R. B., King, R., & Klein, D. F. (1986). Prevalence of mitral valve prolapse in panic disorder: Effect of echocardiographic criteria. *Psychosomatic Medicine, 48,* 167–171. **[63]**

Gorsuch, R. L. **[48, 113]**

Gossard, D. **[13, 17, 24, 27, 29, 42, 43, 52, 64, 181, 182, 239]**

Gracely, E. J. **[19, 207]**

Gray, J. (1981). *The psychology of fear and stress.* London: Weidenfeld. **[308]**

Gray, J. A. (1975). *Elements of a two-process theory of learning*. London: Academic Press. **[126]**

Gray, R. **[239, 241]**

Green, D. M., & Swets, J. A. (1966). *Signal detection theory and psychophysics*. New York: Wiley. **[311]**

Greenberg, R. **[7, 18, 48, 71, 73, 122, 135, 155, 219, 266, 290, 305]**

Greenberg, R. L. (1986). *Ideational components of distress in panic disorder*. Doctoral dissertation, in progress, University of Pennsylvania, Philadelphia. **[97]**

Greenwald, D. **[142, 144]**

Greenwald, M. **[142, 144]**

Grey, S. **[84, 87, 127, 169, 170, 172, 173, 176, 177, 182, 183]**

Griez, E. **[18, 39, 72, 81, 83, 242–246, 249–252]**

Griez, E., & van den Hout, M. A. (1986). CO_2 inhalation in the treatment of panic attacks. *Behaviour Research & Therapy, 24,* 145–150. **[80, 83, 84, 244]**

Griez, E., & van den Hout, M. A. (1984). *Carbon dioxide and anxiety. An experimental approach to a clinical claim*. Unpublished Doctoral dissertation, State University of Limburg, Maastricht, Netherlands. **[73, 87, 244]**

Griez, E., & van den Hout, M. A. (1983). Treatment of phobophobia by exposure to CO_2 induced anxiety symptoms. *Journal of Nervous & Mental Disease, 171,* 506–508. **[83, 242]**

Griez, E., & van den Hout, M. A. (1982). Effects of carbon dioxide-oxygen inhalations on subjective anxiety and some neurovegetative parameters. *Journal of Behavior Therapy & Experimental Psychiatry, 13,* 27–32. **[242]**

Griez, E., Lousberg, H., van den Hout, M. A., & van der Molen, G. M. (1987). Carbon dioxide vulnerability in panic disorder. *Psychiatry Research, 20,* 87–95. **[242]**

Grossman, P. **[80, 126]**

Grosz, H. J., & Farmer, B. B. (1972). Pitt's and McClure's lactate-anxiety study revisited. *British Journal of Psychiatry, 120,* 415–418. **[241]**

Grosz, H. J., & Farmer, B. B. (1969). Blood lactate in the development of anxiety symptoms. *Archives of General Psychiatry, 21,* 611–619. **[241]**

Groves, G. A. **[318]**

Gruenberg, E. **[5]**

Gruenhaus, L. **[57]**

Gruenhaus, L., & Gloger, S. (1982). Mitral valve prolapse in patients with panic attacks. *Israeli Journal of Medical Science, 18,* 221–223. **[63]**

Guidano, V. F., & Liotti, G. (1983). *Cognitive processes and emotional disorders*. New York: Guilford Press. **[155]**

Gursky, D. M. **[48, 248]**

Guttmacher, L. B., Murphy, D. L., & Insel, T. R. (1983). Pharmacologic models of anxiety. *Comprehensive Psychiatry, 24,* 312–326. **[60]**

Hager, J. L. **[326]**

Hajioff, J. **[169]**

Hall, R. C. (1983). Psychiatric effects of thyroid hormone disturbance. *Psychosomatics, 24,* 7–18. **[2, 3]**

Hallam, R. S. (1985). *Anxiety: Psychological perspectives on panic and agoraphobia*. London: Academic Press. **[184]**

Hallam, R. S. (1978). Agoraphobia: A critical review of the concept. *British Journal of Psychiatry, 133,* 314–319. **[84, 205]**

Hamra, B. J. **[128]**

Hare, N., & Levis, D. J. (1981). Pervasive ("free-floating") anxiety: A search for a cause and treatment approach. In S. M. Turner, K. S. Calhoun, & H. E. Adams (Eds.), *Handbook of clinical behavior therapy* (pp. 41–67). New York: Wiley. **[39]**

Harris, E. L. **[128]**

Harris, E. L., Noyes, R., Jr., Crowe, R. R., & Chaudhry, D. R. (1983). Family study of agoraphobia: Report of a pilot study. *Archives of General Psychiatry, 40,* 1061–1064. **[51, 56]**

Harrison, B. **[45, 53, 54, 117, 163, 262]**

Harrison, J. **[18, 80, 250]**

Harschfield, G. **[52, 57, 64]**

Hartman, N., Kramer, R., Brown, W. T., & Devereux, R. B. (1982). Panic disorder in patients with mitral valve prolapse. *American Journal of Psychiatry, 139,* 669–670. **[63]**

Hasher, L. **[212, 213]**

Hasher, L., & Zacks, R. T. (1979). Automatic and effortful processes in memory. *Journal of Experimental Psychology General, 108,* 386–388. **[94, 101]**

Hauch, J. **[45, 53, 54, 117, 163, 262]**

Hauri, P., Friedman, M., Ravaris, R., & Fisher, J. (1985). Sleep in agoraphobia with panic attacks. In M. H. Chafe, D. J. McGinty & R. Wilder-Jones (Eds.). *Sleep Research,* (Vol. 14, p. 128). Los Angeles: BIS/BRS. **[29]**

Havvik, D. **[42, 181, 182]**

Heide, F. J., & Borkovec, T. D. (1984). Relaxation induced anxiety: Mechanisms and theoretical implications. *Behaviour Research & Therapy, 22,* 1–12. **[29, 256]**

Heide, F. J., & Borkovec, T. D. (1983). Relaxation induced anxiety: Paradoxical anxiety enhancement due to relaxation. *Journal of Consulting & Clinical Psychology, 51,* 171–182. **[205]**

Hemsley, D. R. **[72, 80, 126]**

Heninger, G. R. **[3, 45, 51, 54, 57, 60–62, 72, 85, 86, 238, 245, 248, 257]**

Henry, J. P., Meehan, J. P., & Stephens, P. M. (1967). The use of psychosocial stimuli to induce prolonged systolic hypertension in mice. *Psychosomatic Medicine, 29,* 408–414. **[68]**

Herscovitch, P. **[47, 54, 60]**

Heseltine, G. F. D. **[168, 171]**

Hibbert, G. A. **[113]**

Hibbert, G. A. (1986). The diagnosis of hyperventilation using ambulatory carbon dioxide monitoring. In H. Lacey & J. Sturgeon (Eds.), *Proceedings of the 15th European Conference on Psychosomatic Medicine* (pp. 245–248). London: John Libbey. **[80, 125]**

Hibbert, G. A. (1984a). Hyperventilation as a cause of panic attacks. *British Medical Journal, 288,* 263–264. **[63, 79, 214]**

Hibbert, G. A. (1984b). Ideational components of anxiety: Their origin and content. *British Journal of Psychiatry, 144,* 618–624. **[46, 66, 80, 96, 97, 207, 214, 256]**

Hill, R. **[84, 87, 127, 169, 170, 172, 173, 176, 182, 183]**

Himle, J. **[40, 128, 205, 260, 261]**

Hinrichs, J. V. **[38, 43, 60, 87]**

Hodgson, R. **[266, 267]**
Hoehn-Saric, R. (1983). Anxiety, panic, and agoraphobia. *Delaware Medical Journal, 55,* 333–339. **[40]**
Hoehn-Saric, R. (1982). Comparison of generalized anxiety disorder with panic disorder patients. *Psychopharmacology Bulletin, 18,* 104–108. **[53]**
Hoehn-Saric, R., Merchant, A. F., Keyser, M. L., & Smith, U. K. (1981). Effects of clonidine on anxiety disorders. *Archives of General Psychiatry, 38,* 1278–1282. **[60]**
Hofer, M. A. **[68]**
Hofer, M. A. (1983). Relationships as regulators: A psychobiologic perspective on bereavement. *Psychosomatic Medicine, 45,* 1–14. **[68]**
Hollon, S. D., & DeRubeis, R. J. (1981). Placebo-psychotherapy combinations: Inappropriate representation of psychotherapy in drug-psychotherapy comparative trials. *Journal of Consulting & Clinical Psychology, 90,* 467–477. **[180, 181]**
Hollon, S. D., & Kriss, M. R. (1984). Cognitive factors in clinical research and practice. *Clinical Psychology Review, 4,* 35–76. **[155]**
Holzer, C. E., III. **[5, 20, 46]**
Honig, W. K. **[305]**
Huber-Smith, M. J. **[62, 72]**
Huggins, P. **[169]**
Hulse, S. H., Fowler, H., & Honig, W. K. (1978). *Cognitive processes in animal behavior.* Hillsdale, NJ: Lawrence Erlbaum Associates. **[305]**

Ianni, P. **[14, 25, 42, 52, 64, 182, 205, 240]**
Ingram, R. E. **[47]**
Insel, T. R. **[60]**

Jacob, R. G., Moller, M. B., Turner, S. M., & Wall, C., III. (1985). Otoneurological examination in panic disorder and agoraphobia with panic attacks: A pilot study. *American Journal of Psychiatry, 142,* 715–720. **[2, 48, 63]**
Jacob, R. G., & Rapport, M. D. (1984). Panic disorder: Medical and psychological parameters. In S. M. Turner (Ed.), *Behavioral theories and treatment of anxiety* (pp. 187–237). New York: Plenum Press. **[47]**
Jacobsen, G. **[32, 51, 169, 170, 183]**
James, W. (1884). What is emotion? *Mind, 19,* 188–205. **[224]**
Jansson, L., & Ost, L. (1982). Behavioral treatment for agoraphobia: An evaluative review. *Clinical Psychology Review, 2,* 311–336. **[184]**
Jasin, S. **[19]**
Jatlow, P. I. **[72]**
Jenner, F. A. **[85]**
Johnston, D. W. **[84, 127, 130, 170, 174, 182, 184, 260]**
Johnston, J. **[262, 263, 265, 296, 297]**
Jones, B. A. **[2, 63]**
Jones, D. R. O. **[80, 82, 83, 112, 116, 125–128, 200]**
Josephson, S. **[58]**

Kahn, R. J. **[38, 87, 177]**
Kahn, R. J., McNair, D. M., Covi, L., Downing, R. W., Fisher, S., Lipman, R. S., Rickels, K., & Smith, V. (1981). Effects of psychotropic agents on high anxiety subjects. *Psychopharmacology Bulletin, 17,* 97–100. **[38]**

Kamin, L. J. (1969). Predictability, surprise, attention and conditioning. In B. A. Campbell & R. M. Church (Eds.), *Punishment and aversive behavior* (pp. 279–296). New York: Appleton–Century–Crofts. **[324]**

Kantor, J. S., Zitrin, C. M., & Zeldis, S. M. (1980). Mitral valve prolapse syndrome in agoraphobic patients. *American Journal of Psychiatry, 137,* 467–469. **[63]**

Karno. M. **[5]**

Kanton, W. (1985). Panic disorder and somatization: A review of 55 cases. *American Journal of Medicine, 77,* 101–106. **[121]**

Kaufman, C. **[68]**

Kavanagh, D. J., & Bower, G. H. (1985). Mood and self-efficacy: Impact of joy and sadness on perceived capabilities. *Cognitive Therapy & Research, 9*(5), 507–525. **[178]**

Keir, R. **[48]**

Kelly, D. **[169]**

Kelly, D., Mitchell-Heggs, N., & Sherman, D. (1971). Anxiety and the effects of sodium lactate assessed clinically and physiologically. *British Journal of Psychiatry, 119,* 129–141. **[43, 58, 176, 239, 240, 250]**

Kennedy, S., & Shear, M. K. (1987). Unpublished data. **[54]**

Kerr, W. J., Dalton, J. W., & Gliebe, P. A. (1937). Some physical phenomena associated with anxiety states and their relation to hyperventilation. *Annals of Internal Medicine, 11,* 961–992. **[80, 114]**

Keyl, P. M. **[47]**

Keyser, M. L. **[60]**

Kihlstrom, J. **[296, 297]**

King, D. L. **[3]**

King, R. **[63]**

Kinney, J. M. **[3, 18, 80, 244, 245, 246]**

Kirch, I. **[208]**

Klein, D. F. **[2, 3, 14, 18, 27, 32, 39, 41, 43, 51–54, 56, 58, 60, 63, 67, 71, 72, 80, 81, 87, 125, 126, 167–171, 174, 176, 183, 238–241, 244, 245, 246, 250, 267, 296, 317]**

Klein, D. F. (1984). Psychopharmacologic treatment of panic disorder. *Psychosomatics, 25,* 32–36. **[168, 169]**

Klein, D. F. (1982). Medication in the treatment of panic attacks and phobic states. *Psychopharmacology Bulletin, 18,* 85–90. **[51, 57]**

Klein, D. F. (1981). Anxiety reconceptualized. In D. F. Klein & J. Rabkin (Eds.), *Anxiety: New research and changing concepts* (pp. 235–264). New York: Raven Press. **[3, 23, 32, 56, 68, 71, 84, 126, 222, 234, 311]**

Klein, D. F. (1980). Anxiety reconceptualized. *Comprehensive Psychiatry, 21,* 411–427. **[167, 296]**

Klein, D. F. (1967). Importance of psychiatric diagnosis in prediction of clinical drug effects. *Archives of General Psychiatry, 16,* 118–126. **[169, 170]**

Klein, D. F. (1964). Delineation of two drug-responsive anxiety syndromes. *Psychopharmacologia, 5,* 397–408. **[3, 23, 37–39, 51, 53, 71, 170]**

Klein, D. F., & Fink, M. (1962). Psychiatric reaction patterns to imipramine. *American Journal of Psychiatry, 119,* 432–438. **[23, 37, 40, 168]**

Klein, D. F., Rabkin, J. G., & Gorman, J. M. (1985). Etiologic and pathophysiologic inferences from the pharmacologic treatments of anxiety (pp. 501–532). In A. H.

Tuma & J. D. Maser (Eds.), *Anxiety and the anxiety disorders*. Hillsdale, NJ: Lawrence Erlbaum Associates. **[60, 260, 261]**

Klein, D. F., Zitrin, C. M., & Woerner, M. G. (1977). Imipramine and phobia. *Psychopharmacological Bulletin, 13,* 24–27. **[170]**

Klein, D. F., Zitrin, C. M., Woerner, M. G., & Ross, D. C. (1983). Treatment of phobias: II. Behavior therapy and supportive psychotherapy: Are there any specific ingredients? *Archives of General Psychiatry, 40,* 139–145. **[53]**

Kleiner, L., & Marshall, W. L. (in press). Training in problem-solving and exposure treatment for agoraphobics with panic attacks. *Journal of Anxiety Disorders.* **[313, 317]**

Klerman, G. L. (1986). Current trends in clinical research on panic attacks, agoraphobia and related anxiety disorders. *Journal of Clinical Psychiatry, 47*(Suppl.), 37–39. **[136]**

Kligfeld, P. **[52, 57]**

Klimes, I. **[113]**

Klosko, J. S. **[27, 51, 58, 129, 313]**

Ko, G. N., Elsworth, J. D., Roth, R. H., Rifkin, B. G., Leigh, H., & Redmond, D. E. (1983). Panic induced elevation of plasma MHPG levels in phobic-anxious patients. *Archives of General Psychiatry, 40,* 425–430. **[52]**

Knitter, E. **[72, 80]**

Koehler, K. **[88]**

Koelling, R. A. **[255]**

Kopell, B. S. **[43, 239]**

Kopell, M. L. **[43, 239]**

Kopp, M., Mihaly, K., Tringer, K., & Vadasz, P. (1986). Agorafobias es panikneurotikus betegek legzesi kontroll kezelese. *Ideggyogyaszati Szemle, 39,* 185–196. **[83, 114, 115, 125]**

Kornblith, S. **[142, 144]**

Kouretas, N. **[172, 179, 183]**

Kozak, M. J. **[65, 228, 229, 234]**

Knott, V. J. **[239, 241]**

Kramer, M. **[20, 46]**

Kramer, R. **[63]**

Kramer-Fox, R. **[63]**

Kriss, M. R. **[155]**

Lacey, J. I. (1956). The evaluation of autonomic responses: Toward a general solution. *Annals of the New York Academy of Sciences, 67,* 123–164. **[316]**

Lader, M. H. (1980). Psychophysiologic studies in anxiety (pp. 73–88). In G. D. Burrows & B. Davies (Eds.), *Handbook of Studies in Anxiety.* Amsterdam: Elsevier, North Holland. **[56]**

Lader, M., & Mathews, A. (1970). Physiological changes during spontaneous panic attacks. *Journal of Psychosomatic Research, 14,* 377–382. **[14, 41]**

Lader, M., & Wing, L. (1966). *Physiological measures, sedative drugs and morbid anxiety.* London: Oxford University Press. **[230, 267]**

Lane, T. W. **[30]**

Lang, P. J. **[228, 229, 231, 235]**

Lang, P. J. (1985). The cognitive psychophysiology of emotion: Fear and anxiety. In A. H. Tuma & J. D. Maser (Eds.), *Anxiety and the anxiety disorders* (pp. 131–170). Hillsdale, NJ: Lawrence Erlbaum Associates. **[226, 227]**

Lang, P. (1968). Fear reduction and fear behavior. In J. Schlein (Ed.), *Research in psychotherapy* (pp. 90–103. Washington, DC: American Psychological Association, *3*. **[3, 259]**

Lang, P. J., Kozak, M. J., Miller, G. A., Levin, D. N., & McLean, A., Jr. (1980). Emotional imagery: Conceptual structure and pattern of somato-visceral response. *Psychophysiology, 17,* 179–192. **[228, 229]**

Lang, P. J., Levin, D. N., Miller, G. A., & Kozak, M. J. (1983). Fear behavior, fear imagery, and the psychophysiology of emotion: The problem of affective response integration. *Journal of Abnormal Psychology, 92,* 276–306. **[228]**

LaPierre, Y. **[173, 183]**

LaPierre, Y. D., Knott, V. J., & Gray, R. (1984). Psychophysiological correlates of sodium lactate. *Psychopharmacological Bulletin, 20,* 50–57. **[239, 241]**

Last, C. G. **[184, 313, 317]**

Last, C., Barlow, D., & O'Brien, G. T. (1984). Precipitants of Agoraphobia: Role of stressful life events. *Psychological Reports, 54,* 567–570. **[56, 68]**

Last, C. G., O'Brien, G. T., & Barlow, D. H. (1985). The relationship between cognitions and anxiety: A preliminary report. *Behavior Modification, 9,* 235–241. **[208]**

Last, J. M. (1983). *A dictionary of epidemiology*. New York: Oxford University Press. **[5]**

Laude, R. **[3, 66, 95, 206, 214]**

Lazarus, R. S. (1975). The self-regulation of emotion. In L. Levi (Ed.), *Emotions: Their parameters and measurement* (pp. 47–67). New York: Raven Press. **[219]**

Leaf, P. J. **[6, 20, 46]**

Leckman, J. F., Weissman, M. M., Merikangas, K. R., Pauls, D. L., & Prusoff, B. A. (1983). Panic Disorder and major depression. *Archives of General Psychiatry, 4,* 1055–1060. **[23]**

Ledwidge, B. **[169, 171]**

Leigh, H. **[52]**

Leitch, I. M. **[169]**

Lesser, I. M., & Rubin, R. T. (1986). Diagnostic considerations in panic disorders. *Journal of Clinical Psychiatry, 47,* 4–10. **[115]**

Leventhal, H. (1980). Toward a comprehensive theory of emotion. In L. Berkowitz (Ed.), *Advances in experimental social psychology* (Vol. 13, pp. 139–207). New York: Academic Press. **[221]**

Levin, A. P., Liebowitz, M. R., Fyer, A. J., Gorman, J. M., & Klein, D. F. (1984). Lactate induction of panic: Hypothesized mechanisms and recent findings (pp. 81–99). In J. C. Ballinger (Ed.), *Biology of Agoraphobia*. Washington, DC: APA Press. **[54]**

Levin, D. N. **[228, 229]**

Levin, D. N. (1982). *The psychophysiology of fear reduction: Role of response activation during emotional imagery*. Unpublished PhD dissertation. **[228]**

Levine, S. (1968). Influence of infantile stimulation on the response to stress during preweaning development. *Developmental Psychobiology, 1,* 67–78. **[68]**

Levis, D. J. **[39]**

Levitt, E. E. **[228]**

Levitt, K. **[34, 35, 268, 269, 271, 273, 280, 287, 290, 293–295, 298]**

Levitt, M. **[3, 14, 27, 41, 43, 52, 58, 60, 72, 80, 81, 167, 176, 238–241, 245, 246, 250, 267, 317]**

Levy, G. **[3, 14, 27, 41, 43, 52, 60, 72, 80, 81, 167, 176, 238, 240, 241, 245, 246, 267]**

Levy, H. B. (1984). Delirium and seizures due to abrupt alprazolam withdrawal. *Journal of Clinical Psychiatry, 45,* 38–39. **[179]**

Lewis, B. I. (1954). Chronic hyperventilation syndrome. *Journal of the American Medical Association,* July 31, 1204–1208. **[80]**

Ley, R. (1987). Panic disorder. In L. Michelson & M. Ascher (Eds.), *Anxiety and stress disorders: Cognitive-behavioral assessment and treatment.* New York: Guilford Press. **[13]**

Ley, R. (1985). Agoraphobia, the panic attack and the hyperventilation syndrome. *Behaviour Research & Therapy, 23,* 79–82. **[63, 79, 256]**

Ley, R., & Walker, H. (1973). Effects of carbon dioxide-oxygen inhalation on heart rate, blood pressure and subjective anxiety. *Journal of Behavior Therapy & Experimental Psychiatry, 4,* 223–228. **[242]**

Liebowitz, M. R. **[2, 3, 18, 43, 54, 80, 125, 126, 238–241, 244–246]**

Liebowitz, M. R. (1985a). Imipramine in the treatment of panic disorder and its complications. *Psychiatric Clinics of North America, 8,* 37–47. **[38, 169, 173]**

Liebowitz, M. R. (1985b). *Pharmacological treatment of panic attacks.* Paper presented at the annual meeting of the American College of Neuropsychopharmacology, Maui, Hawaii, December. **[24]**

Liebowitz, M. R., Fyer, A. J., Gorman, J. M., Dillon, D., Appleby, I. L., Levy, G., Anderson, S., Levitt, M., Palij, M., Davies, S. O., & Klein, D. F. (1984). Lactate provocation of panic attacks: I. Clinical and behavioral findings. *Archives of General Psychiatry, 41,* 764–770. **[3, 41, 43, 72, 80, 167, 176, 240, 267]**

Liebowitz, M. R., Fyer, A. J., Gorman, J. M., Dillon, D., Davies, S., Stein, J. M., Cohen, B. S., & Klein, D. F. (1985). Specificity of lactate infusions in social phobia versus panic disorders. *American Journal of Psychiatry, 142,* 947–950. **[80, 239, 241]**

Liebowitz, M. R., Gorman, J. M., Fyer, A. J., Levitt, M., Dillon, D., Levy, G., Appleby, I. L., Anderson, S., Palij, M., Davies, S. O., & Klein, D. F. (1985). Lactate provocation of panic attacks: II. *Archives of General Psychiatry, 42,* 709–719. **[14, 27, 52, 60, 80, 81, 238, 241, 245, 246]**

Liebowitz, M. R., & Klein, D. F. (1982). Unresolved issues in the treatment of agoraphobia with panic attacks. *Psychopharmacology Bulletin, 18,* 109–114. **[53]**

Liebowitz, M. R., & Klein, D. F. (1979). Assessment and treatment of phobic anxiety. *Journal of Clinical Psychiatry, 40,* 486–492. **[39]**

Lindemann, C. G., Zitrin, C. M., & Klein, D. F. (1984). Reports of thyroid dysfunction in phobic disorders. *Psychosomatics, 25*(8), 603–606. **[3]**

Liotti, G. **[155]**

Lipman, R. S. **[38, 157]**

Lipsedge, M. S., Hajioff, J., Huggins, P., Napier, L., Pearce, J., Pike, D. J., & Rich, M. (1973). The management of severe agoraphobia: A comparison of iproniazid and systematic desensitization. *Psychopharmacologia, 32,* 667–680. **[169]**

Litner, J. S. **[308, 309]**

Loke, J. **[245, 248]**

LoLordo, V. M. (1969). Positive conditioned reinforcement from aversive situations. *Psychological Bulletin, 72,* 193–203. **[308]**

Lopatka, C. **[287, 288, 290, 293–295, 298]**

Lousberg, H. **[39, 242, 243, 249–252]**

Lum, L. C. (1981). Hyperventilation and anxiety state. *Journal of the Royal Society of Medicine, 7,* 1–4. **[245]**

Lum, L. C. (1976). The syndrome of habitual chronic hyperventilation. In O. W. Hill (Ed.), *Modern trends in psychosomatic medicine* (Vol. 3, pp. 196–230). London: Butterworths. **[27, 80, 114, 125]**

Lushene, R. E. **[48, 113]**

MacLeod, C. **[94, 164, 211, 214–216]**

Macleod, C., Mathews, A., & Tata, P. (1986). Attentional bias in emotional disorders. *Journal of Abnormal Psychology, 95,* 15–20. **[214–216]**

Maddock, R. J. **[13, 17, 24, 27, 29, 42, 43, 52, 64, 181, 182, 239]**

Mahoney, M. J. (1974). *Cognition and behavior modification.* Cambridge, MA: Ballinger. **[223]**

Mandler, G. (1984). *Mind and body: Psychology of emotion and stress.* New York: Norton. **[219, 221, 224]**

Mandler, G. (1975). *Mind and emotion.* New York: Wiley. **[219]**

Mann, J. J. **[51, 52, 57, 63, 64]**

Marangos, P. J. **[54]**

Marchione, K. **[84, 144, 156, 157]**

Margraf, J. **[13, 17, 24, 27, 29, 42, 43, 52, 64, 181, 182, 205, 239, 244, 252–254]**

Margraf, J., Ehlers, A., & Roth, W. T. (1986a). Biological models of panic disorder and agoraphobia: A review. *Behaviour Research & Therapy, 24*(5), 553–567. **[3, 113, 167, 231]**

Margraf, J., Ehlers, A., & Roth, W. T. (1986b). Sodium lactate infusions and panic attacks: A review and critique. *Psychosomatic Medicine, 48*(1–2), 23–51. **[41, 43, 80, 123, 176]**

Marinez, J. M. **[125, 126]**

Marion, R. J. **[114, 115]**

Marks, I. M. **[157, 173, 182]**

Marks, I. M. (1983). Are there anticompulsive or antiphobic drugs? Review of evidence. *British Journal of Psychiatry, 143,* 338–347. **[169, 170, 173, 174, 177, 317]**

Marks, I. M. (1980). *Cure and care of neurosis.* New York: Wiley. **[127]**

Marks, I. M. (1971). Phobic disorders four years after treatment. *British Journal of Psychiatry, 118,* 683–688. **[182]**

Marks, I., & Gelder, M. G. (1965). A controlled retrospective study of behavior therapy in phobic patients. *British Journal of Psychiatry, 111,* 561–573. **[157]**

Marks, I. M., Grey, S., Cohen, S. D., Hill, R., Mawson, D., Ramm, E. M., & Stern, R. S. (1983). Imipramine and brief therapist-aided exposure in agoraphobics having self exposure homework: A controlled trial. *Archives of General Psychiatry, 40,* 153–162. **[84, 87, 127, 169, 170, 172, 173, 176, 182, 183]**

Marks, I. M., & Mathews, A. M. (1979). Brief standard self-rating for phobic patients. *Behaviour Research & Therapy, 17,* 263–267. **[157, 230]**

Marks, S. L. (1984). Agoraphobia and panic disorder: Treatment with alprazolam. *Texas Medicine, 80,* 50–52. **[169]**

Marlatt, G. A., & Gordon, J. R. (Eds.). (1985). *Relapse prevention: Maintenance strategies in the treatment of addictive behaviors.* New York: Guilford Press. **[180]**
Marshall, W. L. **[313, 317]**
Marshall, W. L. (1985). The effects of variable exposure in flooding therapy. *Behavior Therapy, 16,* 117–135. **[307, 318]**
Marshall, W. L., & Gauthier, J. (1983). Failures in flooding. In E. B. Foa & P. M. G. Emmelkamp (Eds.), *Failures in behavior therapy* (pp. 82–103). New York: Wiley. **[313]**
Marshall, W. L., Gauthier, J., Christie, M. M., Currie, D. W., & Gordon, A. (1977). Flooding therapy: Effectiveness, stimulus characteristics, and the value of brief in vivo exposure. *Behaviour Research & Therapy, 15,* 115–117. **[307]**
Marshall, W. L., Gauthier, J., & Gordon, A. (1979). The current status of flooding therapy. In M. Hersen, R. Eisler, & P. Miller (Eds.), *Progress in behavior modification* (Vol. 7, pp. 205–275). New York: Academic Press. **[318]**
Marshall, W. L., & Segal, Z. (in press). Behavior therapy. In C. G. Last & M. Hersen (Eds.), *Handbook of anxiety disorders.* New York: Pergamon Press. **[307]**
Marshall, W. L., & Segal, Z. (1986). Phobia and anxiety. In M. Hersen (Ed.), *Pharmacological and behavioral treatment: An integrative approach* (pp. 260–288). New York: Wiley. **[316]**
Marshall, G. D., & Zimbardo, P. G. (1979). Affective consequences of inadequate explained physiological arousal. *Journal of Personality and Social Psychology, 37,* 953–969. **[46]**
Martin, J. **[58]**
Martin, M., Ward, J. C., & Clark, D. M. (1983). Neuroticism and the recall of positive and negative personality information. *Behaviour Research & Therapy, 21,* 495–503. **[213]**
Martinez, J. M. **[2, 240]**
Maser, J. D. **[1]**
Mathews, A. **[14, 41, 46, 118, 157, 210, 211, 214–216, 230, 263, 297]**
Mathews, A. M., Gelder, M. G., & Johnston, D. W. (1981). *Agoraphobia: Nature and treatment.* New York: Guilford Press. **[84, 127, 130, 170, 174, 184, 260]**
Mathews, A., & MacLeod, C. (1986). Discrimination of threat cues without awareness in anxiety states. *Journal of Abnormal Psychology, 95,* 131–138. **[94, 164, 214, 216]**
Mathews, A., & MacLeod, C. (1985). Selective processing of threat cues in anxiety states. *Behaviour Research & Therapy, 23,* 563–569. **[211, 214, 215]**
Mathews, A. M., & Shaw, P. (1973). Emotional arousal and persuasion effects in flooding. *Behaviour Research & Therapy, 11,* 587–598. **[318]**
Mathews, A. M., Teasdale, J., Munby, M., Johnston, D., & Shaw, P. (1977). A home-based treatment program for agoraphobia. *Behavior Therapy, 8,* 915–924. **[174]**
Mattick, R. **[18, 124, 126]**
Matuzas, W., & Glass, R. M. (1983). Treatment of agoraphobia and panic attacks. *Archives of General Psychiatry, 40,* 220–222. **[174]**
Mavissakalian, M. **[84, 142, 144, 154, 156, 157, 169, 179]**
Mavissakalian, M., & Barlow, D. H. (1981). *Phobia: Psychological and pharmacological treatment.* New York: Guilford Press. **[317]**
Mavissakalian, M., & Michelson, L. (1986a). Agoraphobia: Relative and combined effectiveness of therapist-assisted in vivo exposure and imipramine. *Journal of Clinical Psychiatry, 47,* 117–122. **[84, 86, 127, 139, 169, 172, 176, 183, 186]**

Mavissakalian, M., & Michelson, L. (1986b). Two-year follow-up of exposure and imipramine treatment of agoraphobia. *American Journal of Psychiatry, 143,* 1106–1112. **[127]**

Mavissakalian, M., Michelson, L., & Dealy, R. S. (1983). Pharmacological treatment of agoraphobia: Imipramine versus imipramine with programmed practice. *British Journal of Psychiatry, 143,* 348–355. **[142, 176]**

Mavissakalian, M., & Perel, J. (1985). Imipramine in the treatment of agoraphobia: Dose-response relationships. *American Journal of Psychiatry, 142,* 1032–1036. **[183]**

Mavissakalian, M., Salerni, R., Thompson, M. E., & Michelson, L. (1983). Mitral valve prolapse and agoraphobia. *American Journal of Psychiatry, 140,* 1612–1614. **[63]**

Mawson, D. **[84, 87, 127, 169, 170, 172, 173, 176, 177, 182, 183]**

Mayer, J. D. **[226]**

McCann, D. S. **[62, 72]**

McChesney, C. M. **[128]**

McClenahan, K. L. **[43, 239]**

McClure, D. J. **[169, 171]**

McClure, J. N. **[3, 42, 167, 239–241]**

McDonald, B. **[177]**

McEvoy, L. **[5]**

McGrath, P. **[43]**

McLaren, S. **[182]**

McLean, A., Jr. **[228, 229]**

McLean, A., Jr. (1981). *Emotional imagery: Stimulus information, imagery, ability and patterns of physiological response.* Unpublished PhD dissertation. **[228]**

McNair, D. M. **[38]**

McNair, D. M., & Kahn, R. J. (1981). Imipramine compared with a benzodiazepine for agoraphobia. In D. F. Klein & J. G. Rabkin (Eds.), *Anxiety: New research and changing concepts* (pp. 69–80). New York: Raven Press. **[38, 87, 177]**

McNally, R. J. **[48, 248]**

McNally, R. J., & Foa, E. B. (in press). Cognition and agoraphobia: Bias in the interpretation of threat. *Cognitive Therapy & Research.* **[211]**

McNeil, D. N. **[228]**

McPherson, F. M., Brougham, L., & McLaren, S. (1980). Maintenance of improvement in agoraphobic patients treated by behavioural methods—A four-year follow-up. *Behaviour Research & Therapy, 18,* 150–152. **[182]**

Meduna, L. (Ed.). (1955). *Carbon dioxide therapy. A neurophysiological treatment of nervous disorders.* Springfield, IL: Charles Thomas. **[241]**

Meehan, J. P. **[68]**

Meichenbaum, D. (1977). *Cognitive-behavior modification: An integrative approach.* New York: Plenum. **[143]**

Meichenbaum, D. (1974). *Cognitive behavior modification.* Morristown, NJ: General Learning Press. **[223]**

Melamed, B. G. **[228]**

Mellinger, G. D. **[20]**

Mendelsohn, M. **[157]**

Merikangas, K. R. **[23]**

Merchant, A. F. **[60]**

Merckelbach, H. **[255]**
Mezzich, J. E. **[40]**
Michelson, L. **[63, 84, 86, 127, 139, 142, 158, 169, 172, 176, 183, 186, 209, 210]**
Michelson, L., Marchione, K., & Mavissakalian, M. (1985). Cognitive and behavioral treatments of agoraphobia: Clinical, behavioral and psychophysiological outcome. *Journal of Consulting & Clinical Psychology, 53,* 913–926. **[84, 156]**
Michelson, L., & Mavissakalian, M. (1985). Psychophysiological outcome of behavioral and pharmacologic treatments in agoraphobia. *Journal of Consulting & Clinical Psychology, 53,* 229–236. **[169]**
Michelson, L., & Mavissakalian, M. (1983). Temporal stability of self-report measures in agoraphobia research. *Behaviour Research & Therapy, 21,* 695–698. **[154]**
Michelson, L., Mavissakalian, M., Greenwald, D., Kornblith, S., & Greenwald, M. (1983). *Cognitive-behavioral treatment of agoraphobia: Paradoxical intention versus self-statement training.* Paper presented at the annual meeting of the Association for the Advancement of Behavior Therapy, Los Angeles. **[142, 144]**
Michelson, L., Mavissakalian, M., & Marchione, K. (1985). Cognitive-behavioral treatments of agoraphobia: Clinical behavioral, and psychophysiological outcome. *Journal of Consulting & Clinical Psychology, 53,* 913–925. **[144, 156, 157]**
Mihaly, K. **[83, 114, 115, 125]**
Miller, G. A. **[228, 229]**
Miller, G. A., Levin, D. N., Kozak, M. J., Cook, E. W., III, McLean, A., & Lang, P. J. (in press). Individual differences in emotional imagery. *Cognition and Emotion.* **[228, 229]**
Mineka, S. (1985). Animal models of anxiety-based disorders: Their usefulness and limitations. In A. H. Tuma & J. D. Maser (Eds.), *Anxiety and the anxiety disorders* (pp. 199–244). Hillsdale, NJ: Lawrence Erlbaum Associates. **[296]**
Mineka, S., Davidson, M., Cook, M., & Keir, R. (1984). Observational conditioning of snake fear in rhesus monkeys. *Journal of Abnormal Psychology, 93,* 355–372. **[48]**
Mineka, S., & Hendersen, R. (1985). Controllability and predictability in acquired motivation. *Annual Review of Psychology.* Palo Alto, CA: Annual Reviews, Inc. **[297]**
Mineka, S., & Kihlstrom, J. (1979). Unpredictable and uncontrollable events. *Journal of Abnormal Psychology, 87,* 256–271. **[296, 297]**
Mitchell-Heggs, M. **[43, 58, 176, 239, 240, 250]**
Mock, J. **[157]**
Moller, M. B. **[2, 48, 63]**
Monteiro, W. **[173, 182]**
Morton, L. **[173, 183]**
Mountjoy, C. Q., Roth, M., Garside, R. F., & Leitch, I. M. (1977). A clinical trial of phenelzine in anxiety depressive and phobic neuroses. *British Journal of Psychiatry, 131,* 486–492. **[169]**
Mowrer, O. H. (1939). Stimulus response theory of anxiety. *Psychological Review, 46,* 553–565. **[265]**
Munby, M. **[174]**
Munby, M., & Johnston, D. W. (1980). Agoraphobia: The long-term follow-up of behavioural treatment. *British Journal of Psychiatry, 137,* 418–427. **[127, 182]**
Murphy, D. L. **[60]**
Murrell, E. **[18, 124, 126]**

Myers, J. K., Weissman, M. M., Tischler, G. L., Holzer, C. E., Leaf, P. J., Orvaschel, H., Anthony, J., Boyd, J. H., Burke, J. D., Kramer, M., & Stoltzman, R. (1984). Six-month prevalence of psychiatric disorders in three communities: 1980–1982. *Archives of General Psychiatry, 41,* 959–967. **[20, 46]**

Napier, L. **[169]**

Nasar, S. **[57]**

Nesse, R. M. **[40, 51, 63, 128, 205]**

Nesse, R. M., Cameron, O. G., Curtis, G. C., McCann, D. S., & Huber-Smith, M. J. (1984). Adrenergic function in patients with panic anxiety. *Archives of General Psychiatry, 41,* 771–775. **[62, 72]**

Nestadt, G. **[5]**

Norton, G. R., Dorward, J., & Cox, B. J. (1986). Factors associated with panic attacks in nonclinical subjects. *Behavior Therapy, 17,* 239–252. **[20, 117, 118]**

Norton, G. R., Harrison, B., Hauch, J., & Rhodes, L. (1985). Characteristics of people with infrequent panic attacks. *Journal of Abnormal Psychology, 94,* 216–221. **[45, 53, 54, 117, 163, 262]**

Noyes, R. **[20, 27, 51, 56, 64, 114, 167]**

Noyes, R., Anderson, D. J., Clancy, M., Crowe, R. R., Slymen, D. J., Ghoneim, M. M., & Hinrichs, J. V. (1984). Diazepam and propranolol in panic disorder and agoraphobia. *Archives of General Psychiatry, 41,* 287–292. **[38, 43, 60, 87]**

Noyes, R., Clancy, J., Coyrell, W. H. (1985). A withdrawal syndrome after abrupt discontinuation of alprazolam. *American Journal of Psychiatry, 142*(1), 114–116. **[179]**

Noyes, R., Crowe, R. R., Harris, E. L., Hamra, B. J., McChesney, C. M., & Chaudhry, D. R. (1986). Relationship between panic disorder and agoraphobia. *Archives of General Psychiatry, 43,* 227–232. **[128]**

Nunn, J. D., Stevenson, R. J., & Whalan, G. (1984). Selective memory effects in agoraphobic patients. *British Journal of Clinical Psychology, 23,* 195–201. **[213]**

Nutt, D. J. (1986). Increased central $alpha_2$-adrenoceptor sensitivity in panic disorder. *Psychopharmacology, 90,* 268–269. **[86]**

O'Brien, G. T. **[20, 22, 24, 25, 26, 33, 46, 53, 56, 68, 115, 184, 208, 313, 317]**

Öhman, A. (1986). Presidential address to International Society for Psychophysiological Research. Houston, Texas. **[327]**

Öhman, A. (1979). Fear relevance, autonomic conditioning, and phobias: A laboratory model. In P. O. Sjoden & S. Bates (Eds.), *Trends in behavior therapy* (pp. 107–133). New York: Academic Press. **[225]**

Ortiz, A., Rainey, J. M., Frohman, R. (1985, Sept.). Effects of imipramine on lactate induced panic anxiety. *Abstract 519.4,* Philadelphia World Congress of Biologic Psychiatry, p. 389. **[58]**

Orvaschel, H. **[20, 46]**

Ost, L. **[184]**

Ost, L. G., & Hugdahl, K. (1981). Acquisition of phobias and anxiety response patterns in clinical patients. *Behaviour Research & Therapy, 19,* 439–447. **[323]**

Oswald, I. (1966). *Sleep.* Harmondsworth, England: Penguin Books. **[75]**

Ottaviani, R., & Beck, A. T. (1987). Cognitive aspects of panic disorders. *Journal of Anxiety Disorders, 1*(1), 15–28. **[96, 97]**

Padawer, W. **[213]**
Palij, M. **[3, 14, 27, 41, 43, 52, 60, 72, 80, 81, 167, 176, 238, 240, 241, 245, 246, 267]**
Pariser, S. F., Pinta, E. R., & Jones, B. A. (1978). Mitral valve prolapse syndrome and anxiety neurosis/panic disorder. *American Journal of Psychiatry, 135,* 246–247. **[2, 63]**
Patel, J. **[54]**
Pauley, J. D. **[68]**
Pauls, D. C. **[64, 167]**
Pauls, D. L. **[20, 23]**
Pearce, J. **[169]**
Pearce, K. **[47]**
Pecknold, J. **[173, 183]**
Peeke, H. V. S. **[53]**
Pennebaker, J. W. (1982). *The psychology of physical symptoms.* New York: Springer-Verlag. **[46, 85, 123]**
Perel, J. **[183]**
Perlmutter, J. **[47]**
Peterson, R. A. **[48, 248]**
Pickering, T. **[51, 52, 57, 64]**
Pietromonaco, P. **[164]**
Pike, D. J. **[169]**
Pinsker, H. **[53]**
Pinta, E. R. **[2, 63]**
Pitts, F. N., Jr. (1969). The biochemistry of anxiety. *Scientific American, 220* (2), 69–75. **[222]**
Pitts, F. N., Jr., & McClure, J. N., Jr. (1967). Lactate metabolism in anxiety neuroses. *New England Journal of Medicine, 227,* 1328–1336. **[3, 42, 167, 239–241]**
Pohl, R. B. **[72, 80, 205, 240]**
Polan, J. J. **[52, 57, 64]**
Pollard, A. (1985, November). *Agoraphobic panic: Catastrophic cognitions, physical symptoms, and their interrelationships.* Paper presented at the meeting of the Association for the Advancement of Behavior Therapy, Houston. **[207]**
Post, R. M. **[3, 54, 63, 72]**
Prusoff, B. A. **[23]**
Pruzinsky, T. **[212]**
Puthezhath, N. **[14, 25, 42, 52, 64, 182]**

Rabkin, J. G. **[60, 260, 261]**
Rachman, S. J. **[19, 262, 300]**
Rachman, S. J. (in preparation). *The Fear of Enclosed Spaces Questionnaire.* **[270–282]**
Rachman, S. J. (1984a). Agoraphobia: A safety-signal perspective. *Behaviour Research & Therapy, 22,* 59–70. **[128, 263, 269, 310]**
Rachman, S. J. (1984b). The experimental analysis of agoraphobia. *Behaviour Research & Therapy, 22,* 631–640. **[260, 268]**
Rachman, S. J. (1983). The modification of agoraphobic avoidance behaviour. *Behaviour Research & Therapy, 21,* 567–574. **[297, 298, 310]**
Rachman, S. (1980). Emotional Processing. *Behaviour Research & Therapy, 18,* 51–60. **[165]**

Rachman, S. (1978). *Fear and courage*. San Francisco: W. H. Freeman. **[3, 19, 259, 260, 262, 265, 282]**

Rachman, S. (1976). The passing of the two-stage theory of fear and avoidance. *Behaviour Research & Therapy, 14,* 125–131. **[265]**

Rachman, S., Cobb, J., Grey, S., McDonald, B., Mawson, D., Sartory, G., & Stern, R. (1979). The behavioural treatment of obsessional-compulsive disorders, with and without clomipramine. *Behaviour Research & Therapy, 17,* 467–478. **[177]**

Rachman, S., Craske, M., Tallman, K., & Solyom, C. (1986). Does escape behavior strengthen agoraphobic avoidance? A replication. *Behavior Therapy, 17,* 366–384. **[264]**

Rachman, S., & Hodgson, R. (1974). Synchrony and desynchrony in fear and avoidance. *Behaviour Research & Therapy, 12,* 311–318. **[266, 267]**

Rachman, S. J., & Levitt, K. (1985). Panics and their consequences. *Behaviour Research & Therapy, 23,* 585–600. **[34, 35, 268, 269, 271, 273, 280, 287, 295, 298]**

Rachman, S., Levitt, K., & Lopatka, C. (in preparation). *Safety and panic: An experimental analysis.* **[287, 290, 293, 294]**

Rachman, S., Levitt, K., & Lopatka, C. (1987). A simple method for distinguishing between expected and unexpected panics. *Behaviour Research & Therapy, 25,* 149–154. **[287, 295]**

Rachman, S., & Lopatka, C. (1986a). Match and mismatch in the prediction of fear—I. *Behaviour Research & Therapy, 24,* 387–393. **[287, 288, 294, 298]**

Rachman, S., & Lopatka, C. (1986b). Match and mismatch of fear in Gray's theory—II. *Behaviour Research & Therapy, 24,* 395–401. **[288, 294, 298]**

Rae, D. S. **[5]**

Raiche, M. E. **[47, 54, 60]**

Rainey, J. M. **[58, 205, 240]**

Rainey, J. M., Frohman, C. E., Freedman, R. R., Pohl, R. B., Ettedgui, E., & Williams, M. (1984). Specificity of lactate infusion as a model of anxiety. *Psychopharmacological Bulletin, 20,* 45–49. **[240]**

Rainey, J. M., & Nesse, R. M. (1985). Psychobiology of anxiety and anxiety disorders. *Psychiatric Clinics of North America, 8,* 133–144. **[51]**

Rainey, J. M., Pohl, R. B., Williams, M., Knitter, E., Freedman, R. R., & Ettedgui, E. (1984). A comparison of lactate and isoproterenol anxiety states. *Psychopathology, 17* (Suppl. 1), 74–82. **[72, 80]**

Ramm, E. M. **[84, 87, 127, 169, 170, 172, 173, 176, 182, 183]**

Rapee, R. (1986). Differential response to hyperventilation in panic disorder and generalized anxiety disorders. *Journal of Abnormal Psychology, 95,* 24–28. **[17, 18, 114, 122, 125, 126, 195, 205]**

Rapee, R. (1985). Distinctions between panic disorder and generalized anxiety disorder. *Australian & New Zealand Journal of Psychiatry, 19,* 227–232. **[27, 66, 79, 114, 120, 121]**

Rapee, R., Mattick, R., & Murrell, E. (1986). Cognitive mediation in the affective component of spontaneous panic attacks. *Journal of Behavior Therapy & Experimental Psychiatry, 17,* 245–253. **[18, 124, 126]**

Raskin, A., Marks, I. M., & Sheehan, D. V. (1983). The influence of depressed mood on the antipanic effects of antidepressant drugs. Unpublished data. **[173]**

Raskin, M., Peeke, H. V. S., Dickman, W., & Pinsker, H. (1982). Panic and generalized anxiety disorders: Developmental antecedants and precipitants. *Archives of General Psychiatry, 39,* 687–689. **[53]**

Ravaris, R. **[29]**

Razran, G. (1961). The observable unconscious and the inferable conscious in current Soviet psychophysiology. Interoceptive conditioning, semantic conditioning, and the orienting reflex. *Psychological Review, 68,* 81–147. **[39]**

Redmond, D. E. **[52, 245, 248]**

Redmond, D. E. (1979). New and old evidence for the involvement of a brain norepinephrine system in anxiety (pp. 153–200). In W. E. Fann, I. Karacan, A. D. Pokorny, & R. L. Williams (Eds.), *Phenomenology and treatment of anxiety.* New York: Spectrum Medical and Scientific Books. **[54]**

Rees, W. L. **[18, 80, 250]**

Reiman, E. M., Raichle, M. E., Butler, F. K., Herscovitch, P., & Robins, E. (1984). A focal brain abnormality in panic disorder, a severe form of anxiety. *Nature, 310,* 683–685. **[47, 54, 60]**

Reiman, E. M., Raichle, M. E., Robins, E., Butler, K., Herscovitch, P., Fox, P. O., & Perlmutter, J. (1986). The application of positron emission tomography to the study of panic disorder. *American Journal of Psychiatry, 143,* 469–477. **[47]**

Reiss, S., Peterson, R. A., Gursky, D. M., McNally, R. J. (1986). Anxiety sensitivity, anxiety frequency and the prediction of fearfulness. *Behaviour Research & Therapy, 24,* 1–8. **[48, 248]**

Reite, M., Short, R., Kaufman, I. C., Stynes, A., C., & Pauley, J. D. (1978). Heart rate and body temperature in separated monkey infants. *Biological Psychiatry, 13,* 91–104. **[68]**

Rescorla, R. A., & Wagner, A. R. (1972). A theory of Pavlovian conditioning. In A. H. Black & W. F. Prokasy (Eds.), *Classical Conditioning II* (pp. 64–99). New York: Appleton–Century–Crofts. **[298, 322, 324, 325]**

Rhodes, L. **[45, 53, 54, 117, 163, 262]**

Rich, M. **[169]**

Rickels, K. **[38, 157]**

Rickels, K., Case, W. G., & Diamond, L. (1980). Relapse after short-term drug therapy in neurotic outpatients. *International Pharmacopsychiatry, 15,* 186–192. **[313]**

Rickels, K., & Schweizer, E. E. (1986). Benzodiazepines for treatment of panic attacks: A new look. *Psychopharmacology Bulletin, 22,* 93–99. **[38]**

Rifkin, A., Klein, D. F., Dillon, D., & Levitt, M. (1981). Blockade by imipramine or desipramine of panic induced by sodium lactate. *American Journal of Psychiatry, 138,* 676–677. **[58, 239, 240, 250]**

Rifkin, B. G. **[52]**

Riskind, J. H. **[209]**

Riskind, J. H., & Castellon, C. S. (1986). *Spontaneous causal explanations in unipolar depression and generalized anxiety: A content analysis in outpatients.* Manuscript submitted for publication. **[209]**

Robbins, E. **[47, 54, 60]**

Robins, C. J. **[213]**

Robins, L. M., Helzer, J. E., Croughan, J., & Ratcliff, K. S. (1981). National Institute of Mental Health Diagnostic Interview Schedule: Its history, characteristics, and validity. *Archives of General Psychiatry, 38,* 381–389. **[46]**

Robinson, E. **[212]**

Rohs, R. G., & Noyes, R. (1978). Agoraphobia: Newer treatment approaches. *Journal of Nervous & Mental Disease, 166,* 701–708. **[51]**

Rosenbaum, J. F. **[38]**

Ross, C. A. (1986). Biological tests for mental illness: Their use and misuse. *Biological Psychiatry, 21,* 431–435. **[38]**

Ross, D. C. **[53, 67, 71, 87, 125, 126, 169, 170, 174]**

Roth, M. **[169]**

Roth, R. H. **[52]**

Roth, W. T. **[3, 41, 43, 67, 80, 87, 113, 167, 169, 174, 176, 177, 178, 181, 205, 239, 244, 252–254, 317]**

Roy-Byrne, P. P. **[3, 72]**

Rubin, R. T. **[115]**

Sachar, E. J. **[39, 72, 80, 81, 167, 176, 240, 317]**

Sakheim, D. K. **[225]**

Salerni, R. **[63]**

Salkovskis, P. M. **[18, 72, 80–84, 88, 89, 114, 120–123, 128–131, 184, 200, 202, 248]**

Salkovskis, P. M. (in preparation). The effects of brief hyperventilation in panic patients with and without agoraphobia. **[128]**

Salkovskis, P. M., & Clark, D. M. (1987). Cognitive factors determining affective response to hyperventilation: A test of the cognitive model of panic. Submitted for publication. **[89, 124]**

Salkovskis, P. M., & Clark, D. M. (1986a). Cognitive and physiological processes in the maintenance and treatment of panic attacks (pp. 90–103). In I. Hand & H.-U. Wittchen (Eds.), *Panic and phobias.* Springer–Verlag. **[111, 114]**

Salkovskis, P. M., & Clark, D. M. (1986b). *Hyperventilation and interpretations.* Unpublished manuscript. **[251]**

Salkovskis, P. M., Clark, D. M., & Jones, D. R. O. (1986). A psychosomatic mechanism in anxiety attacks: The role of hyperventilation in social anxiety and cardiac neurosis (pp. 239–245). In H. Lacey & J. Sturgeon (Eds.), *Proceedings of the 15th European Conference in Psychosomatic Medicine.* London: John Libbey. **[80, 112, 127]**

Salkovskis, P. M., & Dent, H. R. Intrusive thoughts, impulses and imagery: Cognitive and behavioural aspects. Manuscript in preparation. **[122]**

Salkovskis, P. M., Jones, D. R. O., & Clark, D. M. (1986). Respiratory control in the treatment of panic attacks: Replication and extension with concurrent measurement of behaviour and pCO_2. *British Journal of Psychiatry, 148,* 526–532. **[82, 83, 116, 125, 126, 128, 200]**

Salkovskis, P. M., & Warwick, H. M. C. (1986). Morbid preoccupations, health anxiety and reassurance: A cognitive-behavioural approach to hypochondriasis. *Behaviour Research & Therapy, 24,* 597–602. **[121, 131]**

Salkovskis, P. M., Warwick, H. M. C., Clark, D. M., & Wessels, D. J. (1986). A demonstration of acute hyperventilation during naturally occurring panic attacks. *Behaviour Research & Therapy, 24,* 91–94. **[80, 112, 121, 125, 130, 135, 194]**

Sanderson, W. **[18]**

Saranson, I. F. (1979). Life stress, self-preoccupation and social supports. Office of Naval

Research (code 452) Organizational Effectiveness Research Program, Arlington, VA 22217. Contract No. N00014-75-C-0905, NR170-804. **[47]**

Sartory, G. **[177]**

Shachter, S., & Singer, J. E. (1962). Cognitive, social and physiological determinants of emotional state. *Psychological Review, 69,* 379–399. **[123, 219]**

Schraoeder, D. J. **[47]**

Schwartz, G. E., Davidson, R. J., & Coleman, D. J. (1978). Patterning of cognitive and somatic processes in the self-regulation of anxiety: Effects of medication versus exercise. *Psychosomatic Medicine, 40,* 321–328. **[27]**

Schwartz, R. N. (1982). Cognitive–behavioral modification: A conceptual review. *Clinical Psychology Review, 2,* 267–293. **[154]**

Schwartz, R. N., & Michelson, L. (in press). State of Mind model: Cognitive balance in the treatment of agoraphobia. *Journal of Consulting & Clinical Psychology.* **[158]**

Schweizer, E. E. **[38]**

Segal, Z. **[307, 316]**

Seligman, M. E. P. (1980). A learned helplessness point of view. In L. Rehm (Ed.), *Behavior therapy for depression* (pp. 123–142). New York: Academic Press. **[325]**

Seligman, M. E. P. (1975). *Helplessness: On depression, development, and death.* San Francisco: W. H. Freeman. **[225, 296, 297]**

Seligman, M. E. P. (1971). Preparedness and phobias. *Behavior Therapy, 2,* 307–320. **[326]**

Seligman, M. E. P. (1970). On the generality of the laws of learning. *Psychological Review, 77,* 406–418. **[326]**

Seligman, M. E. P. (1968). Chronic fear produced by unpredictable shock. *Journal of Comparative and Physiological Psychology, 66,* 402–411. **[296, 297]**

Seligman, M. E. P., & Binik, Y. (1977). The safety signal hypothesis. In H. Davis & H. Hurwitz (Eds.), *Operant-Pavlovian Interactions* (pp. 165–180). Hillsdale, NJ: Lawrence Erlbaum Associates. **[263, 265, 296, 297, 299]**

Seligman, M. E. P., & Hager, J. L. (1972). *Biological boundaries of learning.* New York: Appleton–Century–Crofts. **[326]**

Seligman, M. E. P., & Johnston, J. (1973). A cognitive theory of avoidance learning. In J. McGuigan & B. Lumsden (Eds.), (pp. 69–110). *Contemporary approaches to conditioning and learning.* New York: Wiley. **[262, 263, 265, 296, 297]**

Seuss, W. M., Alexander, A. B., Smith, D. D., Sweeney, H. W., & Marion, R. J. (1980). The effects of psychological stress on respiration: A preliminary study of anxiety and hyperventilation. *Psychophysiology, 17,* 535–540. **[114, 115]**

Sewitch, T. S., & Kirch, I. (1984). The cognitive content of anxiety: Naturalistic evidence for the predominance of threat-related thoughts. *Cognitive Research & Therapy, 8,* 49–58. **[208]**

Shader, R., Goodman, M., & Gever, J. (1982). Panic disorders: Current perspectives. Cited in Margraf, J., Ehlers, A., & Roth, W. T. (1986). Sodium lactate infusions and panic attacks: A review and critique. *Psychosomatic Medicine, 48,* 23–51. **[245]**

Shaw, P. **[174, 318]**

Shear, M. K. **[54, 56, 58, 63]**

Shear, M. K. (1986). Pathophysiology of panic: A review of pharmacologic provocative tests and naturalistic monitoring data. *Journal of Clinical Psychiatry, 47*(Suppl.), 18–26. **[239, 250]**

Shear, M. K., Devereux, R. B., Kramer-Fox, R., Frances, A. J., & Mann, J. J. (1984). A low prevalence of mitral valve prolapse in panic disorder patients. *American Journal of Psychiatry, 14,* 302–304. **[63]**
Shear, M. K., Kligfeld, P., Harschfield, G., Devereux, R. B., Polan, J. J., Mann, J. J., Pickering, T., & Frances, A. J. (1987). Cardiac rate and rhythm in panic disorder patients. *American Journal of Psychiatry, 144,* 633–637. **[52, 57]**
Shear, M. K., Polan, J., Harschfield, G., Frances, A. J., Mann, J. J., & Pickering, T. *Ambulatory monitoring of blood pressure in panic disorder patients.* Unpublished manuscript. **[52, 64]**
Sheehan, D. V. **[3, 51, 54, 56, 173, 222, 245]**
Sheehan, D. V. (1985). Monoamine oxidase inhibitors and alprazolam in the treatment of panic disorder and agoraphobia. *Psychiatric Clinics of North America, 8,* 49–62. **[38, 168, 169]**
Sheehan, D. V. (1983). *The anxiety disease.* New York: Scribner's. **[168]**
Sheehan, D. V. (1982). Panic attacks and phobias. *New England Journal of Medicine, 307,* 156–158. **[167–169, 172, 173, 179, 182, 234]**
Sheehan, D. V., Ballenger, J., & Jacobsen, G. (1980). Treatment of endogenous anxiety with phobic, hysterical, and hypochondriacal symptoms. *Archives of General Psychiatry, 37,* 51–59. **[32, 51, 169, 170, 183]**
Sheehan, D. V., Claycomb, J. B., & Kouretas, N. (1980). MAO inhibitors: Prescription and patient management. *International Journal of Psychiatry and Medicine, 10,* 99–121. **[172, 179, 183]**
Sheehan, D. V., & Sheehan, K. H. (1984). The classification of anxiety and hysterical states. Part I: Historical review and empirical delineation. *Journal of Clinical Psychopharmacology, 2,* 235–244. **[53]**
Sheehan, K. H. **[53]**
Sheehan, P. W. (1967). A shortened form of Betts' questionnaire upon mental imagery. *Journal of Clinical Psychology, 223,* 380–389. **[229]**
Sheikh, J. **[13, 17, 24, 27, 29, 42, 43, 52, 64, 181, 182, 239]**
Sherman, D. G. **[43, 58, 62, 176, 239, 240, 250]**
Shigetomi, C. **[165]**
Short, R. **[68]**
Simons, R. F. **[228]**
Singer, J. E. **[123, 219]**
Slater, S. L., & Levy, A. (1966). The effects of inhaling a 35% CO_2 65% O_2 mixture upon anxiety in neurotic patients. *Behaviour Research & Therapy, 4,* 309–316. **[242]**
Slymen, D. J. **[20, 38, 43, 60, 64, 87, 167]**
Smith, D. D. **[114, 115]**
Smith, T. W. **[47]**
Smith, V. K. **[38, 60]**
Sokol-Kessler, L. **[99]**
Sokol-Kessler, L., & Beck, A. T. (May 14, 1987). *Cognitive treatment of panic disorders.* Paper presented at the 140th Annual Meeting of the American Psychiatric Association, Chicago. **[86, 99, 106]**
Solyom, C. **[38, 169, 171, 264]**
Solyom, C., Solyom, L., LaPierre, Y., Pecknold, J., & Morton, L. (1981). Phenelzine and exposure in the treatment of phobias. *Biological Psychiatry, 16,* 239–247. **[173, 183]**

Solyom, L. **[38, 57, 72, 173, 183]**

Solyom, L., Heseltine, G. F. D., McClure, D. J., Solyom, C., Ledwidge, B., & Steinberg, G. (1973). Behaviour therapy versus drug therapy in the treatment of phobic neurosis. *Canadian Psychiatric Association, 18,* 25–31. **[169, 171]**

Spence, E. L., Vrana, S. R., & Lang, P. J. (in press). Effects of attention and emotion on the acoustic startle response. *Psychophysiology.* **[235]**

Spielberger, C. (1973). *Manual for the state-trait inventory for children.* Palo Alto, CA: Consulting Psychologists Press. **[48]**

Spielberger, C. D., Gorsuch, R. L., & Lushene, R. E. (1970). The state-trait anxiety inventory: Test manual for form X. Palo Alto, CA: Consulting Psychologists Press. **[48, 113]**

Spier, S. E., Tesar, G. E., Rosenbaum, J. F., & Woods, S. W. (1986). Treatment of panic disorder with clonazepam. *Journal of Clinical Psychiatry, 47,* 238–242. **[38]**

Spira, N. **[57]**

Starkman, M. N., Zelnik, T. C., Nesse, R. M., & Cameron, O. G. (1985). Anxiety in patients with pheochromocytoma. *Archives of Internal Medicine, 154,* 248–252. **[63]**

Stein, J. **[3, 18, 80, 238, 239, 241, 244–246]**

Steinberg, D. **[171]**

Steinberg, G. **[169, 171]**

Stephens, P. M. **[68]**

Stern, R. S. **[84, 87, 127, 169, 170, 172, 173, 176, 177, 182, 183]**

Sternberg, D. E. **[61]**

Stevenson, R. J. **[213]**

Stokes, P. (1985). The neuroendocrinology of anxiety. In A. H. Tuma & J. D. Maser (Eds.), *Anxiety and the anxiety disorders* (pp. 53–76). Hillsdale, NJ: Lawrence Erlbaum Associates. **[266]**

Stoltzman, R. **[5, 20, 46]**

Strosahl, K. D., & Ascough, J. C. (1981). Clinical uses of mental imagery: Experimental foundations, theoretical misconceptions and research issues. *Psychological Bulletin, 89,* 422–438. **[227]**

Stynes, A. C. **[68]**

Surman, O. S., Sheehan, D. V., Fuller, T. C., & Gallo, J. (1983). Panic disorder in genotype HRL identical sibling pairs. *American Journal of Psychiatry, 140,* 237–238. **[51, 56]**

Svebak, S., & Grossman, P. (1985). How aversive is hyperventilation? Submitted for publication. **[80, 126]**

Sweeney, H. W. **[114, 115]**

Swets, J. A. **[311]**

Tabachnik, N. **[297]**

Tallman, K. **[19, 262, 264]**

Tata, P. **[214–216]**

Taylor, C. B. **[43, 67, 87, 169, 170, 174, 176, 177, 178, 180, 181, 185, 239, 253, 254, 317]**

Taylor, C. B., Sheikh, J., Agras, W. S., Toth, W. T., Margraf, J., Ehlers, A., Maddock, R. J., & Gossard, D. (1986). Ambulatory heart rate changes in patients with panic attacks. *American Journal of Psychiatry, 143,* 478–482. **[13, 17, 24, 27, 29, 42, 52, 64, 181, 182, 205]**

Taylor, C. B., Telch, M. J., & Havvik, D. (1983). Ambulatory heart rate changes during panic attacks. *Journal of Psychiatric Research, 17,* 261–266. **[42, 181, 182]**

Taylor, J. A. (1953). A personality scale of manifest anxiety. *Journal of Abnormal & Social Psychology, 48,* 285–290. **[157]**

Taylor, M. A. **[240]**

Taylor, S. E. **[212, 213]**

Taylor, W. **[85]**

Tearnan, B. H. **[169, 170, 174, 178, 180, 181]**

Teasdale, J. **[174]**

Teasdale, J. D. (1985). Psychological treatments for depression: How do they work? *Behaviour Research & Therapy, 23,* 157–165. **[197, 201]**

Teasdale, J. D., & Fennell, M. J. V. (1983). Investigating immediate effects on depression of brief interventions: An underused tactic in depression treatment research (pp. 200–214). In M. Rosenbaum, C. M. Franks, & Y. Jaffe (Eds.), *Perspective on behaviour therapy in the eighties.* New York: Springer. **[194]**

Telch, M. J. **[42, 181, 182, 185]**

Telch, M. J. (1985). The Panic Assessment Inventory. Unpublished scale. Stanford University, Stanford, CA. **[182]**

Telch, M. J., Agras, W. S., Taylor, C. B., Roth, W. T., & Gallen, C. (1985). Combined pharmacological and behavioral treatment for agoraphobia. *Behaviour Research & Therapy, 23,* 325–335. **[67, 87, 169, 174, 176, 177, 178, 181, 317]**

Telch, M. J., Tearnan, B. H., & Taylor, C. B. (1983). Antidepressant medication in the treatment of agoraphobia: A critical review. *Behaviour Research & Therapy, 21,* 505–517. **[169, 170, 174, 178, 180, 181]**

Tesar, G. E. **[38]**

Thompson, M. E. **[63]**

Thorpe, G., & Burns, L. (1983). *The agoraphobic syndrome.* Chichester: Wiley. **[260, 261]**

Thyer, B. A. (1986). Agoraphobia: A superstitious conditioning perspective. *Psychological Reports, 58,* 95–100. **[123, 128, 256]**

Thyer, B. A., & Himle, J. (1985). Temporal relationship between panic attack onset and phobic avoidance in agoraphobia. *Behaviour Research & Therapy, 23,* 607–608. **[128, 260, 261]**

Thyer, B. A., Himle, J., Curtis, G. C., Cameron, O. G., & Nesse, R. M. (1985). A comparison of panic disorder and agoraphobia with panic attacks. *Comprehensive Psychiatry, 26,* 208–214. **[40, 128, 205]**

Tischler, G. L. **[20, 46]**

Torgersen, S. (1983). Genetic factors in anxiety disorders. *Archives of General Psychiatry, 40,* 1085–1089. **[48, 51, 56]**

Toth, W. T. **[13, 17, 24, 27, 29, 42, 52, 64, 181, 182]**

Tringer, K. **[83, 114, 115, 125]**

Troudart, T. **[57]**

Tuason, V. B. **[40]**

Tuma, A. H., & Maser, J. D. (Eds.). (1985). *Anxiety and the anxiety disorders.* Hillsdale, NJ: Lawrence Erlbaum Associates. **[1]**

Turner, S. M. **[2, 48, 63]**

Turner, S. M., Beidel, D. C., & Costello, A. (1987). Psychopathology in the offspring of anxiety disorder patients. *Journal of Consulting & Clinical Psychology, 55*(2), 229–235. **[48, 49]**

Turner, S. M., Williams, S. L., Beidel, D. C., & Mezzich, J. E. (1986). Panic disorder and agoraphobia with panic attacks: Covariation along the dimensions of panic and agoraphobic fear. *Journal of Abnormal Psychology, 95*(4), 384–388. **[40]**

Tyrer, P. (1984). Classification of anxiety. *British Journal of Psychiatry, 144,* 78–83. **[46]**

Tyrer, P., Candy, J., & Kelly, D. (1973). Phenelzine in phobic anxiety: A controlled trial. *Psychological Medicine, 3,* 120–124. **[169]**

Tyrer, P., & Steinberg, D. (1975). Symptomatic treatment of agoraphobia and social phobias: A follow-up study. *British Journal of Psychiatry, 127,* 163–168. **[171]**

Uhde, T. W. **[54]**

Uhde, T. W., Boulenger, J.-P., Vittone, B. J., & Post, R. M. (1984). Historical and modern concepts of anxiety: A focus on adrenergic function (pp. 1–27). In J. C. Ballenger, (Ed.), *Biology of agoraphobia.* Washington, DC: American Psychiatric Press. **[54, 63]**

Uhde, T. W., Roy-Byrne, P. P., Vittone, B. J., Boulenger, J.-P., & Post, R. M. (1985). Phenomenology and neurobiology of panic disorder. In A. H. Tuma & J. D. Maser (Eds.), *Anxiety and the anxiety disorder.* (pp. 557–576). Hillsdale, NJ: Lawrence Erlbaum Associates. **[3, 72]**

Uhde, T. W., Vittone, B. J., & Post, R. M. (1984). Glucose tolerance testing in panic disorder. *American Journal of Psychiatry, 141,* 1461–1463. **[3, 63]**

Uhlenhuth, E. H. **[157]**

Uhlenhuth, E. H., Balter, M. B., Mellinger, G. D., Cisin, I. H., & Clinthorne, J. (1983). Symptom checklist syndromes in the general population. *Archives of General Psychiatry, 40,* 1167–1173. **[20]**

Vadasz, P. **[83, 114, 115, 125]**

van den Hout, M. A. **[73, 80, 83, 84, 87, 242, 244, 246, 252, 255]**

van den Hout, M. A., & Griez, E. (1985). Peripheral panic symptoms occur during changes in alveolar carbon dioxide. *Comprehensive Psychiatry, 26,* 381–387. **[83, 243–245]**

van den Hout, M. A., & Griez, E. (1984). Panic symptoms after inhalation of carbon dioxide. *British Journal of Psychiatry, 144,* 503–507. **[72, 83, 242]**

van den Hout, M. A., & Griez, E. (1983). Some remarks on the nosology of anxiety states and panic disorders. *Acta Psychiatrica Belgica, 83,* 33–42. **[39]**

van den Hout, M. A., & Griez, E. (1982a). Cardiovascular and subjective responses to inhalation of carbon dioxide. A controlled test with anxious patients. *Psychotherapy & Psychosomatics, 37,* 75–82. **[18, 242]**

van den Hout, M. A., & Griez, E. (1982b). Cognitive factors in carbon dioxide therapy. *Journal of Psychosomatic Research, 26,* 209–214. **[72, 81]**

van den Hout, M. A., Griez, E., & van der Molen, G. M. (1987). PCO_2 and panic sensations after 35% carbon dioxide inhalation: Hypercapnia/hyperoxia versus hypercapnia/normoxia. *Journal of Behavior Therapy & Experimental Psychiatry, 18,* 19–23. **[244, 250, 252]**

van den Hout, M. A., van der Molen, G. M., Griez, E., & Lousberg, H. (1987a).

Reduction of carbon dioxide-induced anxiety after repeated carbon dioxide exposure. *American Journal of Psychiatry, 144,* 788–791. **[243, 249, 251]**

van den Hout, M. A., van der Molen, G. M., Griez, E., & Lousberg, H. (1987b). Specificity of interoceptive fears to panic disorders. *Journal of Psychopathology & Behavioral Assessment, 9,* 99–106. **[39]**

van der Molen, G. M. **[39, 242–244, 249–252]**

van der Molen, G. M., van den Hout, M. A., & Griez, E. (1986). *Does lactate challenge induce a CNS acidosis?* Unpublished data. **[246]**

van der Molen, G. M., van den Hout, M. A., Griez, E., & Lousberg, H. (in press). Cognitive determinants of lactate induced anxiety. *Behaviour Research & Therapy.* **[252]**

van der Molen, G. M., Merckelbach, H., & van den Hout, M. A. (1986). *Susceptibility to conditioning in relation to the menstrual cycle.* Unpublished data. **[255]**

van Oot, P. H., Lane, T. W., & Borkovec, T. D. (1984). Sleep disturbances. In H. E. Adams & P. B. Sutker (Eds.), *Comprehensive handbook of psychopathology.* New York: Plenum Press. **[30]**

van Veenendaal, W. **[63, 115, 241, 251]**

Vermilyea, B. B. **[20–22, 27, 32, 33, 44, 45, 51, 58, 112, 114, 117, 118, 129, 261, 289, 290, 294, 313]**

Vermilyea, B. B. (1987). *A comparison of anxiety and depressive symptomatology in the anxiety and affective disorders.* Unpublished doctoral dissertation, State University of New York at Albany. **[23]**

Vermilyea, J. A. **[20–22, 32, 33, 44, 45, 112, 114, 117, 118, 261, 289, 290, 294]**

Villa, J., & Beech, H. R. (1978). Vulnerability and defensive reactions in relation to the human menstrual cycle. *British Journal of Social & Clinical Psychology, 17,* 93–100. **[255]**

Vittone, B. J. **[3, 54, 63, 72]**

Vogel, C. **[57]**

Volavka, J. **[240]**

von Korff, M. R., Eaton, W. W., & Keyl, P. M. (1985). The epidemiology of panic attacks and panic disorder: Results of three community surveys. *American Journal of Epidemiology, 122,* 970–981. **[47]**

Vrana, S. R. **[235]**

Vrana, S. R., Cuthbert, B. N., & Lang, P. J. (1986). Fear imagery and text processing. *Psychophysiology, 23,* 247–253. **[228]**

Waddell, M. T. **[20, 22, 27, 33, 46, 51, 53, 58, 129, 313]**

Waddell, M. T., Barlow, D. H., & O'Brien, G. T. (1984). A preliminary investigation of cognitive and relaxation treatment of panic disorder: Effects on intense anxiety versus background anxiety. *Behaviour Research & Therapy, 22,* 393–402. **[24–26, 115]**

Wagner, A. R. **[298, 322, 324, 325]**

Walker, L. (1959). The prognosis of affective illness with overt anxiety. *Journal of Neurology, Neurosurgery, & Psychiatry, 22,* 338–341. **[40]**

Wall, C., III **[2, 48, 63]**

Ward, C. H. **[157]**

Ward, J. C. **[213]**

Warwick, H. M. C. **[80, 112, 121, 125, 130, 131, 135, 194]**

Warwick, H. M. C., & Salkovskis, P. M. (1986). *Clinical and research aspects of hypochondriasis: A review of current problems and a suggested psychological solution.* Unpublished manuscript. **[121, 131]**

Warwick, H. M. C., & Salkovskis, P. M. (1985). Reassurance. *British Medical Journal, 290,* 1028. **[131]**

Watson, J. (1924). *Behaviorism.* New York: People's Institute. **[223]**

Watson, J. P., & Marks, I. M. (1971). Relevant and irrelevant fear in flooding—A crossover study of phobic patients. *Behaviour Therapy, 2,* 275–293. **[157]**

Webster's Seventh New Collegiate Dictionary (1969). Gand C. Merriam Co., Springfield, MA. **[52]**

Weerts, T. C., Cuthbert, B. N., Simons, R. F., & Lang, P. J. (in preparation). *Eye movements in visual imagery and recall.* **[228]**

Weiner, H. **[68]**

Weiner, H. (1977a). *Psychobiology and human disease.* New York: Elsevier. **[55]**

Weiner, H. (1977b). Psychobiologic contributions to human disease (pp. 575–641). In H. Weiner (Ed.), *Psychobiology and human disease.* New York: Elsevier. **[68]**

Weisman, R. G., & Litner, J. S. (1972). The role of Pavlovian events in avoidance training. In R. A. Boakes & M. S. Halliday (Eds.), *Inhibition and learning* (pp. 253–270). London: Academic Press. **[309]**

Weisman, R. G., & Litner, J. S. (1969). Positive conditioned reinforcement of Sidman avoidance behavior in rats. *Journal of Comparative and Physiological Psychology, 68,* 597–603. **[308]**

Weissman, M. M. **[20, 23, 46]**

Weissman, M. M., Leaf, P. J., Blazer, D. G., Boyd, J. H., & Florio, L. (1986). Panic disorder: Clinical characteristics, epidemiology, and treatment. *Psychopharmacology Bulletin, 22*(3), 787–791. **[6]**

Wessels, D. J. **[80, 112, 121, 125, 130, 135, 194]**

Westphal, C. (1872). Die Agoraphobie: Eine neuropathische Erscheinung. *Archives für psychiatrische Nervenkrankheiten, 3,* 138–171. **[84, 247]**

Whalan, G. **[213]**

White, P. Q. **[244]**

Williams, C. **[19]**

Williams, M. **[72, 80, 240]**

Williams, S. L. **[40]**

Wilson, G. T. **[209–212]**

Wing, L. **[230, 267]**

Wittchen, H.-U. (1986). Epidemiology of panic attacks and panic disorders. In I. Hand & H.-U. Wittchen (Eds.), *Panic & Phobias.* Berlin: Springer-Verlag. **[117]**

Woerner, M. G. **[32, 51, 53, 67, 71, 87, 168–171, 174, 176, 183, 296, 317]**

Wolpe, J. (1973). *The practice of behaviour therapy* (2nd ed.). New York: Pergamon Press. **[80]**

Wolpe, J. (1958). *Psychotherapy by reciprocal inhibition.* Stanford, CA: Stanford University Press. **[241]**

Wolpe, J., & Lang, P. J. (1964). A fear survey schedule for use in behavior therapy. *Behavior Research Therapy, 2,* 27–30. **[231]**

Woods, S. W. **[38]**

Woods, S. W., Charney, D. S., Goodman, W. K., & Heninger, G. R. (1986). *Pharmacologic challange strategies in anxiety disorder research.* Paper presented at the World Psychiatric Association Regional Symposium, Copenhagen. **[238]**

Woods, S. W., Charney, D. S., Loke, J., Goodman, W. K., Redmond, D. E., & Heninger, G. R. (1986). Carbon dioxide sensitivity in panic anxiety. *Archives of General Psychiatry, 43,* 900–909. **[245, 248]**

Zacks, R. T. **[94, 101]**

Zajonc, R. B. (1980). Feeling and thinking. *American Psychologist, 35,* 151–175. **[221]**

Zeldis, S. M. **[63]**

Zelnik, T. C. **[63]**

Zillman, D. (1983). Treatment of excitation in emotional behavior. In J. T. Cacioppo & R. E. Petty (Eds.), *Social psychophysiology* (pp. 215–240). New York: Guilford Press. **[221, 225]**

Zimbardo, P. G. **[46]**

Zitrin, C. M. **[3, 53, 63, 87, 170, 176]**

Zitrin, C. M. (1983). Differential treatment of phobias: Use of imipramine for panic attacks. *Journal of Behavior Therapy & Experimental Psychiatry, 14,* 11–18. **[53, 72]**

Zitrin, C. M., Klein, D. F., Woerner, M. G. (1980). Treatment of agoraphobia with group exposure *in vivo* and imipramine. *Archives of General Psychiatry, 37,* 63–72. **[32, 51, 53, 71, 87, 168, 169, 171, 176, 317]**

Zitrin, C. M., Klein, D. F., & Woerner, M. G. (1978). Behavior therapy, supportive psychotherapy, imipramine and phobias. *Archives of General Psychiatry, 35,* 307–316. **[169–171, 176, 183, 317]**

Zitrin, C. M., Klein, D. F., Woerner, M. G., & Ross, D. C. (1983). Treatment of phobias. I. Comparison of imipramine hydrochloride and placebo. *Archives of General Psychiatry, 40,* 125–133. **[67, 71, 87, 169, 170, 174]**

Zitrin, C. M., Woerner, M., & Klein, D. F. (1981). Differentiation of panic anxiety from anticipatory anxiety. In D. F. Klein & J. Rabkin (Eds.), *Anxiety: New research and changing concepts* (pp. 114–157). New York: Raven Press. **[71, 296]**

Subject Index

This index was constructed so that panic is assumed to be the object or referent to most items in the index.

A

B

C

D

E

F

G

H

I